Studies in Rewritten Bible 4

Who Is the Servant of the Lord?
Jewish and Christian Interpretations on Isaiah 53 From Antiquity to the Middle Ages

Antti Laato

T0413290

Åbo Akademi University
Eisenbrauns 2012

Studies in Rewritten Bible

Editor in Chief:
Antti Laato (Åbo Akademi University)
Editorial Board:
Jacques van Ruiten (University of Groningen)
Erkki Koskenniemi (Åbo Akademi University)
Gunnar af Hällström (Åbo Akademi University)

Publishers:
Åbo Akademi University, Turku, Finland
Eisenbrauns, Winona Lake, Indiana, U.S.A.

ISSN 1797-3449
ISBN 978-952-12-2785-1

Contents

Preface

This study consists of eleven articles on early interpretations of Isaiah 53 which is the central text in Jewish-Christian encounters through centuries. I have written these articles so that they can be read independently. Nevertheless they all are interconnected and, therefore, I have also included Introduction and Conclusions in this volume.

This study is a fruit of international co-operation in the network Rewritten Bible which was established in 2006. I had possibility to discuss methodological issues and some parts of these articles in our seminaries and meetings. In particular, I want to thank following scholars in our network who have commented details of this study: Dr Michael Becker, Professor Lukas Bormann, Dr Cor de Vos, Dr Erkki Koskenniemi, Dr Pekka Lindqvist, Professor Jacques van Ruiten, Professor Martin Tamcke and Hannu Töyrylä. In addition, I had possibility to discuss section 8 in Göttingen in December 2011. I thank Professors Peter Gemeinhardt and Martin Tamcke for this opportunity. Professor Tryggve N.D. Mettinger read the final version of the manuscript and commented it. Many thanks for him. Thanks for Theodosia Tomkinson who edited my language. I am also grateful to Doctoral Student Lotta Valve read carefully the manuscript in its form and made many good suggestions on it.

Discussions with my wife, Anni Maria, have always been fruitful for my writing process. She has lent me loving support during this study.

Turku September 12 2012

Antti Laato

1 Introduction

Isaiah 53 has been regarded as a difficult passage within the Hebrew Bible because it describes a person who had to suffer and die vicariously in order to atone for the sins of others. Such a view is in strong contrast to the covenant theology which predominates in the Hebrew Bible and lays the foundation for the principle of retribution: Everyone must bear the consequences of his sins. It is for this reason that Klaus Koch called Isaiah 53 the "erratic block" in the Hebrew Bible.[1] However, in some exegetical studies Isaiah 53 has been treated without reference to the vicarious and atoning suffering of the Servant.[2] This new attempt to understand Isaiah 53 received particular attention in Hägglund's dissertation.[3] His interpretation represents a dramatic illustration of the intellectual problems with which the passage confronts modern readers. He writes that "the variety and multitude of interpretations of Isa 53 could lead to despair and in some ways it does for me too" and goes on

---

[1] K. Koch, "Sühne und Sündenvergebung um die Wende von der exilischen zur nackexilischen Zeit," *EvTh* 26 (1966) 217-239. Note also A. Schenker, *Knecht und Lamm Gottes (Jesaja 53): Übernahme von Schuld im Horizont der Gottesknechtslieder* (Stuttgarter Bibelstudien 190, Stuttgart: Katholisches Bibelwerk 2001).

[2] For example, H.M. Orlinsky ['The So Called 'Servant of the Lord' and 'Suffering Servant' in Second Isaiah.' *VTSup* 14 (Leiden: Brill 1967) 1-133, esp. 51-66], G.R. Driver ['Isaiah 52:13-53:12: the Servant of the Lord.' in: M. Black, G. Fohrer (eds) *In Memoriam Paul Kahle* (BZAW 103, Berlin:DeGruyter 1968) 90-105, esp. 104-5], J.A. Soggin ['Tod und Auferstehung des leidenden Gottesknechtes Jesaja 53,8-10.' *ZAW* 87 (1975) 346-55] and R.N. Whybray [*Thanksgiving for a Liberated Prophet. An Interpretation of Isaiah Chapter 53*. (JSOTSS 4, Sheffield: Sheffield Academi Press 1978) 29-106] attempted to read Isaiah 53 without any reference to vicarious and atoning suffering. I criticized such a reading in an earlier publicvation. For criticism of the view and of Whybray's interpretation in particular, see A. Laato, *The Servant of YHWH and Cyrus: A Reinterpretation of the Exilic Messianic Programme in Isaiah 40-55* (ConBOT 35, Stockholm: Almqvist & Wiksell International 1992) 138-50.

[3] F. Hägglund, *Isaiah 53 in the Light of Homecoming After the Exile* (FAT II/31, Tübingen: Mohr Siebeck 2008).

2

"I have argued that the reconciliation between the 'we' and the servant is more important than the atonement."[4] However, on the next page he totally rejects the atonement aspect, saying that "in the analyses of exclusion and embrace in Isa 53, I have questioned the prominent view that the suffering of the servant is an atoning suffering." Indeed, the latter aspect is the thesis which Hägglund seeks to defend in his dissertation.

When Hägglund's thesis is evaluated in the light of the content of Isaiah 53 there are *prima facie* many references which can be interpreted in the light of the Servant's vicarious atoning suffering. First of all there is a reference to אשם in Isa 53:10 which can be related to sacrificial terminology (Lev 5). On this point Hägglund cites Janowski's study and argues that אשם should not be related to sacrificial theology but to "guilt-incurring encroachments and their reparation".[5] Hägglund repeats Janowski's uncritical statement that cultic terminology is lacking in Isaiah 53.[6] However, the question of the primary level is not whether cultic terminology is employed but rather how the terms used in Isaiah 53 should be interpreted. After all אשם can be related to cultic terminology as also the use of the verb נשא.[7] But they are not used exclusively in the cultic context. The imagery of Isa 53:7 according to

---

[4]Both quotations are from p. 175.

[5]B. Janowski, *Stellvertretung: Alttestamentliche Studien zu einem theologischen Grundbegriff* (Stuttgarter Bibelstudien 165, Stuttgart 1997) 88-92; idem, "He Bore Our Sins: Isaiah 53 and the Drama of Taking Another's Place," in: B. Janowski & P. Stuhlmacher (eds), *The Suffering Servant: Isaiah 53 in Jewish and Christian Sources* (Grand Rapids: Eerdmans 2004) 48-74, quotation is from pp. 68-69. See further Hägglund *Isaiah 53 in the Light of Homecoming* 67-73.

[6]Janowski, *Stellvertretung* 89: "... und auch sonst fehlt in Jes 52,13-53,12 kultisches Vokabular."

[7]The Hebrew expression נשא חטא appears in Isa 53:12 and, in addition, in Lev 19:17; 20:20; 22:9; 24:15; Num 9:13; 18:22; Ezek 23:49; and the verb נשא combined with עון is attested in Ex 28:28, 43; 34:7; Lev 5:1, 17; 7:18; 10:17; 16:22; 17:16; 19:8; 20:17, 19; Num 5:31; 14:18, 34; 18:1 (2 x), 23; 30:16; Ezek 4:4-6; 14:10; 44:10, 12; Hos 14:3; Mic 7:18; Ps 32:5; 85:3. This evidence makes it difficult to agree with Janowski who emphasizes that the context does not contain cultic vocabulary.

which the Servant is brought as a lamb to slaughter is not in conflict with a cultic understanding, nor is the imagery of Isa 53:8 according to which the Servant was "cut off from the land of living," because it recalls the fate of the scapegoat in Leviticus 16.[8] Many expressions in Isaiah 53 imply that the "we"-group admits to misunderstanding the purpose of the Servant's sufferings. Moreover, this confession opens to the "we"-group a new possibility of entering into a relationship with Yhwh so that it is difficult to exclude the atoning effect of the Servant's sufferings. Hägglund compares Isa 53:4a with Jer 10:19 and suggests that the whole of Isaiah 53 should be understood on a par with the passage in the Book of Jeremiah, i.e. the Servant must bear the consequences of others' sins.[9] This is problematic because Isa 53:5 mentions "our peace" which the "we"-group will receive in consequence of the sufferings of the Servant. Hägglund tries to connect Isa 53:5b with the wisdom tradition and compares the passage with Prov 20:30 and Job 5:17-18, 24.[10] However, the wisdom tradition in these passages emphasizes that Yhwh disciplines a person and heals him; on the other hand, in Isaiah 53 the reference is to the Servant who has been disciplined, and this will bring peace to the "we"-group.

Despite his vehement argumentation against the atoning interpretation Hägglund, nevertheless, writes of Isa 53:5b: "This is perhaps the verse that comes closest to expressing the idea of an atoning

---

[8]Janowski's ("He Bore Our Sins" 67-69) attempt to emphasize difference between Isaiah 53 and Leviticus 16 is based on the theory that אשם was not originally connected with cultic sacrifice but rather with "guilt-incurring encroachments and their reparation" (pp. 68-69). Nevertheless, he acknowledges that the concept of אשם later found its way to the terminology of cultic sacrifices (p. 69). This being the case the vocabulary and imagery in Isa 52:13-53:12 can be connected with cultic sacrifice at the level of metaphor. Concerning the connection of Isaiah 53 and Leviticus 16 see, e.g., T.N.D. Mettinger, *A Farewell to the Servant Songs: A Critical Examination of an Exegetical Axiom* (Scripta Minora 1982-1983:3, Lund 1983) 41.

[9]Hägglund, *Isaiah 53 in the Light of Homecoming* 53-56.

[10]Hägglund, *Isaiah 53 in the Light of Homecoming* 59-61.

suffering" (p. 56), "This is vicarious suffering ... however, not a statement that the suffering of the servant atones for the sins of the 'we'" (p. 59) ... "This colon could indicate an atoning suffering. However, read in its context, it is more a confession of the guilt of the 'we' than a statement about the atonement achieved by the servant" (p. 60). These formulations are evidence that there is no ultimate reason to rule out the vicarious and atoning sufferings of the Servant.

Hägglund concludes his analysis of the section "Isaiah 53 and Sin Offering" by observing that "Mowinckel has formulated a somewhat similar view," then quotes the following passage from *He That Cometh*:[11]

> The atoning worth of the Servant's action depends on whether his fellow-countrymen appropriate it, so as to see their own guilt and thereby be moved to conversion and penitence.

When reading Mowinckel's *He That Cometh* it is indeed difficult to conclude that his solution is similar to Hägglund's. Already the passage quoted by Hägglund indicates that the sufferings of the Servant have atoning effects. In addition, Mowinckel comments "it is clear that the poet expresses his thought in sacrificial and legal phrases and conceptions."[12]

This introduction to modern interpretive horizons to Isaiah 53 illustrates that the idea of an innocent Servant who had to suffer on the behalf of the "we" and whose sufferings will benefit the "we," seems to contradict the modern Kantian belief that everyone is responsible for his own acts.[13] This intellectual difficulty resulted in exegetical solutions

---

[11]Hägglund *Isaiah 53 in the Light of Homecoming* 73. See S. Mowinckel, *He That Cometh* (Oxford: Blackwell 1956) 211.

[12]Mowinckel, *He That Cometh* 209.

[13]For this see, in particular, Janowski, "He Bore Our Sins" 49-54. A more detailed treatment is to be found in B. Janowski, *Ecce Homo: Stellvertretung und Lebenshingabe als Themen Biblischer Theologie* (Biblisch-Theologische Studien 84, Neukirchen-Vluyn: Neukirchener Verlag 2007).

intended to "censor" the vicarious atoning sufferings of the Servant. My intention in this study is to broaden the perspective on the reception history of Isaiah 53. I want to show how the vicarious atoning suffering has been an integral part of the interpretation tradition of Isaiah 53; indeed when there has been a tendency to deprecate this aspect of Isaiah 53 it is possible to detect textual manipulations (The Septuagint and Targum Jonathan).

The broader methodological framework of this study is Rewritten Bible as it is understood in our international network. "Rewritten Bible" is not a form-historical concept but a modern term which emphasizes the reading process in ancient texts. It opens up a new horizon whereby a modern critical scholar can understand that a reader in antiquity attempted to build up his religious referential world with the aid of the biblical text. He was convinced that as the biblical text mirrors reality it is, therefore, necessary to fill all the gaps therein so that its referential world fits the reader's own social, historical and religious context. This implies that "Rewritten Bible" enables us to see dynamics between the authoritative texts and the social community interpreting them. New social conditions led to the need for new information from authoritative texts. This was possible through interpretive tendencies. Texts hidden in the texts could be discerned through careful reading, sometimes by combining different texts in the Bible. By application of heuristic interpretive tendencies, early scriptures which were seen to reflect reality could speak in a new way to a new audience.[14]

---

[14]See how the concept "Rewritten Bible" has been interpreted in the international Network behind the series Studies in Rewritten Bible: E. Koskenniemi & P. Lindqvist, "Rewritten Bible, Rewritten Stories", in A. Laato & J. van Ruiten (eds), *Rewritten Bible Reconsidered: Proceedings of the Conference in Karkku, Finland, August 24-26 2006* (Studies in Rewritten Bible 1, Åbo Akademi University & Winona Lake: Eisenbrauns 2008) 11-39; A. Laato, "Gen 49:8-12 and Its Interpretation In Antiquity – A Methodological Approach to Understanding of the Rewritten Bible" in: E. Koskenniemi & P. Lindqvist (eds), *Rewritten Biblical Figures* (SRB 3, Turku: ÅAU, Winona Lake: Eisenbrauns 2010) 1-26.

6

The first important question in our study is the traditio-historical background of Isaiah 53, and the interpretation of the passage in the present literary context of the Book of Isaiah (sect. 2). We thereby arrive at a putative original setting of the passage against which we can reflect the later attempts to rewrite and reinterpret it. We shall argue that the suffering Servant is the loyal Israel and that the traditio-historical background of the motif of vicarious suffering and death of the Servant is the dramatic death of king Josiah. Diverse motifs connected with his fate were developed and used in Isaiah 53. The traditio-historical background of the death of Josiah also connects Isaiah 53 with Zechariah 9-14 and helps us to understand certain revisions in the Books of the Chronicles as far as the king's fate is concerned.

During the Maccabean period the Book of Isaiah was understood in an apocalyptic milieu as is implied by the Book of Ben Sira (48:17-25) and the Book of Daniel.[15] In particular, certain passages in the Book of Isaiah (Isa 26:19; 66:24) were seen to corroborate the idea of resurrection. This being the case Isaiah 53 was read in a new light and influenced the contemporary martyr theology (sect. 3).

In section 4 we shall deal with the Septuagint translation of Isaiah 53 which deprecates the vicarious atoning suffering expressed by the Hebrew text on many points. This revision of Isaiah 53 opened the way to interpret the Servant in Isaiah 53 as the suffering righteous whose sufferings have no atoning effects. Such an interpretation of Isaiah 53 is perceptible in the Book of Wisdom 2-5.

Another translation which obviously presents a revised version of the Hebrew text is Targum Jonathan. Scholars have argued that such a "violent" way to translate the Hebrew text may be an attempt to confront the Christian interpretation or even belittle an earlier messianic understanding of Isaiah 53. Therefore, we shall consider the question of whether we can find any example of a messianic interpretation of Isaiah

---

[15]For this see especially J. Blenkinsopp, *Opening the Sealed Book: Interpretations of the Book of Isaiah in Late Antiquity* (Grand Rapids: Eerdmans 2006).

53 before the time of Jesus. This question will be discussed in sect. 5 while the translation of Targum Jonathan is our subject in sect. 6.

The Christian understanding of Isaiah 53 began a new epoch in its interpretation. We could say that the Christians simply used Isaiah 53 as a "fifth" gospel about the sufferings, death and resurrection of Jesus. We can speak of a process of revision here which implies a certain sensitive reading of Isaiah 53. The old well-known text was seen in a new suit (interpretation) which suddenly seemed to offer a very plausible understanding of the Servant.[16] In section 7 we focus on how the idea of the suffering Servant was developed in the Jesus-movement and among the first Christians and then consider how Isaiah 53 was interpreted in the New Testament. In section 8 we shall move on to the patristic literature and present the different literary contexts in which Isaiah 53 came to the fore.

Against the background of the Christian messianic interpretation of Isaiah 53 it is challenging to see how Isaiah 53 has been understood in the rabbinical writings. We shall deal with the relevant Talmudic and Midrashic material in section 9, while in section 10 the focus turns to Pesiqta Rabbati and is approach to the sufferings of the Messiah.

During the Middle Ages, Jewish and Christian biblical exegesis collided in different polemical contexts. Much textual evidence concerning these discussions is available. In sect. 11 and 12 we consider these polemical confrontations and how the interpretation of Isaiah 53 was challenged therein.

This study will explain how Isaiah 53 found its way into the Hebrew Bible, and how this "erratic block" was interpreted in subsequent Jewish and Christian writings. We shall see that this "erratic" passage produced

---

[16]Cf., the discussion in P. Hanson, "The World of the Servant of the Lord in Isaiah 40-55," in: W.H. Bellinger & W.R. Farmer, *Jesus and the Suffering Servant: Isaiah 53 and Christian Origins* (Harrisburg: Trinity Press International 1998) 9-23; R.F. Melugin, "On Reading Isaiah 53 as Christian Scripture," in: Bellinger & Farmer, *Jesus and the Suffering Servant* 55-69.

8

several interesting interpretations which are in the periphery of the covenant theology of the Hebrew Bible. In the Second Temple Jewish writings Isaiah 53 produced martyr theology, then it was used in the Christian message concerning the suffering and dying Messiah and finally again in rabbinical and medieval Judaism as reflecting the sufferings of Israel and longing of the messianic era. In the light of the reception history of Isaiah 53 it can be confirmed that the passage has great relevance in the Jewish-Christian encounter today. I hope that this study will be a contribution to the current dialogue between Judaism and Christianity.

2 The Traditio–historical Background to the Suffering Servant in Isaiah 53

Isaiah 53 is one of the most difficult passages in the Hebrew Bible. Scholars have discussed whether this "erratic block" describes the vicarious suffering of the servant or his real death and resurrection.[1] Therefore, it is no wonder that there is no agreement either concerning the traditio-historical background of the passage. From what tradition was the vivid picture of the suffering and dying servant in Isaiah 53 derived? This question has been treated in many exegetical studies on Isaiah 53.[2] The aim of this chapter is to provide one possible means of

---

[1]See our discussion in sect. 1.

[2]There are different proposals for the traditio-historical background of Isaiah 53. (1) The myth and ritual school suggested that ancient Near Eastern myths on Tammuz and other dying and resurgent deities who were enacted in the New Year festivals and where the sacral kingship played a decisive role would provide a suitable traditio-historical background for Isaiah 53. See, e.g., I. Engnell, "Till frågan om Ebed Jahve-sångerna och den lidande Messias hos 'Deuterojesaja'," *SEÅ* 10 (1945) 31-65; *idem*, "Profetia och tradition: Några synpunkter på ett gammaltestamentligt centralproblem," *SEÅ* 12 (1947) 110-139; *idem*, *The 'Ebed Yahweh Songs and the Suffering Messiah in "Deutero-Isaiah"* (Reprinted from BJRL 31 [1948] 54-93; Manchester: The Manchester University 1948). (2) There are scholars who argue that the prophetic tradition, in particular the Book of Jeremiah, would explain the features of suffering in Isaiah 53. See, e.g., N.R. Whybray, *Thanksgiving for a Liberated Prophet. An Interpretation of Isaiah Chapter 53* (JSOTSS 4, Sheffield: Sheffield Academic Press 1978); H.-J. Hermisson, "Der Lohn des Knechts," In: J. Jeremias & L. Perlitt (eds), *Die Botschaft und die Boten. Festschrift für H.W. Wolff zum 70. Geburtstag*, Neukirchen-Vluyn: Neukirchener 1981) 269-287; *idem*, "Israel und der Gottesknecht bei Deuterojesaja," *ZThK* 79 (1982) 1-24; *idem*, "Voreiliger Abschied von den Gottesknechtsliedern," *TR* NF 49 (1984) 209-222; *idem*, "Deuterojesaja-Probleme: Ein kritischer Literaturbericht," *VF* 31 (1986) 53-84. (3) Finally some scholars argue that the picture of the sufferings of the servant reflects the distress of the people during the exile. See, e.g., T.N.D. Mettinger, "Die Ebed-Jahwe-Lieder. Ein fragwürdiges Axiom," *ASTI* 11 (1977/78) 68-76; *idem*, *A Farewell to the Servant Songs: A Critical Examination of an Exegetical Axiom* (Scripta Minora 1982-1983:3, Lund: Gleerups

solving this traditio-historical problem. Only then can we present an interpretation of Isaiah 53 in the literary context of the Book of Isaiah.

The Fate of Josiah and the Problem of Theodicy

I have suggested in earlier studies that the rise of the vivid picture of the suffering servant in Isaiah 53 must be traced back to an historical, traumatic event which involved an individual who was regarded as righteous. I have proposed that the death of Josiah could explain the new trends in the Israelite royal theology during the period of the exile, and that this particular royal theodicy tradition was then reinterpreted in Isaiah 53.[3] Nevertheless, Isaiah 53 in its present context does not refer to any royal individual, nor to Josiah.

The fate of Josiah represents a difficult problem in the Deuteronomistic History (from Deuteronomy to 2 Kings). Although theodicy is a central theological concept in this history there is evidence that the treatment of the death of Josiah does not follow the work's hermeneutic model. I shall give a brief summary of my findings.[4]

There are five central theological themes in the Deuteronomistic History which have been used in order to solve the theodicean problem

---

1983). Although I agree that the Servant should be interpreted in its Deutero-Isaianic context as referring to the sufferings of the people in the exile I nevertheless think that we cannot understand the *rise* of this intensive *picture* of "suffering individual" in Isaiah 53 only from the perspective of the national catastrophe. The picture goes back to the traumatic historical event at Megiddo when Josiah was killed (see below).

[3]See my studies *Josiah and David Redivivus: The Historical Josiah and the Messianic Expectations of Exilic and Postexilic Times* (Coniectanea Biblica OTS 33; Stockholm: Almqvist & Wiksell International 1992); and *The Servant of YHWH and Cyrus: A Reinterpretation of the Exilic Messianic Programme in Isaiah 40-55* (Coniectanea Biblica OTS 35; Stockholm: Almqvist & Wiksell International 1992).

[4]See also A. Laato, "Theodicy in the Deuteronomistic History," In: A. Laato & J.C. De Moor (eds), *Theodicy in the World of the Bible* (Leiden: Brill 2003) 183-235; idem, "Beloved and lovely! Despised and rejected. Some reflections on the death of Josiah," In: J. Pakkala & M. Nissinen (eds), *Houses Full of All Good Things. Essays in Memory of Timo Veijola* (Göttingen: vandenHoeck & Ruprecht 2008) 115-128.

of the destruction of Jerusalem in 587 BC. These five theological themes are: (1) *The Law of Moses*: the people of Yhwh should have lived according to the divine ordinances. The crisis of the exile emphasized that they had not done this. (2) *The Land*: According to the covenant theology the people of Israel are Yhwh's vassal who have received the land as their grant. They may live in this country as long as they remain loyal to their Lord. The period of the exile was interpreted as the punishment imposed by Yhwh on his rebellious vassal. (3) *The Temple*: The Temple at Jerusalem was a symbol of the presence of Yhwh. The destruction of the Temple was a sign that Yhwh would no longer show benevolence to the people who did not keep the covenant. (4) *The dynasty of David*: 2 Samuel 7 is Yhwh's unconditional promise to the dynasty of David, and this pledge is constitutional in the Deuteronomistic History.[5] The exile put an end to this promise, adducing the sinfulness of the dynasty and the people. (5) *The prophetic mission*: Yhwh had warned his people through his prophets that the exile will befall the people if they continued to transgress his will. This being the case, the exile did not come as a surprise but manifested the logical consequence of the people's disloyalty.

Nevertheless, these five theological themes were not only vehicles of justice and doom but were also interpreted in the Deuteronomistic History as giving hope to the people during an acute historical crisis, the exile. *The Law of Moses* is still in the hands of the people. The people can return to Yhwh and renew the covenant (Deut 4). There is the possibility of returning to the *Land of Israel*. Even though the *Temple* has been destroyed, the promise is given that Yhwh will listen to the prayers of the people which are addressed toward the ruins

---

[5]Cf., D. J. McCarthy, 'II Samuel and the Structure of the Deuteronomistic History.' *JBL* 84 (1965) 131-138. I have argued elsewhere that 2 Samuel 7 contains an old royal tradition which has been modified in the present form of 2 Samuel 7. See A. Laato, '2 Samuel 7 and Ancient Near Eastern Royal Ideology.' *CBQ* 59 (1997) 244-269 and *A Star Is Rising. The Historical Development of the Old Testament Royal Ideology and the Rise of the Jewish Messianic Expectations* (Atlanta: Scholars Press 1997) 33-47.

of the Temple (1 Kings 8). The Deuteronomistic History ends with the release of Jekoniah (2 Kings 25:27-31), suggesting that there is still hope for *the dynasty of David* which received the promise of 2 Samuel 7. Finally, *the prophetic mission* indicates that Yhwh governs the course of history even during the exile. Thus these five theological themes are vehicles of theodicy in the Deuteronomistic History which gave the people hope in the time of tribulation.

It is important to note that these five theological themes also play a major role in the description of the reign of Josiah, and that there are certain tensions between their presentation in 2 Kings 22-23 and their formulation elsewhere in the Deuteronomistic History.

1. The Law of Moses: The detailed account of Josiah's reformation in 2 Kings 22-23 contains many allusions to the laws of Deuteronomy. The following list demonstrates that according to the Deuteronomistic view, Josiah implemented the covenant of Yhwh:

Covenant between Yhwh and Israel	2 Kgs 23:2-4	Deut 5:3; 29:1, 9
Josiah follows the laws of Yhwh	2 Kgs 23:3	Deut 6:1, 5
Elimination of idolatry	2 Kgs 23:4-7	Deut 13
The astral cult was destroyed	2 Kgs 23:5, 11-12	Deut 17:3
Cultic prostitution was eliminated	2 Kgs 23:7	Deut 23:17-18
Centralization of the cult	2 Kgs 23:8-9, 19	Deut 12
Sacrifice of children was prohibited	2 Kgs 23:10	Deut 18:10
Passover festival at the Temple	2 Kgs 23:21-23	Deut 16:1-8
Illegal divination was banned	2 Kgs 23:24	Deut 18:11-14

It is clear from this account that Josiah was regarded as a righteous king who established the Deuteronomic covenant between Yhwh and the people. Josiah's righteousness is also recorded in the Deuteronomistic History. In 2 Kgs 23:25 he is characterized as the king who sought most zealously to follow the commandments of Yhwh given through Moses: "Neither before nor after him was there a king like him who turned to Yhwh as he did—with all his heart and with all his soul and with all his power (בְּכָל־לְבָבוֹ וּבְכָל־נַפְשׁוֹ וּבְכָל־מְאֹדוֹ) in accordance with all the Law of Moses (כְּכֹל תּוֹרַת מֹשֶׁה)." This description of Josiah complies with the Deuteronomic ideal whereby one must "love Yhwh with all his heart and with all his soul and with all his power." This formulation appears, for example, in Deut. 6:5:

וְאָהַבְתָּ אֵת יְהוָה אֱלֹהֶיךָ בְּכָל־לְבָבְךָ וּבְכָל־נַפְשְׁךָ וּבְכָל־מְאֹדֶךָ

This description of Josiah in the Deuteronomistic History implies that he would have merited blessings from Yhwh according to the prescriptions of Deuteronomy 28-29. However, the final analysis of the reign of Josiah does not follow this Deuteronomic principle of retribution. Instead reference is made to all the evil perpetrated by Judah during the reign of Manasseh. It is postulated that Judah must suffer the exile because of Manasseh's ungodly actions (2 Kgs. 23:26-27):

> Nevertheless, Yhwh did not turn away from the heat of his fierce anger, which burned against Judah because of all that Manasseh had done to provoke him to anger. So Yhwh said: I will remove Judah also from my presence as I removed Israel, and I will reject Jerusalem the city I chose, and this temple, about which I said, 'There shall my Name be'.

This text draws on the assumption of the typical Deuteronomistic phraseology and theology presented above. But it is essential to observe that Josiah is not responsible for the destruction of the city; rather the responsibility for the entire debacle is laid upon Manasseh. This suggests that the Deuteronomist experienced great difficulty in applying his retribution theology. The reign of Josiah remains a mystery for his theodicy.

2. The Land: 2 Kings 23 describes how Josiah attempted to purify the land, even the territory of the Northern kingdom. He razed the cult place of Bethel (2 Kgs 23:15) and destroyed sacrificial sites (כָּל־בָּתֵּי הַבָּמוֹת) in Samaria (2 Kgs 23:19). He introduced the Passover festival. When it is stated in 2 Kgs 23:21-22 that the King Josiah exhorted all the people

14

(אֶת־כָּל־הָעָם) to celebrate the Passover, and that none of the Judean or the Israelite kings before him had so done, it is reasonable to believe that this exhortation, according to the Deuteronomist, was also addressed to the inhabitants of the Northern kingdom. All this indicates that Josiah was attempting to purify the land so that it might become the object of divine blessings.

The theme of the exodus from Egypt is often used in Deuteronomy as a symbol of the covenant between Yhwh and Israel, and to provide a rationale for the Law which stipulates how the Israelites should live in the land which God has given to them as an inheritance.[6] This theme is the heart of the Passover festival. Mettinger has emphasized that the role of the Passover festival was central in Deuteronomistic theology and closely connected with the Deuteronomistic Name theology. The Passover was one element in a Copernican revolution which came to pass in the Judean cult around the time of the exile.[7] That this festival, which is emphasized so strongly in Deuteronomy, is closely linked to the reign of Josiah demonstrates the Deuteronomist's desire to portray Josiah as the ideal king.

3. The Temple: Cultic centralization according to the ideal of Deuteronomy 12 is one of the most prominent reforms which Josiah implemented during his reign. 2 Kgs 23:8 emphasizes that Josiah laid waste all the local cult sites in Judah:

> He brought all the priests from the town of Judah and desecrated the high places from Geba to Beersheba, where the priests burned incense.

Josiah adopted similar measures at Bethel and in the districts of Samaria as noted above. Notwithstanding Josiah's actions could not alter the

---

[6]See M. Weinfeld, *Deuteronomy and the Deuteronomic School* (Winona Lake: Eisenbrauns 1992) 326-330.

[7]T. N. D. Mettinger, *The Dethronement of Sabaoth. Studies in the Shem and Kabod Theologies* (ConBOT 18, Lund: Gleerups 1982) 67-79.

destiny of Jerusalem. 2 Kgs 23:27 emphasizes that Yhwh will nevertheless bring about the destruction of the Temple and will expel his people from the Land of Judah. The Deuteronomistic tragedy is thereby placed in high relief. By the time a king appears who seeks to fulfill the Deuteronomic programme and worship Yhwh in the only place which he has chosen and where his Name dwells it is already too late. Yhwh has determined that a catastrophe will fall upon the land and the city and the holy place chosen by himself.

4. The dynasty of Davidic: The Deuteronomic Law of Kingship in Deut 17:14-20 presupposes that the king must make a copy of and read the Law of Moses in order to follow its statutes and ordinances. Josiah is probably the only sovereign in the Books of Kings who read the lawbook and fulfilled its demands. Joash may be another king who did so. In 2 Kings 11 it is stated that Joash received a document הָעֵדוּת (2 Kgs 11:12). This can be interpreted as articulating the Deuteronomist's emphasis that Joash too followed the Deuteronomic law of kingship by receiving a copy of the Law. The problem with this interpretation is that the word עֵדוּת does not occur in Deuteronomy.[8] In 1 Kgs 2:3; 2 Kgs 17:15; 23:3 the plural form is used together with other terms meaning "statutes" (חֻקִּים) "commandments" (מִצְוֹת), "stipulations" (מִשְׁפָּטִים) of Yhwh. In Josh 4:16 we have an expression אֲרוֹן הָעֵדוּת which suggests that the הָעֵדוּת refers to the tablets of the Ten Commandments. In any case, Joash undertook a reformation which, on many points, adhered to the Deuteronomic ideals.[9] Nevertheless, it is noted in 2 Kgs 12:4 that

---

[8]It is possible that עֵדוּת in 2 Kgs 11:12 (in pre-Deuteronomistic tradition) represents a royal covenant document reminiscent of the one Esarhaddon received on the occasion of his coronation festival. See this neo-Assyrian prophecy document, NAP 3, in *State Archives of Assyria* 9. See further the interpretation of 2 Kgs. 11:12 in its relation to NAP 3 in A. Laato, *A Star Is Rising* 88-92.

[9]For this see H.-D. Hoffman, *Reform und Reformen: Untersuchungen zu einem Grundthema der deuteronomistischen Geschichtsschreibung* (ATANT 66, Zürich: Theologischer Verlag 1980) 104-13.

16

'cult places (הַבָּמוֹת) were not removed but the people continued to sacrifice and burn incense (מְזַבְּחִים וּמְקַטְּרִים) there'. In this light it is clear that Joash did not fulfill the Deuteronomic ideal as Josiah did. We may say that Josiah was a king who should have received blessings from Yhwh, an expectation which stems from the dynastic promise of 2 Sam 7:14-16. In 2 Sam 7:14 it is stated that Yhwh will punish disobedience (בְּהַעֲוֹתוֹ וְהֹכַחְתִּיו בְּשֵׁבֶט אֲנָשִׁים וּבְנִגְעֵי בְּנֵי אָדָם) but never remove his mercy from the dynasty. It seems clear that the fate of Josiah, his death at Megiddo, was not easily reconciled with Deuteronomistic retribution theology.

5. The prophetic mission: The Deuteronomic cultic actions of Josiah are also justified with the support of the prophetic mission. The only prophecy in the whole Deuteronomistic History which *expressis verbis* names a person whose appearance is predicted concerns Josiah. 1 Kgs 13:2 contains a prophecy of judgement from the unnamed prophet of Judah who polemizes against the altar of Bethel, that Judah will crown a king named Josiah and that this king will raze the altar:

> O altar, altar! This is what Yhwh says: 'A son will be born to the house of David—Josiah will be his name. On you he will sacrifice the priests of the high places who now make offerings here, and human bones will be burned on you.'

2 Kgs 23:15-16 record that this prophecy was fulfilled when Josiah destroyed the altar of Bethel and burned thereon the bones removed from the tombs of the priests of Bethel 'in accordance with the word of Yhwh proclaimed by the man of God who foretold these things'. This prediction-fulfilment account in the Deuteronomistic History asserts that Josiah's cultic reformation was foreseen by Yhwh. Such a rhetorical manoeuvre is difficult to interpret if not as a Deuteronomistic attempt to legitimate the reformation of Josiah as a fulfilment of the Deuteronomic programme in the history of the Judean monarchy. But 1 Kgs 13:2 is not the only prophetic text related to the reign of Josiah. Another prophecy, that of Huldah, gives pride of place to the problem of theodicy.

Huldah's prophecy (2 Kgs 22:15-21) in its present form contains many phrases typical of Deuteronomic and Deuteronomistic language.[10] Huldah's prophecy elicits out the startling dissonance between Josiah's righteousness and the catastrophe of Megiddo. This prophecy is consciously inserted between the account of the discovery of the lawbook and the report on Josiah's reformation. Huldah proclaimed the inevitable doom of Jerusalem and Judah (2 Kgs 22:16-17, 19) because the people had rejected the commandments of Yhwh written in the lawbook just found in the Temple. Thus Huldah confirms the prediction presented in 2 Kgs 21:7-14, which is subsequently reiterated in 2 Kgs 23:25-27. Having heard this proclamation of doom, Josiah tries in vain to effect a reversal by implementing a Deuteronomic reformation in Judah and in Israel. But Yhwh had already decided to send a catastrophe upon Judah and Jerusalem because of the sins committed during Manasseh's reign. On the other hand, Huldah's prophecy clearly stresses that Josiah is a righteous king and that Yhwh will not send the catastrophe of the exile during his lifetime. The pronouncement that Josiah will be carried to his grave in peace (2 Kgs 22:20) is at odds with the events described in 2 Kgs 23:28-30.[11] It is difficult to interpret this tension between Huldah's prophecy and the historical events at Megiddo in 2 Kings 22-23 save as an attempt to highlight the fact that Josiah's untimely death was not the result of his own wickedness. Instead it is asserted that Josiah suffered

---

[10]See e.g. Weinfeld, *Deuteronomy and the Deuteronomic School* 320-365. I refer to the following formulations: IA:9; IB:7; VII:16, 21; VIII:5.

[11]Hoffmann (*Reform und Reformen*, 181-189) has argued that the formulation 'you will be gathered into your grave in peace' does not mean that Josiah will die in peace but that he will receive an official burial and not remain unburied which would be a curse (he refers to Deut. 28:26; 1 Sam. 17:44; 1 Kgs. 16:4; 21:24; Prov 30:17; Ezek. 29:5). I regard this argument as unconvincing. More convincing is that of H. Schmid (*Šalôm. 'Frieden' im Alten Orient und im Alten Testament* [SBS 51, Stuttgart 1971] 52) who refers to Jer. 34:5; Gen. 15:15; 1 Kgs. 2:6 and 2 Kgs. 22:20 and notes: '... mit dem Sterben $b^e šalôm$ nichts anderes als das getroste, natürliche Sterben, alt und lebenssatt, gemeint ist, dem ein Sterben etwa in der Fremde (Gen. 15,15) oder durch das Schwert (Jer. 34,5) entgegensteht.'

on account of the sins committed by the people during the reign of Manasseh. In his important study on Josiah, M. Sweeney emphasized that Huldah's oracle concerning the peaceful death of Josiah should be understood in parallel with the Deuteronomist's description of Ahab: "Like Ahab, who repented concerning his actions against Naboth in 1 Kgs. 21:27-29 and thereby did not see evil realized against his house during his lifetime, Josiah repented concerning the deeds of his people and was allowed to die without seeing the punishment that would come upon them."[12] However, this explanation fails to take note of the fact that, according to the Deuteronomistic view, Josiah is regarded as righteous while Ahab was seen as a sinner. In addition, Ahab was killed in battle because of his disloyalty to the prophetic word of Micaiah ben Imla (1 Kings 22). Josiah also met his fate in battle, but there is no indication in 2 Kings 22-23 that he was killed because of his disloyalty, as was Ahab. Therefore, the basic problem of theodicy in the Deuteronomistic presentation remains unsolved.

We have seen that all five themes, the vehicles of theodicy, in the Deuteronomistic History, are actualized in a special way in the account of the reign of Josiah. While these five themes in the Deuteronomistic History are *generally* used to emphasize a retribution theology, in 2 Kings 22-23 they also play another role. They bring out the *mystery* of theodicy. The righteous king who fulfilled the Deuteronomic program did not receive blessings from Yhwh but was obliged to receive the message of inevitable doom: because of Manasseh nothing can be done. The destruction has been decided. What function would such a theology have performed in the time of the exile? In my judgement, the catastrophe of Megiddo led to the rise of a royal theodicy. In what follows I shall present the outlines of this royal theodicy as I believe that it is perceptible in the texts of the Hebrew Bible.

---

[12]M. Sweeney, *King Josiah of Judah: The Lost Messiah of Israel* (Oxford: Oxford University Press 2001) 170; see also pp. 49-50.

The Death of Josiah and Royal Theodicy

The above analysis indicates that against the background of the Deuteronomistic presentation of Josiah's religious and political program, the catastrophe of Megiddo in 609 was a major political and religious setback for Deuteronomic (and Deuteronomistic) circles. This is so whether we explain the events at Megiddo as a consequence of the battle between Josiah and Necho, or as resulting from some sort of internal-political struggle between pro- and anti-Deuteronomists which may have led Necho to eliminate what he perceived to be a dangerous vassal.[13] Either way, *the righteous king who had put his supreme confidence in Yhwh was killed.* I have elsewhere devoted a special study to the traditions surrounding Josiah where I propose that his dramatic end at Megiddo gave rise to new trends in Judaean royal ideology which are reflected in certain passages of the Hebrew Bible.[14] The following texts may be mentioned in support of this hypothesis:

Jer 22:10-12 indicates that the death of Josiah was experienced as a great national trauma in Judah. Mourning songs were sung for Josiah for many months. It is noteworthy that, after the deportation of Shallum (three months after the catastrophe at Megiddo), Jeremiah feels it necessary to exhort the people to mourn no longer for Josiah but rather for Shallum. On the other hand, the Chronicler (2 Chron 35:24-25) recounts that mourning songs were composed over the fate of Josiah and

---

[13]See the different interpretations of the 'battle' of Megiddo in R. N. Nelson, "Realpolitik in Judah (687-609 B.C.E.)," In: W. W. Hallo, J. C. Moyer, L. G. Perdue (eds), *Scripture in Context II. More Essays on the Comparative Method* (Winona Lake: Eisenbrauns 1983) 177-189; N. Na'aman, 'The Kingdom of Judah under Josiah.' Tel Aviv 18 (1991) 3-71, esp. 54-55; Laato, *Josiah and David Redivivus*, 78-79; idem, *A Star Is Rising* 136-138.

[14]Laato, *Josiah and David Redivivus*, 59-68, 361-363; *idem*, "Beloved and lovely! Despised and rejected. Some reflections on the death of Josiah" 115-128.

they were sung even as late as his time i.e. about 400 BC[15] if not even later. This suggests that such laments for Josiah were influential in the royal ideology and may also be reflected in certain texts of the Hebrew Bible.

Assuming that Josiah introduced a Deuteronomic reformation in Jerusalem[16], it is reasonable to expect that his fate at Megiddo and the subsequent trauma would have left its traces in the Deuteronomistic literature. This means that the setback at Megiddo presented proponents of Deuteronomism with considerable theological difficulties, which then prompted an hermeneutic explanation. Such hermeneutic explanations are prominent in 2 Kings 22-23, Psalm 89 and probably also in the Book of Jeremiah.

We have already seen that 2 Kings 22-23 has a tendency to shift responsibility for the catastrophe at Megiddo onto the shoulders of the generation of Manasseh, which had committed so many sins that Yhwh did not forgive his people despite Josiah's righteousness (2 Kgs 23:25-27, 29-30). In 2 Kgs 23:25-27 Josiah's reign is evaluated by observing that, although he was an exceedingly righteous king, Judah could not escape the punishment apportioned by Yhwh on account of Manasseh's sins (2 Kgs 21:7-14). 2 Kgs 23:25-27 is followed by a Deuteronomistic comment containing further reference to the reign of Josiah (2 Kgs 23:28). Immediately after this verse, Josiah's death at the battle of Megiddo is reported (2 Kgs 23:29-30). This gives us reason to believe that the Deuteronomist regarded the catastrophe at Megiddo as a consequence of the sins which Judah committed during the reign of Manasseh. Furthermore, it seems that the Deuteronomist regarded the

---

[15]The date 400 BC is an option if we trust the genealogy of the house of David in 1 Chr 3:17-24 to give us a reliable date. For this see H.G.M. Williamson, *1 and 2 Chronicles* (The New Century Bible Commentary, Grand Rapids: Eerdmans 1982) 15-17.

[16]See the survey of the different opinions in Laato, *Josiah and David Redivivus* 37-52; E. Eynikel, *The Reform of King Josiah and the Composition of the Deuteronomistic History* (OTS 33; Leiden: Brill 1996); Sweeney, *King Josiah of Judah* 40-51.

catastrophe of Megiddo as being the *de facto* end of Judah – a belief which is supported by 2 Kgs 23:25-27: Yhwh has decided to destroy the city and send his people into exile. This characterization of Josiah's reign in 2 Kings 22-23 and the tendency to shift the blame to Manasseh suggests that the text is trying to resolve the problem of theodicy which arose from two circumstances: (i) that Josiah introduced reforms in accordance with the will of Yhwh (according to the Deuteronomistic view) and was thus seen as a righteous king; and (ii) that Josiah was killed at Megiddo, which caused the dissolution of his Deuteronomic programme and ultimately the exile of the people. These two circumstances created a paradox which required explanation since the catastrophe at Megiddo implied that Josiah was not favored by Yhwh and, even worse, that the Deuteronomic programme did not express Yhwh's will.

A corresponding royal theodicy can be found in Psalm 89, which is also connected with the Deuteronomistic ideology. The Psalm should be interpreted in such a way that the collective group is lamenting the demise of the royal house, the very dynasty which laid waste the whole country. This political setback would correspond well to either the events which occurred at Megiddo in 609, or in Judah in 588-586.[17] Seen in this light, the Psalm has royal theodicy as its central theme. Why did Yhwh reject his anointed one to whom he had promised to be faithful? This question was surely one of which the people were acutely aware, both after the fall of the kingdom of Judah and after the catastrophe of Megiddo. This gives us reason to suppose that Josiah became a model for a righteous Davidic king rejected by Yhwh. I read Psalm 89 so that – even if the Psalm does originate from the exilic period – Josiah and his

---

[17]The connection between Psalm 89 and the Deuteronomistic theology has been convincingly shown by Veijola (*Verheissung in der Krise. Studien zur Literatur und Theologie der Exilszeit anhand des 89. Psalms* [AASF B 120, Helsinki 1982] 47-118). I have criticized Veijola's view that the promise of an eternal dynasty given to David has been reinterpreted collectively as referring to the whole people and only to the people. See A. Laato, *Josiah and David Redivivus* 61-67.

reign constitute its focal points. *First*, according to the Deuteronomistic History, the catastrophe of Megiddo was a turning-point in the history of Judah. Yhwh caused this catastrophe in order to prepare for the deportation of the people into exile (see 2 Kgs 23:26-27 and 29-30). Therefore it is reasonable to assume that, according to the Deuteronomist, the Davidic dynasty, in fact, collapsed after the catastrophe at Megiddo. *Second*, Josiah was regarded as a righteous king and it was believed that he would recreate a great empire like that of David. Josiah was a king who came close to realizing the ideals presented in Ps 89:20-38: under his rule the people lived together in peace (vv 23-24); he reigned over a great realm (v 26); he acted righteously (vv 31-38). The setback which Josiah (and Judah) suffered at Megiddo made him a *typos* of the righteous king in the House of David who was rejected by Yhwh.

A similar theological royal theodicy connected with the death of Josiah may also be found in the Book of Jeremiah. In the present form of the Book, the prophet's critical attitude toward Josiah's reform initiatives before 622 (Jer 3:6-13; cf., 2 Chron 34:1-8) may have been cited to show that, although Josiah was a righteous king (Jer 22:15-16), the people did not return whole-heartedly to Yhwh (cf., the summaries in Jer 25:3; 36:2 which have the same tenor). This portrayal of the generation of Josiah and their return to Yhwh indicates that a redactor may have explained the prophet's disappointed expectations (the core of Jeremiah 30-31) in terms of the people's half-hearted attempts to return to Yhwh.[18]

---

[18]Concerning the interpretation of Jeremiah 30-31 in conjunction with the reign of Josiah note the following studies: N. Lohfink, "Der junge Jeremia als Propagandist und Poet. Zum Grundstock von Jer 30-31," in: P. M. Bogaert (ed.) *Le livre de Jérémie. Le prophète et son milieu, les oracles et leur transmission* (BETL 54, Leuven: Peeters 1981) 351-68; idem, "Die Gotteswortverschachtelung in Jer 30-31," in: L. Ruppert, P. Weimar, E. Zenger (eds), *Künder des Wortes: Beiträge zur Theologie der Propheten Josef Schreiner zum 60. Geburtstag* (Würzburg: Echter Verlag 1982) 105-119; W. L. Holladay, *Jeremiah 2* (Hermeneia, Philadelphia 1989); G. Fischer, *Das Trostbüchlein. Text, Komposition und Theologie von Jer 30-31* (SBB 26, Stuttgart: Katholisches Bibelwerk 1993).

The fact that the Chronicler states that laments were sung over the fate of Josiah as late as the Persian period (2 Chron 35:24-25) indicates that his dramatic end at Megiddo could have influenced even very late traditions. In my view, Zech 12:9-13:1 represents one such tradition. Scholars have suggested that behind the "messianic" figure in Zech 9-14 there is a historical personage and his personal fate.[19] However, in Zech 11:4-14 the prophet is enjoined to assume the role of the good shepherd which indicates that the messianic figure in Zechariah 9-14 is one who will come. Zechariah 9-14 explains why the promised messianic age prophesied so vehemently in Zechariah 1-6 did not become reality in the early postexilic period. Zech 11:4-14 turns aside the hopes of Ezekiel 34 and 37:15-28, indicating that because of disobedience of the people the messianic age was not realized. In Zech 12:9-13:1 the postponement of the messianic era is seen as a similar catastrophe which came to pass in Judah in the time of Josiah.[20]

Zech 12:9-13:1 contains three themes which can be connected traditio-historically with the death of Josiah at Megiddo. *First*, according to 2 Chron 35:23 Josiah was pierced by arrows during the battle of Megiddo. Just like Josiah, the figure who is close to Yhwh in Zech 12:10 is pierced (דקר). *Second*, the mourning of the people over the fate of Josiah (see Jer 22:8; 2 Chron 35:24-25) is reminiscent of the mourning over the pierced one (Zech 12:10-13). *Third*, the mourning ritual, according to Zech 12:10-13, will be held at the plain of Megiddo, the very place where Josiah was killed.

The interpretation of 'Hadad-Rimmon' in 12:11 is difficult. The question is whether it refers to the name of a deity or to the name of a place on the plain of Megiddo. The first alternative is the most widely

---

[19]So, for example, M. Hengel, "The Effective History of Isaiah 53 in the Pre-Christian Period," in: B. Janowski & P. Stuhlmacher (eds), *The Suffering Servant: Isaiah 53 in Jewish and Christian Sources* (Grand Rapids: Eerdmans 2004) 75-146, esp. 85-90.

[20]See the detailed interpretation of Zechariah 9-14 in my studies *Josiah and David Redivivus* 260-301 and *A Star Is Rising* 208-218.

accepted view among scholars.[21] The problem with the second is that there is no evidence for the existence of a place name 'Hadad-Rimmon' near Megiddo. Jerome identifies the place with Maximianopolis = *el-leggun*, south of Megiddo, but this identification can neither be confirmed nor excluded by means of other sources.[22] Despite of the difficulty of identifying Hadad-Rimmon, I prefer to regard the term as a toponym for the following reasons. *First*, the grammatical structure of the phrase כְּמִסְפַּד הֲדַד־רִמּוֹן (without the preposition עַל) differs from a similar formulation found in v 10 where we read כְּמִסְפֵּד עַל־הַיָּחִיד. This indicates that v 11 does not refer to weeping for Hadad-Rimmon but the weeping of/in Hadad-Rimmon. A close grammatical parallel to the expression מִסְפַּד הֲדַד־רִמּוֹן is מִסְפַּד בֵּית הָאֵצֶל, found in Mic 1:11. Mic 1:11 uses this similar expression to refer to a place. It is likely that the preposition בְּ was avoided in מִסְפַּד הֲדַד רִמּוֹן due to its occurrence in the phrase בְּבִקְעַת מְגִדּוֹן. *Second*, many place names in the Old Testament contain the word Rimmon: Rimmon, Rimmon-perez, Gath-Rimmon and En-Rimmon. Thus Hadad-Rimmon could well be yet another place name with this element. *Third*, if one attempts to read the name of a pagan mourning-cult deity 'Hadad-Rimmon' here, one has to explain how this fits the text, which is not easy.

The typological use of the fate of Josiah in Zech 12:10-13:1 provides evidence in favour of the theory that Josiah's death at Megiddo was once interpreted as vicarious. In Zech 12:10-13:1 an interesting connection is forged between the typology of Josiah's death (12:10) and Yhwh's forgiveness (13:1) of the people when they return to him (12:11-13). It is reasonable to assume that vicarious interpretations developed from the Deuteronomistic theodicy concerning the death of the righteous Josiah at Megiddo. In 2 Kings 22-23 and Psalm 89 an attempt has been

---

[21]See the overview in W.A. Maier, "Hadadrimmon." *ABD* 3:13.

[22]See J. Simons, *The Geographical and Topographical Texts of the Old Testament. A Concise Commentary in XXXII Chapters* (Leiden: Brill 1959) 479.

made to explain the rejection of the (faithful) Davidic king (against the promise of Yhwh to David) hermeneutically. In 2 Kings 22-23 the fate of Josiah seems to have been connected with the sins of Manasseh and the rejection of the Davidic king in Psalm 89 is understood to militate against the promise of Yhwh which will open the door to the future of the people.

The Fate of Josiah as Traditio-historical Background for Isaiah 53

The concept of the vicarious death of a figure who is closely associated with Yhwh is clearly visible in Isaiah 53. The suffering and death of Yhwh's servant enables a renewed relationship between Yhwh and his people. My theory is that Isaiah 53 is traditio-historically linked with the catastrophe of Megiddo. Isaiah 53, in turn, exhibits several points of formal resemblance to lamentations (2 Chron 35:24-25; see also Zech 12:10-13:1).

Hedwig Jahnow has shown that many of the motifs of Isaiah 53 run parallel to those which occur in lamentation texts, but at same time they are intensified.[23] *First*, a lamentation customarily eulogizes the good character or salutary characteristics of the deceased. In 2 Sam 1:23 we read "Saul and Jonathan, beloved and lovely" but the abhorrent appearance of the servant is depicted in Isa 53:2: 'He had no form or charm, we saw him but he had no beauty to win our hearts'. *Second*, the deceased was depicted as an upright member of society. Saul is praised in 2 Sam 1:24: "O daughters of Israel, weep over Saul, who clothed you with crimson, in luxury, who put ornaments of gold on your apparel." The servant, on the other hand, "was despised, forsaken by the men ... despised, for whom we had no regard" (Isa 53:3). Furthermore, Isa 53:8 states that the contemporaries of the servant paid no attention to (the sufferings of) the servant. *Third*, lamentations over ancient heroes

---

[23]H. Jahnow, *Das hebräische Leichenlied im Rahmen der Völkerdichtung* (Giessen: Töpelmann, 1923) 262-265.

eulogized them for their courage and sometimes compared them to mighty animals: "Saul and Jonathan ... they were swifter than eagles, they were stronger than lions" (2 Sam 1:23). The servant by contrast has been portrayed as a sacrificial lamb: "like a lamb led to slaughter-house, like a bound sheep before its shearers he never opened his mouth" (Isa 53:7). *Fourth*, honorable burial was an essential last rite of the deceased. This becomes apparent in the case of Saul and Jonathan where it is important to show due respect to their dead bodies (2 Sam 2:4-7). However, in Isaiah 53 it is stated that the servant "was given a grave with the wicked."

Isaiah 53's inversion of the normal portrayal of the deceased using lamentations shows that the fate of the servant is being hyperbolized – a feature which probably reflects the profound sorrow and disappointment associated with the problem of the *theodicy*. We have discussed whether it is possible to find traces of lamentation for the death of Josiah in the Hebrew Bible. We have argued that in these laments the righteous king and the political disaster at Megiddo (and later the exilic catastrophe) were seen as diametrical opposites. The mourning for Josiah could well explain the new theological tendency to use the covenant of David to emphasize God's mercy for the people (Isa 55:3-5).

The demise of Josiah, which represented a formidable setback for the Deuteronomic and Deuteronomistic circles, would provide a harmonious traditio-historical background for the degree of disappointment and sorrow reflected in Isaiah 53, even though the passage in its present form does not even mention him or his death at Megiddo. If we assume for a moment that this is so, the origins of a vicarious interpretation of Josiah's death must still be explained. I have argued for a plausible model of such developments in the royal ideology:

The fundamental premise of this *theodicy* was the promise of the eternal dynasty which Yhwh gave to David (2 Sam 7; Ps 89). This promise was seen as an unconditional guarantee that Yhwh would watch over and sustain the Davidic dynasty eternally. While the disobedience of Davidic kings might provoke Yhwh's wrath, it was thought that his punishment would never amount to complete rejection. Josiah was hailed as a righteous king who acted according to Yhwh's will. During Josiah's reign Judah hoped for the restoration of a pan-Israelite kingdom like that of David. Without question Yhwh's promise to the Davidic dynasty played a significant role in contemporary thought. Josiah was regarded by Deuteronomic circles as David Redivivus who was loyal to Yhwh and therefore expected to receive his blessing. Josiah's death at Megiddo was the first major historical event which seriously shook the belief that Yhwh would support the Davidic dynasty eternally. The very same king who had reestablished the Yhwh-cult in the temple and had conducted his reign according to Yhwh's will was killed by the enemies of Yhwh. The dissonance between reality and religious (i.e. Deuteronomic) expectations required an answer to the question: Why did Yhwh not support his righteous one?[24]

The account of the death of Josiah preserved in these lamentations (2 Chron 35:24-25) provided a paradigm for the paradox experienced by Judah (and Israel): a righteous Davidic king was abandoned by Yhwh. Such a reading is feasible in Psalm 89 which is composed of linguistic and stylistic parallels to the servant proclamation in Isaiah 40-55. The central theme in this royal psalm is *theodicy*: Why did Yhwh reject his anointed warrior (see vv 39-46) to whom he had promised to be faithful through the pledge given to David (vv 4-5, 20-38)? In the Deuteronomistic History this *theodicy* concerning Josiah was resolved by asserting that Yhwh rejected the righteous Josiah because of the sins committed by the people during the reign of Manasseh (2 Kgs 23:26-30). Even though 2 Kgs 23:26-27 cannot be interpreted to mean that Josiah's death was vicarious (the punishment of the exile was unavoidable for the people) the notion that it was due to the people's sins does provide a starting-point for a vicarious explanation of the disaster

---

[24]Concerning the dissonance theory see R.P. Carroll, *When Prophecy Failed: Reactions and Responses to Failure in the Old Testament Prophetic Traditions* (London: SCM Press 1979).

at Megiddo. Such a theological explanation of the matter may have prompted further reflection, especially during the subsequent crisis which afflicted the entire nation, the exile.

After the catastrophe of 587/86, when the Davidic dynasty was dethroned, the *theodicy* concerning Josiah's fate was developed further and extended to include the fate of the nation. The historical events of 587/86 seemed to indicate forcefully and indisputably that Yhwh's promise to the Davidic dynasty was no longer valid. Religious belief in an eternal Davidic dynasty conflicted with reality, provoking several attempts to resolve the conflict by means of theological explanation. It is clear that the explanations put forward included one to the effect that Yhwh had revoked his promise to the Davidic dynasty in consequence of the people's sins. This would correspond to the assertions of 2 Kgs 23:26-27, where the death of Josiah was attributed to the sins of the ungodly Manasseh. In light of the fact that the death of Josiah was viewed as tantamount to the dissolution of the kingdom of Judah in that period it is plausible to assume that his death at Megiddo became a symbol of the rejection of the Davidic dynasty. However, the rejection of the Davidic dynasty was not only regarded as an omen of Yhwh's judgement of his people. Since the rejection of the Davidic dynasty ran counter to the promise of Yhwh, a glimmer of hope remained.

Yhwh's promise to David opened the door to the belief that the rejection of the Davidic dynasty (which, according to the Deuteronomist, happened at Megiddo) should be seen as a vicarious rejection. The rejection of the Davidic dynasty of the righteous Josiah at Megiddo was seen as a punishment for the sins of the people. The rejection of the Davidic dynasty and the annulment of the unconditional promise given to David, coupled with the exile of the people were seen as Yhwh's "double punishment for all sins" (cf., Isa 40:2). This belief emerged during the exile when the "vicarious suffering and death" of the Davidic dynasty (intensified by the demise of Josiah) formed the traditio-historical background for Isaiah 53 (and also for Zech 12:9-13:1). This theology would partly explain the exilic interpretation of Yhwh's promise to the Davidic dynasty as applying collectively to the people. This theological emphasis can be found in Isa 55:3-5, in the context of Isaiah 53.

In other words it may be said that the theological interpretation of the promise of an eternal Davidic dynasty as concerning the whole people emphasized the tension between Yhwh's punishment of the dynasty and the people and his pledge. On the one hand, the destruction of the Davidic dynasty might be interpreted as a consequence of the sins committed by the people under the leadership of the Davidic kings during the pre-exilic period. On the other, the destruction of the dynasty was understood to contravene Yhwh's promise to David. This contrast between the *disobedience* of the people, which led to the destruction of the dynasty, and the ultimate *mercy* of Yhwh according to his promise, which would have implied only a limited punishment of the dynasty and not its total dissolution, opens the door to a theological interpretation which sees this collapse as 'vicarious suffering.' In order for Yhwh to show mercy to his disobedient people a severe punishment must be imposed on the dynasty in contravention of the promise. The crescendo of this punishment was seen in the tragic death of Josiah. In proposing that the vicarious interpretation of the "dissolution" of the dynasty was given additional force by reflections on the death of Josiah, I would like to emphasize that we lack *expressis verbis* evidence in the Old Testament. In my view, however, the episode of Josiah at Megiddo provides a traditio-historical background for certain texts, like Isaiah 53 and Zech 12:10-13:1, which are legendary by reason of the difficulties they present to those who attempt to interpret them in historical terms.

In my study *The Servant of YHWH and Cyrus* I also discussed our ability to break the code of the Josianic royal ideology behind the servant figure and the Cyrus proclamation which influenced Isaiah 40-55. In that study I argued, in part following the opinions of other scholars, that the Servant and Cyrus proclamation in Isaiah 40-55 is reminiscent of

Akkadian and Israelite royal ideology at several points.[25] I even tried to reconstruct and report earlier literary layers of the royal texts which overshadowed Isa 42:1-4; 49:1-6 and 52:13-53:12.[26] The role of Josiah is particularly important in the royal ideology which provides the traditio-historical background of Isaiah 40-55.

The vicarious interpretation of Josiah's death was later disparaged as becomes clear from 2 Chronicles 35's assertion that it resulted from his disobedience to the word of Yhwh spoken to him by Pharaoh Necho. The Chronicler attempted thereby to annul all the vicarious interpretations which had previously been advanced concerning Josiah's fate. The description in 2 Chron 35:20-23 is reminiscent of the account of the battle at Ramoth-Gilead in 1 Kgs 22:29-38. Thus the Chronicler tried to portray Josiah as responsible for his own death: Josiah was like Ahab, who did not heed the warnings against going into battle. If this is the case, then the Chronicler, who knew many laments composed over the death of Josiah, wished to put an end to all possible vicarious interpretations connected with the fate of this king. He interpreted Josiah's fate at Megiddo according to the retribution theology which plays so important a role in Chronicles.[27]

---

[25]See J.W. Behr, *The Writings of Deutero-Isaiah and the Neo-Babylonian Royal Inscriptions: A Comparison of the Language and Style* (Publications of the University of Pretoria III:3) Pretoria 1937; S.M. Paul, "Deutero-Isaiah and Cuneiform Royal Inscriptions." *JAOS* 88 (1968) 180-186; Laato, *The Servant of YHWH and Cyrus* 47-68. See further O. Kaiser, *Der königliche Knecht: Eine traditions-geschichtlich-exegetische Studie über die Ebed-Jahwe-Lieder bei Deuterojesaja* (FRLANT 52; Göttingen: Vandenhoeck & Ruprecht 1959).

[26]Laato, *The Servant of YHWH and Cyrus* 249-280.

[27]Concerning the Chronicler's retribution theology see S. Japhet, "Theodicy in Ezra-Nehemiah and Chronicles," In: A. Laato & J.C. De Moor (eds), *Theodicy in the World of the Bible* (Leiden: Brill 2003) 429-469.

The Interpretation of Isaiah 53 in the Hebrew Bible

Isaiah 53 incorporates a vivid picture of the servant who becomes close to Yhwh through his sufferings.[28] In order to understand the nature of theodicy in Isaiah 53 our first question should not concern the identification of the servant in the historical context of Deutero-Isaiah. As Johannes Lindblom astutely says: "Nobody would ask, *Who was* the prodigal son? but, What does the prodigal son *signify?* Nor should we ask, *Who* is the suffering servant in Isa. LIII? The correct question is this: What does the suffering servant *signify?*" and "It is necessary strictly to distinguish between a narrative of historical facts in the strict sense and a symbolical and allegorical picture." and "The decisive question is no longer: *Who* is the Ebed Yahweh in these Songs? but: What are the historical facts which are to be elucidated by the symbols employed."[29] Following Lindblom we shall first describe the ideological setting of Isaiah 53 in order to understand the "symbols employed" therein.

The atonement theology plays a central role in Isaiah 53.[30] The Servant of Isaiah 53 is portrayed in words reminiscent of the description of the scapegoat in Leviticus 16.[31] *First*, the expression עָוֹן נֹשֵׂא in Lev 16:22 indicates that the scapegoat is sent to the place of chaos and destruction (= desert) in order to carry away the sins of the society. In a similar way the servant of Isaiah 53 is described as bearing the sins of the people and annulling them through his own suffering and death. The verb

---

[28]See, e.g., E. Haag, "Die Botschaft vom Gottesknecht. Ein Weg zur Überwindung der Gewalt." in: N. Lohfink (ed), *Gewalt und Gewaltlosigkeit im Alten Testament* (Quaestiones disputatae 96; Freiburg: Herder 1983) 159-213.

[29]The quotations are from J. Lindblom, *The Servant Songs in Deutero-Isaiah: A New Attempt to Solve an Old Problem* (Lund: Gleerups 1951) 48, 51.

[30]See our discussion in sect. 1.

[31]See Mettinger, *A Farewell to the Servant Songs* 42. See also Laato, *The Servant of Yhwh and Cyrus* 144.

32

נָשָׂא is used twice in Isaiah 53 in a manner which emphasizes the servant's vicarious suffering:

אָכֵן חֳלָיֵנוּ הוּא נָשָׂא Isa 53:4

וְהוּא חֵטְא־רַבִּים נָשָׂא Isa 53:12

Second, the phrase אֶל אֶרֶץ גְּזֵרָה in Lev 16:22 is parallelled by the expression כִּי נִגְזַר מֵאֶרֶץ חַיִּים in Isa 53:8. The verbal root גזר occurs in both passages and the expression in Isa 53:8 implies the concept of the "world of the death" to which ארץ in Lev 16:22 refers. Through his suffering the servant becomes a mediator between Yhwh and the people and introduces the new salvation-historical period for Israel.

The problem concerning the identifications of the personae is well defined in Clines' study *I, He, We & They: A Literary Approach to Isa 53*. Clines observes that "he" in Isa 52:13-53:12 "stands in the centre of nexus of relationships" between "I", "we" and "they".[32] He concludes that it is impossible to identify any of these personae with certainty. Moreover that the poem is "open-ended and allows for multiple interpretations"[33] Clines handles the difficult problem of the identity of personae in Isa 52:13-53:12 by referring to the notion of intended ambiguity.

I am not convinced that Clines is correct when he asserts that the author responsible for the present form of Isaiah 53 composed the passage so ambiguously that it is no longer possible to determine precisely whom these personae signify – even though I believe that the aim has never been to identify the persona of the servant or the "we"- and "they"-groups exactly. Before we consider the problem of the identification of the personae in Isaiah 53 we shall first deal with three

---

[32]D.J.A. Clines, *I, He, We, & They: A Literary Approach to Isaiah 53* (JSOTSS 1, Sheffield: Sheffield Academic Press 1983) 38-39. See also K. Joachimsen, *Identities in Transition: The Pursuit of Isa. 52:13-53:12* (SupVT 142, Leiden: Brill 2011).

[33]Clines, *I, He, We, & They* 33; see also 59-65.

themes which – I believe – form the essential background for a correct understanding of Isaiah 53:[34] 1) non-retributive suffering, 2) "blotting out" of the sins and 3) punishment of the people.

The non-retributive suffering motif in Isaiah 40-55: Suffering is often presented in the Hebrew Bible as a consequence of the sins committed by the sufferer. This same view is also to be found in Isaiah 40-55 (see e.g., Isa 42:18-25; 43:22-28). In Isaiah 53, however, the sufferer is one who lives in a right relation to Yhwh. In addition to Isaiah 53, there are two important passages in Isaiah 40-55 where the suffering motif occurs independently of the notion of retribution. The first passage is 49:7, where reference is clearly made to Israel:

> Thus says Yhwh, the redeemer of Israel, its Holy One,
>> to the one who is despised, detested by the nation, to the slave of rulers:
> Kings will stand up when they see, princes will see and bow low,
>> because of Yhwh who is faithful, the Holy One of Israel who has chosen you.

Here the suffering motif serves to strengthen the contrast between Israel and the nations (kings and princes). Israel who is the servant of the nations and who has suffered greatly will in future be honored by its former oppressors. The context reveals that this homage will be paid to Israel because Yhwh will bring back his people from their exile (49:10-12). This exodus is a typological fulfilment of the first exodus from Egypt when Yhwh bore witness to all peoples that he can save the humble who are living amid tribulation. Furthermore, the context of Isa 49:7 demonstrates that the reference is to the loyal Israel which puts its trust in Yhwh. The ideal Israel is given the mission to bring the people back to Yhwh (49:3,5-6; 8-9). The ideal servant Israel (49:3) proclaims among the nations the salvation of Yhwh which will be realized through Cyrus and exhorts the people of Yhwh to trust in the God of Israel. The

---

[34]The following discussion is based on Laato, *The Servant of Yhwh and Cyrus*.

goal of the mission of the ideal Israel is to gather and prepare the people of Yhwh for the new exodus which will ultimately lead to the salvation of the whole world (Isa 49:5-6, 8-9). A similar combination of the new exodus from Babylon and the exalted position of Israel among the nations appears in Isa 45:14-17. Thus we may say that Isa 49:7 presents the sufferings of the loyal Israel as part and parcel of its mission. These sufferings will be ended and the peoples will see how Israel will return from Babylon to the Holy Land. At that time Israel will be honored among the nations. The combination of the three themes: (1) the sufferings of the loyal Israel, (2) the new exodus and (3) the exalted position of Israel among the nations is also manifested in Isa 52:11-15.

Another passage which mentions of suffering in consequence of loyalty to Yhwh is Isa 50:6-7 which describes the ideal Israel:

> I have offered my back to those who struck me,
>> my cheeks to those who plucked my beard;
> I have not hidden my face from insult and spitting.
>> Lord Yhwh comes to my help,
> this is why insult has not touched me,
>> this is why I have set my face like flint
> and I know that I shall not be put to shame.

How can we then explain the reiteration of this theological motif in Isaiah 40-55, whereby the suffering is described as quintessential for one who has a right relationship to Yhwh? The theme of the innocent suffering of the righteous is typical of the Psalter and we may assume that the Psalms – the language of which influenced the style and language of Isaiah 40-55 also in other ways[35] – constitute important background material for the positive suffering motif in Isaiah 40-55.

The theological concept of individual retribution should be given special emphasis in this connection. Lam 5:7 clearly indicates that collective retribution was a popular issue among the Jews of the exilic

---

[35]For these connections see, e.g., J.H. Eaton, *Festal Drama in Deutero-Isaiah* (London: SPCK 1979).

period. The generation born in exile sought an answer to the question: why do we still suffer even though it was our fathers who sinned against Yhwh? This same problem is also reflected in the identical phraseology of Ezek 18:2 and Jer 31:29: "The fathers have eaten unripe grapes; the children's teeth are set on edge." In the contexts of Jeremiah 31 and Ezekiel 18 this saying is dismissed with the help of the theological concept of individual retribution. Every man is responsible only for his own actions, not for his father's. Even though this theological outlook may be articulated to comfort those living amid tribulation because it offers hope, it nevertheless created a new problem namely that of the suffering of the righteous. Why should the righteous suffer the torments of exile if they were not responsible for their fathers' sins? I believe that the positive understanding of the sufferings of the loyal Israel described in Isaiah 40-55 constitutes an attempt to find an answer to this question. The final answer is given in Isaiah 53.

The theological problem of "blotting out" the sins of the people: The exile was interpreted in the Old Testament tradition as Yhwh's punishment of his people. So it is no wonder that the remission of sin became a crucial theological problem among the Jewish people during the exile. Under what circumstances would Yhwh have forgiven his people? This was the vital question which required a theological answer. In the Old Testament this problem is connected with the hopes of restoration. This theme of blotting out sins is also central in Isa 40:1-2 which begins the so-called Deutero-Isaian corpus, Isaiah 40-55 (see also 44:21-22). In order to penetrate this theme in Isaiah 40-55 I first deal with the question of how this theme was interpreted in the texts of the early postexilic period.

In Zech 1-8 the problem of the "blotting out" of sins is connected with the messianic hopes which were not fulfilled. Zech 3:8-10, together with 3:1-7, is a later addition to the cycle of seven visions,[36] which refer to the coming messianic age when the sins of the people will finally be blotted out. Zech 3:8-10 should be read bearing in mind that the reorganization of Jewish society at the beginning of the Persian period did not fulfill the hopes of the religious circle of Zechariah (and Haggai). Even though the Temple was rebuilt, the messianic expectations connected with Zerubbabel were not realized. This was seen as a sign that Yhwh had not yet fully forgiven his people. According to Zech 3:8-10, the appearance of the Messiah would be the final proof of Yhwh's mercy upon his people (when their political freedom would also be restored). At that time the sins of the people will finally be remitted. The theme of Zech 3:8-10 was developed further in Zech 12:10-13:1.[37]

Other postexilic texts, too, contain this tension between Yhwh's mercy upon the people and concrete political freedom. The prayers preserved in Ezra 9 and Nehemiah 9 portray Yhwh withholding the fullness of his mercy towards the people even though he has sent them some signs of his favour. These prayers show clearly that the issue of complete forgiveness was of considerable concern among religious Jews during the Persian period. The prayers reflect a yearning for the political freedom of the Judean people.[38]

The central theme in the sacrificial cult of the postexilic period was the act of *kipper*, which is closely related to the crucial theological emphasis in the Jewish religious community: Yhwh's forgiveness. The

---

[36]This has been shown convincingly in Chr. Jeremias, *Die Nachtgesichte des Sacharja: Untersuchungen zu ihrer Stellung im Zusammenhang der Visionsberichte im Alten Testament und zu ihrem Bildmaterial* (FRLANT 117; Göttingen: Vandenhoeck & Ruprecht 1977).

[37]See further the interpretation of Zech 3:8-10 and 12:10-13:1 in Laato, *Josiah and David Redivivus*, 240-246, 288-293.

[38]See especially A.H.J. Gunneweg, *Esra* (KAT 19/1, Gütersloh: Mohn 1985) 164-172; idem, *Nehemia* (KAT 19/2, Gütersloh: Mohn 1987) 121-129. See further on Ezra's and Nehemiah's religious and political program in Laato, *Josiah and David Redivivus*, 332-341; 346-349.

theological outlook of the Priestly document concerning the sacrificial cult may contain an eschatological dimension – which also accords with Ezekiel 40-48 where the imminent reorganization of the cult is described in a style similar to that of the Priestly Code. In this light it is understandable why a reference to the eschatological expiation of sin may be found also in later Jewish Apocalyptic literature, for example, in Dan 9:24-27 and in the literature of the Qumran community (see CD IV,9-10; XIV,18-19; XX,34 and IQM II,5-6).[39]

These examples from the Old Testament and later Jewish writings show that the final blotting out of the sins of the people constituted a significant eschatological theme in Jewish theology, at least from the beginning of the Persian period. This eschatological event was closely connected with the political independence of the people. Thus it seems that the final proof of Yhwh's forgiveness was a specific salvation-historical event: the delivery of the people from every foreign yoke. Against this background it is not surprising when Isaiah 40-55 proposes the central argument that a new historical beginning for Israel would be realized through Cyrus. Now the hope of an exodus from Babylon and the subsequent miraculous age of salvation preserved in the prophetic traditions were not beyond reach. This yearning for a new beginning for the nation of Israel is regarded by Isaiah 40-55 as an indication that Yhwh would pour out his mercy upon his people and forgive their sins. This theme is expressed in Isa 40:1-2 which begins the macrostructure[40] of Isaiah 40-53; in 44:21-22 which begins the central cycle of Isa 40-53;

---

[39]Concerning the eschatological *kipper* ritual at Qumran see A. Laato, "The Eschatological Act of kipper in the Damascus Document," In: Z.J. Kapera (ed), *Intertestamental Essays in honour of Jósef Tadeusz Milik Volume 1* (Qumranica Mogilanensia 6; Cracow: Enigma 1992) 91-107; *idem*, "The idea of kipper in Judaisms of late antiquity," *Khristianskij Vostok* (= Christian Orient) 1 (1999) 155-193. Concerning the date of Dan 9:24-27 see further A. Laato, "The Seventy Yearweeks in the Book of Daniel," *ZAW* 102 (1990) 212-225.

[40]I have presented one possible macrostructure for Isaiah 40-55. See A. Laato, "The Composition of Isaiah 40-55," *JBL* 109 (1990) 203-224.

and in 52:13-53:12 which concludes the composition. The forgiveness of Yhwh was thought to be based not only on the just punishment of the people but also on the innocent suffering of the righteous, as becomes clear from Isaiah 53.

The theological problem of the punishment of the people: That the people must be punished for their sins is an unbreakable rule in the Old Testament. This same rule also applies in Isaiah 40-55 as we noted above. However, we have also seen that the suffering of the faithful Israel is presented in Isaiah 40-55 in a manner which cannot – in view of the context – be interpreted as a punishment for sin. What then is the significance of the suffering of the righteous in Isaiah 40-55?

Isa 40:1-2 comforts Zion and the people of Yhwh by saying that it has now received "twice" from Yhwh's hand for its sins. The implication of these words of comfort is clear. The sins are now blotted out and therefore the people face a new future. The new future described in Isaiah 40-55 involves the return of the exiles to the Holy Land, and a new glorious period when the people will be honored among the nations. The operative word in Isa 40:1-2 is *kiplayim* which suggests that Zion and the people of Yhwh have experienced more punishment than was required. Because the context of Isaiah 40-55 presents the suffering of the righteous as having a positive effect we may ask whether it is possible that Isa 40:1-2 refers to the innocent suffering of the righteous which will be regarded as the final proof of Yhwh's forgiveness. This hypothesis receives more support in the compositional structure of Isaiah 40-53, where 40:1-2 and 52:13-53:12 were linked together.[41] If this is so, Isaiah 53 would then describe how the sufferings of the righteous will be of benefit to the whole people.

After discussing the three central theological themes we are now ready to deal with the personae in Isa 52:13-53:12 and whom they signify. The

---

[41]Concerning the connection between Isa 40:1-2 and 52:13-53:12 see also Mettinger, *A Farewell to the Servant Songs* 42.

passage refers to five different personae: "I", "he", "we" and "they" and "you" (masc. sing.) in 53:10 (see the textual note to 53:10).

The identification of "I" (and "you") is straightforward. Both Isa 52:13-15 and 53:11-12 are formulated in the first person and Yhwh is obviously the speaker. It is also easy to identify "he". The parallel content between 52:14b and 53:2b shows that "he" in Isaiah 53 is the servant whom Yhwh acclaims in 52:13. But who then is this suffering servant? The answer to this question is based on the following two points.

The *first* point concerns the miraculous event witnessed by the kings and the nations (52:15). Just what is taking place here? That this event was the resurrection of the servant is the most natural conclusion to be drawn from the context of Isaiah 53. This resurrection should not be taken literally but is rather a symbol of how the servant who has died will rise from the dead[42], analogous to the description in Ezek 37:1-14. It seems reasonable to assume that, as elsewhere in Isaiah 40-55 (where the servant is described as faithful to Yhwh), the servant in Isaiah 53 is the ideal Israel. The resurrection in Isaiah 53 can therefore be interpreted as a symbol both of the new exodus which will come to pass under the leadership of the ideal Israel, and of the political reorganization of Israel after "the death of the exile." This interpretation accords with the wider context where this political reorganization is portrayed as astonishing the peoples and kings who see the servant rise from death to vitality and strength. This interpretation of Isa 52:13-15 makes it a good parallel to Isa 49:7.

The *second* point concerns the connection between 52:11-12 and 52:13-15. As stated above 49:7 and its context combine the concepts of the suffering servant, the new exodus and the honoring of Israel among the nations and kings. These same themes are also united in 52:11-15. This being the case, there is good reason to conclude that the servant described in Isa 52:13-15 is the same ideal Israel referred to in 49:1-12.

---

[42]The dogma of the resurrection of the dead was not yet developed in the "Judaism" of the 6th and 5th Centuries B.C.

In more or less problematic treatments of Isaiah 53 it can often be read that Isa 53:8 strongly implies that the servant is an individual because the "people" cannot die for the sins of the people. However, this interpretation is invalid for two reasons:

First, Isa 49:3, 5-6 explicitly states that the servant Israel[43] has a mission to the people Israel/Jacob. This being the case it seems reasonable to postulate two different servant types in Isaiah 40-55: one who is faithful (described as servant and sometimes identified with Israel, but not with Jacob: 42:1-9; 49:1-13; 50:4-11; 51:4-8; 52:13-53:12) and willing to listen to the word of Yhwh, and another who is blind (often identified with "Israel and Jacob": 42:18-25; 43:1-7, 8-13; 44:1-5, 21-22).[44] The task of the faithful servant is to lead the disobedient servant back to Yhwh – which is the theme of Isa 49:1-6. In a corresponding way it can be argued that the sufferings of the righteous servant in Isaiah 53 can benefit the whole people. If we consider the possibility that traditions of the death of the righteous Josiah lie behind Isaiah 53 it is easy to understand the heavy emphasis on the individual features of the Servant. The traditio-historical background of Isaiah 53 explains why the passage has given rise to diverse interpretations.[45]

---

[43]Isa 49:3 states *expressis verbis* that the servant in question is Israel. There is no need to make any text-critical proposals that the word "Israel" was a later addition. For this see N. Lohfink, "Israel in Jes 49,3," in: J. Schreiner (ed), *Wort, Lied und Gottesspruch: Beiträge zu Psalmen und Propheten: FS Joseph Ziegler* (Bd. II; FzB 2; Würzburg: Echter, 1972) 217-229.

[44]Note especially the important studies of J.-H. Hermisson, "Der Lohn des Knechts," In: J. Jeremias & L. Perlitt (eds), *Die Botschaft und die Boten. Festschrift für H.W. Wolff zum 70. Geburtstag*, Neukirchen-Vluyn: Neukirchener Verlag 1981) 269-87; "Israel und der Gottesknecht bei Deuterojesaja" *ZThK* 79 (1982) 1-24; "Voreiliger Abschied von den Gottesknechtsliedern" *TR* NF 49 (1984) 209-22. Hermisson makes a distinction between the loyal servant (= prophet) and the disloyal servant (= the people).

[45]The modern exegetical discussion concerning the Servant as an individual goes back to Bernhard Duhm who in his commentary on the Book of Isaiah proposed that four servant texts in Isaiah 40-55 should be regarded as later additions, Isa 42:1-4(9), 49:1-6(12), 50:4-9(11) and 52:13-53:12, and that these four texts should be interpreted as

Second, Isa 53:8 has a plural suffix in 3rd.plur.masc., לָמוֹ. Concerning this suffix in Isa 53:8 Ibn Ezra writes:

בעבור מלת למו שהוא כמו להם.[46]

This plural suffix is an archaic form which is attested in several passages of the Hebrew Bible, for example Ex 15:10; Deut 32:37; Ps 2:3.[47] Aquila's early translation, which is a very literal rendering of the MT, interpreted this part of the verse 8 as follows: ἀπὸ ἀθεσίας λαοῦ μου ἥψατο αὐτῶν indicating that the word לָמוֹ is regarded as plural 3.masc. suffix.[48] It can be also observed that Rabbi Abraham of Cordova, the proselyte, severely criticizes Jerome's (Hieronymus) translation:[49]

> And who is the man that will not open the eyes of his understanding to discern the craft and guile of the lying Hieronymus, who, in his version, so misused his inkpot as to trample on the word למו, contriving in his usual manner to misapply it to the Messiah (as, in fact, he distorted the sense of the whole prophecy) by the rendering, 'For the transgression of my people was there a stroke upon *him*,' meaning to imply that the Messiah was smitten for the sin of the people?

---

referring to individuals. See B. Duhm, *Das Buch Jesaja* (Göttingen: Vandenhoeck & Ruprecht 1922). See further the discussion in U. Berges, "The Literary Construction of the Servant in Isaiah 40-55: A Discussion about Individual and Collective Identities," *SJOT* 24 (2010) 28-38.

[46]See M. Friedländer, *The Commentary of ibn Ezra on Isaiah* (New York: Feldheim 1948) 92*, 244.

[47]So H.S. Nyberg, "Smärtornas man: En studie till Jes 52:13- 53:12," *SEÅ* 7 (1942) 5-82, esp. 55-56; E.Y. Kutscher, *A History of the Hebrew Language* (Jerusalem: Magnes Press, Hebrew University 1984) 79; F.M. Cross & D.N. Freedman, *Studies in Ancient Yahwistic Poetry* (Grand Rapids: Eerdmans 1997), 41 n. 10.

[48]See H. Hegermann, *Jesaja 53 in Hexapla, Targum und Peshitta* (BFCT 56, Gütersloh: Bertelsmann 1954) 41-42, 112.

[49]S.R. Driver & A. Neubauer, *The Suffering Servant of Isaiah According to the Jewish Interpreters* (Eugene: Wipf and Stock Publishers 1999) 293.

42

This criticism is a good example of the Jewish frustration prompted by the Christian interpretation of the word לָמוֹ as being singular. It is most natural to take "we" in 53:1-10 as referring to the Judeans, the Jewish community, who confess their own guilt vis-à-vis the fate of the servant. Before providing a more precise identification of "we", however, we shall first examine the identity of "they".

The identification of "they" is closely correlated with the question of the identity of the *rabbîm* in 52:13-15 and 53:11-12. That this word refers to the nations and kings in 52:13-15 is clear from the context. However, it is not obvious that *rabbîm* in 53:11-12 denotes nations and kings. Steck, for example, has argued that *rabbîm* in 53:11-12 refers to the people of Yhwh since 53:1-10 and 11-12 contain important linguistic parallels.[50] In my view, Steck's argument is problematic. First, 52:13-15 and 53:11-12 are connected with each other. Yhwh is the speaker in both. Therefore it would be natural for *rabbîm* in both passages to refer to the same group. Second, the word *rabbîm* in 53:12a is on a par with *"ṣûmîm* which reflect the parallelism *rabbîm* and *meʿlakîm* in 52:15. In addition, 53:12 which deals with the sharing of booty, is most naturally interpreted as referring to foreign powers. Third, the servant passages often stress the dual task of the ideal servant vis-à-vis both the people of Yhwh and the nations. For example, in 42:1-9 the faithful servant is assigned to a task which concerns the people of Israel (cf., the connection between 40:27-31 and 42:1-4) and the nations (42:6). This concept of dual mission is also present in 49:5-6. Therefore if 53:11-12 refers to the nations and the kings, then this servant passage emphasizes that the task (i.e. the suffering) of the servant concerns both the people of Yhwh (see esp. Isa 53:8) and the nations. This being the case the proclamation of Yhwh in 53:11-12 not only confirms that the servant has suffered for the people (cf. the word-bridge *yirʾēh* in v. 10 and v. 11) but also asserts that his

---

[50]O.H. Steck, "Aspekte des Gottesknechts in Jes 52,13-53,12," *ZAW* 97 (1985) 36-58.

sufferings will benefit the nations.[51] According to our translation, 52:15 states that the servant "will sprinkle many nations" (see the textual note to 52:15). The ministry of the servant on behalf of the nations may well indicate that they are seen as capable of receiving forgiveness and Yhwh's salvation – as is evident elsewhere in Isa 40-55 (see e.g., 45:22-25; 49:6; 51:5).

In the light of these points, I suggest the following interpretation of Isaiah. The text begins and ends with Yhwh's speech about the servant (52:13-15; 53:11-12). In the middle of the text a community, the "we"-group, bears witness to the fate of the faithful servant, the ideal Israel, whose mission it was to bring the people of Yhwh back to the Holy Land and who, in order to fulfil this task, had to suffer. The "we"-group represents those exiles who put their trust in the proclamation of the ideal Israel as well as those who had remained in the land and who now acclaim the role of the ideal Israel in Yhwh's plan of salvation. They confess that the servant, who was condemned to death in the exile and who, although innocent, must suffer, did so to obtain Yhwh's forgiveness for the whole people and lead it into a new, miraculous era. In 53:10 a question is posed to Yhwh, will he accept the *'āšām* which his faithful servant has offered by his sufferings? Yhwh's answer in 53:11-12 is affirmative. Moreover as in Isa 49:4-6 so also here Yhwh emphasizes that the task of the servant does not pertain only to the Israelites but to all nations. Thus we should translate Isa 52:13-53:12 as follows:[52]

---

[51]See also H.W. Hertzberg, "Die 'Abtrünnigen' und die 'Vielen': Ein Beitrag zu Jesaja 53," in: A. Kuschke, (ed), *Verbannung und Heimkehr. Beiträge zur Geschichte und Theologie Israels im 6. und 5. Jahrhundert v.Chr, Wilhelm Rudolph zum 70. Geburtstage dargebracht von Kollegen, Freunden und Schülern* (Tübingen: Mohr 1961) 97-108.

[52]I have consulted several modern translations. Note, in particular, the New Jerusalem Bible.

44

YHWH'S SPEECH ABOUT THE SERVANT 52:13-15
13   Look, my servant will prosper,
            will be raised and lifted up and highly exalted.
14   As many were aghast at him[53] –
            he was so inhumanly disfigured
            that he no longer looked like a man.
15   So he will sprinkle[54] many nations
       and kings will stay tight-lipped before him,
                 seeing what had never been told them,
       understanding what they had not heard before.

"WE"-GROUP SPEAKS IN 53:1-10
1   Who has believed our message?
                 And the arm of Yhwh – over whom has it been revealed?
2   Like a shoot he grew up before him,
                 like a root in arid ground.
       He had no form or charm,
                 we saw him but he had no appearance that we should
                 desire him;
3   he was despised, forsaken by the men,
                 a man of sorrows, familiar with suffering,
       Like one from whom people hide their faces,
                 he was despised, and we held him in low esteem.
4   Yet ours were the sufferings he was bearing,
                 ours the sorrows he was carrying,
       while we thought of him as someone being punished
                 and struck down by God and afflicted;

---

[53]The MT reads עָלָיו and this reading is attested also by 1QIsaᵃ. This expression can be regarded as a stylistic intensification of the focus on the servant. Nevertheless, I have translated the passage with "at him" because it is difficult to imitate this stylistic phenomenon in translation.

[54]I take the MT's יַזֶּה as a technical term for purificatory rites. The subject of the verb is the servant who performs purificatory rites on behalf of nations (see 53:11-12).

5 whereas he was being pierced for our rebellions,
  crushed because of our guilt;
the punishment which gives us peace fell on him,
  and we have been healed by his wounds.
6 We had all gone astray like sheep,
  each taking his own way,
and Yhwh laid on him
  the iniquity of us all.
7 He was oppressed and afflicted,
  but he never opened his mouth,
like a lamb led to the slaughter-house,
  like a bound sheep dumb before its shearers
he never opened his mouth.
8 Without restraint and without justice he was taken away,
yet who of his generation considered it?
For he was cut off from the land of the living,
for the rebellions of his people he[55] was stricken.
9 He was given a grave with the wicked,
and his tomb is with the rich,
  although he had done no violence,
had spoken no deceit.
10 Yet it was Yhwh's good pleasure to crush him, making
  him sick[56].
If you accept[57] his life as a guilt offering,

---

[55]The suffix in the word לָמוֹ is 3rd plur.masc. but I have translated in the singular because the English translation cannot reveal the dynamic nature of the Hebrew language where the figure of the individual can be used to denote a collective whole.

[56]Or: "piercing him." 1QIsa[a] reads ויחללהו instead of the MT הֶחֱלִי. The Qumran reading is parallel to Isa 53:5 and is, therefore, a good alternative reading.

[57]The MT תָּשִׂים can be 2.sing.masc. or 3.sing.fem (which would refer to נַפְשׁוֹ). I take this form as 2. sing. masc. and interpret it as being a question of the "we"-group to Yhwh. Yhwh gives his answer in verses 11-12 where he emphasizes that he accepts the sacrifice offered by the servant.

46

he will see his offspring and prolong his life,
and through him Yhwh's good pleasure will be done.

YHWH'S SPEECH ABOUT THE SERVANT IN 53:11-12
11   Because of his humiliation he will really see it and be content.
            By his knowledge, the righteous one, my servant will
        justify many
        by taking their guilt on himself.
12   Hence I shall give him a portion with the many,
        and he will share the booty with the mighty,
            because he poured out his life unto death,
        and was numbered with the transgressors.
            For he bore the sin of many,
        and interceded for the rebellious.

As we have already seen the early postexilic texts indicate that the blotting out of sins was still a problem among the people. This gives us reason to suppose that the mission of the Suffering Servant was not successful. Indeed, it can be demonstrated that the Servant of Yhwh plays a role in Isaiah 56-66. Beuken has demonstrated convincingly that the person of Isaiah 61 performs the same function as the faithful servant of Isaiah 40-55.[58] We here mention only some linguistic and thematic parallels in order to illustrate this connection. Isa 61:1 speaks of the Spirit of the Lord (רוח אדני יהוה עלי) which rests upon the messenger of Yhwh; this parallels Isa 42:1: נתתי רוחי עליו. The task of the messenger to proclaim freedom in 61:1-3 is thematically parallel to 42:6-7; 49:8-9. Isa 65:13-15 makes a final distinction between two groups: the group of "my servants (עבדי)" and the group of "you" who have abandoned Yhwh and his prophecy of salvation:

[58]W.A.M. Beuken, "Servant and Herald of Good Tidings: Isaiah 61 as an Interpretation of Isaiah 40-55," in: J. Vermeylen (ed), *The Book of Isaiah* (BETL 81, Leuven 1989) 411-442.

> Therefore Lord Yhwh says this:
>   My servants will eat
> while you go hungry;
>   my servants will drink
> while you go thirsty;
>   my servants will rejoice
> while you are put to shame;
>   my servants will shout for joy of heart
> while you shriek for sorrow of heart
>   and howl with a broken spirit.
> And you will leave your name behind as a curse for my chosen ones,
>   "May Lord Yhwh strike you dead!"
> But to his servants he will give another name.

These connections between Isaiah 40-55 and 56-66 with regard to the identity of the servant bear witness that the servant presented in Isaiah 40-55 was unable to complete his mission. This failure apparently led to the postponement of the great hopes described in Isaiah 40-55 to a future time. Isaiah 40-55's importance in Jewish writings related to the Hebrew Bible (the apocalyptic writings and pseudepigrapha together with the documents from Qumran) and the New Testament is understandable since the magnitude of the expectations defined in Isaiah 40-55 were not fulfilled in reality.

Conclusions

Our examination of Isaiah 53 has prompted the hypothesis that the traditio-historical background of the passage was based on lamentations concerning Josiah which contained a belief in his vicarious suffering and death. These lamentations with which the Chronicler was familiar were rejected both by him and by the theological circles which emphasized covenant theology and its retribution principle. During the period of the exile when there was a great need to explain why the righteous had to suffer Isaiah 53 found its way to Isaiah 40-55. The passage was interpreted as referring to the righteous and faithful Israelites who by their sufferings guarantee that Yhwh will pardon his people and establish it in the Land of Israel. While this "erratic block" was saved in the Hebrew Bible it showed its vitality in reception history. We shall now turn to these interpretive traditions.

3 The Influence of Isaiah 53 on Early Jewish Martyr Theology

The concept "(early) Jewish martyrdom" is usually treated in scholarly studies as a literary phenomenon because there are no reliable historical sources concerning such martyrs. No protocol has been preserved of the trials or executions of martyrs.[1] Thus the martyr theology can be analyzed as a literary phenomenon and its central role in early Jewish writings defined. Scholars agree that the emergence of Jewish martyr theology should be placed within or just before the Maccabean period. The traditio-historical background of the martyr theology has proved to be a crucial question in scholarly discussion.

Scholars tend to emphasize that the idea of martyrdom and human vicarious suffering do not occur in the Hebrew Bible and early Jewish writings. The death of the prophets was not glorified in either the Hebrew Bible or in early Jewish legends.[2] The only exception is Isaiah 53 which K. Koch described as the "erratischer Block" ("erratic block") in the Hebrew Bible.[3] Thus, for example, Hengel postulates that "a representative death to atone for the guilt of others can therefore be found at best on the periphery of the Old Testament – for example in Isa. 53,

---

[1]See J.W. van Henten (ed), *Die Entstehung der jüdischen Martyrologie* (Studia Post-Biblica 38, Leiden: Brill 1989), in particular, the "Einleitung" (pp. 1-19) by B. Dehandschutter & J.W. van Henten.

[2]For this scholarly view see O.H. Steck, *Israel und das gewaltsame Geschick der Propheten* (WMANT 23, Neukirchen-Vluyn: Neukirchener Verlag 1967); van Henten (ed), *Die Entstehung der jüdischen Martyrologie*; A.M. Schwemer, *Studien zu den frühjüdischen Prophetenlegenden Vitae Prophetarum* (Two Volumes, TSAJ 49-50, Tübingen: Mohr Siebeck 1995-1996).

[3]K. Koch, "Sühne und Sündenvergebung um die Wende von der exilischen zur nachexilischen Zeit," *EvTh* 26 (1966) 217-239, esp. p. 237.

which K. Koch rightly describes as an 'erratic block'."[4] We proposed a similar conclusion in section 2, viz. "a representative death to atone for the guilt of others" was deprecated in the periphery of the Old Testament because it was at odds with the covenant theology and its retribution concept. Nevertheless, we have also emphasized that the fate of Josiah was involved in this vicarious theology inasmuch as he was regarded as an ideal king who followed the covenant theology. We have argued that 2 Kings 22-23 contains the root of atonement theology, although such theology was not formulated in the Deuteronomic covenant theology. On the other hand, Isaiah 53 is one exponent of the "vicarious suffering and atonement" theology which was influenced by lamentations over the death of Josiah. This being the case, we could modify Koch's slogan on Isaiah 53 and say that this "erratic block" is derived from covenant theology and the two can be linked whenever theodicy is involved. The aim of this section 3 is to demonstrate that this occurred during the Maccabean period.

Historically the Maccabean period was a significant turning-point in the development of martyr theology. The covenant theology was threatened when Antiochus Epiphanes compelled the Jews to reject the instructions of the Torah and established a new cult at the Temple of Jerusalem. The righteous observers of the Torah were persecuted. This problem of theodicy – when righteous followers of the covenant were tortured and murdered – required a theological solution. While the First Book of Maccabees does not contain any direct traces of martyr theology, the Second and the Fourth Books emphasize the role of the Jewish martyrs in the war for freedom.

Scholars seem to agree that an important theological background for Jewish martyr theology in the Books of Maccabees consists of the suffering righteous in the Hebrew Bible, particularly the Psalter and the

---

[4]M. Hengel, *The Cross of the Son of God Containing The Son of God, Crucifixion, The Atonement* (London: SCM Press 1986) 196.

prophetic books.[5] But what is the background of the idea of the vicarious suffering and compensatory death of the martyrs? According to Wengst, the surrender formula (σῶμα καὶ) ψυχήν προδίδωμι used in 2 Macc 7:37-38 originates from classical and Hellenistic sources concerning heroic deaths for the fatherland.[6] In his important study on early Jewish martyr theology van Henten agrees with Wengst's basic idea but comments that it "requires significantly more nuanced formulation in certain of its aspects."[7] According to van Henten, Wengst places undue emphasis on the distinction between Hellenistic-Jewish and Palestinian culture-Old Testament.[8] In contrast, van Henten combines Greek-Hellenistic beliefs about heroic death with the Old Testament-Jewish background of the suffering righteous. According to van Henten, Euripides' tragedies contain "much attention to the motif of atonement by the death of a human person."[9] In particular, he refers to O'Connor-Visser's study on Euripides.[10] Nevertheless, van Henten emphasizes that the Jewish martyr theology cannot be understood without its Old Testament background. Non-cultic atonement appears in Exodus 32 and

---

[5]See, e.g., the works of L. Ruppert, *Der leidende Gerechte. Eine motivgeschichtliche Untersuchung zum Alten Testament und zwischentestamentlichen Judentum* (FzB 5, Würzburg: Echter Verlag 1972); *Jesus als der leidende Gerechte? Der Weg Jesu im Lichte eines alt- und zwischentestamentlichen Motivs* (SBS 59, Stuttgart: KBW Verlag 1972); *Der leidenden Gerechte und seine Feinde: Eine Wortfelduntersuchung* (Würzburg: Echter Verlag 1973).

[6]K. Wengst, *Christologische Formeln und Lieder des Urchristentum* (Gütersloh 1972) 67-70. Note also R. Tomes, "Heroism in 1 and 2 Maccabees," *Biblical Interpretation* 15 (2007) 171-199 where many parallels between 1 and 2 Maccabees and Greek literature are listed.

[7]J.W. van Henten, *The Maccabean Martyrs as Saviours of the Jewish People: A Study of 2 and 4 Maccabees* (SupSJS 57, Leiden: Brill 1997) 157.

[8]For a critical view of Wengst's distinction between Jewish and Hellenistic see also Hengel, *Cross of the Son of God* 191-192.

[9]Van Henten, *Maccabean Martyrs* 157-159. Quotation is from p. 157.

[10]E.A.M.E. O'Connor-Visser, *Aspects of Human Sacrifice in the Tragedies of Euripides* (Diss. Amsterdam 1987).

Numbers 25 as well as in Psalms 78 and 106.[11] Van Henten concludes that "the description of the martyrs' sacrificial death continues biblical notions of non-cultic atonement as well as Graeco-Roman ideas about sacrificial death."[12] He criticizes Weber's view that martyrs are passive suffering righteous and emphasizes instead that they were active heroes: "The Maccabean martyrs are presented as heroes whose behaviour has led, directly or indirectly, to the defeat of the Seleucid enemy."[13]

I agree with van Henten that the Maccabean martyrs are presented in the Second and Fourth Books of Maccabees as those through whom salvation was realized for the people of Judah. Nevertheless, it should be observed that the fate of Eleazar and the seven brothers in 2 Macc 6-7 is described in terms which indicate their helplessness in the face of Antiochus' persecution. The whole point in the story of 2 Macc 6-7 is that the powerlessness of the Jewish martyrs will be effective because *martyrdom pleases God*. It is exactly this aspect of the martyr theology which is manifested in Isaiah 53. The suffering Servant is helpless when faced with death but he is willing to accept his fate – something which pleases God according to Isa 53:10-12. It is significant that even van Henten remarks that Isaiah 53 may prove vital for the Maccabean martyr theology.[14] Our question here is whether we can prove that Isaiah 53 played a major role in Jewish martyr theology during the Maccabean period and the later related texts (2 and 4 Maccabees). I believe we can.

The Book of Isaiah was connected with an eschatological and apocalyptic milieu in Hellenistic times. This emerged from consideration of how the Isaianic texts were used in Jewish eschatological and

---

[11]Van Henten, *Maccabean Martyrs* 160-163.

[12]Van Henten, *Maccabean Martyrs* 299.

[13]Van Henten, *Maccabean Martyrs* 303.

[14]Van Henten, *Maccabean Martyrs* 160.

53

apocalyptic texts such as, for example, the Book of Daniel.[15] Similar evidence is available in ancient versions of the Book of Isaiah. The text of Isaiah has been translated to correspond to the translator's eschatological and apocalyptic worldview.[16] Such an apocalyptic reading implies that the vivid picture in Isaiah 53 of the Servant who suffers vicariously and dies and will then prolong his days (according to the MT) or sees light (1QIsaᵃ and LXX) was easy to connect with the eschatological drama of resurrection. Thus the suffering and dying servant in Isaiah 53 could be linked with Jewish martyr theology.

Isaiah 53 contains all the relevant elements which play a role in the martyr theology of the Maccabean period. *First*, Isaiah 53 presupposes that the servant is faithful to God. He can be compared with the Jewish martyr who will keep the Torah. *Second*, the servant must suffer and die – a feature which reflects the tortures of the Jewish martyrs described in 2 and 4 Maccabees. *Third*, the idea of the martyr who must die not because he has sinned but because he has kept the Torah and who is consoled by the coming resurrection finds a close parallel in the fate of the servant in Isaiah 53. *Fourth*, the suffering of the servant will benefit others. In the apocalyptic milieu, the martyr theology was easy to modify according to Isaiah 53 which speaks of the servant who suffers and dies without guilt and who then will receive a new life. The Book of Daniel contains evidence that the theology of Isaiah 53 was significant in the Maccabean period.

---

[15]For this see, in particular, J. Blenkinsopp, *Opening the Sealed Book: Interpretations of the Book of Isaiah in Late Antiquity* (Grand Rapids: Eerdmans 2006) 11-27. Cf., also the use of Isaiah 65-66 in 1 Enoch 2-5. For this see G.W.E. Nickelsburg & K. Baltzer, *1 Enoch: A Commentary on the Book of 1 Enoch 1-36; 81-108* (Hermeneia; Minneapolis: Fortress 2011).

[16]For this see I.L. Seeligman, *The Septuagint Version of Isaiah and Cognate Studies* (FAT 40, Göttingen: Mohr Siebeck 2004) and A. van der Kooij, *Die alten Textzeugen des Jesajabuches: Ein Beitrag zur Textgeschichte des Alten Testaments* (OBO 35, Freiburg: Universitätsverlag, Göttingen: Vandenhoeck & Ruprecht 1980) 22-73.

The Book of Daniel

One of the earliest interpretations of Isaiah 53, if not the earliest can be found in the Book of Daniel, which praises the resistance of the pious martyrs who were willing to die for the Torah. According to Dan 11:33-35 the military victories of the Maccabees enjoyed only limited success.[17] The final, decisive victory will come from Yhwh and Yhwh alone. The Book of Daniel glorifies Jewish martyrs who trust in Yhwh and the victory which he will give. This can be seen in Daniel 3, even though Daniel's three friends did not actually die but were miraculously saved.[18] Nevertheless, their willingness to die for the Torah has been presented as exemplary for the Jews in the Maccabean period, which indicates why the story was edited in the Book of Daniel. As a result of martyrs' willingness to die for the Torah "the Son of God" will be with Jews as he was with the three men in Daniel 3. It is attractive to suggest that "the Son of God" (בר אלהין) in Dan 3:25 is parallel to "the Son of Man" in Daniel 7. Both are celestial figures. In Daniel 3 it is emphasized that this celestial figure is like "the Son of God" because the reference pertains to the human beings, the three friends of Daniel. On the other hand, Daniel 7 describes a heavenly vision so that it is important to emphasize that the celestial figure resembles "the Son of Man." It is worth noting that the friends of Daniel are called as "the servants of the Most High (עליא)" and the same title "Most High" is also used in Dan 7:25. Thus there is an

---

[17]J.A. Goldstein, *1 Maccabees* (AB 41, Garden City: Doubleday 1976), 64-65; *idem*, "How the Authors of 1 and 2 Maccabees Treated the 'Messianic' Promises." in: J. Neusner, W.S. Green, E.S. Frerichs (eds), *Judaism and Their Messiahs at the Turn of the Christian Era* Cambridge: Cambridge University Press 1987, 69-96, esp. 74-75.

[18]Daniel 3 has been treated as a martyr text even though the three men did not die. See E. Haag, "Die drei Männer im Feuer nach Dan 3:1-30," in J.W. van Henten (ed), *Die Entstehung der jüdischen Martyrologie* (Studia Post-Biblica 38, Leiden: Brill 1989) 20-50. Haag provides a redactio-historical analysis of the chapter which I do not regard as convincing. See, e.g., J.J. Collins, *Daniel* (Hermeneia, Minneapolis: Fortress 1993) 179-180.

internal link between Daniel 3 and the vision of the Son of Man in Daniel 7.[19] We may say that the willingness of the Jews to die for the Torah will ultimately provoke Yhwh to act and destroy the wicked enemy and establish the heavenly kingdom on earth.[20]

The traditio-historical background of the martyr theology in the Book of Daniel can be traced to the Book of Isaiah. Haag rightly commented that Isaiah 43 provides an important traditio-historical background to Daniel 3.[21] The fate of the suffering servant in Isaiah 53 forms an essential traditio-historical setting to Dan 11:33-12:10.[22] We shall list the relevant parallels here:

The basic concept of resurrection in Dan 12:2 ("many of those who sleep in the dust of the earth will awake") alludes to Isa 26:19 which has apparently been associated with the idea of resurrection (see also Isa 25:8). The word "abhorrence" (דראון) in Dan 12:2 appears otherwise only in Isa 66:24, and this passage of the Book of Isaiah too can easily be reinterpreted as referring to the eternal punishment of the ungodly after the resurrection: "And they will go out and look on the dead bodies of

---

[19]Cf., also Collins, *Daniel* 306.

[20]U. Kellerman ("Das Danielbuch und die Märtyrertheologie der Auferstehung," in J.W. van Henten [ed], *Die Entstehung der jüdischen Martyrologie* [Studia Post-Biblica 38, Leiden: Brill 1989] 51-75) has argued that Dan 7:9-10, 13-14 as an original tradition was a hymn concerning the postmortal fate of the Jewish martyrs. Such an interpretation is difficult to derive from the present form of Daniel 7. Nevertheless, the connection between Daniel 3 and 7 is the key to understanding the function of martyr theology.

[21]Haag, "Die drei Männer im Feuer" 34-50. Isa 43:2 is quoted in 4 Macc 18:14.

[22]See H.L. Ginsberg, "The Oldest Interpretation of the Suffering Servant." *VT* 3 (1953) 400-404; Ruppert, *Der leidende Gerechte* 66-67; J. Day, "*DA`AT* 'Humilation' in Isaiah LIII 11 in the Light of Isaiah LIII 3 and Daniel XII 4, and the Oldest Known Interpretation of the Suffering Servant," *VT* 30 (1980) 97-103; M. Hengel, "The Effective History of Isaiah 53 in the Pre-Christian Period," in: B. Janowski & P. Stuhlmacher (eds), *The Suffering Servant: Isaiah 53 in Jewish and Christian Sources* (Grand Rapids: Eerdmans 2004) 75-146, esp. 90-98; G.W.E. Nickelsburg, *Resurrection, Immortality, and Eternal Life in Intertestamental Judaism and Early Christianity* (Harvard Theological Studies 56, Cambridge: Harvard University Press 2006) 23-42; Blenkinsopp, *Opening the Sealed Book* 261-262.

those who rebelled against me; the worms that eat them will not die, the fire that burns them will not be quenched, and they will be loathsome (דראון) to all mankind." These prophecies indicate that the Book of Isaiah makes an essential traditio-historical contribution to the idea of resurrection in the Book of Daniel.[23]

The third Isaian passage which has been reinterpreted as referring to the idea of resurrection is the Servant passage in Isa 52:13-53:12. The expression וּמַצְדִּיקֵי לָרַבִּים in Dan 12:3: "those who lead many to righteousness" echoes Isa 53:11 which reads לרבים ... יצדיק, "will justify many", while the expression וְהַמַּשְׂכִּלִים in Dan 12:3 is derived from the verb יַשְׂכִּיל in Isa 52:13. The image of the resurrection from the "dust of the earth" in Dan 12:2 is parallel to the fate of the Servant who after his sufferings and burial will again "prolong his days" (MT) or "see light" (LXX and 1QIsa). It is also worth noting that the word הדעת ("knowledge") is used in Dan 12:4: "Daniel, roll up and seal the words of the scroll until the time of the end. Many will go here and there to increase knowledge." The idea of sealing the Book is derived from Isa 8:16-18 where Isaiah sealed his message to his disciples. Isa 29:9-12 indicates that only the true disciple can understand the words of the sealed book. Isa 50:4-5 prophecies the coming time of salvation when true disciples will be able to understand the words of the sealed book.[24] Immediately after these verses there is a reference to the sufferings of the faithful servant (Isa 50:6-7) indicating that those martyrs of the Maccabean time who can understand the secret message of the Book of Isaiah are also ready to die as martyrs. In the light of this evidence we suggest that Isa 53:11 signifies that the martyrs of the Maccabean period understood the secret message of resurrection in the Book of Isaiah and

---

[23]For the Isaianic background to the concept of resurrection in the Book of Daniel see, in particular, Nickelsburg, *Resurrection* 23-42.

[24]For the view of the Book of Isaiah as a sealed book which contains secrets of eschatology that were revealed during the time of the Maccabees see, in particular, Blenkinsopp, *Opening the Sealed Book* 11-27.

57

that it is this "knowledge" that will lead many Jews to righteousness. It is also noteworthy that the LXX translations of Dan 11:35 and 12:3 are reminiscent of the LXX of Isa 52:13-53:12 which proves that these connections between Dan 11-12 and Isaiah 53 were known in antiquity.[25]

We have seen that the Book of Isaiah and its Servant passage in Isaiah 53 played a vital role in the resurrection theology. This being the case we have good reason to assume that the Book of Daniel is a traditio-historical link between Isaiah 53 and the martyr theology in the Second and Fourth Books of Maccabees.[26] This proposal becomes even more plausible when we examine Greek additions to the Book of Daniel.

The old Greek translation of Dan 3:40 is an example of martyr theology. However, it contains two different readings. The so-called Theodotion text renders the passage as follows: "Such may our sacrifice be in your sight today, and may we unreservedly follow you, for no shame will come to those who trust in you." However, the older pre-Hexaplaric Septuagint version (attested in the old and important Papyrus 967) here reads:[27]

οὕτω γενέσθω ἡμῶν ἡ θυσία ἐνώπιόν σου σήμερον
καὶ ἐξιλάσαι ὄπισθέν σου
ὅτι οὐκ ἐστιν αἰσχύνη τοῖς πεποιθόσιν ἐπὶ σοί
καὶ τελειῶσαι ὄπισθέν σου
So let our sacrifice be in your sight today,
   and may it make atonement before you,
for there is no shame to those who trust in you,
   and may it be perfect before you.

---

[25]P. Grelot, *Les Poèmes du Serviteur. De la Lecture Critique a l'Hermeneutique* (Lectio divina 103, Paris: Les Editions du Cerf 1981) 121-125.

[26]This conclusion was also reached by J.A. Goldstein in his commentary *II Maccabees* (AB 41 A; New York: Doubleday 1983). Commenting on 2 Maccabees 7 he writes (p. 293): "Thus, the martyrs in our chapter are portrayed using the vocabulary and ideas of the book of Isaiah, as did the actual victims of the persecution."

[27]Hengel "The Effective History of Isaiah 53," 93-95.

58

Hengel notes that while "the grammar of this version is very difficult and its translation uncertain" it nevertheless contains language of atonement derived from sacrificial cult.[28] The verb ἐξιλάσκομαι is used in the LXX as a translation equivalent to the Hebrew *kipper*. Another important term is θυσία which clearly relates the prayer of Eleazar to the sacrificial atonement theology. While the Hebrew Bible contains vicarious atonement theology connected with the merits of the righteous the elements of sacrificial cult are rarely attested. The only real parallel to Dan 3:40 in the Hebrew Bible is Isaiah 53. There the Servant bears (as a scapegoat) the sins of the people and his life becomes "an offering for sin" (אשם, Isa 53:10). The expression *nāsā' 'āwôn* in Lev 16:22 emphasizes the belief that the sins of the people were remitted by sending an animal into the desert, a place which symbolizes chaos and destruction. The bearing of sin is seen in a similar light in Isaiah 53. The phrase כי נגזר מארץ היים in Isa 53:8 is reminiscent of ארץ גזרה in Lev 16:22. The verb root גזר is used in both passages. The expression in Isa 53:8 calls to mind the concept of the "world of the death" to which ארץ in Lev 16:22 refers. The thematic links between Isaiah 53 and Leviticus 16 explain why the Greek addition in Dan 3:40 introduced the idea of vicarious sacrifice to the Jewish martyr theology.

Scholars agree that the principal theological reflections on the theology of martyrdom are made in the Second and Fourth Books of Maccabees. The ideological aim of the First Book of Maccabees is to glorify the actions of the brothers Maccabees. This glorification is crucially related to the pious martyrs who, according to 1 Maccabees 2, refused to resist against the Seleucids on the Sabbath day and were therefore slaughtered. 1 Maccabees sees the military actions of Maccabees as justified. The question is whether the First Book of Maccabees, is in fact averse Jewish martyr theology because its Torah observance seemed to imply no resistance. If such criticism is manifest

---

[28]Hengel "The Effective History of Isaiah 53," 95.

in 1 Maccabees the situation is strikingly different in 2 and 4 Maccabees. The willingness to die as a martyr for the sake of the Torah will guarantee victory for the Jewish people.[29] These books give martyrs their full due and develop the martyrology of the Book of Daniel. We shall now deal with these two books of Maccabees and their connection of the theology of martyrdom with the idea of *kipper*.

The Second Book of Maccabees

2 Maccabees is an important document of early Jewish martyr theology (2 Macc 6-7). The date of the book is under discussion but it would seem to have originated in the latter half of the second century BC.[30]

2 Macc 6:12-17 introduces the description of the martyrs contemporary with the Maccabees.[31] The passage contains crucial theological reflections on theodicy, why God allows the persecution and torture of his faithful servants (the italics are mine):

> Now, I urge anyone who may read this book not to be dismayed at these calamities, but to reflect that such visitations are intended *not to destroy our race but to discipline* (πρὸς παιδείαν) it. Indeed, when evil-doers are not left for long to their own devices but incur swift retribution, it is a sign of great benevolence. In the case of other nations, the Master waits patiently for them to attain the full measure of their sins before he punishes them, but with us he

---

[29]In the Third Book of Maccabees the theology of martyrdom is not representative. For example, there is no reference to future life, or to retribution in another world. See M. Hadas, *The Third and Fourth Books of Maccabees* (New York: KTAV Publishing House 1953) 25; see further S.R. Johnson, *Historical Fictions and Hellenistic Jewish Identity: Third Maccabees in Its Cultural Context* (Hellenistic culture and society 43; Berkeley: University of California Press 2004) 122-216.

[30]J.J. Collins, *Between Athens and Jerusalem: Jewish Identity in the Hellenistic Diaspora* (New York: Crossroad 1983) 75-81; D.R. Schwartz, *2 Maccabees* (CEJL, Berlin: de Gruyter 2008) 3-15.

[31]Concerning the interpretation of the theology of martyrdom in 2 Maccabees and 4 Maccabees I refer mainly to the analysis in Lohse, *Märtyrer und Gottesknecht* 66-72 and van Henten, *Maccabean Martyrs*.

has decided to deal differently, rather than have to punish us later, when our sins come to full measure. And so he *never entirely withdraws his mercy* (τὸν ἔλεον) from us; *he may discipline* (παιδεύων) us by some disaster but *he does not desert his own people*. Let this be said simply by way of reminder; we must return to our story without more ado.

This passage describes the important relationship between the fact that some of the faithful must suffer and die as martyrs, and that the whole nation is *responsible* for the sins committed by Jews. This collective responsibility leads to *discipline* which is brought to bear only on certain faithful Jews. Even though this notion of discipline is a problematic aspect of theodicy for individuals who face torture, it is a sign bearing some theological significance since it indicates that the Lord has not abandoned his people but continues to *show his mercy*. The following description of the persecution of the martyrs in 2 Macc 6:18-7:42 illustrates this theological paradigm, especially in the case of the seven brothers.

Nickelsburg observed that the fate of Eleazar and the seven brothers is presented in a way resembling the torture of the Servant in Isa 50:4-9 and 52:13-53:12. Even though there is no clear linguistic dependence between passages there are some interesting parallels in content. The brothers are scourged (μάστιγες) and the skin of the head of the second brother and his scalp torn away (2 Macc 7:7) – thus paralleling to the fate of the Servant in Isa 50:6: "I offered my back to those who beat me, my cheeks to those who pulled out my beard; I did not hide my face from mocking and spitting." The third brother says that God has given him his limbs and tongue (2 Macc 7:10-11) – a statement which Nickelsburg relates to the confession of the Servant in Isa 50:4: "The Sovereign Lord has given me a well-instructed tongue, to know the word that sustains the weary. He wakens me morning by morning, wakens my ear to listen like one being instructed." All the brothers are disfigured after torture (2 Macc 7:4, 7) – corresponding to the fate of the Servant in Isa 52:14; 53:2. The king is astonished when he realizes that torture has no effect on the brothers (2 Macc 7:12) – a fact which

Nickelsburg would associate with Isa 52:14. Furthermore, Nickelsburg sees parallels between the fates of the seven brothers and the suffering of the righteous in Wisdom 2-5.[32] The Book of Wisdom is a later work, however, and we shall deal with it in due course (see sect. 4). These parallels to the Servant texts in Isaiah 40-55 support our thesis that the vicarious suffering and atonement in the martyr theology of the Maccabean period are rooted in Isaiah 53.

The first brother refers to Deut 32:36 at the time of his death: "The Lord God is watching over us and in truth has compassion on us, as Moses declared in his song that bore witness against the people to their faces, when he said, 'And he will have compassion on his servants'" (2 Macc 7:6). The passage in Deut 32:36 renders "The Lord will vindicate his people and relent concerning *his servants* when he sees their strength is gone and no one is left, slave or free" and later in Deut 32:43 there is a promise that God "*will avenge the blood of his servants*; he will take vengeance on his enemies and make atonement for his land and people.*" This Deuteronomic passage has played an important role in Jewish martyr theology as can be seen from the fate of Taxo and his seven sons. Taxo commands his sons saying (Testament of Moses 9:6-7): "We shall fast for a three-day period and on the fourth day we shall go into a cave, which is in the open country. There let us die rather than transgress the commandments of the Lord of Lords, the God of our fathers. For if we do this, and do die, *our blood will be avenged before the Lord.*" The Testament of Moses 10 follows immediately after this saying of Taxo and in it the glorious appearance of the kingdom of God is described.[33]

---

[32]G.W.E. Nickelsburg, *Resurrection, Immortality, and Eternal Life in Intertestamental Judaism and Early Christianity* (Harvard Theological Studies 56, Cambridge: Harvard University Press 2006) 119-138, esp. 130-134.

[33]See J. Licht, "Taxo, or the Apocalyptic Doctrine of Vengeance," *JJS* 12 (1961) 95-103. However, note J. Tromp, "Taxo, the Messenger of the Lord," *JSJ* 21 (1990) 200-209 where it is argued that Taxo and *nuntius* in 10:2 should be identified. Taxo is not killed but rehabilitated.

Deut 32:43 is a significant passage in the Torah because it connects the idea of vengeance for the blood of the servants of God with the idea of atonement. In Deuteronomy the meaning of atonement is apparently to guarantee that the blood of the innocent is expiated and the land purged.[34] However, it seems reasonable to assume that this passage has been reinterpreted in the Jewish martyr theology to enable the death of the servant to atone for the people and the land. It is this theology which is manifest in 2 Maccabees as we shall see below. Another important feature of Deut 32:43 is the use of the word "servants" which seems to allude to the suffering servant in Isaiah 53.[35] We may also note that Deuteronomy 32 played a prominent role in the Samaritan ritual of *Yom Kippur*.[36] This connection to Yom Kippur ritual gives pride of place to the idea of atonement.

The second, third and fourth brothers confess their belief in resurrection, another demonstration of the mercy of God. The fifth brother proclaims the coming annihilation of Antiochus' descendants and confirms that God has not deserted his people. In the saying of the sixth brother the theme of suffering and its theological significance is explicit (2 Macc 7:18-19):

> Do not delude yourself: we are suffering like this through our own fault, having sinned against our own God; hence, appalling things have befallen us — but do not think you yourself will go unpunished for attempting to make war on God.

The rhetorical "we" in these verses is the whole people of Israel as is indicated by the fact that the fifth brother speaks of "our race" which God has not deserted (2 Macc 7:16). Thus the seven brothers and their mother suffer on account of the sins committed by the entire nation. The mother

---

[34]Cf., Deuteronomy 21 and the murder of the victim.

[35]See further Goldstein, *II Maccabees* 294-295; Nickelsburg, *Resurrection* 43-46.

[36]See M. Lehmann, "'Yom Kippur' in Qumran," *RdQ* 3 (1961/62) 119-124, esp. 120-121.

encourages the seventh brother to die on behalf of the Torah and expects that she will receive him back "on the day of mercy" (ἐν τῷ ἐλέει, 2 Macc 7:29). The coming day of mercy thereby reflects the present situation in which martyrs were willing to suffer and die – an idea which can easily be related to Isaiah 53. The most obvious connection between God's discipline and the vicarious benefit of the martyrs' death can be found in the words of the youngest brother (2 Macc 7:32-38, the italics are mine):

> We are suffering for our own sins, and if, *to punish and discipline* (παιδείας) us, our living Lord is briefly angry with us, *he will be reconciled with us in due course* (καὶ πάλιν καταλλαγήσεται τοῖς ἑαυτοῦ δούλοις)... Our brothers, having endured brief pain, for the sake of ever-flowing life have died for the covenant of God ... I too, like my brothers, surrender my body and life for the laws of my ancestors, *begging God quickly to take pity on our nation* (ἐπικαλούμενος τὸν θεὸν ἵλεως ταχὺ τῷ ἔθνει γενέσθαι), and by trials and afflictions to bring you to confess that he alone is God, so that with my brothers and myself there *may be an end to the wrath of the Almighty, rightly let loose on our whole nation.*

This saying contains two significant expressions which emphasize the benefit conferred by the suffering and death of martyrs: (1) God will reconcile (καταλλάσσειν) the people to himself and (2) he will be merciful (ἵλεως γιγνέσθαι) to his people.[37] The concept καταλλάσσειν concerns the establishment of the broken relationship between two persons (e.g., a man and a woman, 1 Corinthians 7).[38] On the other hand, ἵλεως γιγνέσθαι is a concept which has its origins in the sacrificial cult and the idea of *kipper*. The only text in the Hebrew Bible to contain the belief that the suffering and death of the righteous may

---

[37]It is worth noting that both concepts, καταλλαγή and the atonement-motif, are prominent in the New Testament when the meaning of the death of Jesus Christ is interpreted.

[38]See a good analysis of these important concepts in J. Thurén, *Sovituspaikka ja sovinto* (Kirkon Tutkimuskeskus Sarja B:65, Pieksämäki 1991).

become a sacrifice which is pleasing to God is in Isaiah 53: "... and though you make his life an offering for sin, he will see his offspring and prolong his days, and the will of the Lord will prosper in his hand" (Isa 53:10). In addition, Isaiah 53 refers to that the broken relationship between Yhwh and the "we"-group can be reconciled through the sacrifice of the Servant.

The connection of the theology of martyrdom and the idea of *kipper* in 2 Maccabees does not exclude the primacy of the sacrificial cult (cf., also Dan 9:24-27 which emphasizes the role of the sanctuary). 2 Macc 3:33 records how the high priest Onias performed the rite of expiation on behalf of Heliodorus and how this ritual gave him life. Another emphasis on the sacrificial cult is found in 2 Macc 2:7 (cf., also 2 Bar 6:5-9) which predicts that the Ark (and so also *kapporet*) will exist in the eschatological age when God will show mercy (ἵλεως γίγνεσθαι) to his people. Later in 2 Macc 2:22 the recovery of the sanctuary by Maccabees is seen as being the precursor of the eschatological event and a sign of God's mercy (ἵλεως γίγνεσθαι). According to 2 Macc 10:2 Judas defeated the enemy when, together with other Jews, he prostrated himself before the altar, imploring God to show mercy (ἵλεως γίγνεσθαι). Finally 2 Macc 12:45 glorifies the central role of the expiation rituals in the Temple when it is said that Judas had an expiatory sacrifice offered for the slain Jewish soldiers, so that they might be released from their sins and rise again from the dead (cf., 1 Cor 15:29).

Van Henten has rightly noted that 2 Maccabees contains "an extensive description of the impact which the martyrdoms have on the political circumstances."[39] This is manifest in 2 Macc 8:1-7. In that episode Jewish soldiers pray to God and ask him to remember all the innocent martyrs (2 Macc 8:2-5): "They besought the Lord to look upon the people who were oppressed by all, and to have pity on the temple which had been profaned by ungodly men, and to have mercy on the city which was being destroyed and about to be leveled to the ground, and to

---

[39] van Henten, *Maccabean Martyrs* 153; see further Schwartz, *2 Maccabees* 329.

hearken to the blood that cried out to him, and to remember also the lawless destruction of the innocent babies and the blasphemies committed against his name, and to show his hatred of evil. As soon as Maccabeus deployed his army, the gentiles could not withstand him, for the wrath of the Lord had turned to mercy (τῆς ὀργῆς τοῦ κυρίου εἰς ἔλεον τραπείσης)." The last phrase is a clear allusion to 2 Macc 7:32-38 quoted above. God hearkened to the prayers of the martyrs and resisted to the enemy of the Jewish people.

The Fourth Book of Maccabees

The fates of Eleazar and the seven brothers with their mother are described in 4 Maccabees. In antiquity the Fourth Book of Maccabees was entitled "On the Sovereignty of Reason." Both Eusebios and Jerome refer to the work by this title and attribute it to the Jewish historian Josephus.[40] The author of the work was assuredly not Josephus.[41] But the title "On the Sovereignty of Reason" receives support from the very first words (4 Macc 1:1): "Thoroughly philosophical is the subject I propose to discuss, namely, whether religious reason is sovereign over the emotions." The martyrs are another important theme. Scholars agree that the genre of 4 Maccabees is related to panegyric orations given at heroes' funerals. That there is a connection to Greek funeral orations (ἐπιτάφιος λόγος) is indicated by 4 Macc 17:8-10: "Indeed, it would be proper to inscribe upon their very tomb the words following as a memorial to those [heroes] of our people: Here lie buried an aged priest, an old woman, and her seven sons, victims of the violence of a tyrant resolved to destroy the polity of the Hebrews. They vindicated their race, looking to God, and

---

[40]Eusebios, *Eccl. Hist.* III.10.6 and Jerome, *De viris illustribus* 13.

[41]Hadas, *The Third and Fourth Books of Maccabees* 114; Ruppert, *Der leidende Gerechte. Eine motivgeschichtliche Untersuchung* 106-107; D.A. deSilva, *4 Maccabees* (Guides to Apocrypha and Pseudepigrapha; Sheffield: Sheffield Academic Press 1998) 12.

66

enduring torments even to death." Nevertheless, van Henten has rightly observed that 4 Maccabees cannot be regarded formally as a funeral oration even though it shares many of its elements.[42] The best way to characterize 4 Maccabees is to say that it is "a philosophical argument supported by laudatory descriptions of martyrdom."[43]

The date of 4 Maccabees is controversial and several theories have been expressed. A prominent aspect in this discussion are the similarities between 4 Maccabees and the New Testament together with the Letters of Ignatios. This prompted the hypothesis that the Christian and Jewish martyr theology developed in parallel at Antioch.[44] However, deSilva has shown that there are such marked parallels between the New Testament and 4 Maccabees that we can also speak of an influence by the latter to the former. In this case we can argue that even Ignatios was dependent on 4 Maccabees.[45] Klauck has argued that there is no interest in the Temple cult in 4 Maccabees which implies that the work must have been written after the destruction of the Second Temple in 70 AD.[46] However, 4 Maccabees was written in a Jewish Hellenistic milieu and it

---

[42]Van Henten, *Maccabean Martyrs* 60-67.

[43]van Henten, *Maccabean Martyrs* 279.

[44]For this see J.W. van Henten, "Datierung und Herkunft des Vierten Makkabäerbuches," in: J.W. Henten & H.J. de Jonge et al. (eds), *Tradition and Re-interpretation in Jewish and Christian Literature* (Leiden: Brill 1986) 136-149; note, however, that van Henten writes (p. 145): "Man darf die Bedeutung dieser Gemeinsamkeiten nicht übertreiben." See further H. Spieckermann, *Martyrium und die Vernunft des Glaubens: Theologie als Philosophie im vierten Makkabäerbuch* (Nachrichten der Akademie der Wissenschaften zu Göttingen. I. Philologisch-Historische Klasse 2004:3, Göttingen: Vandenhoeck & Ruprecht 2004).

[45]See parallels between the New Testament and 4 Maccabees in deSilva, *4 Maccabees* 143-155, and the date of 4 Maccabees in deSilva, *4 Maccabees* 12-18.

[46]H.-J. Klauck, *4. Makkabäerbuch* (JSHRZ III/6, Gütersloh: Gütersloher Verlagshus 1989) 665-669.

is not uncommon for such works to disregard the sacrificial cult even before AD 70.[47]

The author of the book argues that reason should dominate emotions. The concept "divine philosophy" (ἡ θεία φιλοσοφία) and related terms (e.g., εὐσέβεια) are used frequently in 4 Maccabees to show that the Jewish Torah observance enables reason to dominate all emotions.[48] Thus, for example, Eleazar is praised in 4 Macc 7:16: "If, then, an aged man despised tortures unto death, we must acknowledge that religious reason (ὁ εὐσεβὴς λογισμός) is leader over the emotions." The writer argues that the Torah observance must be taken seriously in order to prevail over torture and be able to overrule emotions by reason (4 Macc 7:18-19): "Those who take thought for religion with their whole heart, they alone are able to dominate the passions of the flesh, believing that to God they die not, as neither did our patriarchs Abraham, Isaac, and Jacob, but live to God." 4 Maccabees argues that the Torah piety will lead to the control of all feelings and passions and it "educates us in justice, so that we keep an even balance whatever our tempers; and it instructs us in piety, so that we reverence the sole living God with due magnificence" as Eleazar says in 4 Macc 5:24. The consequences of this pious life are that "even the young, by following a philosophy in accordance with devout reason have prevailed over the most painful instruments of torture" (4 Macc 8:1).

In 4 Maccabees the theology of martyrdom of 2 Maccabees has been developed further. There is an interesting shift from the belief in the

---

[47]So J.J. Collins, *Between Athens and Jerusalem: Jewish Identity in the Hellenistic Diaspora* (New York: Crossroad 1983) 187. Ruppert (*Der leidende Gerechte. Eine motivgeschichtliche Untersuchung* 108) dates the book to the 40's AD.

[48]Scholars have argued which Greek philosophic system lies behind 4 Maccabees. Collins (*Between Athens and Jerusalem* 188) notes rightly: "The author was a rhetorician, not a philosopher, who used philosophical ideas eclectically to embellish his case. The philosophical pronouncements are not consistently thought through. The story of the martyrs is not well integrated with its philosophical framework. 'Reason' is virtually equated with keeping the law."

concrete bodily resurrection in 2 Maccabees to a more sophisticated view of the immortal soul continuing its life after death.[49] At the beginning of the book we encounter a programmatic statement of the important role of the martyrs who "became responsible for the dissolution of the tyranny which oppressed our nation" and "through them the fatherland was purged (καθαρισθῆναι)" (4 Macc 1:11). The two episodes of the torture of Eleazar and the seven brothers are developed and intensified in 4 Maccabees. 4 Macc 6:28-29 is one of the strongest formulations of the theology of martyrdom in Jewish writings (outside the New Testament). The old man Eleazar prays to God saying:

> Be merciful (ἵλεως γενοῦ) to Your people, and let my punishment be sufficient for their sake. Make my blood an expiation (καθάρσιον) for them, and take my life as a ransom for theirs (ἀντίψυχον αὐτῶν).

This saying adopts central motifs and themes from the theology of the sacrificial cult and its idea of *kipper*. The Greek word καθάρσιον in the expression "make my blood an expiation (or: purification)" conveys a concept of the elimination of sin similar to that of the sacrificial cult. That the Greek word καθάρσιον approaches the idea of *kipper* is shown by the LXX which translates כִּפֻּרִים with καθαρισμός in Ex 29:36 (see also Ex 30:10). Further, we may observe that the term καθαρισμός is frequently employed in connection with sacrificial cult in the LXX – an association which may have influenced the range of its use. The usage of the Greek word ἀντίψυχος in 4 Macc 6:28-29 provides a close

---

[49]See deSilva *4 Maccabees* 137: "*4 Maccabees*, like Philo and the Wisdom of Solomon (cf. Wis. 3.9), prefer the immaterial 'immortality of the soul': indeed, *4 Maccabees* expunges all references to resurrection contained in his source (cf. 2 Macc. 7.9, 11,14, 22-23) and replaces this with the more Platonic notion (cf. *4 Macc.* 9.22; 14.5-6; 16.13; 17.12; 18.23). The immortality of the righteous is 'endless life' (17.12), but the immortality of the impious is endless punishment."

equivalent to the Hebrew כֹּפֶר (or perhaps פִּדְיוֹן).[50] For example, in Isa 43:3-4 the possessive suffix 'yours' in the expression כָּפְרְךָ means that the ransom is provided for 'you' (see also Ps 49:8). The Greek expression ἀντίψυχον αὐτῶν is a similar construction, indicating that ἀντίψυχος is given on the behalf of 'them.' These connections indicate that the saying of Eleazar is parallel with the Hebrew expression נתן נפשי כפרהם ("give my soul to be their ransom").

In the description of the seven brothers, a similar emphasis on the idea of *kipper* is perceived. The seven brothers are willing to die for the sake of their religion and their sufferings have a vicarious effect. For example, in 4 Macc 9:8 the brothers say that "we shall be with God, on whose account we suffer," articulating the same belief as in Isaiah 53, whereby the Servant suffers according to the will of God. The atonement theology is visible in 4 Macc 9:24 where the first son says: "Fight the sacred and noble fight for religion's sake. Through it may the just Providence which watched over our fathers also become merciful (ἵλεως γίγνεσθαι) to our people, and exact punishment from the accursed tyrant." The youngest brother prays to the Lord as death approaches: "I call upon the God of my fathers to prove merciful (ἵλεως γίγνεσθαι) to our nation" (4 Macc 12:18).

In his conclusion the author confirms that the martyrs' willingness to suffer and die for the sake of their nation and their religion has benefited the whole people. 4 Macc 17:20-22 states that the martyrs were sanctified by God and through them "our land was purified" because "they having become as it were a ransom (ἀντίψυχον) for the sin of the nation." Verse 22 goes even further, stating that "it was through the blood of these righteous ones, and through the expiation of their death (τοῦ ἱλαστηρίου τοῦ θανάτου αὐτῶν), that divine Providence preserved Israel, which had been ill used."[51] This verse clearly expresses

---

[50]Cf., Lohse, *Märtyrer und Gottesknecht* 70-71.

[51]See deSilva *4 Maccabees* 137-141.

the death of the martyrs as expiation in terms of the Old Testament idea of *kipper*. Finally 4 Macc 18:4 glorifies the martyrs by saying that "it was because of them that our nation obtained peace; they renewed the observance of the Law in their country; and lifted their enemies' siege."

The afterlife of the soul is a crucial element in the theology of 4 Maccabees even though it does not take the form of bodily resurrection as in 2 Maccabees. 4 Macc 17:5 contains an interesting allusion to Daniel 12. The seven brothers are compared with "lightning the way to piety for your seven starlike sons; honored by God, and with them fixed in heaven." A similar comparison to stars is found in Dan 12:3 where the martyrs are described as shining stars in the brightness of the firmament.

4 Maccabees 18 contains references to Old Testament passages. It is significant that Isaiah 53 is not among them. However, the reference pertains to Isa 43:2: "When you walk through fire the flame will not burn you." This text plays a major role in Daniel 3 as we have seen.[52] Another important key-text is Deut 32:39: "I kill and I make alive; for that is your life and the length of your days." This text is from Deuteronomy 32 which is important in both 2 Maccabees 7 and the Testament of Moses 9. The fact that Isaiah 53 is never *expressis verbis* quoted in 4 Maccabees cannot be taken as proof that it is not relevant to the martyr theology. After all, Isaiah 53 seems to be the only Old Testament passage which voices the belief that the suffering and death of the righteous can be compared to a sacrifice which benefits others.[53]

In comparison with 2 Maccabees (written about 100 BC) the theology of martyrdom in 4 Maccabees (written in the first century AD) is developed and intensified through the inclusion of vicarious

---

[52]In 4 Macc 18:6-19 the mother of the seven brothers reminds them how their father taught them about the twelve holy men who had to suffer: Abel, Isaac, Joseph, Phinehas, Hananiah, Azariah, and Mishael in the fire, Daniel, Isaiah, David, Solomon and Ezekiel. The Isa 43:2 quotation befits the context where reference is made to the three friends of Daniel who were cast into the furnace.

[53]The role of Isaiah 53 in the theology of 4 Maccabees has been emphasized by deSilva (*4 Maccabees* 139).

expressions which closely resemble those which define the atoning work of Jesus Christ in the New Testament. Perhaps this development resulted from the increasing influence of Christian proclamation. Thus the proclamation of the vicarious sufferings and death of Jesus Christ, using Old Testament sacrificial-cultic terms, was challenged by emphasizing the role of the martyrs and intensifying the belief that their obedience benefits others. Needless to say, the theology of martyrdom was not developed in Judaism into the view that sins could be wholly eliminated by the death of the martyr(s).

Conclusions

This survey of the early Jewish martyr theology indicates that Isaiah 53 served to give new hope to the martyrs who die for the sake of the Torah. Isaiah 53 is alluded to in the Book of Daniel but never quoted in the Book of Maccabees. Nevertheless, we have argued that Isaiah 53 plays a role in 2 and 4 Maccabees: the death of the martyrs will benefit the whole people and the martyrs themselves will receive their reward in the coming world through resurrection. What is important in this interpretation is the fact that the suffering servant provides a model for a righteous martyr and that the sufferings, death and resurrection of the servant in Isaiah 53 are interpreted literally.

From this interpretive perspective it becomes understandable that during the time of Jesus, Isaiah 53 was regarded as a text *sui generis* which pertains to any righteous who must suffer in this world. The text emphasizes that after his humiliation the Servant will receive his reward in the world to come after the resurrection. In the next section we shall scrutinize the translation of the Septuagint, and the Wisdom of Solomon 2-5, based thereon, and show how Isaiah 53 served as a key text for a righteous sufferer.

4 Isaiah 53 as a Proof Text for a Suffering Righteous

In section 3 we saw that the earliest interpretations of Isaiah 53 which can be traced in the ancient Jewish writings concerned suffering righteous martyrs. A similar interpretation also emerges in Wisdom 2-5 where Isaiah 53 is used to describe the suffering righteous one. But before we deal with that passage we shall examine the Septuagint translation of Isaiah 53 which is used in Wisdom 2-5 and reinterpreted.

The Septuagint Version of Isaiah 53

Isaiah 53 is so crucial a passage in Christian theology that it cannot be assumed that textual traditions transmitted in manuscripts of Christian origin derive from the pre-Christian period. For example, Euler argued that our present text of Isaiah 53 contains many later Christian interpolations.[1] It is therefore necessary to deal first with the Septuagint version of Isaiah 53.[2]

The basic problem is that Isaiah 53 has also been preserved in the documents of early Christian writers and not always in the same form as the established Septuagint version. Consequently, scholars have considered the possibility that the central Christian text, Isaiah 53, may

---

[1]K.F. Euler, *Die Verkündigung vom leidenden Gottesknecht aus Jes 53 in der griechischen Bibel* (BWANT 4:14, Leipzig: Kohlhammer 1934).

[2]A good introduction to the problem is M. Hengel, "Die Septuaginta als 'christliche Schriftensammlung', ihre Vorgeschichte und das Problem ihres Kanons," in: M. Hengel & A.M. Schwemer (eds), *Die Septuaginta zwischen Judentum und Christentum* (WUNT 72, Tübingen: Mohr 1994) 182-284.

contain some later corrections.[3] These problems in textual transmission can be perceived when the texts of Mt 8:17 and 1 Peter 2:24 which quote Isa 53:4 are compared with the accepted Septuagint manuscripts Codex Vaticanus, Codex Sinaiticus and Codes Alexandrinus:[4]

Mt 8:17: Αὐτὸς τὰς ἀσθενείας ἡμῶν ἔλαβεν καὶ τὰς νόσους ἐβάστασεν

1 Peter 2:24:[5] ... τὰς ἁμαρτίας ἡμῶν αὐτὸς ἀνήνεγκεν

Isa 53:4: οὗτος τὰς ἁμαρτίας ἡμῶν φέρει καὶ περὶ ἡμῶν ὀδυνᾶται

The differences between these texts can be explained only by assuming that different Greek translations have been followed. However, this does not suggest that these texts go back to interpolations to the Septuagint. It is conceivable that Christians made their own translations of the key passages of the Hebrew Bible. This may well be true, in particular, of Isaiah 53 because – as we shall see – the Septuagint translation has in many points deprecated vicarious and atoning aspects of the suffering of the servant, so that its wording may have been difficult to accept in the New Testament and Christian texts.[6]

Clemens Romanus quotes Isaiah 53 in his Letter to Corinthians (16:3-14), which contains some important readings which differ from

---

[3]For this discussion see Euler's above mentioned study. See also H.S. Nyberg, "Smärtornas man: En studie till Jes. 52,13-53,12," SEÅ 7 (1942) 5-82; J. Ziegler, *Isaias* (Septuaginta, Vetus Testamentum Graecum, Göttingen: Vandehoeck & Ruprecht 1967).

[4]These three codices are available in A. Rahlfs' edition: *Septuaginta* (Stuttgart: Deutsche Bibelgesellschaft 1982).

[5]1 Peter 2:24 combines quotations from Isa 53:4 and 53:12.

[6]See D.A. Sapp, "The LXX, 1QIsa, and MT Versions of Isaiah 53 and the Christian Doctrine of Atonement," in: W.H. Bellinger & W.R. Farmer (eds), *Jesus and the Suffering Servant: Isaiah 53 and Christian Origins* (Harrisburg: Trinity Press 1998) 170-192.

LXX.[7] In particular, Markschies emphasizes the statement in Isa 53:6 where Clement reads: καὶ κύριος παρέδωκεν αὐτὸν ὑπὲρ τῶν ἁμαρτιῶν ἡμῶν while the Septuagint has καὶ κύριος παρέδωκεν αὐτὸν ταῖς ἁμαρτίαις ἡμῶν. Clement's reading contains the preposition ὑπὲρ which is often used in the New Testament when the vicarious meaning of the death of Jesus is presented.[8]

Another example is Justin Martyr. He often gives two different translations of one and the same Old Testament passages. In as much as quotations from Isaiah 53 appear several times in Justin's work, it is clear that this chapter is one of the most significant proof texts about the suffering, death and resurrection of Jesus Christ.[9] Justin often quotes Isaiah 53 according to the chief Septuagint manuscripts but the text of one quotation in *1 Apol* 50.2 does not follow this tradition. In *1 Apol* 50.2-11 Justin gives the Septuagint version of Isa 52:13-53:8 but it is preceded by a non-LXX version of Isa 53:12:[10]

---

[7]See these differences in C. Markschies, "Jesus Christ as a Man before God: Two Interpretive Models for Isaiah 53 in the Patristic Literature and Their Development," in: B. Janowski & P. Stuhlmacher (eds), *The Suffering Servant: Isaiah 53 in Jewish and Christian Sources* (Grand Rapids: Eerdmans 2004) 225-320. In this same volume D.P. Bailey (pp. 321-323) gives the text of 1 Clement 16:3-4 according to the Codex A. Bailey presents typographically how Clement's text of Isaiah 53 differs from Septuagint manuscripts (in Ziegler's and Rahlfs' editions).

[8]Markschies, "Jesus Christ as a Man before God," 237-239. See further sect. 7.

[9]See the evidence in *Biblia Patristica. Index des citations et allusions bibliques dans la litterature patristique. Centre d'analyse et de documentation patristiques*. See further H.W. Wolff, *Jesaja 53 im Urchristentum. Mit einer Einführung von Peter Stuhlmacher* (Giessen: Brunnen 1984) 123-142; A. Laato, "Isaiah 53 and the Biblical Exegesis of Justin Martyr," in: A.Laato & J. Van Ruiten (eds), *Rewritten Bible Reconsidered: Proceedings of the Conference in Karkku, Finland August 24-26 2006* (SRB 1, Winona Lake: Eisenbrauns; Turku: Åbo Akademi University 2008) 215-229.

[10]See the texts by Justin Martyr in E.J. Goodspeed (ed.), *Die ältesten Apologeten. Texte mit kurzen Einleitungen*. Göttingen: Vandenhoeck & Ruprecht 1984; M. Marcovich (ed.), *Iustini Martyris Apologiae pro christianis*. Berlin: de Gruyter 1994; idem, *Iustini Martyris Dialogue cum Tryphone*. Berlin: de Gruyter 1997. Translations are from *Ante-Nicene Fathers*. See also *St. Justin Martyr: Dialogue with Trypho*.

ἀνθ ὧν παρέδωκαν εἰς θάνατον τὴν ψυχὴν αὐτοῦ καὶ μετὰ τῶν ἀνόμων ἐλογίσθη αὐτὸς ἁμαρτίας πολλῶν εἴληφε καὶ τοῖς ἀνόμοις ἐξιλάσεται

There are three differences between this text and the LXX rendering. *First*, there is a parallel to Lk 22:37 which reads καὶ μετὰ ἀνόμων ἐλογίσθη while the LXX has καὶ ἐν τοῖς ἀνόμοις ἐλογίσθη but the meaning is the same. The *second* difference is that *1 Apol* 50.2 states "they delivered his soul" while the LXX uses a passive construction "his soul was delivered" which is a better alternative to the Hebrew expression הֶעֱרָה לַמָּוֶת נַפְשׁוֹ. It is plausible that the third person plural refers to the executioners (Romans or Jews) of Jesus in the textual tradition (testimonia source) transmitted by Justin. The *third* difference is the most striking, when the Hebrew יַפְגִּיעַ is rendered by the Greek verb ἐξιλάσεται, emphasizing the expiation and atonement. Because the verb ἐξιλάσκομαι does not appear in Justin's writings Skarsaune's conclusion that he is dependent on an early Christian testimony source seems reasonable. Justin's use of such an early Christian source is a strong indication of how Isaiah 53 was connected with the interpretation that the death of Jesus was expiatory.[11]

Scholars seem to regard these differences as evidence that in the early Church the quotation of central theological Old Testament texts was controlled by the Hebrew text. This is a plausible assumption, particularly in the case of Isaiah 53 which in its Septuagint version has shifted from the vicarious suffering (so clearly present in the Hebrew text) to the innocent suffering of the righteous. This being the case, we have good reason to agree with Ziegler who in his edition of the Book of

---

Transl. by Thomas B. Falls; rev. and with a new introduction by Thomas P. Halton; ed. by Michael Slusser. Washington: Catholic University of America Press 2003.

[11]O. Skarsaune, *The Proof from Prophecy. A Study in Justin Martyr's Proof-Text Tradition: Text-Type, Provenance, Theological Profile* (SupNT 56, Leiden: Brill 1987) 62-63.

Isaiah considers renderings in the Septuagint manuscripts as generally reliable.[12] Nevertheless, there is one peculiar reading in Ziegler's edition which we cannot overlook here. Against all manuscripts Ziegler reads in Isa 53:2 ἀνέτειλε μὲν instead of ἀνηγγείλαμεν. Ziegler argues for this conjecture that particularly in the transmission process of the Septuagint version of Isaiah there are several examples where ἀναγγέλλειν and ἀνατέλλειν are interchanged. He lists the following texts: 42:9; 43:19; 45:8; and 47:13. This being the case a similar copying error may have arisen in Isa 53:2 – apparently at an early stage of the Septuagint tradition so that it occurs in all the manuscripts.[13]

Ekblad criticized this theory because ἀνατέλλειν is never used to translate the Hebrew verb עלה. He regards the reading ἀνηγγείλαμεν as *lectio difficilior* and therefore original.[14] Ziegler's conjecture has its basis in textual evidence. In the Septuagint version of Isaiah ἀνατέλλειν stands for the Hebrew verb צמח in Isa 42:9; 43:19; 44:4; 45:8; 58:8; 61:11 and in 45:8 תִּפְתַּח־אֶרֶץ וְיִפְרוּ־יֶשַׁע is translated with ἀνατειλάτω ἡ γῆ ἔλεος καὶ δικαιοσύνην ἀνατειλάτω ἅμα. In Isa 58:10; 60:1 the Hebrew verb זרח and in 66:14 פרח are translated with ἀνατέλλειν. There are two passages which support Ziegler's view that in Isa 53:2 the verb עלה could have been translated by ἀνατέλλειν. In Isa 13:10 the verb יצא and in 44:26 the verb קום are translated with this verb. Both Hebrew verbs are semantically related to עלה. In addition, it should be mentioned that the metaphor of Isa 53:2 concerns the growth

---

[12]Hengel ("The Effective History of Isaiah 53 in the Pre-Christian Period," in: B. Janowski & P. Stuhlmacher (eds), *The Suffering Servant: Isaiah 53 in Jewish and Christian Sources* (Grand Rapids: Eerdmans 2004) 75-146, esp. 119-121) agrees with Ziegler that the Septuagint textual tradition on Isaiah 53 is relatively reliable. Concerning critical evaluation of Euler's thesis note also H. Hegermann, *Jesaja 53 in Hexapla, Targum und Peschitta* (Gütersloh: Bertelsmann 1954).

[13]Ziegler, *Isaias* 99.

[14]E.R. Ekblad, *Isaiah's Servant Poems According to the Septuagint* (CBET 23, Leuven: Peters 1999) 198-199.

of a shoot and comes close to the Hebrew צֶמַח. Nevertheless, we must remember that Ziegler's suggestion is a conjecture.

The Greek translation of the Book of Isaiah which later became a part of the Septuagint was made in the second century BC. The introduction of Ben Sira's Greek version indicates that the translation of Isaiah was completed before the end of the second century BC. Seeligman made a careful examination of the translation and discovered several allusions to the Maccabean period.[15] He starts with Isa 14:19-20 which is translated in the LXX as follows:[16]

> But you will be cast out on the mountains (ἐν τοῖς ὄρεσιν),
> like an abominable corpse
> with many dead, those pierced with daggers
> who go down into Hades.
> As a cloak stained with blood will not be clean
> so neither will you be clean,
> because you have destroyed my land
> and killed my people.

Seeligman notes that in 2 Macc 9:28 the death of Antiochus IV Epiphanes is reported as taking place "on the mountains":[17]

---

[15]The use of the prophecies of Isaiah in the Book of Daniel are good parallels. For this see I.L. Seeligman, *The Septuagint Version of Isaiah and Cognate Studies* (FAT 40, Göttingen: Mohr Siebeck 2004) 238-240 – Seeligman's original study was published in 1948; see further J. Blenkinsopp, *Opening the Sealed Book: Interpretations of the Book of Isaiah in Late Antiquity* (Grand Rapids: Eerdmans 2006) 14-27.

[16]Seeligman *The Septuagint Version of Isaiah* 240-251.

[17]A. Van der Kooij (*Die alten Textzeugen des Jesajabuches: Ein Beitrag zur Textgeschichte des Alten Testaments* [OBO 35, Freiburg: Universitätsverlag, Göttingen: Vandenhoeck & Ruprecht 1981] 40) notes that 2 Macc 9:28 is later than the LXX translation of Isaiah, so that it is not self-evident that the translator referred to the death of Antiochus IV Epiphanes.

So the murderer and blasphemer, having endured the most intense suffering, such as he had inflicted on others, came to the end of his life by a most pitiable fate among the mountains in a strange land (ἐπὶ ξένης ἐν τοῖς ὄρεσιν).

There are other interesting readings which reveal that the translator of the Septuagint version of the Book of Isaiah has the Maccabean period in mind. The Hebrew expression in Isa 8:8 which describes the Assyrian flood penetrating into Judah and flooding up to the neck has been reinterpreted and translated: "... and he will cause the disappearance from Judah of the man who is able to raise his head and achieve something." This translation speaks of a man from Judah who is capable of righteous deeds – and Seeligman identifies him as being Onias III.[18] A similar tendency is visible in Isa 10:5-6 which in the Hebrew text mentions Assyrians who have been sent against the "lawless nation", i.e. Judah, in the LXX translation this has been changed so that the Lord's anger is against "a lawless nation", i.e. the Seleucids, and he sent against them "my people" who will win the war: "I will send my anger against a lawless nation and I will instruct my people to take spoils and plunder ..."

There is a significant detail also in Isa 10:24 where the Hebrew expression בדרך מצרים is not translated literally ἐν ὁδῷ Αἰγύπτου as in Am 4:10 but "so that you may see the way of Egypt (ἐπὶ σὲ τοῦ ἰδεῖν ὁδὸν Αἰγύπτου)." Such a translation indicates that Assyrians (i.e. Selucids) compel the people of Zion to emigrate to Egypt. According to Seeligman the famous passage in the Passover Haggadah, "the Aramean wanted to destroy my Father" and forced him to move to Egypt

---

[18]It is worth noting that Seeligman (*The Septuagint Version of Isaiah* 252-257) argues that Onias III was not murdered but moved to Egypt and established the temple at Leontopolis when he fled Antiochus IV Epiphanes to Philometor sometime before 170 BC. This view receives support from Josephus (*Bell Jud* 7:423-432) but contradicts what Josephus states elsewhere, indicating that the temple of Leontopolis was established by Onias IV (*Ant* 13:62-73 and 20:236) when he fled to Ptolemaeus VI Philometor after Alcimus had been appointed high priest in 161 BC. According to Seeligman, the story in 2 Macc 4:33-38 originally tells about the murder of Seleucos IV by Andronichus.

is a similar tradition describing the Jews' emigration to Egypt in consequence of persecutions during the Maccabean period. Josephus remarks (*Ant* XIII 3:1) that Isa 19:19 was used to explain the existence of the Judean Temple at Leontopolis.

Seeligman would date the Septuagint translation of Isaiah to the mid-second century BC because he takes Isa 23:10 as referring to the destruction of Carthage (146 BC) when the city lost its ships: "Work you land, for indeed ships no longer come from Carthage."[19]

Van der Kooij argues that the Septuagint translation of Isaiah originates from Leontopolis and was written to glorify the priestly generation of Oniads. Following Seeligman he regards the translation of Isa 23:10 as evidence that Carthage was already destroyed. In his view Isa 21:1-9 confirms the date of its destruction. The translation was made with the events of the year 141 BC in mind when Babylon, the city of the Seleucid kingdom, was captured by Mithridates I.[20]

These two suggested dates in the 140's BC imply that the translation was made after the Maccabean revolt. Therefore, we may assume that the Jewish martyr theology was well known to the translator(s).[21]

The Greek translation of Isaiah 53 makes consistent use of tense. Isa 52:13-15 has been translated in the future and Isa 53:1-7 in the aorist. In Isa 53:8-12 the future tense is again used. This being the case, the

---

[19]Seeligman, *The Septuagint Version of Isaiah* 250-251.

[20]Van der Kooij, *Die alten Textzeugen des Jesajabuches* 71-73.

[21]In addition, scholars have argued that many details in the Septuagint translation of Isaiah point to Egyptian (Alexandrian) background. See J. Ziegler, *Untersuchungen zur Septuaginta des Buches Isaias* (Altestamentlichen Abhandlungen XII:3, Münster: Aschendorff 1934) 175-212. Ziegler writes (p. 211): "Ein Rückblick auf diesen Abschnitt: 'Der alexandrinisch-ägyptische Hintergrund der Js-LXX' zeigt uns, dass der Übers. aus dem Wortschatz der alexandrinischen Umwelt seine Ausdrücke und Wendungen holte. Wie die einzelnen Beispiele zeigen, ist er in den Fragen der Landwirtschaft, der Bodenbeschaffenheit, der Pflanzen- und Tierwelt, des gewerblichen Lebens, des Rechtswesens und sogar der Frauenmode gut bewandert." See also Seeligman, *The Septuagint Version of Isaiah* 258-294.

translator of the LXX seems to have in mind a past event to which Isa 53:1-7 refer. This event will prove to benefit not only the servant himself but also the "we"-group, as implied by the use of the future tense in Isa 52:13-15; 53:8-12. In what follows, a translation of the Septuagint version of Isaiah 53 is presented and comments are included as footnotes.

The future glorification of the servant

13   Look, my servant (ὁ παῖς μου)[22] will become wise (συνήσει)[23], will be exalted and greatly glorified (ὑψωθήσεται καὶ δοξασθήσεται σφόδρα)[24].

14   As many will be astonished at you (ὃν τρόπον ἐκστήσονται ἐπὶ σὲ πολλοί)[25] so will your outlook be dishonored by human beings and your glory[26] by human beings.

15   So many peoples will wonder (θαυμάσονται)[27] about him and kings will shut their mouths because they will see what they had never been told about him, and understand what they had not heard before.

---

[22]In Isa 48:20; 49:3,5 the word δοῦλος is used.

[23]LXX interprets יַשְׂכִּיל as referring to the servant's intellectual growth.

[24]The same two verbs are also used in Isa 4:2; 5:16; 10:15; 33:10. These translations connect Isaiah 53 to two important theological concepts. First, Isa 33:10-11 speak of the final judgment when the Lord will rise and "will be glorified and be exalted." Second, Isa 4:2 refers to the remnant of Israel which "will be exalted and glorified." See W. Zimmerli & J. Jeremias, *The Servant of God* (SBT 20, London: SCM Press 1965) 44; Hengel "The Effective History of Isaiah 53," 121-122.

[25]Cf., the reading in Wisd 5:2.

[26]The only Hebrew word which can be related to δόξα is תֹּאַר, a poor equivalent, indeed. It seems that the Greek translation of Isa 52:13 influenced the interpretation even here.

[27]Aquila and Theodotion translate the MT word יַזֶּה med ῥαντίσει. The LXX reading may be based on different Hebrew reading, i.e., יִרְגְּזוּ (from the verb רגז).

82

The description of the fate of the servant

1   O Lord! Who has understood what we have heard? And the arm of the Lord, to whom has it been revealed?

2   He grew up before him as a child, like a root in arid ground (ἀνέτειλε μὲν ἐναντίον αὐτοῦ ὡς παιδίον, ὡς ῥίζα ἐν γῇ διψώσῃ)[28]. He had no comeliness or glory. We saw him but he had no comeliness or beauty,

3   rather his comeliness was despised and deprecated in comparison with the sons of men. A man who was in pain and who knew what is to bear illness. His faces were turned away, he was dishonored and regarded as nothing.

4   This (man) bore our sins and was tormented on our behalf (οὗτος τὰς ἁμαρτίας ἡμῶν φέρει)[29], and we regarded him as being in toil, in pain and in oppression.

5   But he was wounded for our sins (αὐτὸς δὲ ἐτραυματίσθη διὰ τὰς ἀνομίας ἡμῶν), he fell ill (μεμαλάκισται) because of our

---

[28]The use of the word παιδίον is interesting here because the same word is used in the translation of Isa 9:5. As noted above, all Septuagint manuscripts here otherwise read (cf., also Clement in 1 Cor 16:3-15): ἀνηγγείλαμεν ἐναντίον αὐτου ὡς παιδίον, ὡς ῥίζα ἐν γῇ διψώσῃ. This Greek interpretation is difficult to understand. Justin Martyr gives one very sophisticated interpretation of this enigmatic translation (Dial 42): "And Isaiah speaks as if he were personating the apostles, when they say to Christ that they believe not in their own report, but in the power of Him who sent them. And so he says: 'Lord, who hath believed our report? and to whom is the arm of the Lord revealed? We have preached before Him **as if** [we were] **a child**, as if a root in a dry ground.' (And what follows in order of the prophecy already quoted.) But when the passage speaks as from the lips of many, 'We have preached before Him', and adds, **'as if a child'**, it signifies that the wicked shall become subject to Him, and shall obey His command, and that all shall become as one child. Such a thing as you may witness in the body: although the members are enumerated as many, all are called *one*, and are a *body*. For, indeed, a commonwealth and a church, though many individuals in number, are in fact as one, called and addressed by one appellation."

[29]As Hengel ("The Effective History of Isaiah 53," 124) has noted the vicarious atoning suffering is softened in many parts of the LXX translation of Isaiah 53 but it is, nevertheless, clearly present in verses 53:4-5.

evil deeds; the punishment of our peace was on him, and we have been healed by his bruises.

6   All we went astray like sheep, each followed his own path, and the Lord gave him up for our sins.

7   And he did not open his mouth when he was tormented, like a lamb which is led to the slaughter, and like a sheep is dumb before its shearers he never opened his mouth.

The future of the servant

8   His justice was taken away through humiliation. And who will tell his generation? For his life was taken up from the earth, for the lawless deeds of my people he was led to death (ὅτι αἴρεται ἀπὸ τῆς γῆς ἡ ζωὴ αὐτοῦ ἀπὸ τῶν ἀνομιῶν τοῦ λαοῦ μου ἤχθη εἰς θάνατον).[30]

9   And I will give[31] the wicked instead of his grave, and the rich instead of his death (καὶ δώσω τοὺς πονηροὺς ἀντὶ τῆς ταφῆς αὐτοῦ καὶ τοὺς πλουσίους ἀντὶ τοῦ θανάτου αὐτοῦ), because he did no wrong nor was deceit found in his mouth.

10   And the Lord desires to cleanse him of the plague; if you make a sin offering, your[32] soul will see long-lived offspring (ἐὰν δῶτε περὶ ἁμαρτίας ἡ ψυχὴ ὑμῶν ὄψεται σπέρμα μακρόβιον)[33].

---

[30]It is worth noting that the passage refers to an individual.

[31]The Hebrew text has וַיִּתֵּן but the Greek has δώσω which implies that the verse 9 constitutes a promise.

[32]It is worth noting that Codex B here reads ἡμῶν instead of ὑμῶν. The idea in B seems to be that "The Lord desires to cleanse him of the plague if you make an offering. Our soul will see long-lived offspring."

[33]In the Hebrew text it is the servant who gives his life as אָשָׁם sacrifice, but in the LXX those who have erred are exhorted to make a sacrifice.

11 And the Lord desires to take away the agony of his soul[34], to show to him light and to fill [him] with understanding, to vindicate the righteous one who well serves the many and their sins he will take on himself (δικαιῶσαι δίκαιον εὖ δουλεύοντα πολλοῖς καὶ τὰς ἁμαρτίας αὐτῶν αὐτὸς ἀνοίσει)[35].

12 Hence he will inherit many, and he will take the booty of the mighty[36], as recompense for that his soul was exposed to death and he was counted as one of the rebellious, and he bore the sins of many and was given for their evil deeds (ἀνθ᾽ ὧν παρεδόθη εἰς θάνατον ἡ ψυχὴ αὐτοῦ καὶ ἐν τοῖς ἀνόμοις ἐλογίσθη καὶ αὐτὸς ἁμαρτίας πολλῶν ἀνήνεγκεν καὶ διὰ τὰς ἁμαρτίας αὐτῶν παρεδόθη)[37].

Scholars agree generally that the translator of the Septuagint version of Isaiah 53 softened the vicarious atoning suffering of the servant in many places but this aspect is not totally censored as is the case in the Targum Jonathan (see sect. 6). After all, the vicarious suffering is still present in

---

[34]The subject of the verbs at the end of 53:10 and 53:11 is the Lord. The meaning of Isa 53:10-11 in the LXX is strikingly different from that of the MT.

[35]The end of verse 11 is strikingly different from the MT. This must be due to the fact that the translator of the LXX read the participle form עֹבֵד instead of the Hebrew word עַבְדִּי. For this see L. Ruppert, *Der leidende Gerechte. Eine motivgeschichtliche Untersuchung* 60.

[36]Ekblad, *Isaiah's Servant Poems* 263: "In contrast to the servant of the MT who divides the spoil with the mighty, in the LXX the servant divides the spoils of the strong."

[37]As already noted, Justinus Martyr renders Isa 53:12 in 1 Apol 50.2 as ἀνθ᾽ ὧν παρέδωκαν εἰς θάνατον τὴν ψυχὴν αὐτοῦ καὶ μετὰ τῶν ἀνόμων ἐλογίσθη. αὐτὸς ἁμαρτίας πολλῶν εἴληφε καὶ τοῖς ἀνόμοις ἐξιλάσεται. This translation may have been taken from some testimony source. Skarsaune, *Proof from Prophecy* 63; Markschies, "Jesus Christ as a Man before God," 248-249. In 1 Apol 51.5 the text of Isa 53:12 is quoted according to the LXX.

the translation of Isa 53:4-5. A prominent problem in the Greek translation concerns its reference to the death and resurrection of the servant.

In Hengel's opinion the LXX version of Isa 53:8-10 and, in particular, the statement about the Servant in verse 8 (ὅτι αἴρεται ἀπὸ τῆς γῆς ἡ ζωὴ αὐτοῦ) should be understood as signifying that the servant and his congregation will inherit eternal life.[38] However, Sapp holds another view. He observes that in both Isa 53:8 and 53:12 the Greek translation softens the Hebrew expression about the death of the servant. He concludes that the LXX text "leaves some doubt as to whether the Servant was actually put to death or only led up to the point of possible death."[39] In Sapp's opinion the translation of Isa 53:9-11 casts doubt on whether the servant would really die. The translator of the LXX has interpreted verse 9 so that the servant was not buried among the ungodly, rather that the Lord will give the grave which was prepared for the servant to the wicked. Thus Sapp argues that "the LXX, unlike the Hebrew, understands the Servant to have been *led to the verge of death but not subjected to it.*"[40] Sapp concludes that the Septuagint version of Isa 53:8-11 contains strikingly different theology from the MT. While in the Hebrew "*the righteous one, the Lord's Servant, gives righteousness to the many through a divinely intended sacrificial death inflicted on him by wicked people*" in the LXX "*the Lord vindicates the righteous one*

---

[38]Hengel "The Effective History of Isaiah 53," 126: "The statement about the congregation's seed or posterity in verse 10c ... corresponds to the Servant's 'generation' in verse 8b, which is so large that nobody can 'declare' it ... The restoration of the true Israel through the resurrection of the dead is presupposed. That the Servant himself has received a share in God's eternal life may already be hinted at in verse 8c ... 'for he is *taken up* (removed) from the earth'."

[39]Sapp, "Versions of Isaiah 53," 177. Cf., also E. Fascher, *Jesaja 53 in christlicher und jüdischer Sicht* (Aufsätze und Verträge zur Theologie und Religionswissenschaft 4; Berlin: Evangelische Verlagsanstalt 1958) 13-15.

[40]Sapp, "Versions of Isaiah 53," 176-184, the quotation is from p. 179.

who serves the many well by cutting short his agony and saving him from death at the hands of wicked people."[41] Sapp's interpretation is not the first possibility which comes to mind when we read the content of verse 8. After all the Septuagint verse states that the life of the Servant was taken away from the earth. This is difficult to understand in any other way than as a reference to his death. Hengel proposes a specific explanation of the LXX version of Isaiah 53. He criticizes Hahn's self-evident view whereby a messianic expectation cannot be discerned in Isaiah 53 (LXX). Hengel refers to "messianic" titles in the translation of Isaiah 53. The first is the conjecture in Isa 53:2 suggested by Ziegler. The verb ἀνατέλλω is cognate to the messianic title ἀνατολή which is the Septuagint translation of צמח in Jer 23:5; Zech 3:8; 6:12. Another term is παιδίον in Isa 53:2 which is the word used in the messianic prophecy in Isa 9:5.[42] Hengel argues that the text can be related to the death of Onias III who was regarded as the last legitimate Zadokite High priest. Hengel refers to Dan 9:26; 11:22 and 1 Enoch 90:8 which probably describe the death of Onias III. According to 2 Macc 15:12,16 the High Priest revealed himself after his death to Judas Maccabeus in a vision, indicating that he was regarded as living among God (cf., the translation of the LXX to Isa 53:8). According to Hengel, such an interpretation of Isaiah 53 is plausible because the son of Onias III, Onias IV, who established a Jewish military colony in Egypt, was acting when the Greek translation of the Book of Isaiah was made. Against this historical background the Greek interpretation of Isa 19:18 can be regarded as referring to Leontopolis where Onias IV established his temple[43] – a theory which receives support also from Josephus' understanding of Isa 19:18 as already mentioned.

---

[41]Both quotations are from Sapp, "Versions of Isaiah 53," 182; italics are Sapp's.

[42]On the individual or messianic interpretation see Hegermann, *Jesaja 53 in Hexapla* 128-130; Zimmerli, *Servant of God* 43-44.

[43]Hengel, "The Effective History of Isaiah 53," 136-137.

Hengel assumes an individual interpretation which is optional. Nevertheless, if this concrete identification between the Servant and Onias III ever existed, it does not seem to have any Wirkungsgeschichte in subsequent documents. Therefore, it is justified to ask whether the readers of the Septuagint Isaiah connected the content of Isaiah 53 with other Servant texts. If so then the collective understanding of the servant figure in Isaiah 53 becomes highly relevant. The words "Jacob" and "Israel" have been added in 42:1, suggesting that 42:1-4 was interpreted collectively. In Isa 49:1-6 the word "Israel" is preserved in v 3, indicating that here, too, "servant" was understood collectively.[44] An interpretation which is on a par with Isa 42:1-4; 49:1-6 has been proposed by Nyberg. He argues that the LXX refers generally to a righteous person who lives among the ungodly and is compelled to bear the consequences of the sins of the world. In 53:4 the MT expression "struck by God" has been translated "we regarded him as being in toil." The translation does not say who is responsible for the suffering of the righteous but 53:6 emphasizes that the Lord allowed this to happen. The righteous one will ultimately be rewarded by God (53:10-12). Nyberg's thesis receives support from the Book of Wisdom which – as Nyberg also remarks – incorporates Isaiah 53 in its descriptions of the trials and tribulations of the righteous.[45] This interpretive tendency becomes more prominent now as we shall deal with this book.

---

[44]For the collective interpretation of Isa 42:1-4 and 49:1-6 in the LXX see, e.g., C.R. North, *The Suffering Servant in Deutero-Isaiah: An Historical and Critical Study* (Oxford: Oxford University Press 1963) 8; Zimmerli, *Servant of God* 42-43; H. Haag, *Der Gottesknecht bei Deuterojesaja* (EdF 233, Darmstadt: Wissenschaftliche Buchgesellschaft 1985) 44-47.

[45]H.S. Nyberg, "Smärtornas man" 5-82, esp. 5-33.

The Wisdom of Solomon and the Interpretation of Isaiah 53

The Wisdom of Solomon was written at Alexandria. It contains an attempt to modify the Jewish religion to accord with the principles of the Greek philosophy. Philo's writings contain many parallels to the Wisdom of Solomon.[46] The concept of an immortal soul is a tenet of the theology of the Wisdom of Solomon, being particularly visible in Chapters 2-5, which describe the righteous one who must suffer in the world at the hands of the wicked. The Septuagint version of Isaiah 53 plays an important role in Wisdom 2-5.[47] It can be demonstrated that even Isaiah 54, 56-57 are quoted and alluded to in Wisdom 2-5.[48]

Wisd 2:1-5:23 forms a single literary unit and deals with theodicy:[49] Why do the righteous suffer?[50] At the beginning and the end of this textual complex there is a quotation from the Book of Isaiah: Wisd 2:12 and Isa 3:10; Wisd 5:18 and Isa 59:17. The servant of Isaiah 52-53 is interpreted in the Wisdom of Solomon as a righteous man who

---

[46] D. Winston, *The Wisdom of Solomon* (AB 43, Garden City: Doubleday 1979), 59-63.

[47] See Nyberg, "Smärtornas man" 5-33; M.J. Suggs, "Wisdom of Solomon 2:10-5: A Homily based on the fourth Servant Song." *JBL* 76 (1957) 26-33; J. Jeremias, *The Servant of God* 54-55; Ruppert *Der leidende Gerechte. Eine motivgeschichtliche Untersuchung* 70-105; Hengel, "The Effective History of Isaiah 53," 129-132.

[48] Ruppert *Der leidende Gerechte. Eine motivgeschichtliche Untersuchung* 80; P.C. Beentjes, "Wisdom of Solomon 3,1-4,19 and the Book of Isaiah," in: J. Van Ruiten & M. Vervenne (eds), *Studies in the Book of Isaiah: Festschrift Willem A.M. Beuken* (BETL 132, Leuven: University Press 1997) 413-420.

[49] For a general overview of the problem of theodicy see D. Winston, "Theodicy in the Wisdom of Solomon," in: A. Laato & J.C. De Moor (eds), *Theodicy in the World of the Bible* (Leiden: Brill 2003) 525-545.

[50] Ruppert (*Der leidende Gerechte. Eine motivgeschichtliche Untersuchung* 72-73) gives a neat overview of how the word *dikaios* and its parallel expressions in the singular and plural are used in Wisdom 1-6. He argues that there are redactional layers. Note also A.G. Wright, "Numerical Patterns in the Book of Wisdom," *CBQ* 29 (1967) 524-538 where he argues that there are numerical patterns in Wisdom including Wisd 1-6.

is scorned and oppressed by sinners and the ungodly. They regard the righteous as a mad man. However, at the last judgment the wicked will realize that the righteous man suffered by the will of the Lord and that he will receive his reward. At the final judgment the sinners will realize what they have done (Wisd 4:20): "They shall come, when their sins are reckoned up, with coward fear; And their lawless deeds shall convict them to their face" (Wisd 4:20). We shall examine the Greek text of the Wisdom of Solomon 2-5 and seek out its connections to Isaiah 52-57 and, in particular, to Isaiah 53.[51] In the following translations (the basic text which is followed here is RSV) my footnotes refer to the text of Isaiah 53 which is parallel to the text in Wisdom 2-5:[52]

2:1 For they reasoned unsoundly, saying to themselves, "Short and sorrowful is our life, and there is no remedy when a man comes to his end, and no one has been known to return from Hades.[53] 2:2 Because we were born by mere chance[54], and

---

[51]Concerning the parallels and for discussion see P.W. Skehan, "Isaias and the Teaching of the Book of Wisdom," *CBQ* 2 (1940) 289-299; Suggs "Wisdom of Solomon"; Jeremias, *Servant of God* 55; Ruppert *Der leidende Gerechte. Eine motivgeschichtliche Untersuchung* 70-105; Winston, *Wisdom of Solomon* 111-150; Beentjes, "Wisdom of Solomon"; L.L. Grabbe, *Wisdom of Solomon* (Guides to Apocrypha and Pseudepigrapha, Sheffield: Sheffield Academic Press 1997) 44-47; G.W.E. Nickelsburg, *Resurrection, Immortality, and Eternal Life in Intertestamental Judaism and Early Christianity* (Harvard Theological Studies 56, Cambridge: Harvard University Press 2006) 83-88. Winston (p. 114) argued that the arguments of the wicked parallel in some measure Epicurean philosophy (e.g., the finality of death, the denial of Divine Providence and the legitimacy of pleasure) but there is no basis for an idea that they could be identified with the Epicureans.

[52]The Greek text is from J. Ziegler, *Sapientia Salomonis* (Septuaginta: Vetus Testamentum Graecum, Auctoritate Societatis Litterarum Gottingensis editum XII,1; Göttingen: Vandenhoeck & Ruprecht 1962).

[53]In Wisd 2:1-5 the ungodly argue that they have no hope of afterlife – something which the righteous have and there is reason to believe that the end of Isaiah 53 has been interpreted as referring to this hope of eternal life.

[54]The Servant "grew up before" God according to LXX Isa 53:2.

hereafter we shall be as though we had never been; because the breath in our nostrils is smoke, and reason is a spark kindled by the beating of our hearts. 2:3 When it is extinguished, the body will turn to ashes, and the spirit will dissolve like empty air. 2:4 Our name will be forgotten in time and no one will remember our works[55]; our life will pass away like the traces of a cloud, and be scattered like mist that is chased by the rays of the sun and overcome by its heat. 2:5 For our allotted time is the passing of a shadow, and there is no return from our death, because it is sealed up and no one turns back. 2:6 Come, therefore, let us enjoy the good things that exist, and make use of the creation to the full as in youth. 2:7 Let us take our fill of costly wine and perfumes, and let no flower of spring pass by us. 2:8 Let us crown ourselves with rosebuds before they wither. 2:9 Let none of us fail to share in our revelry, everywhere let us leave signs of enjoyment, because this is our portion, and this our lot.[56] 2:10 Let us oppress the righteous (δίκαιον)[57] poor man; let us not spare the widow nor regard the gray hairs of the aged. 2:11 But let our might be our law of right, for what is weak proves itself to be useless. 2:12 Let us lie in wait for the righteous man, because he is useless to us (ἐνεδρεύσωμεν τὸν δίκαιον ὅτι δύσχρηστος ἡμῖν ἐστιν)[58] and opposes our actions; he reproaches us for sins

---

[55]The fate of the Servant is different. His actions will be commemorated and he will have a marvelous future and afterlife.

[56]D. Winston (*The Wisdom of Solomon* [AB 43, Garden City: Doubleday 1981] 118-119) has noted that the enjoyment of life is an ancient and popular motif which goes back to ancient Near Eastern texts and the Old Testament (e.g., Isa 22:13; Qoh 9:7) so that there is no need to attempt to reconstruct any underlying Greek philosophical background. Nevertheless, Winston notes that "the Cyrenaic philosophy would undoubtedly come much closer to the views of the wicked" (p. 114).

[57]The Servant in Isaiah 53 has been called righteous: LXX Isa 53:11.

[58]This is an almost verbatim quotation from Isa 3:10: δήσωμεν τὸν δίκαιον ὅτι δύσχρηστος ἡμῖν ἐστιν. In the Letter of Barnabas (6:7) this text is quoted and

against the law, and accuses us of sins against our training (ἁμαρτήματα παιδείας ἡμῶν).[59] 2:13 He professes to have knowledge of God (γνῶσιν ἔχειν θεοῦ)[60], and calls himself a child of the Lord (παῖδα κυρίου)[61]. 2:14 He became to us a reproof of our thoughts; the very sight of him is a burden to us (βαρύς ἐστιν ἡμῖν καὶ βλεπόμενος)[62], 2:15 because his manner of life is unlike that of others, and his ways are strange. 2:16 We are considered by him (ἐλογίσθημεν αὐτῳ)[63] as something base, and he avoids our ways as unclean; he calls the

---

interpreted as referring to Christ. See also Justin Martyr (*Dial* 17) and the Pseudo-Cyprian tractate De duobus montibus Sina et Sion 7.1 (concerning this text see A.M. Laato, *Jews and Christian in De duobus montibus Sina et Sion: An Approach to Early Latin Adversus Iudaeos Literature* [Åbo: Åbo Akademi University Press 1998]). Ruppert (*Der leidende Gerechte. Eine motivgeschichtliche Untersuchung* 78) has noted that the oppression against the righteous one is intensified in Wisd 2:12-20 until the murder plan is presented in v. 20: "In den soeben behandelten fünf, sich kunstvoll steigernden Selbstaufforderungen (ἐνεδρεύσωμεν; V.12a; ἴδωμεν: V.17a; πειράσωμεν: V.17b; ἐτάσωμεν: V.19a; καταδικάσωμεν: V.20a) konkretisiert sich ihre Feindschaft gegen den Gerechten bis zum Mordplan (V.20)."

[59]Isa 53:5 says of the Servant that he is παιδεία εἰρήνης ἡμῶν. It is possible that Isa 53:5 has given inspiration to formulate the antithetic expression of the godless in Wisd 2:12.

[60]LXX Isa 52:13; 53:11 emphasize that the servant will receive σύνεσις. In Isa 53:11 the Hebrew word *da'at* is also a good equivalent to the Greek *gnosis*.

[61]This is a clear allusion to παῖς κυρίου in Isaiah 53. The Servant is even called παιδίον in 53:2. In Wisd 5:5 the ungodly had to confess that the righteous is numbered among the sons of God. Ruppert (*Der leidende Gerechte. Eine motivgeschichtliche Untersuchung* 78) notes that the writer of Wisd 2:12-20 must have a particular righteous in mind when he applies Isaiah 53 to him, but adds "oder doch wenigstens das Urbild des Gerechten meinen".

[62]Isa 53:2 contains a corresponding idea i.e. the Servant is hard to gaze upon: εἴδομεν αὐτόν καὶ οὐκ εἴχεν εἶδος οὐδὲ κάλλος.

[63]In Isa 53:4 there is a same verb ἐλογισάμεθα αὐτόν.

last end of the righteous happy (μακαρίζει ἔσχατα δικαίων)[64], and boasts that God is his father.[65] 2:17 Let us see (ἴδωμεν) if his words are true, and let us test what will happen at the end of his life; 2:18 for if the righteous man is God's son[66], he will help him (ἀντιλήμψεται αὐτοῦ)[67], and will deliver him from the hand of his adversaries. 2:19 Let us test him with insult and torture (ὕβρει καὶ βασάνῳ ἐτάσωμεν αὐτόν)[68], that we may find out how gentle he is, and make trial of his forbearance.[69] 2:20 Let us condemn him to a shameful death (θανάτῳ ἀσχήμονι καταδικάσωμεν αὐτόν)[70], for, according to what he says, he will be protected."

2:21 Thus they reasoned, but they were led astray (ἐπλανήθησαν)[71], for their wickedness blinded them (ἀπετύφλωσεν γὰρ αὐτοὺς ἡ κακία αὐτῶν)[72], 2:22 and they did not know the secret purposes (μυστήρια) of God, nor hope

---

[64]This is the key idea in Wisd 2-5. The righteous one emphasizes that the final end of the righteous one will be happy – something which corresponds well to the content of Isaiah 53.

[65]The term *pais theou* implies that God is the father of the Servant.

[66]The term "God's son" can be regarded as parallel to *pais theou* which can also be translated "the child of God".

[67]The same expression in the first person singular (ἀντιλήμψομαι αὐτοῦ) appears also in Isa 42:1 which also speaks of the Servant of the Lord.

[68]The content of LXX Isa 53:4 emphasizes that the servant is tortured and in great distress.

[69]The righteous is gentle and meek as the Servant in Isaiah 42:1-4 and 52:13-53:12.

[70]LXX Isa 53:8-9 speaks of the death of the servant (or the threat to kill the servant).

[71]The same verb is used in Isa 53:6 where the "we"-group confess that they have gone astray: ἐπλανήθημεν.

[72]The Wisdom of Solomon describes how the wicked became blind like the "we"-group in Isaiah 53. The wicked think that the righteous will receive no help from God.

for the wages of holiness, nor discern the prize for blameless souls (ψυχῶν ἀμώμων)[73]; 2:23 for God created man for incorruption, and made him in the image of his own eternity, 2:24 but through the devil's envy death entered the world, and those who belong to his party experience it.

3:1 But the souls of the righteous are in the hand of God, and no torment will ever touch them. 3:2 In the eyes of the foolish they seemed to have died, and their departure was thought to be an affliction (καὶ ἐλογίσθη κάκωσις ἡ ἔξοδος αὐτῶν)[74], 3:3 and their going from us to be their destruction; but they are at peace (οἱ δέ εἰσιν ἐν εἰρήνῃ)[75]. 3:4 For though in the sight of men they were punished (καὶ γὰρ ἐν ὄψει ἀνθρώπων ἐὰν κολασθῶσιν)[76], their hope is full of immortality. 3:5 Having been disciplined a little (καὶ ὀλίγα παιδευθέντες)[77], they will receive great good (εὐεργετηθήσονται)[78], because God tested them (ὁ θεὸς ἐπείρασεν αὐτούς)[79] and found them worthy of

---

[73]It is emphasized that the righteous are blameless and that the wicked do not understand their secret life. It will remain a mystery for them until the last judgment. In this respect the wicked represent the "we"-group in Isaiah 53 who did not understand the distress and torments of the servant of the Lord.

[74]The phrase presents a typical antithesis in Isaiah 53: the fate of the righteous (the Servant in Isaiah 53) seems to be seen by the wicked (the "we"-group in Isaiah 53) as an affliction but they do not know the secret plans of the Lord.

[75]While the righteous must suffer the wicked can be at peace – something which is parallel to the fates of the servant and "we" in Isaiah 53.

[76]This idea is a fitting parallel to the end of verse 4 in LXX Isaiah 53.

[77]It is worth noting that LXX Isa 53:5 uses the word παιδία.

[78]Isa 53:12 states that the Servant will receive a great reward after his sufferings. The idea that affliction will endure a little while after which God will give a great reward appears also in Isa 54:7-8 and 57:17.

[79]This idea of God's wish to test his servants is taken from Isaiah 53. This being the case God allows his righteous to be tested by ungodly sinners.

himself; 3:6 like gold in the furnace he tried them, and like a sacrificial burnt offering he accepted them (ὡς ὁλοκάρπωμα θυσίας προσεδέξατο αὐτούς).[80] 3:7 In the time of their visitation they will shine forth, and will run like sparks through the stubble.[81] 3:8 They will govern nations and rule over peoples (κρινοῦσιν ἔθνη καὶ κρατήσουσιν λαῶν)[82], and the Lord will reign over them for ever. 3:9 Those who trust in him will understand truth (συνήσουσιν ἀλήθειαν)[83], and the faithful will abide with him in love, because grace and mercy are upon his elect, and he watches over his holy ones.

3:10 But the ungodly will be punished as their reasoning deserves (καθὰ ἐλογίσαντο)[84], who disregarded the righteous man (ὁι ἀμελήσαντες τοῦ δικαίου)[85] and rebelled against the Lord; 3:11 for whoever despises wisdom and instruction (παιδείαν) is miserable. Their hope is vain, their labors are unprofitable, and their works are useless. 3:12 Their wives are foolish, and their children evil; their offspring are accursed.

---

[80]In the Second and Fourth Books of Maccabees as well as in the prayer of Azariah similar sacrificial terminology is used. The righteous are ready to sacrifice their lives for the sake of God and his Torah. See sect. 3.

[81]The same image of the star-like brilliance of the righteous recurs in Dan 12:3 where Isaiah 53 is also used.

[82]This passage is parallel to LXX Isa 52:13-15, 53:12 where it is promised that the servant will receive his reward among nations and kings and the mighty ones.

[83]Isa 52:13 says of the Servant that he will receive understanding: συνήσει ὁ παῖς μου (see also LXX Isa 53:11). Even here good parallels can be found to Dan 11:33 and 12:10 both of which are also related to Isa 52:13.

[84]This key verb is also used in the LXX Isaiah 53. The point is that the ungodly have a wrong attitude to the righteous. While in Isaiah 53 the "we"-group confess their sin, in Wisdom the ungodly will realize their error only in the Day of Judgement.

[85]The ungodly disregard the righteous as the "we"-group the Servant in Isaiah 53.

3:13 For blessed is the barren woman who is undefiled[86], who has not entered into a sinful union; she will have fruit when God examines souls. 3:14 Blessed also is the eunuch whose hands have done no lawless deed (καὶ εὐνοῦχος ὁ μὴ ἐργασάμενος ἐν χειρὶ ἀνόμημα)[87], and who has not devised wicked things against the Lord; for special favor will be shown him for his faithfulness, and a place of great delight in the temple of the Lord (δοθήσεται γὰρ αὐτῷ τῆς πίστεως χάρις ἐκλεκτὴ καὶ κλῆρος ἐν ναῷ κυρίου θυμηρέστερος).[88] 3:15 For the fruit of good labors is renowned, and the root (ἡ ῥίζα)[89] of understanding does not fail. 3:16 But children of adulterers will not come to maturity, and the offspring of an unlawful union will perish. 3:17 Even if they live long they will be held of no account (εἰς οὐθὲν λογισθήσονται)[90], and finally their old age will be without honor. 3:18 If they die young, they will have no hope and no consolation in the day of decision. 3:19 For the end of an unrighteous generation is grievous. 4:1 Better than this is childlessness with virtue, for in the memory of virtue is

---

[86]Cf., Isa 54:1.

[87]This runs parallel with that in Isa 56:2: μακάριος ἀνὴρ ὁ ποιῶν ταῦτα καὶ ἄνθρωπος ὁ ἀντεχόμενος αὐτῶν καὶ φυλάσσων τὰ σάββατα μὴ βεβηλοῦν καὶ διατηρῶν τὰς χεῖρας αὐτοῦ μὴ ποιεῖν ἀδίκημα, "Blessed is the man that does these things, and the man that holds by them, and keeps the sabbaths from profaning them, and keeps his hands from doing unrighteousness."

[88]The end of this same verse in Wisd 3:14 continues the idea presented in Isa 56:5: δώσω αὐτοῖς ἐν τῷ οἴκῳ μου καὶ ἐν τῷ τείχει μου τόπον ὀνομαστὸν κρείττω υἱῶν καὶ θυγατέρων ὄνομα αἰώνιον δώσω αὐτοῖς καὶ οὐκ ἐκλείψει, "I will give them in my house and within my walls an honourable place, better than sons and daughters; I will give them an everlasting name, and it shall not fail."

[89]The same Greek word is also used in Isa 53:2.

[90]The intention is to compare the fate of sinners with the fate of the Servant. While the Servant will receive reward finally; the ungodly will not.

immortality, because it is known both by God and by men. 4:2 When it is present, men imitate it, and they long for it when it has gone; and throughout all time it marches crowned in triumph, victor in the contest for prizes that are undefiled. 4:3 But the prolific brood of the ungodly will be of no use, and none of their illegitimate seedlings will strike a deep root (οὐ δώσει ῥίζαν εἰς βάθος)[91] or take a firm hold. 4:4 For even if they put forth boughs for a while, standing insecurely they will be shaken by the wind, and by the violence of the winds they will be uprooted (ἐκριζωθήσεται).[92] 4:5 The branches will be broken off before they come to maturity, and their fruit will be useless, not ripe enough to eat, and good for nothing. 4:6 For children born of unlawful unions are witnesses of evil against their parents when God examines them.

4:7 But the righteous man, though he die early, will be at rest (δίκαιος δὲ ἐὰν φθάσῃ τελευτῆσαι ἐν ἀναπαύσει ἔσται).[93] 4:8 For old age is not honored for length of time, nor measured by number of years; 4:9 but understanding is gray hair for men, and a blameless life is ripe old age. 4:10 There was one who pleased God and was loved by him, and while living among sinners he was taken up (εὐάρεστος θεῷ γενόμενος ἠγαπήθη

---

[91]In Isa 53:2 we read ὡς ῥίζα ἐν γῇ διψώσῃ. Again the aim is to compare the coming fate of the sinners with that of the Servant in his distress.

[92]In Wisd 4:3-4 the ungodly will be uprooted. The imagery of the "root" goes back to Isa 53:2 where it is said that the Servant grew up before God as a root.

[93]This parallels well with the fate of the suffering righteous Servant in Isaiah 53. Isa 53:8 uses words which describe the death and the burial of the Servant. It is worth noting that even Isa 57:20 (οἱ δὲ ἄδικοι οὕτως κλυδωνισθήσονται καὶ ἀναπαύσασθαι οὐ δυνήσονται, "But the unrighteous shall be tossed as troubled waves, and shall not be able to rest") is parallel to Wisd 4:7.

καὶ ζῶν μεταξὺ ἁμαρτωλῶν μετετέθη)[94]. 4:11 He was caught up lest evil change his understanding (μὴ κακία ἀλλάξῃ σύνεσιν αὐτοῦ)[95] or guile deceive his soul. 4:12 For the fascination of wickedness obscures what is good, and roving desire perverts the innocent mind. 4:13 Being perfected in a short time[96], he fulfilled long years (ἐπλήρωσεν χρόνους μακρούς)[97]; 4:14 for his soul was pleasing to the Lord (ἀρεστὴ γὰρ ἦν κυρίῳ ἡ ψυχὴ αὐτοῦ)[98], therefore he took him quickly from the midst of wickedness. 4:15 Yet the peoples saw and did not understand, nor take such a thing to heart (οἱ δὲ λαοὶ ἰδόντες καὶ μὴ νοήσαντες μηδὲ θέντες ἐπὶ διανοίᾳ τὸ τοιοῦτο)[99], that God's grace and mercy are with his elect, and he watches over his holy ones.[100] 4:16 The righteous man who has died will

---

[94] A similar idea is presented in LXX Isa 53:8 which could have been interpreted so that the death of the servant was realized through the wicked actions of the ungodly. The text contains linguistic parallels to Isa 57:1: ἴδετε ὡς ὁ δίκαιος ἀπώλετο καὶ οὐδεὶς ἐκδέχεται τῇ καρδίᾳ καὶ ἄνδρες δίκαιοι αἴρονται καὶ οὐδεὶς κατανοεῖ ἀπὸ γὰρ προσώπου ἀδικίας ἦρται ὁ δίκαιος, "See how the just man has perished, and no one lays it to heart: and righteous men are taken away, and no one considers: for the righteous has been removed out of the way of injustice."

[95] Isa 52:13 indicates that the Servant will receive understanding through sufferings. According to Wisd 4:11 God prevents the righteous from losing understanding by snatching him away from the world.

[96] The Servant in Isaiah 53 will receive understanding through his sufferings. This is interpreted in Wisdom as that the righteous will be perfected.

[97] Compare LXX Isa 53:10 where the servant will see long-lived offspring.

[98] The idea is in some way parallel to Isaiah 53 where the Lord desires to oppress his Servant. In Wisd 4:14 God allows the righteous to die in order to remove him from the middle of wickedness. However, the LXX has modified the MT Isa 53:11 so that the Lord does not allow the Servant to be oppressed but takes away his agony.

[99] This inability of the wicked to understand the plans of God is equivalent well to the inability of "we" in Isaiah 53 to understand the fate of the servant.

[100] Wisd 4:15b is identical with Wisd 3:9b.

condemn the ungodly who are living, and youth that is quickly perfected will condemn the prolonged old age of the unrighteous man. 4:17 For they will see the end of the wise man, and will not understand what the Lord purposed for him (καὶ οὐ νοήσουσιν τί ἐβουλεύσατο περὶ αὐτοῦ)[101], and for what he kept him safe. 4:18 They will see, and will have contempt for him (ὄψονται καὶ ἐξουθενήσουσιν)[102], but the Lord will laugh them to scorn. 4:19 After this they will become dishonored corpses, and an outrage among the dead for ever; because he will dash them speechless to the ground[103], and shake them from the foundations; they will be left utterly dry and barren, and they will suffer anguish, and the memory of them will perish.[104] 4:20 They will come with dread when their sins are reckoned up (ἐλεύσονται ἐν συλλογισμῷ ἁμαρτημάτων αὐτῶν δειλοί)[105], and their lawless deeds will convict them to their face.

5:1 Then the righteous man will stand with great confidence in the presence of those who have afflicted him, and those who make light of his labors (τοὺς πόνους αὐτοῦ).[106] 5:2 When they

---

[101]Cf., the use of the verb βούλομαι in LXX Isa 53:10. The content corresponds to the "we"-group's inability to understand why the Lord allowed the righteous to be distressed.

[102]The theme in LXX Isa 53:3 is similar.

[103]According to Isa 52:15 many will be astonished and speechless when they see the fate of the Servant.

[104]The coming fate of the ungodly will be similar to the fate of the Servant when he was in distress.

[105]LXX Isa 52:15 is interpreted so that the wicked will come to judgment when they realize that the righteous will be rewarded. The whole episode in Wisd 4:20-5:2 describes this scene of judgment. The vocabulary is the same: πόνος (LXX Isa 53:11) and ἐκστήσονται (LXX Isa 52:14).

[106]At the last judgment the ungodly will realize that the afflicted righteous will receive his reward.

see him, they will be shaken with dreadful fear, and they will be amazed at his unexpected salvation (καὶ ἐκστήσονται ἐπὶ τῷ παραδόξῳ τῆς σωτηρίας).[107] 5:3 They will speak to one another in repentance (μετανοοῦντες)[108], and in anguish of spirit they will groan, and say, 5:4 "This is the man whom we once held in derision and made a byword of reproach – we fools! We thought that his life was madness (τὸν βίον αὐτοῦ ἐλογισάμεθα μανίαν)[109] and that his end was without honor. 5:5 Why has he been numbered among the sons of God? And why is his lot among the saints (καὶ ἐν ἁγίοις ὁ κλῆρος αὐτοῦ ἐστιν)[110] ? 5:6 So it was we who strayed from the way of truth (ἄρα ἐπλανήθημεν ἀπὸ ὁδοῦ ἀληθείας)[111], and the light of righteousness did not shine on us, and the sun did not rise upon us. 5:7 We took our fill of the paths of lawlessness and destruction, and we journeyed through trackless deserts, but the way of the Lord we have not known (τὴν δὲ ὁδὸν κυρίου οὐκ ἐπέγνωμεν). 5:8 What has our arrogance profited us? And what good has our boasted wealth brought us? 5:9 All those things have vanished like a shadow, and like a rumor that passes by; 5:10 like a ship that sails through the billowy water, and when it has passed no trace can be found, nor track of its keel in the

---

[107]The same verb ἐκστήσονται is used in Isa 52:14. In both cases the fate of the righteous causes amazement. Another Servant text which is echoed by Wisd 5:1-2 is Isa 49:7.

[108]The whole speech in Wisd 5:4-13 is presented in the "we"-form which is parallel to Isaiah 53. This speech indicates how the wicked will realize at the last judgment that they have mocked the righteous who will now receive his reward. But there is no vicarious atonement for the sinners.

[109]Cf., the verb form ἐλογισάμεθα in LXX Isa 53:4.

[110]Cf., the use of the verb κληρονομέω in LXX Isa 53:12.

[111]Cf., LXX Isa 53:6: πάντες ὡς πρόβατα ἐπλανήθημεν ἄνθρωπος τῇ ὁδῷ αὐτοῦ ἐπλανήθη. Wisd 5:7, too, contains a parallel to Isa 53:6.

100

waves; 5:11 or as, when a bird flies through the air, no evidence of its passage is found; the light air, lashed by the beat of its pinions and pierced by the force of its rushing flight, is traversed by the movement of its wings, and afterward no sign of its coming is found there; 5:12 or as, when an arrow is shot at a target, the air, thus divided, comes together at once, so that no one knows its pathway. 5:13 So we also, as soon as we were born, ceased to be, and we had no sign of virtue to show, but were consumed in our wickedness." 5:14 Because the hope of the ungodly man is like chaff carried by the wind, and like a light hoarfrost driven away by a storm; it is dispersed like smoke before the wind, and it passes like the remembrance of a guest who stays but a day.

5:15 But the righteous live for ever, and their reward is with the Lord (δίκαιοι δὲ εἰς τὸν αἰῶνα ζῶσιν καὶ ἐν κυρίῳ ὁ μισθὸς αὐτῶν)[112]; the Most High takes care of them. 5:16 Therefore they will receive a glorious crown and a beautiful diadem from the hand of the Lord, because with his right hand he will cover them, and with his arm he will shield them (ὅτι τῇ δεξιᾷ σκεπάσει αὐτοὺς καὶ τῷ βραχίονι ὑπερασπιεῖ αὐτῶν)[113]. 5:17 The Lord will take his zeal as his whole armor, and will arm all creation to repel his enemies; 5:18 he will put on righteousness as a breastplate, and wear impartial justice as a helmet (ἐνδύσεται θώρακα δικαιοσύνην καὶ περιθήσεται

---

[112]The belief that God will reward the servant and that the servant will live is expressed in LXX Isaiah 53:10-11 (notice that the subject has been changed in the Greek text in comparison with the MT). Another close parallel is LXX Isa 49:4-5. The following verse, Wisd 5:16, is also parallel to LXX Isa 53:10-12.

[113]Apparently the idea is that "the right arm of the Lord (βραχίων Κυρίου)" mentioned in LXX Isa 53:1 has been revealed to the righteous. Cf., also Isa 42:1 which speaks of how God's arm supports the Servant.

κόρυθα κρίσιν ἀνυπόκριτον)[114]; 5:19 he will take holiness as an invincible shield, 5:20 and sharpen stern wrath for a sword, and creation will join with him to fight against the madmen. 5:21 Shafts of lightning will fly with true aim, and will leap to the target as from a well-drawn bow of clouds, 5:22 and hailstones full of wrath will be hurled as from a catapult; the water of the sea will rage against them, and rivers will relentlessly overwhelm them; 5:23 a mighty wind will rise against them , and like a tempest it will winnow them away. Lawlessness will lay waste the whole earth, and evil-doing will overturn the thrones of rulers.

This text in the Wisdom of Solomon shows clearly how Isaiah 53 could have been interpreted in ancient Jewish texts without any reference to the vicarious atoning suffering of the servant. The translation of the Septuagint version of Isaiah 53 was an important stage in this process. With its aid the writer of Wisdom expresses his interpretation of Isaiah 53. The righteous one is oppressed, even killed, but in the last judgment he will receive his reward and his oppressors must confess like the "we"-group in Isaiah 53 that they totally misunderstood his fate. In the last judgment they must confess that God supports his servant even though he allowed him to suffer tribulation. This result is important because it means that the tendency to avoid vicarious atoning suffering in the exegesis of Isaiah 53 is not a phenomenon which came to pass as a reaction to the outcome of the Christological interpretation. This conclusion should be considered when in sect. 6 we examine the Targum interpretation of Isaiah 53.

---

[114]This expression is clearly modified according to Isa 59:17: καὶ ἐνεδύσατο δικαιοσύνην ὡς θώρακα καὶ περιέθετο περικεφαλαίαν σωτηρίου ἐπὶ τῆς κεφαλῆς, "And he put on righteousness as a breast-plate, and placed the helmet of salvation on his head."

Conclusions

Summing up, we may note that the LXX translation of Isaiah 53 reveals two important interpretive tendencies. First, Isaiah 53 contains such clear references to vicarious suffering that it is impossible to censor it in a translation which attempts in some measure to follow the content of the Hebrew text. Second, the LXX translation shows a tendency to deprecate the *vicarious* atoning suffering. This tendency emerges more clearly in the Wisdom of Solomon. In that text the suffering of the righteous is significant but his suffering is not regarded as being vicarious and atoning.

That the Greek version does not emphasize the vicarious suffering and death of the servant as markedly as the Hebrew text is symptomatic in ancient Jewish interpretations.[115] We have argued that this tendency is dependent on the covenant theology and its principle of retribution. This interpretive tendency is visible in Jewish texts already before the time of Jesus – which explains the later traditions in the targumic and rabbinical exegesis. This being the case the deceptive move of avoiding vicarious and atoning interpretation of Isaiah 53 cannot be primarily connected to the Christian interpretation of Isaiah 53. The main reason to avoid vicarious atonement theology in the interpretation of Isaiah 53 seems to be the covenant theology and its principle of retribution. On the other hand, the vicarious atoning dimension of the passage has been interpreted fully in the Jewish martyr theology when there was need to explain the persecution of the righteous and their martyrdom.

---

[115]Cf., Hengel, "The Effective History of Isaiah 53 in the Pre-Christian Period" 145-146.

5 A Messianic Interpretation of Isaiah 53 in Pre-Christian Time?

The Thesis of Joachim Jeremias

Dalman and Billerbeck postulated between the 1800's and 1900's that the messianic interpretation of Isaiah 53 was developed relatively late in Judaism. According to Dalman, the first references to the messianic interpretation of Isaiah 53 can be traced from the 3rd century AD.[1] Billerbeck presents a similar view.[2] At the beginning of 1900's Klausner analyzed the messianic logia of tannaim in the rabbinical literature on the basis of Dalman's study and concluded that early rabbinical Judaism contained no references to the suffering Messiah who must die for the sins of the people.[3]

Joachim Jeremias opened the scholarly discussion from a new viewpoint when he proposed that the eschatological hope concerning a

---

[1]The thesis was presented in G.H. Dalman, *Der leidende und sterbende Messias der Synagoge im ersten nachchristlichen Jahrtausend* (Berlin 1888) 91. This work was in a sense a corrective to Driver's and Neubauer's monumental project where the Jewish parallel material was collected. Dalman wanted to establish the precise date of the suffering Messiah in Judaism. In his later work *Jesaja 53: das Prophetenwort vom Sühnleiden des Gottesknechtes mit besonderer Berücksichtigung des jüdischen Literatur* (Leipzig: Hinrischs'sche Buchhandlung 1914) – originally published in 1890 – Dalman presented the Jewish text material with a somewhat different aim. He tried to demonstrate that the Jewish interpretation tradition provides many good parallels to the Christian concept of the suffering Messiah.

[2]P. Billerbeck, *Kommentar zum Neuen Testament aus Talmud und Midrasch von Hermann L. Strack und Paul Billerbeck Vol I-V* (Munich: Oskar Beck 1922-1928) I:481-485.

[3]See Kalusner's view in his later published work where his studies on Messiah were collected. J. Klausner, *The Messianic Idea in Israel: From Its Beginning to the Completion of the Mishnah* (New York: MacMillan Co. 1956) 405-407.

Messiah who must suffer and die for the sins of the people was known in Palestinian Judaism already before the time of Jesus.[4] The Christians incorporated such a messianic hope in their proclamation. As a result Jews began to censor their sources concerning the suffering Messiah. According to Jeremias the situation was different in Hellenistic Judaism where, for example, Wisdom 2-5 show that Isaiah 53 was interpreted collectively. In order to justify his thesis on the suffering and dying Messiah in pre-Christian Palestinian Judaism Jeremias quoted the following Jewish texts in his article presented in TWNT (1954):[5]

1. Sirach 48:10 refers to Elijah, the forerunner of the Messiah, and the formulations of this passage are taken from Isa 49:6. This shows, according to Jeremias, that the servant text in Isa 49:1-6 defined the messianic task, viz. the reestablishment of the twelve tribes. Nevertheless, Jeremias comments that this is only a free allusion.

2. Jeremias interprets the Testament of Benjamin 3:8 (according to the Armenian version which is free from Christian interpolations) so as to refer to the messianic individual from the tribe of Joseph (in later rabbinical literature this person is known as Messiah ben Ephraim): "In

---

[4]It is worth noting that Jeremias made a clear distinction between the Palestinian and the Hellenistic Judaism. Such a dichotomy is difficult to maintain in the light of recent research. See M. Hengel, *Judentum und Hellenismus: Studien zu ihrer Begegnung unter besonderer Berücksichtigung Palästinas bis zur Mitte des 2. Jh.s v. Chr.* (WUNT 10, Tübingen: Mohr 1988). Qumran finds have made it also clear that the Old Testament textual traditions which are close to the Hebrew Vorlage of the Septuagint translations were transmitted there.

[5]Jeremias first presented his ideas in his article "Erlöser und Erlösung im Spätjudentum und Urchristentum" published in 1929. Later he developed his ideas and published them in his article παῖς θεοῦ in *TWNT* (1954) 676-713 where he formulates (685): "Die messianische Deutung einzelner Gottesknechtabschnitte des Deuterojesaja ist mit hoher Wahrscheinlichkeit bis in vorchristliche Zeit züruckverfolgbar." The latest version of Jeremias' theories can be found in the study which he published together with W. Zimmerli in 1965: W. Zimmerli & J. Jeremias, *The Servant of God* (SBT 20, London: SCM Press 1965). Jeremias there also considered the severe criticism presented by M. Rese, "Überprüfung einiger Thesen von Joachim Jeremias zum Thema des Gottesknechtes im Judetum," *ZTK* 60 (1963) 21-41.

you [Joseph] will be fulfilled the heavenly prophecy which says that the spotless one will be defiled by lawless men and the sinless one will die for the sake of impious men." According to Jeremias this text must refer to Isaiah 53.[6]

3. 1 Enoch 37-71 contains texts where the Son of Man – who is a messianic figure – is called the servant of the Lord. Jeremias refers to several passages in 1 Enoch 37-71 which contain allusions to, and quotations from, the servant passages of Isaiah 40-55, in particular Isa 42:1-6; 49:1-2, 5-6 and 52:13-15; 53:11. Jeremias regards these allusions as crucial for Jesus' mission and self-understanding.

4. Jeremias refers to Hegermann's study[7] and argues that (a) the Syriac translation of the Hebrew Bible, the Peshitta, as well as the ancient Greek translations (b) Aquila, and (c) Theodotios, and (d) the Aramaic translation in Targum Jonathan contain a messianic interpretation of Isaiah 53. These translations are dependent on interpretive traditions which can be traced back to pre-Christian times.

5. Interestingly, Jeremias also uses a single New Testament text to argue for the messianic understanding of Isaiah 53 in pre-Christian Palestinian Judaism. This passage is Lk 23:35 which contains an ancient Jewish messianic title "the chosen one (ὁ ἐκλεκτός)" the origin of which is in the servant texts in the Book of Isaiah (see Isa 42:1: *bāḥîr*). Those who crucified Jesus used this title when they scorned him. According to Jeremias, the title was rarely used among Christians; it appears only in John 1:34.

6. Finally, Jeremias refers to the rabbinical evidence and singles out the logion of the Galilean rabbi Jose (who lived before 135 AD, i.e., clearly before the compilation of the Mishnah about 200 AD) which has

---

[6]Jeremias writes (p. 685): "Mit der 'Weissagung des Himmels' muss Js 53 gemeint sein."

[7]See H. Hegermann, *Jesaja 53 in Hexapla, Targum und Peschitta* (Gütersloh: Mohn 1954). Hegermann attempted to show that behind the Targum-Jonathan version of Isaiah 53 there was an older text which spoke of the suffering Messiah.

been transmitted in Sifra Leviticus: *Wayyiqra Dibura Dehoba Parasha* 12.[8] This logion has two different versions, one presented in the rabbinical tradition which led to the Vienna edition (in 1545) and a second extant in Raymundus Martini's *Pugio Fidei* (1278, Folio 674-675; pages 866-867 in Carpzov's edition). According to the logion preserved in *Pugio Fidei* the Messiah would suffer on behalf of the sins of the peoples and expiate them by annulling the destruction caused by Adam:[9]

> R. Yosé the Galilean said, Come forth and learn the righteousness of the King Messiah and the reward of the just from the first man who received but one commandment, a prohibition, and transgressed it: consider how many deaths were inflicted upon himself, upon his own generations, and upon those that followed them, till the end of all generations. Which attribute is the greater, the attribute of goodness, or the attribute of vengeance? He answered, The attribute of goodness is the greater, and the attribute of vengeance is the less; how much more, then, will the King Messiah, who endures affliction and pains for the transgressors (as it is written, "He was wounded") justify all generations and this is what is meant when it is said, "And the Lord made the iniquity of us all meet upon him."

---

[8]Sifra Leviticus is an early Halakhic commentary on the instructions of the Torah. Sifra comments on every verse in Leviticus. Originally it was divided into nine tractates (*dibburim*), which in turn were divided into texts (*parashiyot*) and every parasha into two or three chapters (*peraqim*). In the Babylonian tradition Sifra was divided into 14 parts. See G. Stemberger, *Introduction to the Talmud and Midrash* (Minneapolis: Fortress 1996) 283-289. The Hebrew text can be found in L. Finkelstein, *Sifra on Leviticus: According to Vatican Manuscript Assemani 61 with Variants from the Other Manuscripts, Genizah Fragments, Early Editions and Quotations by Medieval Authorities and with References to Parallel Passages and Commentaries. Volume 2* (New York: The Jewish Theological Seminary of America 1983) 206-207. The English translation can be found in J. Neusner, *Sifra: An Analytical Translation Volume One* (BJS 138, Atlanta: Scholars Press 1988) 327; *idem, The Components of the Rabbinic Documents From the Whole to the Parts I: Sifra* (South Florida Academic Commentary Series 75; Atlanta, Ga.: Scholars Press 1997) Part 1: 249.

[9]The English translation is from A. Neubauer & S. Driver, *The "Suffering Servant" of Isaiah According to the Jewish Interpreters Translated by S.R. Driver and A. Neubauer* (Eugene: Wipf and Stock 1999) 10-11.

The Vienna edition mentions only the sufferings of the righteous, which are not connected with the fall caused by Adam:[10]

> R. Yosé says, "If you want to know how great a reward is coming to the righteous in the coming time, go and take heed of the case of the original Adam, who was commanded only concerning a single commandment, involving merely refraining from a given action, and he violated that commandment. Now see how many deaths were exacted for him and his generations and for all generations to the end of all generations. Now which divine trait is the more abundant, the trait of bestowing benefit or the trait of exacting punishment? You must say that it is the trait of bestowing benefit, while the trait of exacting punishment is the lesser of the two. Now see how many deaths were exacted for him and his generations and for all generations to the end of all generations. The trait of bestowing benefit is greater: one who merely refrains from consuming sacrificial meat that has been subjected to an improper intention on the part of the officiating priest and from meat that is left over [beyond the time allotted to eat it], who afflicts himself on the Day of Atonement, how much the more so that such a one, and his generations, and all generations to the end of all generations, will receive merit!"

Jeremias discusses another rabbinical text in his TWNT article, viz. the passage in bSanh 98b according to which the Messiah is called the "sick one" or the "leprous" according to Isa 53:4. Finally, reference is made to the interpretation of Isa 53:5 as referring to the Messiah in the rabbinical writings, the earliest evidence of which is Ruth Rabbah. Moreover, according to Jeremias, Justin Martyr's partner in his *Dialogue with Tryphon* is Rabbi Tarfon, known in the rabbinical tradition as a close friend of Rabbi Jose. When Justin Martyr recounts Tryphon's belief that the Messiah must suffer even according to the Jewish view (*Dial* 36.1; 39.7; 49.2; 68.9; 76.6-77.1; 89.1-2; 90.1), this stance was for Jeremias an argument that Raymundus Martin transmitted a reliable Jewish tradition.

---

[10]The English translation is from Neusner, *Sifra: An Analytical Translation Volume One* 327; idem, *The Components of the Rabbinic Documents: Sifra* Part 1: 249.

The problems of Jeremias' atomistic exegesis were assigned pride of place by Rese.[11] His criticism can be summarized as follows: *First*, Jeremias' exegesis is atomistic. When ancient Jewish texts refer to a servant text in Isaiah 40-55, for example Isa 42:1-4 or 49:1-6, the idea of vicarious atoning suffering and the death of the servant (from Isaiah 53) cannot automatically be incorporated. A good example is 1 Enoch 37-71 where references can be found to the servant texts in the Book of Isaiah (42:1-6; 49:1-6 and 52:13-15). However, the passages comprising 1 Enoch 37-71 do not deal with the vicarious atoning suffering and death of the Son of Man. *Second*, Jeremias' claim that the Peshitta and early Jewish translations (Aquila and Theodotion) have interpreted Isaiah 53 messianically are not clearly formulated in the translations. *Third*, even though Targum Jonathan contains a messianic interpretation of Isaiah 53 the problem is how to date and interpret Targums.

Rese's criticism annulled much of the fundamental basis for Jeremias' thesis, and it did not win acceptance among scholars.[12] In 1965 Jeremias modified his own view. He no longer considered T.Benjamin 3:8 as evidence for his thesis because the text is text-critically problematic.[13] Another significant change is that Jeremias now regarded the tradition of Raymundus Martin as secondary.[14] We shall return to this

---

[11]Rese "Überprüfung einiger Thesen" 21-41.

[12]See, for example, the survey in H. Haag, *Der Gottesknecht bei Deuterojesaja* (EfF 233, Darmstadt: Wissenschaftliche Buchgesellschaft 1985) 36-43. The starting-point in M. Hengel's article ("Zur Wirkungsgeschichte von Jes 53 in vorchristlicher Zeit," in: B. Janowski & P. Stuhlmacher, *Der leidende Gottesknecht. Jesaja 53 und seine Wirkungsgeschichte mit einer Bibliographie zu Jes 53* [FAT 14, Tübingen: Mohr 1996] 49-91, esp. 49-54) is that Jeremias' thesis was not regarded as convincing among scholars. I refer to M. Hengel's updated article "The Effective History of Isaiah 53 in the Pre-Christian Period," in: B. Janowski & P. Stuhlmacher (eds), *The Suffering Servant: Isaiah 53 in Jewish and Christian Sources* (Grand Rapids: Eerdmans 2004) 75-146, esp. 76-82.

[13]Jeremias, *Servant of God* 7.

[14]Jeremias, *Servant of God* 7, 73-74.

Pugio Fidei reading later in section 9. In 1965 Jeremias also rejected his earlier view that Tryphon could be identified with Rabbi Tarfon. In particular, he refers to Hyldahl's article.[15] Now Jeremias also emphasizes that Justin comments *expressis verbis* that Tryphon refutes the theory that the Messiah will suffer on the cross as cursed by God (*Dial.* 32.1; 89.2; 90.1).[16]

Hengel has revised yet again Jeremias' thesis. Even though he regards many of Jeremias' viewpoints as problematic he, nevertheless, observes that Jeremias "has encountered fierce and partly unobjective criticism."[17] Hengel discusses the following Jewish texts which antedate the New Testament: Zechariah 12-13; the Book of Daniel; 1 Enoch 37-71; Qumran's Isaiah Scrolls; the translation of the Septuagint, Qumran text 4Q540/41 (which is a part of the Aramaic Testament of Levi); the Septuagint translation of Isaiah 53 together with Wisdom 2-5; T.Benjamin 3:8; Qumran text 4Q491.

We have already discussed Zechariah 12-13 and determined that it is hardly an interpretation of the servant texts in the Book of Isaiah. Rather it reflects the same traditio-historical background as Isaiah 53, i.e. it is related to old traditions concerning Josiah, lamentations which were composed after his death at Megiddo.[18] We have also examined Daniel 11-12 and observed that it refers to martyrs of the Maccabean period.[19] Concerning the translation of the Septuagint we have seen that there is no evidence that the translator associated the passage with the coming

---

[15]N. Hyldahl, "Tryphon und Tarphon," *StTh* 10 (1956) 77-88. See further the basic study on Tarphon: J. Gereboff, *Rabbi Tarfon: The Tradition, the Man, and Early Rabbinic Judaism* (Brown Judaic studies 7, Missoula: Scholars Press 1979).

[16]See further A.J.B. Higgins, "Jewish Messianic Belief in Justin Martyr's Dialogue with Trypho," *NT* 9 (1967) 298-305 which is reprinted in L.Landman, *Messianism in the Talmudic Era* (New York: KTAV Publishing House 1979) 182-189.

[17]Hengel, "The Effective History of Isaiah 53," 79.

[18]See sect. 2.

[19]See sect. 3.

eschatological savior or messiah.[20] Hengel offers an hypothesis that the translator of Isaiah 53 may have had Onias III in mind.[21] In what follows we shall scrutinize the texts presented by Jeremias and Hengel and discuss the extent of their support for the belief that pre-Christian Judaism encompassed an expectation that the Messiah must suffer (vicariously) and die in order to atone for the sins of the people (peoples).

The Use of the Servant Texts in 1 Enoch 37-71

Jeremias has demonstrated convincingly that the servant passages of Isaiah were used in 1 Enoch 37-71 when the Son of Man was depicted. These parallels are commonly accepted and, in particular, Isa 49:1-6 is a key text which is often cited.[22] In what follows we shall summarize scholarly discussion and quote several texts in 1 Enoch 37-71 where terminological parallels have been underlined and the parallels to Isaianic servant texts are mentioned (partly in footnotes).[23]

1 Enoch 39:6-7 contains for the first time an important title "the Elect One" which here is the head of the elect and the righteous:

> 6 And in those days my eyes saw *the Elect One* of righteousness and of faith, and righteousness shall prevail in his days,

---

[20]See sect. 4.

[21]Hengel, "The Effective History of Isaiah 53," 136: "If we wish to draw a connection between the Servant in the Septuagint version of Isaiah 53 and a concrete historical figure, we *could* – very hypothetically – think of Onias III, the last legitimate Zadokite high priest."

[22]Jeremias, *The Servant of God* 60-61. A most important study where the Old Testament background for 1 Enoch 37-71 and Isaiah 40-55, in particular, was treated is J. Theisohn, *Der auserwählte Richter: Untersuchungen zum traditionsgeschichtlichen Ort der Menschensohngestalt der Bilderreden des äthiopischen Henoch* (SUNT 12, Göttingen: Vandenhock & Ruprecht 1975) esp. 114-126; see also M. Black, *The Book of Enoch or 1 Enoch: A New English Edition* (SVTP 7, Leiden: Brill 1985); Hengel, "The Effective History of Isaiah 53," 99-101.

[23]The translations are from OTP 1.

and the righteous and elect ones shall be without number before him forever and ever.

7 And I saw *a dwelling place underneath the wings of the Lord of the Spirits*; and all the righteous and the elect before him shall be as intense as the light of fire.
Their mouth shall be full of blessing;
and their lips praise the name of the Lord of the Spirits,
and righteousness before him will have no end;
and uprightness before him will not cease.

The "Elect One" appears several times in the Book of Enoch but only in the section on Parables (40:5; 45:3, 4 ["my Elect One"]; 49:2, 4; 51:3, 5; 52:6, 9; 53:6; 55:4 ["my Elect One"]; 61:5, 8, 10; 62:1) in order to denote the Son of Man. It is apparently taken from the servant passages in Isaiah 40-55. The servant is chosen by Yhwh (the verb בחר) in Isa 41:8-9; 43:10; 44:1-2; 49:7. Isa 42:1 uses the title "my elect one" for the servant which indicates that the election of the servant is expressed not only with the help of the verb but also of the title "Elect One". The corresponding title is used in the New Testament for Jesus (Lk 23:35; see also Lk 9:35; John 1:34). The key words "righteousness" or "righteous" which are often associated with the servant are also worthy of note. For example, Isa 53:11 calls the servant "my righteous servant."

Theisohn refers to Billerbeck's article and mentions parallels between 1 Enoch 39:6 and Isa 50:6-10; 53:9, 11 but I am at a loss to see any clear connection here.[24] There is a more obvious parallel between 1 Enoch 39:7 and Isa 49:2, which recurs in 1 Enoch 48 and 62, as we shall see. The expression "as intense as the light of fire" is reminiscent of Dan 12:3 and, as we have seen in section 3, Daniel 11-12 contains an early interpretation of Isaiah 53.

---

[24]P. Billerbeck, "Hat die alte Synagoge einen präexistenten Messias gekannt?" *Nathanael* 19 (1903) 97-125; *Nathanael* 21 (1905) 89-150. See Theisohn, *Der auserwählte Richter* 115. All parallels listed by Theisohn (without 1 Enoch 46:4 and Isa 52:15) are presented in Hengel, "The Effective History of Isaiah 53," 99 n. 77.

112

1 Enoch 46:4-6 speaks about the Son of Man who will come to judge the world. The passage includes possible, vague, allusions to Isa 50:11 where the servant confronts his opponents and condemns them to their fate, "lie down in torment" and to Isa 52:15 where the servant is associated with the kings and nations:

> 4 This Son of Man whom you have seen is the One who would remove the *kings* and the *mighty ones* from their comfortable seats and the *strong ones* from their thrones. He shall loosen the reins of the strong and crush the teeth of the sinners.
>
> 5 He shall depose the *kings* from their thrones and kingdoms. For they do not extol and glorify him, and neither do they obey him, the source of their kingship.
>
> 6 The faces of the strong will be slapped and be filled with shame and gloom. Their dwelling places and their beds will be worms. They shall have no hope to rise from their beds, for they do not extol the name of the Lord of the Spirits.

More prominent parallels to the Deutero-Isaianic servant texts can be found in 1 Enoch 48:2-6. The text contains many parallels to Isaiah 49:1-6 and this text was obviously used in the description of the Son of Man:[25]

> 2. At that hour, that Son of Man *was given a name*, in the presence of the Lord of Spirits, the Head of Days[26]
>
> 3. even before the creation of the sun and the moon, before the creation of the stars, *he was given a name* in the presence of the Lord of the Spirits.[27]
>
> 4. He will become a staff for the righteous ones in order that they may lean on him and not fall. He is *the light of the gentiles* and he will become the hope of those who are sick in their hearts.[28]

---

[25]See, in particular, Theisohn, *Der auserwählte Richter* 119-121.

[26]Isa 49:1: "Yhwh *called* me when I was in the womb ..."

[27]Isa 49:1: "... before my birth he had *pronounced my name*."

[28]Isa 49:6: "He said: It is not enough for you to be my servant, to restore the tribes of Jacob and bring back the survivors of Israel; I shall make you *a light to the nations* so that my salvation may reach the remotest parts of earth." See also Isa 42:6.

5. All those who dwell upon the earth *shall fall* and worship before him; they shall glorify, bless, and sing the name of the Lord of the Spirits.[29]

6. For this purpose he became the *Chosen One*; he *was concealed* in the presence of (the Lord of the Spirits) prior to the creation of the world, and for eternity.[30]

The calling of the servant is articulated many times in Isaiah 40-55: 43:1 (Israel); 45:3 (Cyrus); 49:1 (the servant Israel) and it is used when a particular task is set. In Isa 49:1-6 this task is to be "the light of the nations" which is also the title given to the Son of Man in 1 Enoch 48:4. The idea that the Son of Man was concealed in the presence of the Lord of the Spirits is interesting because this concept is implied in Daniel 7 and recurs later in the messianic features of rabbinical traditions.[31] According to 1 Enoch 48:5 the Son of Man plays the eschatological and universal role of the Isaianic servant. Nowhere does the text say that the Son of Man must suffer.

The last passage in the Parables to contain clear references and allusions to the Isaianic servant traditions is 1 Enoch 62:1-9. Again the principal servant passage is Isa 49:1-12. Theisohn notes two significant parallels in the content of the texts. *First*, the content of 1 Enoch 62:6 is parallel to Isa 49:7. The kings and the exalted ones are humbled and will be compelled to confess that the Lord is the true Ruler of the world. *Second*, even though no terminological connections exist between 1 Enoch 62:8 and Isa 49:12, both verses deal with how the Israelites will be gathered to the Holy Land.[32] The Enochic text begins with an

---

[29]Isa 49:7: "Kings will stand up when they see, princes will see and *bow low*, because of Yhwh who is faithful, the Holy One of Israel." See further 1 Enoch 46:4; 48:10; 55:4; 62:1,3,9.

[30]Isa 49:1-2: He made my mouth like a sharp sword, *he hid me* in the shadow of his hand. He made me into a sharpened arrow and *concealed me* in his hand. Isa 49:7: "...the Holy One of Israel who *has chosen you*."

[31]See further sects. 9 and 10. The idea is developed, in particular, in Pesiqta Rabbati.

[32]Theisohn, *Der auserwählte Richter* 121-123.

exhortation to kings and the mighty to acknowledge the Elect One. It is easy to recognize that in Isaiah 40-55 the fate of the servant is often related to the kings and the mighty:

> 1. Thus the Lord *commanded the kings, the governors, the high officials, and the landlords and said:* "*Open your eyes,* and lift up your eyebrows – if you are able to *recognize the Elect One.*"
> 2. The Lord of Spirits has sat down on the throne of his glory, and *the spirit of righteousness has been poured upon him*[33]. The word of his mouth will do the sinners in; and all the oppressors shall be eliminated from before his face.
> 3. On the day of judgment, all the *kings,* the *governors,* the *high officials,* and the *landlords shall see* and *recognize* him – how he sits on the throne of his glory, and righteousness is judged before him, and that no nonsensical talk shall be uttered in his presence.
> 4. Then pain shall come upon them as on a woman in travail with birth pangs – when she is giving birth (the child) enters the mouth of the womb and she suffers from childbearing.
> 5. *One half portion of them shall glance at the other half; they shall be terrified and dejected*[34]; and pain shall seize them when they see that Son of Man sitting on the throne of his glory.
> 6. (These) *kings, governors,* and all the *landlords* shall (try to) bless, glorify, extol him who rules over everything, him who has been *concealed.*[35]

---

[33]Isa 42:1: "*My chosen* (= the Elect One) ... *I have laid my spirit upon him.*" It is also worth noting that the servant in Isa 42:1-4 executes judgement among nations – a circumstance which is mentioned in 1 Enoch 41:9; 45:3; 49:4; 55:4; 61:9; 62:2-3; 69:27.

[34]Cf., Isa 52:14-15.

[35]Isa 49:7: "*Thus says Yhwh,* the redeemer, the Holy One of Israel, to the one who is despised, detested by the nation, to the slave of despots: *Kings* will stand up when they *see, princes* will *see* and bow low because of Yhwh who is faithful, the Holy One of Israel who has chosen you." Cf., also Isa 52:13. It is worth noting that Jeremias (*The Servant of God* 61) rightly comments that in Wisd 2-5 the scene of Isa 52:13-53:12 is the final judgment as in 1 Enoch 62. This connection to Wisdom is also cited in Hengel, "The Effective History of Isaiah 53," 100.

7. For the Son of Man *was concealed* from the beginning, and the Most High One preserved him in the presence of his power; then he revealed him to the holy and the elect ones.[36]

8. The congregation of the holy ones shall be planted, and all the elect ones shall stand before him.

9. On that day, *all the kings, the governors, the high officials, and those who rule the earth shall fall down before him on their faces*[37], and worship and raise their hopes in that Son of Man; they shall beg and plead for mercy at his feet.

Nickelsburg mentioned many correspondences between Isaiah 53 and 1 Enoch 62-63 but none indicate that the Son of Man will be a suffering and dying figure.[38] Rather, we may say that the adversaries of the Son of Man are depicted as the opponents of the righteous one in Wisdom 2-5.[39] In conclusion we can adduce sufficient evidence to argue that the servant passages, Isa 49:1-12 in particular, were in the Parables to refer to the Son of Man. Isaiah 49 befits the description of the Son of Man because it incorporates the idea of the concealment of the servant (Isa 49:2). A similar concept is prominent in the Parables' depiction of the Son of Man. The Son of Man is hidden from the beginning of the world until the end of time.[40] Furthermore, the universal view in Isa 49:1-13, i.e., the confrontation between the servant and the kings of the world accords with the portrayal of the Son of Man both in the Parables and Daniel 7. Thus the individual interpretation of the servant figure of Isaiah 49:1-12 is attested in 1 Enoch 37-71 notwithstanding that the word "Israel" is the

---

[36]Isa 49:2. ... he *hid* me in the shadow of his hand. He made me into a sharpened arrow and *concealed* me in his quiver.

[37]Cf., Isa 49:7; 52:13-15.

[38]G.W.E. Nickelsburg, *Resurrection, Immortality, and Eternal Life in Intertestamental Judaism and Early Christianity* (Harvard Theological Studies 56, Cambridge: Harvard University Press 2006) 93-97.

[39]So Hengel, "The Effective History of Isaiah 53," 100.

[40]So E. Sjöberg, *Der Menschensohn im äthiopischen Henochbuch* (SMHVL 41, Lund: Gleerup 1946) 102-115; Theisohn, *Der auserwählte Richter* 123-124.

reading in almost every manuscript of Isa 49:3 (including ancient translations). The text has been read so that there is a single figure, i.e. the righteous servant who has a task vis-à-vis the Israelites and all peoples.

On the other hand, we have seen that there is no evidence that the Son of Man could have been presented as the suffering Servant who must die in order to atone for the sins of the people(s) in 1 Enoch 37-71. This does not mean that certain motifs and themes of Isaiah 53 could have been included in the presentation of the Son of Man in 1 Enoch 37-71. 1 Enoch 47:1, 4 refers to the blood of martyrs and may be an allusion to Isaiah 53, but the reference is made to many, not to the martyr death of the Son of Man.[41] Individual references and allusions to Isaiah 53, mainly to Isa 52:13-15, do not imply that the Son of Man will suffer and die for the sins of the people.[42] Rather the text refers to the sufferings of the righteous in this world – something which is parallel to Wisdom 2-5.[43] This being the case 1 Enoch 37-71 may be used to support the view that

---

[41]Black (*The Book of Enoch* 209) writes concerning the expression "the blood of the righteous": "Isa 53.11 lies as certainly behind this passage as it does Wis 2.12-18." See also Hengel, "The Effective History of Isaiah 53," 100.

[42]So, for example, Theisohn, *Der auserwählte Richter* 33-34. Sjöberg (*Menschensohn* 128-129 and note 37) writes that Jeremias presented a lecture in Uppsala in 1938, where he built up on 1 Enoch 47:1, 4 and argued that the Parables contain an idea of a suffering and dying servant according to the model of Isaiah 53. Sjöberg writes concerning 1 Enoch 47:1-4 (p. 129): "Jeremias legt Gewicht auf den Singular und meint, dass 'der Gerechte' hier Bezeichnung des Menschensohnes ist, dessen Blut also ausgegossen worden ist." Sjöberg notes further that this idea has not been presented in Jeremias' article from 1929; it does neither appear in the TWNT article from 1954, nor in the 1965 version.

[43]Hengel writes ("The Effective History of Isaiah 53," 101): "The Son of Man of the Similitudes shares traits of the Servant, but only by functioning as the righteous judge of the ungodly, never by discharging human guilt through vicarious suffering." Hengel adds that this is one indication why 1 Enoch 37-71 cannot be a Christian text.

Isaiah 53 was used in ancient Jewish texts to describe the sufferings of the righteous or the death of martyrs.[44]

This survey indicates that we have no evidence that the Son of Man was regarded as a suffering and dying savior figure in 1 Enoch 37-71. This implies that the Parables do not provide any support for Jeremias' thesis. Hengel agrees on this point.

The Servant Passages in the Qumran Writings

Jeremias wrote in 1965 that "the Qumran texts have been given due attention. The result is, however, negative; they show no trace of a collective application of the servant of Deutero-Isaiah to the Essene community, nor of an individual application to the teacher of Righteousness."[45] Ever since the discovery of the Qumran scrolls some scholars have attempted to find evidence that these writings contain the concept of a suffering and dying servant, the Messiah.[46] One of the latest misinterpretations was that of 4Q285 which was regarded as referring to the death of the Messiah.[47] Even this attempt was convincingly refuted by scholars who commented that in the text reference is made to the way in which the Messiah will destroy his enemies. After all, 4Q285

---

[44]Cf., Hengel "The Effective History of Isaiah 53," 100 where he notes that 1 Enoch 47:1, 4 may be an allusion to Isaiah 53 and "be interpreted collectively" as referring to martyrs.

[45]The quotation is from Jeremias, *The Servant of God* 7. See also pp. 57 n. 225a and 57 n. 240.

[46]One early attempt identified the suffering servant figure with the Teacher of Righteousness, but as Hengel ("The Effective History of Isaiah 53," 118) notes, J. Carmignac ("Les Citations de l'Ancien Testament et spécialement des Poèmes du Serviteur dans les Hymnes de Qumran," *RevQ* 2 [1960] 357-394) and G. Jeremias (*Der Lehrer der Gerechtigkeit* [WUNT 2, Göttingen: Vandenhoeck & Ruprecht 1963] 299-307) convincingly refuted this theory.

[47]R. Eisenman & M. Wise, *The Dead Sea Scrolls Uncovered* (Shaftesbury: Element 1992) 24-29 and M.G. Abegg, "Messianic Hope and 4Q285: A Reassessment," *JBL* 113 (1994) 81-91.

interprets Isaiah 10-11 and is parallel to 4Q161 where the Messiah is presented as victorious over his enemies.[48] In what follows we shall deal with significant possible allusions to the servant passages.[49]

A plausible collective interpretation of the servant figure can be found in 1QpHab 5:4: "... in the hand of his chosen ones (בחירו) God will place the judgment (משפט) over all the peoples (גוים)." This text shares three important terms with Isa 42:1: בחיר, משפט and גוים. The Qumran passage is also parallel in terms of content: the elected one(s) will bring משפט to גוים. As far as the interpretation of IQpHab 5:4 is concerned, the *crux interpretum* is the word בחירו. Does this term have an individual ("his elect") or a plural ("his elected ones") referent? For example, Gaster and Vermes translate the passage "his elect."[50] However, Elliger has proposed that this word is defective and we must read בְּחִירָו.[51] If this is true, as I believe, then 1QpHab 5:4 shows that Isa 42:1-4(9) was interpreted collectively, referring to the ideal Israel, i.e., to the Qumran community itself (cf., the collective interpretation in the LXX). Unfortunately no *pesher* interpretation of the Deutero-Isaian servant texts has been found at Qumran. Only two fragments deal with Deutero-Isaian passages: 4QpIsa[d] (4Q164) contains a *pesher* on Isa 54:11-12 and

---

[48]See G. Vermes, "The Oxford Forum for Qumran Research: Seminar on the Rule of the War from Cave 4 (4Q285)," *JJS* 43 (1992) 85-90; J.J. Collins, *The Scepter and the Star : The Messiahs of the Dead Sea Scrolls and other Ancient Literature* (New York: Doubleday 1995) 123-126.

[49]References to the texts and translations are mainly from F. García Martínez & E.J.C. Tigchelaar, *The Dead Sea Scrolls: Study Edition 1-2* (Leiden: Brill, Grand Rapids: Eerdmans 1997-1998) with additional references in footnotes.

[50]T.H. Gaster, *The Dead Sea Scriptures in English Translation with Introduction and Notes* (Garden City: Doubleday 1957) 251; G. Vermes, *The Dead Sea Scrolls in English* (Revised and Extended Fourth Edition; London: Penguin Books 1995) 342.

[51]K. Elliger, *Studien zum Habakuk-Kommentar vom Toten Meer* (BHT 15, Tübingen: Mohr 1953) 182. The passage was thus translated in García Martínez, F. & Tigchelaar, E.J.C. *The Dead Sea Scrolls: Study Edition 1-2* (Leiden: Brill, Grand Rapids: Eerdmans 2000) 15.

4QpIsa[e] (4Q165) a pesher on Isa 40:11-12.[52] However, it is possible that the *pesher* of 4QpIsa[d] is somehow connected with a *pesher* of Isa 49:1-6 – if such a text ever existed. 4QpIsa[d] interprets the passage "and all your gates as stones of beryl" as follows: "The interpretation of it concerns the heads of the tribes of Israel at the e[nd of days]."[53] It is possible, but by no means certain, that Isa 49:5-6 is connected with this *pesher* (cf., the word-bridge "tribes of Israel"), i.e., the verses refer to the coming restoration of Israel – a reference which would run parallel to 1QpHab 5:3-5. Thus Isa 49:1-6 may have been interpreted along the lines of Isa 42:1-4, i.e., as referring to the ideal Israel (cf., 1QIsa[a] where the word "Israel" is preserved in 49:3). However, this proposal is merely a plausible hypothesis which cannot be verified.

Some scholars have attempted to discern messianic interpretations of the servant texts of Isaiah 40-55 on the basis of 1QIsa[a]. One such suggestion is that Isa 51:4-8 (which is a close parallel to Isa 50:4-9 and can be regarded as a servant text) would have been interpreted messianically.[54] The view is firmly based on the argument that the change of person in Isa 51:5 from 1.sing (MT) to 3.sing (1QIsa[a]) indicates that the text refers to the Messiah. Such an argument has not been accepted without reservations. For example, van der Kooij considers that the Qumran reading pertains to Cyrus.[55] However, all putative references to

---

[52]Concerning the *pesher* interpretations of Isaiah see J.M. Allegro (ed.), *Qumran Cave 4, I (4Q 158 - 4Q 186)* (DJD 5; Oxford: Clarendon 1968); M.P. Horgan, *Pesharim: Qumran Interpretations of Biblical Books* (CBQMS 8, Washington: The Catholic Biblical Association of America 1979).

[53]Horgan, *Pesharim* 126.

[54]W.H. Brownlee, "The Servant of the Lord in the Qumran Scrolls," *BASOR* 132 (1953) 8-15, esp. 10-12; J.V. Chamberlain, "The Functions of God as Messianic Titles in the Complete Qumran Isaiah Scroll," *VT* 5 (1955) 366–72, esp. 366-369.

[55]See this discussion in A. van der Kooij, *Die alten Textzeugen des Jesajabuches: Ein Beitrag zur Textgeschichte des Alten Testaments* (OBO 35, Freiburg: Universitätsverlag; Göttingen: Vandenhoeck & Ruprecht 1981) 90-92.

textual differences in 1QIsaᵃ are so confused that we cannot reach any firm opinion of how the servant passages were interpreted in 1QIsaᵃ.[56]

Hengel has brought to the fore the reading of Isa 52:14 in the Isaiah Scroll at Qumran. He comments that the MT reading in Isa 52:14 *mšḥt*, which can be vocalized as *mišḥat* or *mašḥēt*, is a *hapax legomenon*. In the Qumran Isaiah Scroll it has an additional *yod*, which gives the possible reading *māšaḥtî*, "I have anointed". Thus the text is interpreted by Hengel as follows:[57]

כאשר שממו עליכה רבים
כן משחתי מאיש מראהו ותוארו מבני האדם
Just as many were astonished at you,
so have I anointed his appearance beyond that of any (other) man, and his form beyond that of the sons of humanity.

Hengel remarks that a grammatical parallel is Ps 45:8 which also contains the word כֵּן, the verb מָשַׁח and the comparative adjective with מִן. It is more difficult to arrive at an adequate interpretation of Isa 52:14. According to Hengel, the reference may also pertain to an eschatological priest or prophet. It is worth noting that the Qumran interpretation of Isa 61:1 speaks of a prophetic person, and Isaiah 53 could then be regarded as referring to the sufferings of the prophet who is anointed for his task. Isa 61:1 is interpreted in Qumran as referring to the eschatological period.[58] Nevertheless, I wonder what is the meaning of the expression that God anoints the appearance of the servant? It goes without sayings that the object of the anointing is the person, not his appearance. All these problems indicate that without any other evidence it is impossible to claim that the Qumran reading of Isaiah 53 in 1QIsaᵃ refers to a

---

[56]See, e.g., A.S. van der Woude, *Die messianischen Vorstellungen der Gemeinde von Qumran* (SSN 3; Assen: van Gorcum 1957), 166-169; H. Haag, *Der Gottesknecht* 47-51; Hengel, "The Effective History of Isaiah 53," 101-102.

[57]Hengel, "The Effective History of Isaiah 53," 102-105.

[58]Isaiah 61 plays a major role in 4Q521 and in the Melchizedek fragment (11Q13).

specific messianic individual who must suffer and die for the sins of the people. Inasmuch as there are too many possible interpretations of Isaiah 53 in Judaism we can conclude that no proof of the suffering and dying Messiah can be derived from Qumran's Isaiah manuscript.

Hengel also deals with two texts from Qumran, 4Q540/41 and 4Q491, which, however, do not present any *explicit* statement that the saviour or the messianic individual in these texts would suffer vicariously and die in order to atone for the sins of the people. The crux of 4Q541 (frag. 9 col I) reads as follows:

> 2 ... And he will atone for all the children of his generation
> (ויכפר על כול בני דרה),
> and he will be sent to all the children of 3 his [people].
> His word is like the word of the heavens,
> and his teaching, according to the will of God.
> His eternal sun will shine
> 4 and its fire will burn in all the ends of the earth;
> above the darkness it will shine.
> Then, darkness will vanish 5 [fr]om the earth,
> and gloom from the dry land.
> They will utter many words against him,
> and an abundance of 6 [lie]s;
> they will fabricate fables against him,
> and utter every kind of disparagement against him.
> His generation will be evil and changed 7 [and ...] will be,
> and his position of deceit and violence.
> [And] the people will go astray in his days
> and they will be bewildered ...

Hengel refers to the interpretation of Puech who believes that the 4Q540/41 is an early midrash on Isaiah 53 taken to refer to the eschatological Priest-Messiah. Puech even thinks it possible that the Priest-Messiah will experience a violent death.[59] Hengel concludes:[60]

---

[59] E. Puech, "Fragments d'un apocryphe de Levi et le personnage eschatologique: 4QTestLevi[c-d] (?) et 4QAJa." in: J.T. Barrera & L.V. Montaner (eds), *The Madrid Qumran Congress Volume 2* (STDJ 11/2 Leiden: Brill 1992) 449-501; and the edition

> For Puech – and we can hardly contradict him here, despite all the remaining uncertainties – our text contains "the first and oldest midrashic exploitation of the Servant Songs of Isaiah interpreted in terms of an individual, in a current of Palestinian Judaism which more or less dates from the second century B.C.E. at the latest."

Despite of this possible individual interpretation Hengel notes that there is no reference to the vicarious suffering and the atoning death of the servant:[61]

> Nevertheless, no vicarious surrender of life is evident in the fragments, though one could associate יכפר ("he will atone") of fragment 9 line 2 with the אָשָׁם (NRSV "an offering for sin") of Isaiah 53:10.

This theory is somewhat bizarre because later in his summary Hengel writes that "the motif of vicarious atoning death ... perhaps plays a role in the *Aramaic Apocryphon of Levi*[b] (4Q541)."[62] In my judgment, Hengel's "perhaps" is too strong a formulation for the evidence we possess.

First, we could interpret יכפר as referring to the eschatological *kipper* rite which the priestly Messiah will perform at the beginning of the eschatological period. Such references to the eschatological rite of *kipper* can be found in Qumran writings (see CD 4:9-10; 20:34; 12:23-13:1; 1QM 2:5-6) and it is easy to interpret 4Q540/41 in conjunction with these texts.[63] So the most natural interpretation of יכפר is that it has

---

in *DJD* 31.

[60]Hengel, "The Effective History of Isaiah 53," 118.

[61]Hengel, "The Effective History of Isaiah 53," 117.

[62]Hengel, "The Effective History of Isaiah 53," 146.

[63]See A. Laato, "The Eschatological Act of kipper in the Damascus Document," in: Z.J. Kapera (ed), *Intertestamental Essays in Honour of Józef Tadeusz Milik Volume 1* (Qumranica Mogilanensia 6; Cracow: Enigma 1992) 91-107; idem, *A Star Is Rising: The Historical Development of the Old Testament Royal Ideology and the Rise of the*

nothing to do with the belief that the messianic priest would offer his life in order to atone for the sins of the people.

Second, Hengel (following Puech) observed that a good parallel to 4Q540/41 is the Testament of Levi 18; they even state that the Qumran text is a pre-stage of this T.Levi 18.[64] However, T.Levi 18 does not refer to the idea that the priestly Messiah ben Levi would offer his life for the sins of the people. If this idea was originally part of the Testament of Levi it goes without saying that the Christian interpreters who were responsible for the final edition of the Testament of Patriarchs would certainly have preserved it. The fact that such an idea is not present in T.Levi 18 strongly suggests that it was not present in 4Q540/41 either. Indeed, T.Levi 18 indicates that the priestly office of the eschatological Messiah ben Levi is connected with the Temple and the elimination of the sins rather refers to the *kipper* rituals performed at the Temple than to the vicarious death of the priestly Messiah:

> 2. And then the Lord will raise up a new priest
> to whom all the words of the Lord will be revealed.
> He shall effect the judgment of truth over the earth for many days.
> 3. And his star shall rise in heaven like a king;
> kindling the light of knowledge as day is illumined by the sun.
> And he shall be extolled by the whole inhabited world.
> 4. This one will shine forth like the sun in the earth;
> he shall take away all darkness from under heaven,
> and there shall be peace in all the earth.
> 5. The heavens shall greatly rejoice in his days
> and the earth shall be glad;
> the clouds will be filled with joy
> and the knowledge of the Lord will be poured out on the earth like the water of the seas.
> And the angels of glory of the Lord's presence will be made glad by him.

Jewish Messianic Expectations (International Studies in Formative Christianity and Judaism, Atlanta: Scholars Press 1997) 299-307; idem, "The idea of *kipper* in Judaisms of late antiquity." *Khristianskij Vostok* 1 (= *Christian Orient*) 1999, 155-193.

[64]See Hengel, "The Effective History of Isaiah 53," 115-116.

> 6. The heavens will be opened,
> and *from the temple of glory sanctification will come upon him*
> with a fatherly voice, as from Abraham and Isaac ...
> 9. ... *In his priesthood sin shall cease*
> and lawless men shall rest from their evil deeds
> and righteous men shall find rest in him.

As far as 4Q491 is concerned, Hengel notes that the vicarious suffering and death "is not visible at all"[65] even though he rightly observes that the Qumran text contains allusions to Isa 50:4-9; 52:13-53:12. Hengel also writes that it is not self-evident to whom reference is made in 4Q491. He regards the collective interpretation as "possible" and as the best alternative.[66]

This survey has shown that we have no example of interpretation in Qumran where the vicarious atoning suffering or death of the servant was interpreted individually. Summing up we may agree with Jeremias who reached the same conclusion in 1965.

The Testament of Benjamin

Hengel again promotes the relevance of T.Benjamin 3:8, which was the heart of Jeremias' argumentation in 1954 but which he then rejected in 1965 by maintaining that the passage is a Christian interpolation. Hengel refers to the studies of Becker and Hultgård according to which the Testaments of Joseph and Benjamin contain only a few Christian interpolations. In particular, both scholars argue that T.Benjamin 3:8 is probably not a Christian interpolation.[67] This being the case Hengel

---

[65]Hengel, "The Effective History of Isaiah 53," 146.

[66]Hengel, "The Effective History of Isaiah 53," 145-146.

[67]See, e.g., J. Becker, *Untersuchungen zur Entstehungsgeschichte der Testamente der zwölf Patriarchen* (AGJU 8, Leiden: Brill 1970), 51-56; A. Hultgård, *L'eschatologie des Testaments des Douze Patriarches II: Composition de l'ouvrage textes et traductions* (Acta Universitatis Upsaliensis, Historia Religionum 7; Stockholm: Almqvist & Wiksell International 1982) 39-40.

considers that T.Benjamin 3:8 contains the following pre-Christian text concerning the offspring of Joseph:

> In you [Joseph] will be fulfilled the heavenly prophecy which says that the spotless one will be defiled by lawless men and the sinless one will die for the sake of impious men.

The interpretation of this text is more complicated. We have already maintained that during the Maccabean period Isaiah 53 was used to refer to the death of martyrs (the righteous men) and the idea of atonement is presented in this connection. There are many possible interpretations of this text. The *first* problem concerns the connection with a specific eschatological saviour. It could also refer to the righteous offspring of Joseph, i.e. the spotless and the sinless is Joseph (and his offspring).[68] The situation is similar in Wisdom 2-5 where the singular "the righteous one" is used (beside the plural) but the idea is that the passages can be applied to everyone who is righteous and must suffer in the world at the hands of the ungodly. The *second* interpretive problem pertains to the kind of theology reflected in this passage. We have already seen that in ancient Jewish texts Isaiah 53 may have been associated with the sufferings of the righteous and this same interpretive tradition is also visible in the rabbinical traditions. Therefore, if we assume that T.Benjamin 3:8 originates from the pre-Christian period we cannot confirm any theological concept whereby Isaiah 53 could have been associated with the saviour or the Messiah who must suffer and die for the sins of the people, expiating them. The text could also be interpreted so that the "spotless" or the "sinless" must suffer and die in consequence of the lawless and impious men. As Hegel writes:[69]

---

[68]Hengel ("The Effective History of Isaiah 53," 139-140) refers to his study *The Zealots* (1989) 256-271, remarking that there were many martyrs or political and prophetic agitators who died, and an expectation in T.Benjamin 3:8 may in some way be related to them.

[69]Hengel, "The Effective History of Isaiah 53," 140.

Simply sticking this text with the label "Joseph as the suffering righteous one" does not explain its uniqueness as a "heavenly prophecy" and testimony to vicarious atonement. Moreover, Joseph himself is not sinless, nor does he die for his brothers.

Conclusions

We have examined Jeremias' thesis which has come to the fore again through Hengel's informative analysis of some Jewish key texts from the Second Temple period which can be regarded as influenced by Isaiah 53. We have seen how Hengel himself formulates cautiously and does not find any clear evidence for Jeremias' thesis. We have also emphasized that some texts which Hengel regards as "perhaps" containing the idea of a vicarious suffering and death of an eschatological saviour or messianic individual can easily, and more aptly be interpreted in another way.[70] This means that we have no evidence in ancient Jewish texts that Isaiah 53 was interpreted as referring to the messiah or saviour who must suffer and die for the sins of the people and expiate them. The interpretation of Isaiah 53 in Targum Jonathan will be treated in the following section. Nor does the Targum contain any atonement theology connected with the mission of the Messiah, moreover it originates from the time after the destruction of the Temple in 70 AD so that it can be regarded as irrelevant in this context. The only way to relate the Targum Jonathan to the discussion of the thesis of Jeremias is to emphasize that it contains an early pre-stage where the vicarious suffering and death of the Messiah is mentioned. We shall see that this is not the case.

---

[70]Hengel ("The Effective History of Isaiah 53," 146) formulates very carefully and speculatively: "Nevertheless, I believe we are not entirely without grounds for the hypothesis that already in the pre-Christian period, traditions about suffering and atoning eschatological messianic figures were available in Palestinian Judaism (as well as in the Diaspora; the two cannot be strictly separated), and that Jesus and the Early Church *could* have known and appealed to them." Note his expressions "I believe", "not entirely without grounds" and "*could*" with italics.

This survey of the interpretation of the servant texts and the suffering servant of Isaiah 53 in the Jewish texts of late antiquity have significant consequences for the exegesis of the New Testament. Scholars have often discussed how the New Testament's description of Jesus of Nazareth as the servant of Isaiah 40-55 (especially Isa 42:1-4 and Isaiah 53 were applied to him) may relate to Jesus' own messianic self-understanding. We have seen that there is no evidence that Isaiah 53 was understood to refer to the Messiah before the time of Jesus. On the other hand, there is only one text in the Synoptic Gospels where Jesus applies Isaiah 53 to himself and this text is a part of the passion history (see sect. 7). This implies that we cannot regard Isaiah 53 as being the text which generated the idea of the suffering Messiah. This is not to say that Isaiah 53 was not a crucial text among the first Christians when they attempted to understand the meaning of the death of Jesus.

The issue of just how Isaiah 53 was thought to refer to Jesus leaves in its wake another important question, viz. how is the collective interpretation of the servant passages in Isaiah 40-55 reflected in the New Testament. After all, this was the most common interpretation of these passages in contemporary Jewish writings as we have seen in sections 3-5. The New Testament stresses that Jesus suffered, thus fulfilling the expectations of Isaiah 53, and that he also gave the great commission with its worldwide scope (cf., Isa 49:5-6). However, a collective interpretation of the servant is in full accord with many theological tendencies in the New Testament. Indeed, the Christian Church is viewed by the New Testament as constituting the new Israel. That it is the Church which is to proclaim salvation throughout the world is already implied in Jesus' Great Commission. Therefore it is no wonder that Isa 49:6 is applied to the Christian Church in the New Testament (Acts 13:47). On the other hand, it is often stressed in the Gospels that those who follow Jesus must also take up their cross and suffer in his name. The Christian Church is thus easily identified with the suffering servant of God described in Isaiah 40-55. Especially in the *Corpus Paulinum*, the sufferings of Jesus and those of the Christians in general are presented as

128

closely intertwined (2 Cor 1:5-7; Phil 3:10 and Col 1:24). Col 1:24 emphasizes this relationship most clearly:

> It makes me happy to be suffering for you now, and in my own body to make up all the hardships that still have to be undergone by Christ for the sake of his body, the Church.

The writer of the letter to the Colossians applies the collective interpretation of Isaiah 53 to the Christian Church. Jesus, the Head of the body, has first gone through hardships and suffered; now it is the turn of his body, the Church. And when all the hardships and torments are fulfilled, the time will be ripe for the final judgment and the glorious era of the Christian Church. It is also interesting to note that Isaiah 53 was used in the New Testament as a parenetic exhortation to Christians to follow in the footsteps of their Master, he who first walked the path described in Isaiah 53 (see Phil 2:5-11; 1 Peter 2:18-25).[71] This collective interpretation of Isaiah 53 in the New Testament shows that the New Testament is deeply rooted in the Jewish interpretive traditions of the Old Testament.

But if the origin of the suffering and dying Messiah cannot be traced back to Isaiah 53 whence did this idea come? In my view, the roots for this idea are in Zechariah 9-14 and we shall turn to this question in section 7.

---

[71]See Jeremias παῖς θεοῦ 709; *Servant of God*, 97-99.

6 The Targum Interpretation of Isaiah 53

Isaiah 53 has been interpreted in Targum Jonathan as referring to the Messiah but the translation in no way implies that he must suffer and die for the sins of the people. Therefore, this peculiar interpretation has prompted vehement scholarly discussions of whether this tendency to avoid mention of the sufferings of the messianic Servant is dependent on an anti-Christian bias. Both Jeremias and Hegermann argued that the Targum Jonathan Isaiah 53 reflected an older translation where the Servant was depicted as the suffering and dying Messiah. However, the text in its present form is an anti-Christian modification of that earlier translation.[1] Our aim in this section is to examine the "translation" of Isaiah 53 in the context of the whole Targum Jonathan and discuss its date and meaning. We shall also take a stand on its possible relation to the anti-Christian beliefs.

The first printed edition of the Isaiah Targum was included in the First Rabbinic Bible (1515-1517), *Miqraot Gedolot*.[2] However, it became clear that earliest manuscripts of the Targum do not always correspond to the versions of these rabbinical Bibles. Therefore, one of the most important tasks in the Targum studies is to construct a reliable edition of the text. Nowadays scholars agree that the best edition of the Targums is that of Sperber. Sperber chose the manuscript B.M. 2211 as a basic text in his edition but it must be corrected according to other manuscripts "in

---

[1]J. Jeremias, παῖς θεοῦ in *TWNT* (1954) 676-713; idem, in: W. Zimmerli & J. Jeremias, *The Servant of God* (SBT 20, London: SCM Press 1965); H. Hegermann, *Jesaja 53 in Hexapla, Targum und Peschitta* (Gütersloh: Mohn 1954) 66-94, 115-126.

[2]Concerning these rabbinical Bibles see E.L. Greenstein, "Medieval Bible Commentaries" in: B.W. Holtz (ed), *Back to the Sources. reading the Classic Jewish Texts* (New York: Touchstone 1992) 212-259.

respect of grammar, style and harmonization."[3] His edition is also a starting-point for our study on the interpretation of the Targum Jonathan on Isaiah 53.

The Messianic Nature of Targum Isaiah 53

There are a further servant passages in Isaiah 40-55 which have been interpreted messianically: In Isa 42:1; 43:10 the title "Messiah" has been inserted after "my Servant" as it was added in Isa 52:13 and in 53:10. The translation of Targum Jonathan to Isa 52:13-53:12 given below follows that of Chilton (all statements extraneous to the MT are written in italics):[4]

52:13 Behold, my servant, *the Messiah*, shall prosper, he shall be exalted and *increase*, and shall be very *strong*.

52:14 *Just* as *the house of Israel hoped for him many days – their* appearance *was so dark*[5] *among the peoples*, and *their aspect* beyond that of *the* sons of men –

52:15 so he shall *scatter* many *peoples*; kings shall *be silent* because of him, *they shall place their hands upon* their mouth; for *things*

---

[3] B. Chilton, *The Isaiah Targum* (The Aramaic Bible 11, Wilmington: Glazier 1987) xxx.

[4] See B. Chilton, *The Isaiah Targum* 103-105. See further the English translations in J.F. Stenning, *The Targum of Isaiah* (Oxford: Clarendon Press 1949) 178-181; R. Syrén, "Targum Isaiah 52:13-53:12 and Christian Interpretation," *JJS* 40 (1989) 201-212, esp. 201-202.

[5] K. Koch ("Messias und Sündenvergebung in Jesaja 53 – Targum: Ein Beitrag zu der Praxis der aramäischen Bibelübersetzung," *JSJ* 3 [1972] 117-148, esp. p. 125 n. 2) has noted that Sperber's edition should be corrected here: the verb form must be read in the singular *dahawā* according to many manuscripts and the plural 3rd person suffixes should be attached to the words "their appearance" and "their aspect." Stenning (*The Targum of Isaiah* 178-179) translates "his appearance" and "his countenance" but notes that in the Aramaic text the suffixes are in the plural.

which have not been told to them they have seen, and that which they have not heard they have understood.

53:1 Who has believed *this* our *report*? And to whom has *the strength of* the *mighty* arm of the LORD been so revealed?

53:2 And *the righteous[6] shall be exalted* before him, *behold*, like *tufts which sprout*, and like *a tree which sends its* roots *by streams of waters, so holy generations will increase on the* land *which was needing him; his appearance is* not *a common appearance* and *his fearfulness is* not *an ordinary fearfulness*, and *his brilliance will be holy brilliance*, that *everyone who* looks at him will *consider* him.

53:3 *Then the glory of all the kingdoms will be for contempt* and *cease[7]; they will be faint and mournful, behold, as* a man of sorrows and *appointed for* sicknesses; and as when *the face of the Shekinah was taken up from us, they are* despised and not esteemed.

53:4 *Then* he *will beseech concerning our sins* and our *iniquities for his sake will be forgiven*; yet we *were* esteemed *wounded*, smitten *before the LORD* and afflicted.

53:5 And he *will build the sanctuary which was profaned* for our *sins, handed over* for our iniquities; and *by his teaching his* peace *will increase* upon *us*, and in *that we attach ourselves to his words our sins will be forgiven* us.

53:6 All we like sheep have *been scattered*; we have *gone into exile*, every one his own way; and *before* the LORD *it was a pleasure* to forgive the *sins* of us all *for his sake*.

53:7 He *beseeches*, and he *is answered*, and *before* he opens his mouth *he is accepted; the strong ones of the peoples he will hand over* like a lamb to the *sacrifice*, and like a ewe *which* before its

---

[6]Sperber's edition has the plural form צדיקיא but he has documented that even the singular form is well attested in the manuscripts.

[7]The text here has two important variant readings. See below.

shearers is dumb, so *there is* not *before him one who* opens his mouth, *or speaks a saying.*

53:8 From *bonds* and *retribution* he *will bring our exiles near; the wonders which will be done for us in his days,* who *will be able to recount?* For he *will take away the rule of the Gentiles* from the land of *Israel; the sins which* my people *sinned he will cast on to them.*

53:9 And he *will hand over the* wicked *to Gehenna* and *those* rich *in possessions which they robbed to the* death *of the corruption, lest those who commit sin be established,* and *speak of possessions* with *their* mouth.

53:10 Yet *before* the LORD *it was a pleasure to refine* and *to cleanse the remnant of his people, in order to purify their* soul *from sins; they* shall see *the kingdom of their Messiah, they shall increase sons and daughters, they* shall prolong days; *those who perform the law of* the LORD shall prosper in his *pleasure;*

53:11 from *the slavery of the Gentiles he shall deliver their* soul, *they* shall see *the retribution of their adversaries. They shall* be satisfied *with the plunder of their kings;* by his *wisdom* shall *he* make *innocents* to be accounted *innocent, to subject* many *to the law;* and he shall *beseech concerning* their *sins.*

53:12 Then I will divide him *the plunder of* many *peoples,* and he shall divide the spoil, *the possessions of* strong *fortresses;* because he *handed over* his soul to the death, and *subjected the rebels to the law;* yet he *will beseech concerning* the *sins* of many, and *to the rebels it shall be forgiven for him.*

The beginning of Isa 53:3 is problematic as far as its textual transmission is concerned. There are two different readings which yield two strikingly different interpretations.[8] The reading יַפְסִיק is in *aph'el,* "he will make to cease," and the text should be interpreted so that the Messiah is the

---

[8]See Jeremias, *The Servant of God* pp. 69-70 n. 296.

subject of both verbs: "Then he will be despised and will make to cease the glory of all the kingdoms." On the other hand, the reading יִפְסוֹק (*qal*) is also attested in the manuscripts, when the subject must be "the glory of all the kingdoms," being the received translation presented by Chilton. It is clear that both readings are feasible and can well be combined with messianic emphases in the rabbinical writings. That the messiah's suffering (in pre-existence) guarantees victory in the coming eschatological battle is attested in relatively late Pesikta Rabbati and Zohar (see sect. 10). Hegermann argued that the first reading reflects an earlier Targum rendering where the concept of the suffering and dying Messiah was described.[9] However, the whole construction remains hypothetical and lacks concrete evidence.

Even though the idea that the Messiah would be a subject of both verbs has almost categorically been refuted in recent studies it is worth noting that medieval rabbinical Bibles preserved this reading – apparently because the idea of the Messiah as despised has many parallels to other rabbinical texts and Zohar. Such a reading should not be excluded because of Hegermann's unjustified hypothesis of the Messiah who suffers and dies vicariously for the sins of the people. After all in Isa 53:12 the Targum describes the Messiah as one who is ready to die: "He handed over his soul to death." Therefore, I cannot see any difficulty in taking the reading of the Servant as subject as an acceptable alternative to Chilton's translation. But in that case I do not understand the text according to Hegermann's and Jeremias' hypothesis. The Messiah may face tribulation when trying to fulfil his task vis-à-vis the nations but he will finally have success.

The basic problem in the interpretation of Isaiah 53 is that it deviates so markedly from the content of the MT. We stated already in section 5 that this deviation was tentatively explained as a consequence of the anti-Christian polemics. While we shall discuss this problem at the end of this section we shall first envisage how the translation of the

---

[9]Hegermann, *Jesaja 53 in Hexapla* 75-77.

Targum Jonathan to Isaiah 53 was made and how its messianic content follows typical emphases of the Targum Isaiah and other targums. Only after having first attempted to understand Targum Isaiah 53 on its own merits and in conjunction with other targums and Jewish (mainly rabbinical) traditions we shall postulate in how this text is related to the Christian interpretation, if at all.

According to Koch, the meturgeman read a Hebrew *Vorlage* which contained ʻ*ālāyw* instead of the ʻ*ālekā* in verse 52:14.[10] However, other scholars have rightly noted that this person change from the third to the second person in 52:14 enabled the meturgeman to apply the references to suffering in 52:14 and 53:3-9 to an individual other than the Servant the Messiah.[11]

The meturgeman has interpreted the verb שׁמְמוּ as the *poʻlel* form from the verb שׂים with the meaning "put (trust) in him."[12] Thus the subject is the people who put its trust in him (the Messiah). The end of the verse 52:14 should therefore be interpreted as referring to the distress of the people. This reading of the first verse which refers to the sufferings of the servant illustrates how the meturgeman understood the whole passage of Isaiah 53. As we have seen in sections 3 and 4 there is a tendency in the Second Temple period to see the servant as representing the sufferings of the (righteous) members of the nation. This being the case, it follows that the meturgeman attributed the sufferings mainly to

---

[10]Koch, "Messias und Sündenvergebung in Jesaja 53," 125.

[11]O. Betz, "Die Übersetzung von Jes 53 (LXX, Targum) und die Theologia Crucis des Paulus," in: O. Betz, *Jesus, der Herr der Kirche: Aufsätze zur biblischen Theologie II* (WUNT 52, Tübingen: Mohr 1990) 197-216, esp. 202; J. Ådna, "The Servant of Isaiah 53 as Triumphant and Interceding Messiah: The Reception of Isaiah 52:13-53:12 in the Targum of Isaiah with Special Attention to the Concept of the Messiah," in: B. Janowski & P. Stuhlmacher (eds), *The Suffering Servant: Isaiah 53 in Jewish and Christian Sources* (Grand Rapids: Eerdmans 2004) 189-224, esp. 199-200.

[12]Koch, "Messias und Sündenvergebung in Jesaja 53," 125. Hegermann (*Jesaja 53 in Hexapla* 68) comments: "Wie Tg nun zu der Wiedergabe von שָׁמְמוּ mit סָבְרוּ gekommen ist, ist dunkel; es handelt sich wohl um eine freie Übersetzung."

those living in tribulation while the description of the Messiah follows the main stream of the Second Temple Jewish messianic expectations which offer hope to the oppressed (see, e.g., the Psalms of Salomon 17-18). The only problem in the meturgeman's interpretation is that he identifies the servant with the Messiah in Isa 52:13 but does not regard the passages with reference to the sufferings of the Servant as concerning the Messiah – which is true of many rabbinical passages, and of Pesiqta Rabbati as well as Zohar.

In his interpretation the meturgeman combined two interpretive streams: (1) Isaiah 53 speaks of the (righteous) members of the people who are suffering. However, the meturgeman does not emphasize their innocence. His interpretation on this point diverges from how the text was understood during the Maccabean period when reference was made to the righteous martyrs. (2) The meturgeman introduces the Messiah among these righteous ones and accepts the typical messianic expectations of Second Temple Judaism and rabbinical writings and reads this eschatological expectation into Isaiah 53. Only in some cases does the meturgeman translate the suffering passages of Isaiah 53 so as to refer to the Messiah's intercession for the people (e.g. Isa 53:5). This inconsistency indicates that the meturgeman's translation is not coherent as far as the suffering passages in the Masoretic text are concerned. Some of them refer to the sufferings of the nation while other are reinterpreted to concern the Messiah's intercession for the people.

Apparently under the influence of Isa 52:7 the meturgeman translates the "message" (שְׁמוּעָה) in 53:1 by the "gospel, good tidings" (בְּסוֹרתָא). Isa 52:7-8 introduces the idea of the coming of the Kingdom of God, which in the Isaiah Targum concerns God's "divine and saving revelation, particularly on Mount Zion."[13] The meturgeman translates Isa 52:7-8 as follows:

---

[13]See B. Chilton, *The Glory of Israel. The Theology and Provenience of the Isaiah Targum* (JSOTSS 23, Sheffield: JSOT Press 1983) 77-81. The quotation is from p. 77.

> How beautiful upon the mountains of *the land of Israel* are the feet of him who announces, who publishes peace, who announces good tidings, who publishes salvation, who says to *the congregation of* Zion, "*The kingdom of* your God *is revealed*." The voice of your *guardians, who* lift up *their* voice, together they sing for joy; for *with their* eyes they will see *the prodigies which* the LORD *will do* when he *will* return *his Shekinah* to Zion.

In light of this connection between 52:7-8 and 53:1 it was natural for the meturgeman to interpret the distress of the people described in Isaiah 53 as referring to the destruction of the Temple whence the Shekinah of the Lord has vanished.[14] This belief is planted in Isa 53:3 by the meturgeman. The meturgeman has interpreted וּכְמַסְתַּר פָּנִים מִמֶּנּוּ so that reference is made to "the divine faces of Shekinah" (= פָּנִים) which has rejected "us"! Indeed the suffix in מִמֶּנּוּ can also be interpreted as referring to 1. plural.[15] It is significant that a similar idea is presented in the MT Isa 8:17 where the prophet remarks that the LORD hides (the verb סתר) his face from the people:

וְחִכִּיתִי לַיהוָה הַמַּסְתִּיר פָּנָיו מִבֵּית יַעֲקֹב וְקִוֵּיתִי־לוֹ

In the interpretation of Isa 8:17, Targum Jonathan has added the idea of Shekinah as follows:

> *The prophet said, For this reason* I *prayed before* the LORD, who *threatened to take up his Shekinah* from *those of* the house of Jacob, and I *besought before him.*

---

[14]It is customary to express the destruction of the Temple by referring to the departure of the Shekinah of the LORD from its resting place. Its biblical background is Ezekiel 8-11. See Chilton, *Glory of Israel* 69-75; Ådna, "The Servant of Isaiah 53," 210-213

[15]See Hegermann, *Jesaja 53 in Hexapla* 76; Koch, "Messias und Sündenvergebung in Jesaja 53," 133, Ådna, "The Servant of Isaiah 53," 200-201.

The Targum of Isaiah 53:3 has been interpreted so as to imply that "our situation" (the situation of the Jews) and "the situation of the foreign peoples" are compared. The meturgeman takes the verb forms at the end of verse 3 as a collective singular, leading to the interpretation: "we" i.e. oppressed Jews "are despised and not esteemed" when the Shekinah is taken up from them through the destruction of the Temple.

Isa 53:5, too, has been interpreted by the meturgeman as referring to the destruction of the Temple. He interprets the MT's מְחֹלָל as deriving from the verb חָלַל, "profane". The translation of the MT's מְדֻכָּא as "hand over (אִתְמְסַר)" can be understood so that reference is made to the Temple which was surrendered to Romans (gentiles) who profaned it and destroyed it.[16] The idea that the servant Messiah will rebuild the Temple is the meturgeman's conclusion with no real textual basis. But because he could understand verse 3 as referring to the destruction of the Temple it was easy to find suitable words and idioms which were open to the idea of rebuilding.

There are other instances where the meturgeman succeeded in altering by minimal reinterpretations (intentionally or not) the meaning of the MT which refers to the sufferings of the servant. In verse 7 the MT's נִגַּשׂ is regarded as deriving from the verb נָגַשׁ which denotes cultic attendance: come near (to God). In this way the meturgeman shifted the meaning of the text to the cultic role of the Messiah. His prayers are effectual. In consequence, the meturgeman regards the Hebrew verb ענה as coming from the verb "answer" and נענה could then signify "being heard" (by God).[17] Consequently, the end of the verse is understood so that foreigners will be led to the slaughter. Similarly the meturgeman has modified verse 4 so that the Messiah does not "bear our sins" but "beseech concerning our sins" and this prayer is the reason why "our

---

[16]See Koch, "Messias und Sündenvergebung in Jesaja 53," 135-136; Ådna, "The Servant of Isaiah 53," 207-209 and n. 70.

[17]Koch, "Messias und Sündenvergebung in Jesaja 53," 137; Ådna, "The Servant of Isaiah 53," 201-202.

138

iniquities for his sake will be forgiven."[18] A similar belief that "our sins" will be forgiven because the Messiah will beseech God is emphasized in vv. 6, 11-12. The end of verse 4 is interpreted anew when the meturgeman translates the MT's חֲשַׁבְנֻהוּ with חֲשִׁיבִין without the suffix. In this case it is "we" who are wounded and smitten and afflicted, not the servant.

In Isa 53:7-8 too the meturgeman has amended the MT by diverse minor readings. He has vocalized passive verb forms יוּבָל and לֻקַּח as active. Thus it is not the servant who will be led to the slaughter but he himself will deliver the peoples to destruction. Furthermore, the servant is not taken from imprisonment and judgement but he himself will lead the exiles from bonds and retribution. It is worth noting that in verse 6 the meturgeman has interpreted the MT so that it refers to the exile.

An important detail is also the meturgeman's misinterpretation of the Masoretic מוּסַר as referring to the teaching of the Messiah. He has thereby introduced a significant dogmatic detail into the text: listening and following the Torah guarantees forgiveness.

These examples indicate how the meturgeman has an interpretive tendency to identify the sufferings of the servant with the distress of the people. His execution is often skilful, exploiting the openness of the Masoretic text. Nevertheless, this interpretive tendency has produced some markedly forced interpretations of the MT. One example is verse 2 where the reference to the disfigured nature of the servant has yielded to the glorious appearance of the servant Messiah. There is a controversy

---

[18]Koch "Messias und Sündenvergebung in Jesaja 53," 134-135; Ådna, "The Servant of Isaiah 53," 214-215. Koch (pp. 137-138, 141-142, 148) interprets the Messiah in Isaiah 53 as being a priest. Ådna opposes this view by noting (p. 215) that "the Book of Zechariah is tradition-historically important for the Messiah's ministry as temple builder, and this book with its reception in *Targum of Zechariah*, as well as *Targum Jonathan* as a whole, differentiate precisely between the competencies of the Messiah and those of the high priest or the priests."

as to whether or not the Hebrew Vorlage of verse 2 was different[19] but it is difficult to speculate about the Vorlage on the basis of these free translations of the Targum. Nevertheless, Hegermann suggests that the meturgeman may have vocalized the MT's נִרְאֵהוּ as נִרְאֵהוּ (niphal participle "his fearfulness" from the verb יָרֵא) which accurately translates the Aramaic אֵימְתֵיהּ, while the MT's מַרְאֶה is taken to be the hiphil participle from the verb רָאָה. The problem is the last negation וְלֹא before מַרְאֶה. According to Hegermann, the meturgeman would have read the text as if לֹו was written instead of וְלֹא.[20] But this is difficult to verify. In any case, verse 2 has been interpreted in the Targum as being at odds with all other ancient translations and this is true of other verses too so that we should rather speak of an interpretive tendency than a different Hebrew Vorlage.

This survey indicates that the Messiah in TgIsa is not reminiscent of the Servant of the Lord in the MT of Isaiah 53 who must suffer and die for the sins of the people. Rather, the Messiah is a victorious warrior who teaches the people the Torah, rebuilds the Temple and prays for his people. How should we understand the mode of interpreting Isaiah 53 in Targum Jonathan?

It has been suggested that the translation of the Targum was intentionally censorious, and that its aim was to oppose the Christian interpretation.[21] As already noted, Hegermann and Jeremias went so far

---

[19]See Hegermann, *Jesaja 53 in Hexapla* 73-74; Koch, "Messias und Sündenvergebung in Jesaja 53," 130-131.

[20]Hegermann, *Jesaja 53 in Hexapla* 73.

[21]G. Dalman, *Jesaja 53: das Prophetenwort vom Sühnleiden des Gottesknechtes mit besonderer Berücksichtigung des jüdischen Literatur* (Leipzig: Hinrischs'sche Buchhandlung 1914); P. Billerbeck, *Kommentar zum Neuen Testament aus Talmud und Midrasch von Hermann L. Strack und Paul Billerbeck Vol I-V* (Munich: Oskar Beck 1922-1928) I:482-483; Hegermann, *Jesaja 53 in Hexapla* 66-94, 115-126; Jeremias, παις θεου 690-693; H.W. Wolff, *Jesaja 53 im Urchristentum. Mit einer Einführung von Peter Stuhlmacher* (Giessen: Brunnen 1984) 52.

as to suggest that originally (before the Christian interpretation was established) the Targum described the Messiah who died for the sins of the people. They note that the translation technique in this passage stands out in its unusual freedom. There is no compelling explanation for this, unless the translator wished to attack Christian interpretations of the passage as referring to the vicarious suffering and death of Jesus Christ.[22] Further, they suppose that the original Targumic version which originated in pre-Christian times was closer to the Hebrew text than the contemporary Targumic version and included the idea of the vicarious suffering and death of the Servant.[23] Jeremias explains the nature of this Targumic interpretation as follows:[24]

> The whole section was indeed messianically explained because the messianic interpretation of Isa. 52.13-53.12 was so firmly rooted that *Targ*.Isa. could not escape it, but the passages about suffering, in brusque contradiction to the original, are replaced by the current view of the Messiah.

Hegermann's and Jeremias' view is problematic. We have already seen that in ancient Jewish texts from the Second Temple period there is no example of interpretation that the Servant of Isaiah 53 would be the Messiah who must die for the sins of the people. The servant may symbolize the righteous who must suffer in the world, and his death may benefit the people. But this concept has never been connected with messianic expectations. We have no example of any atoning death of the Messiah which would call to mind at all the death of Jesus Christ in the New Testament. Against this background it is natural that if the Targum interprets Isaiah 53 as referring to the Messiah, it makes no mention of

---

[22]The Targumic version makes no mention of the vicarious suffering and death of the Servant, which is the central theme of the Hebrew text.

[23]Hegermann *Jesaja 53 in Hexapla* 115-126; Jeremias, παις θεου 690-693; *Servant of God* 69-72.

[24]Jeremias, *Servant of God* 72.

the vicarious atoning death of the Messiah. But the problem remains. Why on earth choose Isaiah 53 to describe the victorious Messiah? Far-reaching analysis of the translation technique of Targums has enabled scholars to take a stand against such a one-sided anti-Christian interpretation of the Targum translation of Isaiah 53. For example, in 1972 Koch maintained that the Targum interpretation of Isaiah 53 follows the principles which can be discerned in other targumic messianic interpretations.[25] In particular, Koch refers to Churgin who, in his opinion, shows that typical tendencies of interpretation are followed even in Isaiah 53. This same conclusion has been emphasized by Ådna.[26] However, Churgin's approach to the interpretation of Isaiah 53 diverges from the statements of Koch and Ådna. He observes that there are four main principles of exegesis in the Targum: 1) the allegorical, 2) the metaphorical, 3) the complementary and 4) the lexical. He characterizes the interpretation of Isaiah 52:13-53:12 as a good example of allegorical interpretation which, nevertheless, has its own peculiarities. First, he deals with two other examples of allegorical interpretations, Ezekiel 16 and Hosea 1-3, and remarks that they receive support from Aggadic material in rabbinical writings. But in the case of Isaiah 53 Churgin writes:[27]

> But the targumist is strikingly singular. Assured that this prediction is about the Messiah, the targumist reverses the simple meaning of the words, transforming the gloomy portraiture of the Messiah into an image of magnificence and splendor, unlike the Agadist contemporaries, who would rather play thoughtfully on the humbleness and sufferings of the Messiah. He

---

[25] Koch, "Messias und Sündenvergebung in Jesaja 53," 117-148. See also Syrén, "Targum Isaiah 52:13-53:12," 201-212; Ådna, "The Servant of Isaiah 53," 189-224.

[26] Koch, "Messias und Sündenvergebung in Jesaja 53," 123, 147-148; Ådna, "The Servant of Isaiah 53," 193.

[27] P. Churgin, *Targum Jonathan to the Prophets* (New York: KTAV Publishing House, Baltimore: The Baltimore Hebrew College 1983) 78-84, the quotation is from pp. 83-84. Churgin's work was originally from 1927.

was influenced by the great national movements of his time, which assumed a Messianic character.

We can see that Churgin here *expressis verbis* comments that the Targum interpretation seems to be unique, differing from the way in which the messianic interpretation of Isaiah 53 is presented in rabbinical writings. In addition, he emphasizes the targumist's custom of reversing the simple meaning of the words. Churgin's thesis is that Isaiah 53 reflects fervent messianic hopes during the time of Bar Kochba. He formulates his thesis more precisely when he deals with the Targum interpretation of Ezek 39:16 which interprets Gog as referring to Rome. He writes:[28] "I am also led to believe that this was the reason why the T. turns the gloomy and miserable description of the 'Servant' (Is. ch. 53) into a most glorious presentation. The targumist, living in a time when the Messiah stood at the head of warring armies, could hardly have conceived those objectionable features in a literal sense. V. 5 points clearly to Bar Kochba." We shall turn to the question of the anti-Christian character of the Targum translation later but first we shall deal with the date of Targum Isaiah 53.

---

[28]Churgin, *Targum Jonathan* 26. Cf., also p. 42 where Churgin writes: "Although the official Targumim were in a definite shape in the time of R. Akiba, the process of transformation had been still going on to a comparatively late date." On p. 30 Churgin writes "the progressive composition of the targum until it assumed its present form."

The Date of Targum Isaiah 53

Churgin does not argue more precisely for his dating of the Isaiah Targum to Bar Kochba's time but many scholars have adopted his date with some modifications.[29] For example, Isaiah Targum incorporates

---

[29] The dating of Targums was greatly benefitted when the Targum Neofiti was "found" in 1956 and its relation to Pentateuch, Pseudo-Jonathan Targum, the so-called Fragment-Targum and Targum fragments discovered at Cairo Geniza was examined. Targum Neofiti proved what Paul Kahle had emphasized at the beginning of 1900's that it is impossible to reconstruct one normative Palestinian Targum. Different versions existed which were more or less reminiscent of each other. See M. McNamara, *The New Testament and the Palestinian Targum to the Pentateuch* (AnBib 27A, Rome: Biblical Institute Press 1978). Even the finds from Qumran have influenced scholars in their discussion of the dates of Targums. Among Qumran writings there are old Aramean translations to the Book of Job (11QTgJob and 4QTgJob) and Leviticus (4QTgLev). See *DJD* 6:86-90. These early (from about 100 BC) texts are not only translations but contain several additions, like Targums do. The Qumran texts show that translations like Targums were produced to the books of the Hebrew Bible already before the time of Jesus. This being the case scholars cannot *prima facie* exclude the possibility that Targums reflect old traditions which are rooted in Second Temple Judaism. See, e.g., R. Syrén, *The Blessings in the Targums: A Study on the Targumic Interpretations of Genesis 49 and Deuteronomy 33* (Åbo: Åbo Akademi Press 1986) where Targum interpretations are seen partly as parallel to the ideas presented in Qumran writings. On the basis of this Qumran evidence, scholars discuss the way in which Targum interpretations to the Hebrew Bible have influenced Jesus' preaching in the New Testament. Chilton's view seems plausible to me. The evidence from the Babylonian Talmud indicates that Targums are the result of a complicated transmission process. Already during the Tannaitic period there were Targum translations which were completed in the Amoraite period. This being the case, we can date the final composition of Targum Jonathan to the period 300-500 AD. See further P. Alexander, "Targum, Targumim," *ABD* 6:320-331 where it is rightly noted that Targum translations were composed outside rabbinical circles – an observation which explains the fact (already noted by Churgin) that Targums sometimes contradict rabbinic halakha – and rabbis tried to control them and their use in synagogal service. These circumstances must imply that the composition of Targums was in progress during the Talmudic era. For example, P. Schäfer ("Bibelübersetzung II. Targumim," *TRE* 6:216-228, espec. 223) argues that Targum Jonathan was originally composed in Palestine and then edited in Babylonia during the period 300-500 AD, before the Islamic era. See also E. Levine, "The Biography of the Aramaic Bible," *ZAW* 94 (1982) 353-379 where a date before the rise of Islam is given for the end redaction of Targums.

passages which *expressis verbis* refer to the historical conditions of later times. Isa 34:9 and 54:1 contain references to Rome.[30] Levey agrees with Churgin and comments that the Targum interpretation of Isaiah 53 shows beyond doubt that "there is no room whatsoever for a suffering and dying Messiah. If there were such, the targumist would have to look no farther for biblical support than the Suffering Servant passages, yet from what he does with them, it is obvious what his thoughts are."[31] However, this date of Isaiah 53 does not pertain to the entire Targum, according to Levey. He refers to the translation of 2 Sam 22:32 in Targum Jonathan: "There is no god but Yhwh" which is formulated according to the basic confession in Islam and should imply that Targum Jonathan has received its final form only after the rise of Islam.[32] This *terminus ad quem* date for the Targum Jonathan is not convincing, however. Van der Kooij has referred to 1 Sam 2:2 which may well be behind the formulation for Targum 2 Sam 22:32.[33]

Van der Kooij also suggests the date just before Bar Kochba war for Targum Isaiah. He argues that both the prophet Targum and Onqelos have been composed by the high priest Eleazar from Modein.[34]

---

[30]For a detailed discussion of the historical references in the Isaiah Targum see A. van der Kooij, *Die alten Textzeugen des Jesajabuches* 161-175, 192-197; Chilton *Glory of Israel*; idem, *The Isaiah Targum*.

[31]S.H. Levey, *The Text and I: Writings of Samson H. Levey* (edited by S.F. Chyet; South Florida Studies in the History of Judaism 166, Atlanta: Scholars Press 1998) 120-127, the quotation is from p. 126. Levey's original work "The Messiah, An Aramaic Interpretation – The Messianic Exegesis of the Targum" was from 1974.

[32]Levey, *The Text and I* 93-102. This date was followed also by M. Pickup, "The Emergence of the Suffering Messiah in Rabbinic Literature." In: *Approaches to Ancient Judaism. New Series Vol 11* (ed. by J. Neusner. South Florida Studies in the History of Judaism 154, Atlanta: Scholars Press 1997) 143-162, esp. 155.

[33]van der Kooij, *Die alten Textzeugen des Jesajabuches* 189-190. See also Koch, "Messias und Sündenvergebung in Jesaja 53," 119 n. 1.

[34]van der Kooij, *Die alten Textzeugen des Jesajabuches* 161-213. He also refers to TgIsa 32:14 and texts where Shekinah was taken away (TgIsa 1:15; 5:5; 8:17; 53:3; 54:8; 57:17; 59:2; 64:6) and notes that Koch's ("Messias und Sündenvergebung in

Chilton began his discussion concerning the date of Targum Jonathan from the rabbinical tradition according to which Jonathan ben Uzziel was a student of Rabbi Hillel who flourished in the time of Jesus (bMeg 3a). On the other hand, the Babylonian Talmud connects Rabbi Joseph bar Hijja (active in the Babylonian Academy in Pumbedita in 4th century AD) to Targums. According to traditions preserved in the Talmud, Joseph rendered an Aramaic translation to Sef 3:18 (bBer 28a) and Isa 5:17 (bPes 68a) which are very close to the wording of the Targum Jonathan. On the other hand, bSanh 94b (Isa 8:6) and bMQ 28b (Zech 12:11) refer to how Joseph discusses the Aramaic translations close to Targum Jonathan and the context reveals that they are not Joseph's own translations but were taken from some earlier texts.[35] This evidence gives Chilton reason to argue that the first Tannaitic version of the Isaiah Targum was composed before the Bar Kochba war in 132-135 AD. and that it was later complemented by an Amoraic meturgeman.[36] The Isaiah Targum – like Targumim in general – is related to the theological emphases of rabbis who sought to increase the influence of their teachings in synagogal services. Targumim are not literal translations but translations which incorporate expanded theological interpretations and therefore reveal how the Hebrew text has been interpreted ideologically.

This being the case, Chilton argues that there are two major periods when the Isaiah Targum was composed. The messianic

---

Jesaja 53," 120) statement that Targum Isaiah never mentions the destruction of the Temple is not convincing.

[35] Chilton, *Glory of Israel* 2-3, 120 n. 10-11.

[36] Chilton, *Glory of Israel*; see also idem, *The Isaiah Targum* xiv-xxv; idem, "Two in One: Renderings of the Book of Isaiah in Targum Jonathan," in: C.C. Broyles & C.A. Evans (eds), *Writing & Reading the Scroll of Isaiah: Studies of an Interpretive Tradition, Volume Two* (VTSup 70:2, Leiden: Brill 1997) 547-562; idem, "Targum Jonathan of the Prophets I," in: J. Neusner & A.J. Avery-Peck (eds), *Encyclopaedia of Midrash: Biblical Interpretation in Formative Judaism Volume II* (Leiden: Brill 2005) 889-908.

146

expectations in Isaiah Targum originate mainly from the Tannaitic period (70-135 AD) when it was expected that the Messiah would destroy the enemies of Israel (the Romans) and rebuild the Temple.[37] Chilton finds many expressions in the Targum of Isaiah 53 which indicate that, by and large, the passage was composed by an early Tannaitic meturgeman. No parallels from the rabbinic literature can be found to the manner in which the concepts "Shekinah," "sanctuary," "exile" and "messiah" are treated in the Targum.[38] Chilton concludes:[39]

> In a word, the hopes of the primitive meturgeman centered on a messiah as he looked forward to recovery from the disaster of 70. The gospel of Jesus was not yet of sufficient concern to make him alter his interpretation for apologetic reasons, and it is permissible to infer that, in his messianic understanding of the Isaian servant, the meturgeman attests a primitive exegesis common to Judaism and the Christianity.

Chilton speculates even that the Targumic tradition of the messianic interpretation of Isaiah 53 originated in pre-Christian times.[40]

Chilton's thesis provoked criticism by Ådna who observed that "the need for caution regarding these sorts of theological distinctions as dating criteria is urged by the juxtaposition of both present and future eschatological understandings of the kingdom of God in Qumran as well as the New Testament."[41] Ådna himself follows the general view among scholars that Targum Isaiah 53 dates from shortly before the Bar-Kochba revolt. The main arguments for this date are that the passage refers to the destruction of the Temple and to glowing messianic expectations.[42]

---

[37]See Chilton, *Glory of Israel* 86-96, 110.

[38]Chilton, *Glory of Israel* 93, 104-107.

[39]Chilton, *Glory of Israel* 94.

[40]Chilton, *Glory of Israel* 91.

[41]Ådna, "The Servant of Isaiah 53" 196 n. 22.

[42]Ådna, "The Servant of Isaiah 53" 197.

This survey offers evidence that scholars agree that Targum Isaiah 53 is connected with the Tannaitic period, often dated just before the time of the Bar Kochba revolt. This does mean that the essential passages of Targum Jonathan may go back to the Tannaitic period – as Chilton has suggested.[43]

The Messianic Targum Isaiah

We shall now deal with the nature of the messianic exegesis of TgIsa 53 in its relation to the overall messianic interpretation in Targum Isaiah. According to Chilton, many of the messianic passages of the Isaiah Targum go back to the Tannaitic meturgeman, and the Amoraic meturgeman interpreted the Messiah in a new framework by emphasizing his role as the eternal witness (TgIsa 43:10-12) and by depreciating his political status (TgIsa 59:16; 63:5, 9).[44] Like Chilton other scholars too have emphasized that TgIsaiah 53 conveys a coherent picture of the Messiah. Ådna summarizes these features by speaking of three central themes: The Messiah is 1) teacher of the Law; 2) builder of the Temple and 3) intercessor, which does not mean that the Messiah himself was a priestly figure (so Koch) who by cultic performances forgives sins, but rather that God for the sake of the Messiah will forgive. These three

---

[43]A gradual development has been suggested for Targum Jonathan in many studies in the series The Aramaic Bible. See, e.g., D.J. Harrington & A.J. Saldarini, *Targum Jonathan of the Former Prophets* (The Aramaic Bible 10; Wilmington: Michael Glazier 1987) 13-14 with reference to the classical studies of Churgin (*Targum Jonathan*) and L. Smolar & M. Aberbach (*Studies in Targum Jonathan to the Prophets* [New York: KTAV; Baltimore: Baltimore Hebrew College 1983]); C.T.R. Hayward, *The Targum of Jeremiah* (The Aramaic Bible 12, Wilmington: Michael Glazier 1987) 34-38; S.H. Levey, *The Targum of Ezekiel* (The Aramaic Bible 13; Wilmington: Michael Glazier 1987) 2-4; K.J. Cathcart & R.P. Gordon, *The Targum of the Minor Prophets* (The Aramaic Bible 14, Edinburgh: Clark 1989) 16-18. It is worth noting that this basic idea of gradual development of Targumim is indicated already in early studies of Churgin and Smolar & Aberbach.

[44]For this see Chilton, *The Glory of Israel* 86-96; idem, "Two in One," 550-561 and passages *ad loc* in Chilton's translation of Targum Isaiah.

aspects of the messianic view in TgIsaiah 53 mean that the Davidic Messiah is the sole mediator of salvation.[45] The list of Ådna should be complemented by at least a fourth theme, viz. that the Messiah is he who subjugates nations. Targum Isaiah contains many texts where the messianic era is related to obedience to the Torah, and the final battle against the nations at the time of their subjugation.

The first messianic text in the Isaiah Targum is 4:2-6. It summarizes the content of chapters 1-3 where hope is given to the righteous who will keep the Torah and who will see consolation of Jerusalem. Isaiah Targum opens with severe criticism of the men of Judah. TgIsa 1:6 says that "from *the remnant of the people* even to *the* heads there is not among *them one that is perfect in my fear. All of them are disobedient and rebellious; they defiled themselves with sins as* a dripping wound." It goes on to describe how the sacrifices performed in the temple are futile. The Shekina will be taken away (TgIsa 1:15): "And when *the priests* spread forth *their* hands *to pray for you*, I take up *the face of my Shekinah* from you." After this criticism and condemnation there is a passage which introduces the possibility of repentance (Tg 1:16-20). This opens a new hopeful perspective to the fate of Jerusalem. Jerusalem will receive its consolation but the sinners will be annihilated (TgIsa 1:24): "*The city of Jerusalem I am about to comfort, but woe to the wicked when I am revealed to take just retribution* from the enemies *of the people*, and I will *return* vengeance to *the adversary.*" Those who will keep the Torah will be saved (TgIsa 1:27-28): "Zion shall be redeemed *when judgment is performed in her*, and the *ones who have performed the law will* return *to* her in righteousness. But rebels and *sinners will be* shattered together, and those who *have* forsaken *the law of* the LORD will be consumed."

TgIsa 2:1-5 presents an eschatological vision whereby the Shekinah of God will return to the temple which will be established on the Mount of Zion. The Torah of God will be established and every

---

[45] Ådna, "The Servant of Isaiah 53," 207-224.

nation will "walk *in the teaching of his law.*" This same willingness concerns also the house of Jacob: "Come, and let us walk in *the teaching of the law* of the LORD." TgIsa 2:6-22 contains harsh criticism of the men of Jerusalem who have forsaken the law and walk according to the customs (*nomos*) of Gentiles. The use of the Greek loan word *nomos* illustrates here how the meturgeman regarded the Greek style of life as dangerous.[46] This lifestyle is particularly manifest in TgIsa 3:16-26 where ornaments of the daughters of Zion are depicted with the aid of Greek loanwords.[47] TgIsa 3 continues the criticism of the sinners but in verse 10 it is noted: "Tell the righteous, '*You are blessed,*' for the fruits of their deeds will *be repaid.*" When TgIsa 4:2-6 introduces the messianic promise it is intimately related to the themes of TgIsa 1-3. We shall here quote the whole passage of TgIsa 4:2-6:

> 2 In that *time the Messiah* of the LORD shall be for *joy* (לחדוא) and for glory, and *those who perform the law* for pride and for praise *to* the survivors of Israel. 3 And it shall come to pass that he who is left *will return to* Zion and who *has performed the law will be established* in Jerusalem; he will be called holy, every one who has been recorded for *eternal* life *will see the consolations of Jerusalem,* 4 when the LORD shall have *taken away* the filth of the daughters of Zion and *banished those who shed innocent* blood *who are in* Jerusalem from its midst, by a *command* of judgment and by *a command of extirpation.* 5 And then the LORD will create over the whole *sanctuary of the* Mount *of* Zion and over *the place of the house of the Shekinah* a cloud *of glory* – it will be covering it by day, and *the dense cloud will be as* a flaming fire by night; for *it shall have glory greater than was promised he would bring upon it, the Shekinah will be sheltering it as* a canopy. 6 And *over Jerusalem there will be the covering of my cloud to cover* it by day from heat and for a refuge and *for* shelter from storm and from rain.

---

[46]Elsewhere in Targum Jonathan the Greek *nomos* is used to denote the law of foreigners which is used in courts against Jews – something which is regarded as punishment. See Smolar & Aberbach, *Studies in Targum Jonathan* 40-41.

[47]Chilton, *The Isaiah Targum* 7, 9.

This messianic passage indicates that the Shekinah of God will again appear in the sanctuary of Jerusalem during the time of the Messiah. Those who have complied with the ordinances of the Torah will rejoice in Jerusalem because the Messiah will be their joy. The words צמח יהוה in the MT have been interpreted in the Targum as משיחא דיוי, an interpretation apparently generated by Jer 23:5-6; 33:15; Zech 3:8-10; 6:9-15. The MT of Isa 4:2 is linguistically reminiscent of Isa 28:5 and therefore even TgIsa 28:5 was interpreted in terms of the Messiah: "In that *time the Messiah of* the LORD of hosts will be a *diadem* of *joy* (כליל דחדוא) and a *crown* of praise, to the remnant of his people." It seems that also Isaiah 61 has been interpreted in messianic terms, even though the word Messiah does not appear in the Targum. But the word כליל is added in TgIsa 61:3:

> ... to *confuse* those who mourn in Zion—to give them a *diadem* (כליל) instead of ashes, oil of joy (משח דחדוא) instead of mourning, a prais*ing spirit* instead of *their* spirit *which was* dejected; that *they* may call *them true princes*, the *people* of the LORD, that he may be glorified.

It is significant that beside the word "diadem" also the keyword "joy" (חדוה) is attested in TgIsa 61:3 as it is in TgIsa 4:2; 28:5. TgIsa 61:1 begins with an addition "the prophet said" indicating that the speaker is not the Messiah but the prophet himself who foresees כליל.

From chapter 5 onwards the Isaiah Targum begins a new more concrete theme of the punishment of the sinners. References to the armies of gentiles are found and they will realize the judgment of God against his people. The song of the vineyard in TgIsa 5:1-7 is introduced by an addition that Israel "*is like a vineyard, the seed of Abraham, my friend.*" This is an allusion to Isa 41:8 which promises a new beginning to Israel. But in TgIsa 5 the vineyard will be destroyed, the Shekinah of God will be taken away and the enemy army will be sent against it. It is emphasized that in the middle of the invasion of the enemy army God will distinguish between the righteous and the sinners (TgIsa 5:30): "And he will *thunder* against it at that *time* like the roaring of the sea, *so that even if the wicked seek help from the inhabitants of* the land, *he has brought* distress *and breaking upon them, but the righteous that are in that hour will be hidden from the evil.*" The question is how the meturgeman understood that this protection of the righteous would be realized at a time of enemy invasion?

In a study on the ideology of the Book of Isaiah I suggested that Sennacherib's invasion in Isaiah 36-37 plays an important role in the overall structure of the book.[48] It seems to me that the meturgeman was aware of the existence of many internal connections between Isaiah 36-37 and Isaiah 1-35. This indicates that the Assyrian invasion was a paradigmatic event which will implement the judgement of God against sinners. In order to illustrate this, we may mention some essential links which the meturgeman discerned between Isaiah 36-37 and other texts in Isaiah 1-35.

We can begin the wording of TgIsa 37:32: "*By the Memra* of the LORD of hosts this will *be* accomplish*ed.*" The Hebrew text here is identical with the end of Isa 9:6 and even that text is translated word for word in the Isaiah Targum. This means that the meturgeman saw an internal link between the "messianic" text in Isaiah 9:1-6 and Sennacherib's invasion in Isaiah 36-37.

TgIsa 37:32 is also interesting from another point of view. It contains a promise to the righteous: "*...* for out of Jerusalem shall go forth a remnant *of the righteous,* and out of *the* Mount *of* Zion a survival *of those who uphold the law.*" This indicates that the survival of Jerusalem during the time of Hezekiah was seen by the meturgeman as the typological salvation of the righteous who will keep the Torah of God. The Torah plays an important role also in TgIsa 9:5-6 which renders the four Hebrew titles of the royal child so that the first three concern the Lord and only the fourth the Messiah (TgIsa 9:3-6):

---

[48] A. Laato, *About Zion I Will Not be Silent: The Book of Isaiah as an Ideological Unity* (ConBOT 44; Stockholm: Almqvist & Wiksell International 1998).

3 For *you have removed* the yoke of his *mastery* and the *rule* of his *tribulation, the ruler* who was *subjugating* him *is* broken as on the day of Midian. 4 For *all their dealing is with wickedness; they are defiled with sins, even as* a garment *kneaded* in blood *whose stain marks are not cleansed from it, just as there is no use for it except to be burned in the fire. Therefore the Gentiles who are strong as the* fire *will come upon them and kill them.* 5 *The prophet said to the house of David,* For to us a child has been born, to us a son has been given; and *he has taken the law* upon *himself to keep it,* and his name has been called *before the* Wonderful Counselor, *the* Mighty God, existing forever, *the messiah in whose days* peace *will increase upon us.*[49] 6 *Great pride will belong to those who perform the law,* and for *those who keep* peace there will be no end, upon the throne of David and upon his kingdom, to establish it and to *build* it with judgment and with *virtue* from this time forth and forever. *By* the *Memra* of the LORD of hosts this will *be* done.

According to Levey, it is possible that the meturgeman understood the passage as referring to Hezekiah (bSanh 94a; RuthR 7:2; GenR 97) because perfect tenses are used so that the reference is to a child who has already been born.[50] The view that Isa 9:5-6 reports the birth of Hezekiah is common in rabbinical writings which also emphasize Hezekiah's eagerness to instigate Torah studies (CantR 4:8,3).

TgIsa 9:3 refers to the day of Midian (already in the MT) which will occur in Judah when its oppressor will be annihilated. The same imagery of the day of Midian is used in TgIsa 10:25-34 (already in the MT) and in this text denotes the armies of Sennacherib which will be destroyed before the Messiah:

26 And the LORD of hosts will *bring upon him* a *stroke,* as when he struck Midian at the *cleft* of Oreb; and his *stroke will pass from you as the mastery*

---

[49] מְשִׁיחָא דִשְׁלָמָא יִסְגֵי עֲלָנָא בְּיוֹמוֹהִי.

[50]Levey, *The Text and I* 110-111. Chilton (*The Isaiah Targum* 21) translates in TgIsa 9:5: "for to us a child is born, to us a son is given; and he will accept the law ... and his name will be called ..." but because Aramaic perfect tenses have been used here I follow Levey (*The Text and I* 111-112) who translates here the passage in the English perfect. It is worth noting that Chilton earlier (*Glory of Israel* 87) translated the passage in the English perfect.

of Pharaoh passed from you at the sea, *for prodigies are done for you as* in the manner of Egypt. 27 And it will come to pass in that time that his *stroke* will *pass* from you, and his yoke from your neck, *and the Gentiles will be shattered before the Messiah* ... 32 *While* the day *was* still *young and he had much time to enter, behold Sennacherib the king of Assyria came and* stood at Nob, *the city of the priests, opposite the wall of Jerusalem. He answered and said to his forces, 'Is not this Jerusalem, against which I stirred up all my armies? Behold it is fainter than all the fortresses of the peoples which I have suppressed with the strength of my hands.' He stood over it* shaking *his head, waving back and forth with* his hand *against* the mount *of the sanctuary which is in* Zion, *and against the courts which are in* Jerusalem. 33 Behold, the master *of the world,* the LORD of hosts *casts slaughter among his armies as grapes trodden in the press*; and the great in stature will be hewn down and the *strong will be humbled.* 34 And he will slay the *mighty men of his armies who make themselves mighty* with iron, and *his warriors* will *be cast on the land of Israel.*

This description of the destruction of the Assyrian army will then be presented in TgIsa 37:36. It is worth noting that the Assyrian hubris is depicted as rebellion against the Memra of the Lord (TgIsa 37:29) and the destruction of the Assyrian army is realized through the Memra of the Lord (TgIsa 37:32, 35). This Assyrian hubris against Memra is also reported elsewhere in the Isaiah Targum. A good example is TgIsa 10:5-19 where the Assyrian king boasts and will receive punishment from the Memra of the Lord.[51] TgIsa 30:27-33 is another text which mentions the destruction of the Assyrian army by the Memra of the Lord. Moreover TgIsa 31:8-9 speaks of the destruction of Assyrians by the Memra of the Lord. Finally, we can mention TgIsa 14:24-27 which describes the destruction of the Assyrian army in Judah – apparently referring to the events in Isaiah 36-37.

Thus the interpretation of Isaiah 9-10 in Targum Jonathan contains an idea that Sennacherib's invasion was a typos for a coming

---

[51]The pride of the Assyrian king in TgIsa 10:5-15 and Rabshakeh's speech in TgIsa 36 are good parallels already in the Masorretic text.

eschatological struggle, Gog and Magog.[52] There is one text where the name Gog appears, in TgIsa 33. The text speaks of the invasion of Judah and of Jerusalem by an enemy army. In this invasion, the sinners of Jerusalem are annihilated (TgIsa 33:14) while the righteous will find refuge in the city of the Shekinah of the Lord (TgIsa 33:15-18). As the Assyrian army was shattered before the Messiah Hezekiah so will the enemy army of Gog be destroyed in the messianic period. We have a neat text in the rabbinical writings where this typolocial comparison between Sennacherib and Gog, on the one hand, and Hezekiah and the Messiah, on the other are presented (bSanh 94a):

> *Of the increase of his government and peace there shall be no end.* R. Tanhum said: Bar Kappara expounded in Sepphoris, Why is every *mem* in the middle of a word open, whilst this is closed?—The Holy One, blessed be He, wished to appoint Hezekiah as the Messiah, and Sennacherib as Gog and Magog; whereupon the Attribute of Justice said before the Holy One, blessed be He; 'Sovereign of the Universe! If Thou did not make David the Messiah, who uttered so many hymns and psalms before Thee, wilt Thou appoint Hezekiah as such, who did not hymn Thee in spite of all these miracles which Thou wroughtest for him?' Therefore it (the *mem*) was closed. Straightway the earth exclaimed: 'Sovereign of the Universe! Let me utter song before Thee instead of this righteous man (Hezekiah), and make him the Messiah.' So it broke into song before Him, as it is written, *From the uttermost part of the earth have we heard songs, even glory to the righteous.* Then the Prince of the Universe said to Him: 'Sovereign of the Universe! It (the earth) hath fulfilled Thy desire (for songs of praise) on behalf of this righteous man.' But a heavenly Voice cried out, *'It is my secret, it is my secret.'* To which the prophet rejoined, *'Woe is me, woe is me*: how long (must we wait)?' The heavenly Voice (again) cried out, *'The treacherous dealers have dealt treacherously; yea, the treacherous dealers have dealt very treacherously'*: which Raba—others say, R. Isaac—interpreted: until there come spoilers, and spoilers of the spoilers.

---

[52]The interpretation of Isaiah 10-11 as referring to the eschatological battle against the enemies of Israel is reminiscent of the pesher interpretations at Qumran (see 4Q161 and 4Q285). The evidence from Qumran indicates that such an interpretation of these chapters in the Book of Isaiah is deeply rooted in Jewish traditions.

Assuming that the Isaiah Targum describes the annihilation of the enemy army during the reign of Hezekiah we can also understand the "heretic" viewpoint that perhaps Hezekiah was the promised Messiah as indicated in Isa 9:5-6 (bSanh 99a):

> R. Hillel (a brother of Juda II) said: There shall be no Messiah for Isaiah, because they have already enjoyed him in the days of Hezekiah. R. Joseph said: May God forgive him (for saying so). Now, when did Hezekiah flourish? During the first Temple. Yet Zechariah, prophesying in the days of the second, proclaimed, *Rejoice greatly O daughter of Zion, shout, O daughter of Jerusalem; behold thy king cometh unto thee; he is just, and having salvation; lowly and riding upon an ass, and upon a colt the foal of an ass.*

But the Isaiah Targum seems to indicate that Hezekiah is a typos for the coming Messiah. Therefore TgIsaiah 11 continues the theme of TgIsaiah 9-10 by describing the appearance of the Messiah in the eschatological age. The fourth title of the royal child in TgIsa 9:5 parallels the translation of another messianic passage in TgIsa 11:6: *"In the days of the Messiah of Israel shall peace increase in the land*[53]." Thus even this detail indicates that Hezekiah was regarded as a typos for the coming Messiah. It is also worth noting that the eschatological thanksgiving in the messianic era is presented in Isaiah 12. It was precisely the lack of such thanksgiving which, according to bSanh 94a, prevented Hezekiah's recognition as the Messiah. This eschatological thanksgiving speaks of the consolation of Jerusalem, the loyalty to the Torah of God, many prodigies which the Lord will realize and the presence of the Shekinah of God in the midst of the people.

The defeat of the Pharaoh of Egypt (TgIsa 10:26) and that of Sennacherib (TgIsa 10:32) are thus interpreted as prefiguring the eschatological destruction of the enemy armies before Jerusalem. Likewise TgIsa 27:1 also regards the conquest of Pharaoh and of Sennacherib as typoi for the eschatological destruction of the coming evil

---

[53]ביומוהי דמשיחא דישראל יסגי שלמא בארעא

king (apparently identical with Gog): "In that *time* the LORD with his *great* and *strong* and hard sword will punish *the king who exalts himself like Pharaoh the first king, and the king who prides himself like Sennacherib the second king*, and he will slay *the king who is strong as* the dragon that is in the sea." TgIsa 52:4-6 is also significant, telling of the oppression of Israel by Egypt and Assyria and how the Lord and his Memra will appear against the enemies of the people of God.

Another text in the Book of Isaiah which has been interpreted as referring to Hezekiah in the rabbinical writings is the Immanuel prophecy in Isa 7:14-17. There is no clear evidence in Targum Isaiah that the Immanuel sign there has been interpreted as concerning Hezekiah. TgIsa 8:8 adds the word "Jerusalem" when it envisages the Assyrian flood as reaching to the neck and replaces the MT expression "your land O Immanuel" with "your land, O *Israel*." TgIsa 8:6 reads: "Because this people despised *the kingdom of the house of David which leads them gently* as the waters of Shiloah that flow gently, and *are pleased with* Rezin and the son of Remaliah." This implies that during the reign of Ahaz (Rezin and Pekah were Ahaz' enemies) the reign of the House of David was favourably regarded. This may well support the view that the meturgeman interpreted the Immanuel sign as a promise of the coming Davidic king, Hezekiah, and TgIsa 8:5-8 is a prophecy of doom against the people which does not put its trust in this plan of salvation. Therefore the Lord will demonstrate his power by allowing Assyria to attack Judah during the reign of Hezekiah and then destroying this enemy. TgIsa 8:14 warns the people because "*those of the house of Israel have been divided against those of the house of Judah.*" This expression reiterates the theme of TgIsa 7:17, revealing that the Immanuel sign signifies an internal division among the people of Israel. Such a division may take place when the new, pious royal child, Hezekiah, is born. He did not follow his father's (Ahaz') ungodly religious policy of destroying the Torah studies in the land (GenR 42:3; y.Sanh 10:2; b.Sanh 103b).

After the account of the destruction of the Assyrian army in TgIsa 14:24-27 follows a text which was probably regarded by the meturgeman as referring to Hezekiah. It is directed against Philistea and in verse 29 the meturgeman has inserted a significant addition which indicates that the coming scourge of Philistea will appear from among the sons of Jesse:[54] "Rejoice not, all you *Philistines*, because *the ruler* who was *subjugating* you is broken, for from *the sons of the sons of Jesse the Messiah* will come forth, and his *deeds* will be *among you* as a *wounding serpent*." In the context, i.e., in TgIsa 14:32, it is stated that "the LORD has founded Zion, and in her the *needy* of his people will *trust and rejoice*." Such an association of the advent of the Messiah with the salvation of Zion is attested also in TgIsaiah 10-11.

In rabbinical writings there is an enigmatic utterance of Johanan ben Zakkai according to which Hezekiah will appear in the future (bBer 28b): "At the moment of his departure he said to them: Remove the vessels so that they shall not become unclean, and prepare a throne for Hezekiah the king of Judah who is coming." In the light of what we have said above it seems reasonable to assume that Johanan ben Zakkai's utterance is connected with the great eschatological drama which is depicted in the Isaiah Targum. Hezekiah is a typos for the coming Messiah, and the destruction of the Assyrian army in his days prefigures the destruction of the army of Gog. In bSanh 98b different messianic names appear, all of them being justified by a biblical passage. One of these names is Menachem, the son of Hezekiah. This name is somewhat surprising because Menachem is known as one of the most evil kings in Judah (2 Kings 21). However, if Hezekiah has been seen as typos for the coming Messiah then the name of his son could well have been interpreted in a new light, in this case in conjunction with Lam 1:16 which says: "The comforter who should refresh my soul is far from me." The point at issue here is that the consolation of Jerusalem is a central concept in the Isaiah Targum. In TgIsa 1:24 we read: "*The city of Jerusalem I am about to comfort* (לנחמותה) ..." The first messianic text in the Isaiah Targum contains the concept "*the consolations* (נחמת) *of*

---

[54]So Levey, *The Text and I* 117-118.

Jerusalem" (TgIsa 4:3). So even though bSanh 98b refers to Lam 1:16 there is good reason to argue that the name Menachem is in fact closely connected with the content of the Isaiah Targum. The original meaning of Menachem was "the one who gives consolation to Jerusalem" and it was intimately linked with the role of Hezekiah in the Isaiah Targum.

Another text in Isaiah 13-23 which (in addition to Isa 14:28-32) is interpreted in terms of the Messiah is Isaiah 16 which already in the MT includes a reference to the House of David. Now it seems that the reference is no longer to Hezekiah but rather to the eschatological Messiah. TgIsa 16:1 presents a creative reinterpretation inasmuch as the Moabites must submit to the yoke of the Messiah: "*They will offer tribute to the Messiah of Israel who prevailed over the one as the* desert, the mount of the *congregation* of Zion." The Lord will send the gentiles against the proud princes of Moab (TgIsa 16:6-11), but in the messianic age these plunderers will be destroyed and even Moabites can find protection under the shadow of the Messiah: "When the *one who distresses comes to an end*, the *plunderer* is *destroyed*, and *all those who were* trampling the land *come to an end, then the* throne *of the Messiah of Israel* will be established in *goodness* and he will sit on it in truth in the *city* of David, a judge and seeking judgment and *doing truth*" (TgIsa 16:4-5).

TgIsa 55:3-5 also describes the messianic kingdom. TgIsa 55:5 has an intratextual reference to TgIsa 16:1, saying that foreign peoples will bring their tribute. TgIsa 16:1 reads "*They will offer tribute to the Messiah of Israel* (יהון מסקי מסין למשיחא דישראל)" which is a good parallel to the expression in TgIsa 55:5: "Behold, *people* that you know not shall *serve you*, and people that knew you not shall run *to offer tribute* to you (לאסקא לך מסין)."

A new perspective to the messianic expectations is presented in TgIsa 43:10. The passage does not mention the coming Messiah but refers to his pre-existence. He is already now the Lord's witness: "You are witnesses *before me*, says the LORD, and my servant *the Messiah with* whom I *am pleased*, that you might know and believe *before* me and

159

understand that I am He. *I am he that was from the beginning, even the ages of the ages are mine*, and there *is* no God *besides me.*" According to Chilton, such an idea of pre-existence is of an Amoraic origin.[55] Furthermore he argues that the political role of the Messiah is deprecated in 59:16 and 63:5, 9. It is alleged that no man was seen as righteous before the Lord, so that the Lord himself was forced to help his people. Chilton remarks that even the messianic interpretation of 66:7 (*"her king will be revealed"*) was augmented by an Amoraic meturgeman with the addition of the slogan in v 9: "I, *God, created the world from creation*, says the LORD; I *created every man*; I *scattered them among the peoples*; *I am also about to gather your exiles*, says your God."[56] However, it is questionable whether we can elicit so much from these texts. After all the MT of 59:16; 63:5, 9 already emphasize concepts similar to those attested in the Targum translations. The Targum interpretation seems rather to be a rhetorical recognition of the Lord's sovereignty and faithfulness contra human treachery. The slogan in 66:9 also stresses the sovereignty of Yhwh and should not be read as disparaging the messianic ideas. We could also observe that if the aim of an Amoraic meturgeman was to belittle the political status of the Messiah, why did he not alter the status of the Messiah in Tannaitic sayings as, for example, in Isa 10:27-11:16?

The messianic era and the Torah observance may be related even in TgIsa 42:1-9. In many manuscripts the word "Messiah" has been added after the word "servant" in 42:1 but it is lacking in B.M. 2211 (on

---

[55]Chilton, *Glory of Israel* 90-91; idem, *The Isaiah Targum* 85. Concerning the view that pre-existence was not mentioned by the Tannaim, see J. Klausner, *The Messianic Idea in Israel from Its Beginning to the Completion of the Mishnah* (New York: Macmillan 1956) 460. However, Klausner's opinion that the idea of the pre-existence of the Messiah was not represented in 1 Enoch 48:3 is problematic. For this see A. Laato, *A Star Is Rising: The Historical Development of the Old Testament Royal Ideology and the Rise of the Jewish Messianic Expectations* (International Studies in Formative Christianity and Judaism, Atlanta: Scholars Press 1997) 387-388.

[56]Chilton, *Isaiah Targum* 115, 121.

which Sperber's edition is based). Even without this addition TgIsa 42:1-7 can be interpreted in terms of the Messiah. The servant establishes justice (TgIsa 42:1-3; cf., TgIsa 11:4 which refers to the Messiah) and brings to pass salvation by breaking the enemies of the people (TgIsa 42:7; cf., TgIsa 10:27; 14:29; 16:1; 53:11 which are interpreted in terms of the Messiah). The servant in TgIsa 42:1-7 also teaches the Torah (TgIsa 42:3-4, 7) which illustrates the character of the Messiah in TgIsa 9:5 ("*he will accept the law* upon *himself to keep it*") and TgIsaiah 53.

In the MT, Isaiah 49:1-6 is a close parallel to Isa 42:1-9. Therefore, also the Targum interpretation of Isa 49:1-6 emphasizes ideas similar to those in Isa 42:1-9. The faithful servant is thought to be a group of loyal Israelites who will bring God's people into the right cultic service of God. Isa 49:3 is a literal translation of the MT which preserves the word "Israel". Thus the Servant is Israel. That this Servant is a group of Israelites becomes clear from the beginning of Isa 49:6 where the translation uses the plural expression "you *are called my* servants" but at the end of the verse the reading is again in the singular (apparently in a collective sense): "I will give you as a light to *peoples* (עממין; the MT has גויים) that my salvation may be to the ends of the earth."

Abraham is portrayed as the father of the Israelites who are faithful adherents of the Torah. There is an interesting tendency in the Isaiah Targum to prefer the Abraham interpretation in the passages which modern scholars interpret in terms of the Persian king, Cyrus. Isa 41:2 has been understood as referring to the Lord's summons of Abraham from the East to take possession of the Land of Canaan:[57] "Who *brought Abraham openly* from *the* east, *a select one of* righteousness *in truth*? He *brought him to* his *place, handed over peoples* before him and *shattered* kings; he *cast the slain* like dust *before* his sword, *he pursued them* like chaff *before* his bow." This interpretation is apparently derived from Isa 41:8-13 where reference is made to Abraham. Another "Cyrus passage"

---

[57]The Abraham interpretation is also attested in the rabbinical literature: bBaba Batra 15a; Gen R 2:3; 43:3; cf., also Num R 2:13. See further Billerbeck 1922, 49; 1928, 425.

which has been interpreted in terms of Abraham is 48:15-16: "I, even I, *by my Memra decreed a covenant with Abraham your father* and *exalted* him, I brought him *to the land of my Shekinah's house* and *I* prospered his way. Draw near to *my Memra*, hear this: from *the* beginning I have not spoken in secret, from the time *the Gentiles separated from my fear, from* there I *brought Abraham near to my service*." On the other hand, in the Isaiah Targum, verse 41:25 is interpreted as referring to the gentile king: "I *will bring a king openly who is strong as* the north *wind*, and he *will* come *as the going forth* of the sun *in its might* from the east, and *I will make him mighty* by my name: he will come *and trample the* rulers *of the Gentiles as those who trample the dust*, as *the* potter *who kneads the* clay." Apparently the Cyrus mentioned in TgIsa 44:28; 45:1 is a typos for this pagan king in TgIsa 41:25.

We have argued that there are four exegetic traditions in the Isaiah Targum which are connected with the messianic interpretation of Isaiah 53: *First*, in TgIsa 1-35 we can find many internal connections with TgIsa 36-37, which indicates that the meturgeman sees a relation between Hezekiah and "messianic" texts (in particularly, TgIsa 9:5-6; 10:27). *Second*, Hezekiah and the miraculous rescue of Jerusalem from the clutches of Sennacherib is a typos for an eschatological war when Gog and his armies will be defeated by the Messiah. Moreover, Hezekiah is a typos for the Messiah by disseminating the Torah observance. There are also references to the presence of the Shekinah in Jerusalem when Jerusalem was protected against the invasion of the Assyrian army. The *third* exegetic perspective is that the Servant of TgIsa 49:1-6 denotes the faithful Israelites who will bring all other Israelites to the right cultic service of God. *Finally*, we have seen that even Abraham is presented as God's servant whom God protected. This goodness of God toward Abraham is a typos for the coming salvation.

All four traditions probably flourished during the Tannaitic period. Some of them were also known to non-Jews who learnt these interpretive perspectives from Jews attending the synagogal service.

Indeed, Targums represent the prevalent interpretive traditions as Chilton comments: "The Prophets' Targum, both to the Former and the Latter Prophets, has received renewed attention as the best source for the explication of Scripture in synagogues during periods of early Judaism and Rabbinic Judaism."[58] The association of Hezekiah with the Immanuel prophecy is well attested in Justin's *Dialogue with Trypho*.[59] The collective perspective on the Servant figure is mentioned by Origen in *Contra Celsum* where some Jews interpreted Isaiah 53 as referring to righteous Jews who must suffer. This collective perspective is attested in TgIsaiah 53 without any reference to vicarious sufferings. Of course, we cannot assume that Targum interpretations were consistent in late antiquity.

Conclusions

After this survey of the messianic character of the Targum Jonathan of Isaiah we are now ready to propose some conclusions. We have seen that the messianic interpretation in TgIsaiah 53 follows typical patterns in the Targum Jonathan. The content of the messianic expectation is straight-forward. The question is, however, why the meturgeman chose Isaiah 53 for his messianic interpretation. It is clear that there were other possibilities. In particular, the collective interpretation which is attested in TgIsa 49:1-13 and well documented in pre-Targumic Jewish interpretations could have been in accord with TgIsaiah 53. It seems obvious that the Masoretic text of Isaiah 53 does not lend itself to the description of the Messiah according to the model presented in Targums. Indeed – as emphasized by Churgin – the meturgeman frequently interprets the MT too freely and in many points his vocalizations and explanations do not receive support from other early translations, apart from the Masoretic tradition. The Targum interpretation of Isaiah 53 also

---

[58]Chilton, "Targum Jonathan of the Prophets I," 892.

[59]*Dial* 43.8; 67.1; 71.3.

differs from those preserved in the Talmud and early midrashim (see sect. 9). Although it is an exaggeration to say that the main aim of the passage was to find fault with the Christian interpretation, it is difficult to imagine that the meturgeman was unfamiliar with the Christian use of Isaiah 53's narrative as referring to the vicarious suffering and death of the Messiah.[60] We may well assume that Jewish Christians visited synagogues and the messianic interpretation of Isaiah 53 neatly formulated the simple questions posed by the hearers: here in the synagogue we do not accept the Christian view of the fate of the Messiah but adopt the traditional Jewish approach. The author who created the Targum interpretation of Isaiah 53 used imaginative and wonderful intellectual maneuvers when the suffering Servant became the victorious Messiah. The main aim was to teach Jewish messianic expectation to hearers, not to refute the Christian interpretation. But by using one of the Christian key-texts for the suffering Messiah the meturgeman was willing to provoke his hearers. Whosoever believes that the proposed interpretation is controversial will be revealed and excommunicated.

The discussion in this section has also made clear that we can exclude the translation of Isaiah 53 in the Targum Jonathan as reflecting a messianic interpretation of the suffering servant before the time of Jesus. So the hypothesis that TgIsaiah 53 once contained the concept of a vicarious and atoning suffering and death of the Messiah is irrelevant.

---

[60]Cf., M. Hengel, *The Cross of the Son of God Containing The Son of God, Crucifixion, The Atonement* (London: SCM Press 1986) 245-246.

7 Isaiah 53 in the New Testament

The aim of this section is to survey how Isaiah 53 has been interpreted in the New Testament, and how the atonement theology associated with messianic expectation can be explained as originating from that chapter. The index in Nestle-Aland's edition reveals that the texts of Isaiah 40-66 are often quoted in the Greek New Testament. Isa 52:13-53:12 is one of the most frequently cited texts therein. Direct quotations occur in Rom 15:21 (Isa 52:15); Joh 12:38; Rom 10:16 (Isa 53:1); Mt 8:17; 1 Peter 2:24 (Isa 53:4); 1 Peter 2:6 (Isa 53:6); Acts 8:32-33 (Isa 53:7-8); 1 Peter 2:22; Rev 14:5 (Isa 53:9); Lk 22:37; 1 Peter 2:24 (Isa 53:12).

The seven direct New Testament quotations from Isaiah 53 can be divided into four groups: 1) the healing ministry of Jesus in Mt 8:17; 2) the passion of Jesus in Lk 22:37; in Acts 8:32-33; in Rom 10:16; 3) the preaching of the gospel to the gentiles in Rom 15:21 and 4) moral exhortation in 1 Pet 2:18-25.[1] In addition to this list several allusions and echoes from Isaiah 53 can be found.[2] This evidence has been variously

---

[1] Cf., K.D. Litwak, "The Use of Quotations from Isaiah 52:13-53:12 in the New Testament," *JETS* 26 (1983) 385-394. Litwak divides passages into three different groups, arguing that Mt 8:17 is related to the passion.

[2] For example, "to bear the sins of many" (εἰς τὸ πολλῶν ἀνενεγκεῖν ἁμαρτίας) in Hebr 9:28 is apparently related to the Septuagint version of Isa 53:12: "he bore the sins of many" (αὐτὸς ἁμαρτίας πολλῶν ἀνήνεγκεν). John the Baptist says of Jesus "Here is the Lamb of God who takes away the sin of the world" (Joh 1:29). This is probably also from Isaiah 53 where the Servant of Yhwh is equated with the Lamb. These allusions and echoes are documented well in W. Zimmerli & J.Jeremias, *The Servant of God* (SBT 20, London SCM Press 1965) 88-99; O. Betz, "Jesus and Isaiah 53," in: W.H. Bellinger & W.R. Farmer, *Jesus and the Suffering Servant: Isaiah 53 and Christian Origins* (Harrisburg: Trinity Press International 1998) 70-87; P. Stuhlmacher, "Isaiah 53 in the Gospels and Acts," in: B. Janowski & P. Stuhlmacher (eds), *The Suffering Servant: Isaiah 53 in Jewish and Christian Sources* (Grand Rapids: Eerdmans 2004) 147-162; O. Hofius, "The Fourth Servant Song in the New Testament Letters," in: B. Janowski & P. Stuhlmacher (eds), *The Suffering*

treated by exegetes. There are scholars who regard this evidence as proof that the historical Jesus identified himself with the suffering and dying servant in Isaiah 53.[3] However, Hooker and Bultmann *inter alia* argued that Jesus never identified himself with the Servant of Yhwh. There are only two quotations from Isaiah 53 in the synoptic Gospels. Mt 8:17 is the evangelist's comment on Jesus' healing ministry and not a saying of Jesus. Lk 22:37 is the only passage where Jesus quotes Isaiah 53 with regard to himself[4] but this is a part of the passion history and, according to Hooker and Bultmann, not derived from the historical Jesus.[5]

We must give credit to Hooker and Bultmann for their evaluation. There is no clear evidence that the historical Jesus ever described himself as the servant in Isaiah 53. He never used the title "Servant" and there is no explicit logion of Jesus where he identifies himself with the Servant of Isaiah. Nevertheless, the discussion concerning Jesus' self-understanding as a suffering messianic figure is not limited to Isaiah 53.

Servant: Isaiah 53 in Jewish and Christian Sources (Grand Rapids: Eerdmans 2004) 163-188.

[3]See, e.g., Betz, "Jesus and Isaiah 53" and Stuhlmacher, "Isaiah 53 in the Gospel and Acts."

[4]Isaiah 53 plays an important role in the soteriology of Luke as an explanation for the atonement death of Jesus. For this see U. Mittmann-Richert, *Der Sühnetod des Gottesknecht: Jesaja 53 im Lukasevangelium* (WUNT 220, Tübingen: Mohr Siebeck 2008).

[5]M.D. Hooker, *Jesus and the Servant* (London: SPCK 1959); idem, "Did the use of Isaiah 53 to Interpret His Mission Begin with Jesus?" in: W.H. Bellinger & W.R. Farmer, *Jesus and the Suffering Servant: Isaiah 53 and Christian Origins* (Harrisburg: Trinity Press International 1998) 88-103; R. Bultmann, *Theologie des Neuen Testament* (Tübingen: Mohr 1965) 31-33. Note also W. Grimm, *Weil ich dich liebe: Die Verkündigung Jesu und Deuterojesaja* (ANTJ 1, Frankfurt: Lang 1976). Grimm (pp. 306-307) gives a summary and observes that Isaiah 53 played a role in the proclamation of Jesus, but nevertheless has reservations (p. 306): "Doch ist sogleich anzumerken, dass 2 Anspielungen (Lk. 11,22; 10,23f) einen erfolgreichen Knecht voraussetzen und einige andere, die auf das Leiden des Knechts reflektieren, entweder nicht mit Sicherheit jesuanisch sind (Mk. 2,20; Lk. 22,37; 23,34.39-43) oder aber gar nicht ausschliesslich Jes. 53 meinen (Mk. 8,33; 10,45b; 14,8.24.35f; Lk. 22,53b)."

After all, there are many other individual expectations in the Old Testament that can be considered. In particular, two characters play a central role in Jesus' teaching and symbolic actions, viz. the Son of Man and the messianic figure of Zechariah 9-14.[6] As we have seen in previous chapters Isaiah 53 became a key-text for the understanding of Jewish martyrology. This being the case, if Jesus spoke of his coming martyrdom in terms of the Son of Man or the messianic figure of Zechariah 9-14, then Isaiah 53 may loom behind the scene. And this has no bearing on whether or not Jesus explicitly claimed to be the servant in Isaiah 53. He could well have considered that Isaiah 53 describes righteous sufferers in general terms and uses its imagery to depict the Son of Man as an example.[7]

The idea of the suffering of the Son of Man can be perceived in Daniel 7 because the chapter describes the sufferings of the holy people under the pressure of the fourth and most evil kingdom (Dan 7:25): "He will speak against the Most High and oppress his holy people and try to change the set times and the laws. The holy people will be delivered into his hands for a time, times and half a time." Because the Son of Man can be regarded as the king of the community of the holy people it is reasonable to infer that he too must suffer. So that even though the sufferings of the Son of Man are not reported *expressis verbis* in Daniel 7 it is possible that their nature can be envisaged.[8]

---

[6]Evans observed that it has been difficult for scholars to take a stand on Jesus's own self-understanding because he has been identified with so many eschatological figures in the New Testament. See C.A. Evans, "Prophet, Sage, Healer, Messiah, and Martyr: Types and Identities of Jesus," in: T. Holmén & S.E. Porter (eds), *Handbook for the Study of the Historical Jesus Vol 2: The Study of Jesus* (Leiden: Brill 2011) 1217-1243.

[7]Note, in particular, Stuhlmacher, "Isaiah 53 in the Gospels and Acts" where he argues that Isaiah 53 looms behind Jesus' teaching.

[8]Concerning this see J. Thurén, *Markuksen evankeliumi* (Helsinki: SLEY-Kirjat 1996).

The Origin of the Concept of the Suffering Messiah

In this subsection my aim is not to contradict the view that Isaiah 53 has already been relevant to Jesus. However, because Jesus never described himself in the synoptic gospels as the servant of Yhwh it seems reasonable to start from another perspective when we deal with his self-understanding. The best starting-point comprises his two symbolic actions when he invoked Jerusalem. He fulfilled Zech 9:9-10 and 14:21 and, as we have seen, these texts are closely linked to the theme of Isaiah 53 (sect. 2).[9] I shall discuss how these Deutero-Zecharian texts are related to the Son of Man utterances and ask how these texts reflect the idea of the Suffering Messiah in the New Testament.[10]

All the gospels report that Jesus rode to Jerusalem on an ass, and we may assume that this event was linked to the prophecy in Zech 9:9-10. Another symbolic action which (according to the Synoptic Gospels) followed immediately was the cleansing of the Temple. This action is best explained by Zech 14:20-21 where it is said that the Temple will be

---

[9]It is worth noting that we cannot assume that our historical interpretation of Zechariah 9-14 as presented in sect. 2 was accepted in antiquity. The messianic interpretation of Zechariah 9-14 may well have sought new trends in the proclamation of the gospel and our proposal in this section is that Jesus associated it with the Jewish martyr theology (sect. 3).

[10]Scholars have long disputed whether or not Jesus predicted his own death. See, e.g., the survey of research in H. Haag, *Der Gottesknecht bei Deuterojesaja* (EdF 233, Darmstadt: Wissenschaftliche Buchgesellschaft 1985) 66-78; N.A. Dahl, "Messianic Ideas and Crucifixion of Jesus," in: J.H. Charlesworth (ed), *The First Princeton Symposium on Judaic and Christian Origins. The Messiah: Developments in Early Judaism and Christianity* (Minneapolis: Fortress 1992) 382-403. Concerning Jesus' messianic self-understanding and the passion history in Mark see M. Hengel, "Jesus, the Messiah of Israel. The Debate about the 'Messianic Mission' of Jesus." In: B. Chilton & C.A. Evans, *Authenticating the Activities of Jesus* (Leiden: Brill 1999), 323-349.

holy place and no merchants will be there.[11] In the context of Zechariah this implies that the Temple will be the place of worship for all peoples (Zech 14:16-19), and Jesus' quotation of Isa 56:7 befits this occasion because according to it, the Temple will be a house of universal prayer. These two symbolic actions of Jesus have traditionally been regarded as historical[12] although some scholars have voiced doubts.[13] The two symbolic actions just before Easter embody the significant aspects of the self-understanding of the historical Jesus which pertain to his logia of the Son of Man.

Because Jesus executed the two symbolic actions mentioned in Zechariah 9-14 there is reason to believe that his messianic self-understanding was related to these texts. According to Zechariah 9-14, Jerusalem and the Temple will be sanctified and become the center of universal worship (Zech 9:10; 14:16-19). This universalism closely connected with the kingdom of God is a favourite theme in the teaching

---

[11]LXX reads in Zech 14:21 Χαναναῖος but the Hebrew word כְּנַעֲנִי is open to other interpretations, too. It can mean "merchant" and this interpretation has been taken in the Vulgate (*mercator*) and the Targum (*taggarā'*). In b.Pes 50a there are sayings which support the identification between *kĕna'ăni* and merchant by answering the question: "How do we know that *kena'ani* connotes a merchant (*taggār*)?"

[12]See, for example, the following scholars who represent different viewpoints on the historical Jesus: E.P. Sanders, *The Historical Figure of Jesus* (Allen Lane: The Penguin 1993) 253-264; A.M. Schwemer, in M. Hengel & A.M. Schwemer, *Der messianische Anspruch Jesu und die Anfänge der Christologie* (WMANT 138, Tübingen: Mohr Siebeck 2003) 219-223 and M. Goulder "Jesus without Q," in: T. Holmén & S.E. Porter (eds), *Handbook for the Study of the Historical Jesus Vol 2: The Study of Jesus* (Leiden: Brill 2011) 1287-1311, esp. 1305. Concerning the cleansing of the Temple see, in particular, J. Ådna, *Jesu Stellung zum Tempel: Die Tempelaktion und das Tempelwort als Ausdruck seiner messianischen Sendung* (WMANT 119, Tübingen: Mohr Siebeck 2000).

[13]See, for example, R.W. Funk, R.W. Hoover, and the Jesus Seminar, *The Five Gospels: The Search for the Authentic Words of Jesus* (New York: Scribner 1996); G. Lüdemann, *Jesus after Two Thousand Years: What He Really Said and Did* (London: SCM 2000); J. Dunn, *Jesus Remembered* (Christianity in the Making, vol. 1; Grand Rapids: Eerdmans 2003) esp. 642, 649. Dunn says that the ride into Jerusalem was historical but hardly a conscious attempt to fulfil Zech 9:9-10.

of Jesus. According to Zech 14:9, the kingdom of God will be manifest throughout the earth: "Yhwh will be king over the whole earth. On that day Yhwh will be one, and his name will be one." Jesus saw himself as an important eschatological mediator in this renewal of the world. When riding on an ass to Jerusalem he was aware that he carried a vital message to both Jerusalem and the world (Zech 9:9-10):

> Rejoice greatly, Daughter Zion!
> Shout, Daughter Jerusalem!
> See, your king comes to you,
> righteous and victorious,
> lowly and riding on a donkey,
> on a colt, the foal of a donkey.
> I will take away the chariots from Ephraim
> and the warhorses from Jerusalem,
> and the battle bow will be broken.
> He will proclaim peace to the nations.
> His rule will extend from sea to sea
> and from the River to the ends of the earth.

Zechariah 9-14 warns that the goal of this universal divine kingdom centered around Jerusalem cannot be realized without suffering and death. In three texts, Zech 11:4-14; 13:7-19 and 12:10, it is implied that the Messiah riding to Jerusalem must be prepared to suffer. Responsibility for the rejection and death (by piercing) of the Messiah is laid on the religious leaders and the House of David as is indicated in Zech 12:11-13. The very fact that the thirty shekels of silver – the payment which should be rendered to a slave according to Ex 21:30 – will be thrown back to the temple (Zech 11:13) proves that religious leaders are behind the rejection and "murder" of the Messiah.

According to the Gospel of Mark, Jesus began to reveal his future suffering and death to the disciples when they started their journey to the Passover Festival in Jerusalem (Mk 8:31-33; 9:30-32; 10:32-34). Although these texts in their present form are from post-Easter time they contain plausible historical information according to which Jesus spoke of his own death beforehand – something which can be seen in Mk 10:45

(see below). There are two details in the Gospels which should be considered when we evaluate Jesus' self-understanding of his coming suffering.

First, Jesus' words in the institution of Holy Communion are often regarded as authentic by scholars. They indicate his realisation that his death was imminent. The only feasible explanation of Jesus's words is derived from the Jewish martyr theology (sect. 3). Jesus thought that by giving his own life he could call upon God to intervene decisively in history. The Holy Communion was also a link with the great eschatological banquet in the world to come as is implicit in Luke's account (Lk 22:14-23). The Apostle Paul's version is reminiscent of Luke's (1 Cor 11:23-26) and he also sees a connection between the meal and the eschatological future which in Paul's kerygma corresponds to the second coming of Jesus: "For whenever you eat this bread and drink this cup, you proclaim the Lord's death until he comes." Religio-historical parallels can be found at Qumran where communal meals served as *typoi* for the coming eschatological banquet. Holy Communion was instituted according to a similar pattern, being the meal which will continue to be observed until the eschatological banquet be celebrated in the world to come.[14]

---

[14]Concerning the eschatological nature of the communal meals at Qumran see, in particular, L.H. Schiffman, *The Eschatological Community of the Dead Sea Scrolls* (SBL MS 38, Atlanta: Scholars Press 1989) 53-67. "These meals, conducted regularly as part of the present-age way of life of the sect, were preenactments of the final messianic banquet which the sectarians expected in the soon-to-come end of days. Again, the life of the sect in this world mirrored its dreams for the age to come" (p. 67); idem, *Reclaiming the Dead Sea Scrolls: The History of Judaism, the Background of Christianity, the lost Library of Qumran* (Philadelphia: The Jewish Publication Society 1994) 329-339. See further also J.D.G. Dunn, "Jesus, Table-Fellowship, and Qumran," in: J. Charlesworth (ed), *Jesus and the Dead Sea Scrolls* (The Anchor Bible Reference Library, New York: Doubleday 1992) 254-272.

The *second* detail in the Gospels which should be considered are Jesus' harsh words to Peter in Mk 8:33.[15] This saying is not easy to explain as a fabrication of the early Church where Peter was regarded as the principal apostle. If the story is not fictitious, then Jesus' statement to Peter can only be understood in the context provided by the Gospel: Jesus had predicted that he must go to Jerusalem and die. Peter attempted to avert this catastrophe by rebuking Jesus. Precisely at this point we may assume that Jesus introduced a new idea in the Jewish messianic alternatives (notice the plural). Here it is wise to remember what Collins writes about messianic options: that they "cannot be coined at will".[16] However, Peter's answer to Jesus implies that he experienced his own messianic expectations with which Jesus's saying about the suffering and death of the Son of Man is at odds. This indicates that the concept of the suffering and dying Messiah was difficult to accept for Peter – apparently because it was unknown in Judaisms (see sect. 5).

Zechariah 9-14 emphasize the close relationship between the Good Shepherd (Messiah) and God. When the Good Shepherd was rejected by the people the Lord states that they have also rejected him (Zech 11:13): "Throw it to the smelter—the handsome price at which they valued *me*!" Thus the rejection of the Messiah means the rejection of God himself. Another example is Zech 12:10 where the Lord says: "And I will pour out on the house of David and the inhabitants of Jerusalem a spirit of grace and supplication. They will look on *me*, the one they have pierced, and they will mourn for him as one mourns for an only child, and grieve bitterly for him as one grieves for a firstborn son." The text states that the Lord himself has been pierced when the Good

---

[15]It is worth noting that the Christian tradition connects the Gospel of Mark with the reminiscences of St Peter. Concerning this option see M. Hengel, *Studies in the Gospel of Mark* (Philadelphia: Fortress Press 1985), a detailed discussion which is followed and developed in J. Thurén, *Markuksen evankeliumi* (Helsinki: SLEY-Kirjat 1996), 7-32 (in Finnish).

[16]J.J. Collins, *The Scepter and the Star: The Messiahs of the Dead Sea Scrolls and Other Ancient Literature* (New York: Doubleday 1995) 205.

Shepherd has been killed (Zech 13:7). This close connection between God and Good Shepherd fully explains why high Christology was developed so rapidly after the events of Easter. The crucified Messiah could be related closely to God on the basis of Zech 12:10.

As the synoptic gospels indicate, Jesus did not reveal his fate as the suffering and dying Messiah until just before the Passover festival. When Jesus finally revealed to his disciples that he intended to fulfil Zechariah 9-14 events rolled on so fast that nothing could be done to prevent his death. Nevertheless, the disciples had seen Jesus' symbolic actions in Jerusalem where he fulfilled Zech 9:9-10 and 14:21, and received his teaching in the form of the Son of Man logia that he must suffer and die. These events helped the disciples after Easter to construct the atonement theology related to the death of Jesus.

The logia of the Son of Man closely reflects the content of Zechariah 9-14, and I shall now argue that by using cryptic sayings concerning the Son of Man, Jesus sought to prepare his disciples for his imminent death which would follow the lines predicted in Zechariah 9-14. There are three messianic themes in Zechariah 9-14 which can be related to the sayings of the Son of Man:[17]

(1) The Messiah is present (Zech 9:9) but his power is hidden in such a manner that the people do not perceive it (Zech 11:4-14) but reject him. Scholars have rightly observed that Jesus chose to refer to himself as the Son of Man because he wanted to reveal his humility and

---

[17]For general discussion and analysis of the Son of Man logia see L. Goppelt, *Theologie des Neuen Testaments* (Göttingen: Vandenhoeck & Ruprecht 1978) 226-253; V. Hampel, *Menschensohn und historischer Jesus: Ein Rätselwort als Schlüssel zum messianischen Selbstverständnis Jesu* (Neukirchen-Vluyn: Neukirchener Verlag 1990); B.D. Chilton, "(The) Son of (the) Man, and Jesus." In: B. Chilton & C.A. Evans (eds), *Authenticating the Words of Jesus* (Leiden 1999), 259-287; M. Kreplin, "The Self-Understanding of Jesus," in: T. Holmén & S.E. Porter (eds), *Handbook for the Study of the Historical Jesus Vol 3: The Historical Jesus* (Leiden: Brill 2011) 2473-2516. Note also J.J. Collins, "The Son of Man in Ancient Judaism," in: T. Holmén & S.E. Porter (eds), *Handbook for the Study of the Historical Jesus Vol 2: The Study of Jesus* (Leiden: Brill 2011) 1545-1568.

174

lowliness.[18] In the Gospel of Mark (2:10 par, 2:28 par) the Son of Man has the power to forgive sins and teach *halakha* in a new way. On the other hand, in Q the present Son of Man is described as meek and mild (Mt 8:20 par; 11:19 par; 12:32 par; cf., Zech 9:9; Isa 42:2-3). Taking into account the perception that the Son of Man will be a supreme judge, these logia indicate that his power is in some way hidden. Parallels to this belief can be found in 1 Enoch 48:6; 62:7 where the power of the Son of Man (who is in heaven, however) will only be revealed to the elect.[19] A similar parallel can be found in Jesus' actions which fulfilled Zech 9:9-10 and 14:21. Even though he rode openly on a donkey to Jerusalem and purified the Temple, he did not attempt to establish his political power, an omission which is implied in Zech 9:10.

(2) The Messiah will be rejected by the people (Zech 11:4-14) and he will die (Zech 13:7; 12:10). In the Gospel of Mark (and par) certain logia state that the Son of Man will come to suffer and die. In Mk 8:31; 9:31 and 10:33-34 Jesus predicts the imminent suffering and death of the Son of Man, but as we have already observed the literary form of these passages is connected with the passion accounts. All these logia predict that the Son of Man will rise on the third day. Mk 10:33-34 in particular contains a detailed description of the passion. Therefore, it is difficult to argue that such formulations of the coming death and resurrection of the Son of Man are authentic sayings of the historical Jesus.[20] However, we have discussed the possibility that the content of these passages may suggest an event which Jesus revealed to his disciples before the Passover Festival because the idea of death is compatible with

---

[18]See C. Colpe, ὁ υἱος τοῦ ἀνθρώπου, ThWNT 8 1969 cols. 403-481, esp. 409; Kreplin, "The Self-Understanding of Jesus" 2489: "This concept contains an element of lowliness, as the address of the prophet with בֶּן אָדָם in the Book of Ezekiel shows."

[19]The idea of concealment is also expressed in Isa 49:2 which speaks about the Servant of the Lord. See, e.g., M. Black, *The Book of Enoch or 1 Enoch: A New English Edition with Commentary and Textual Notes* (SVTP 7, Leiden: Brill 1985) 210-211.

[20]See, e.g. discussion in Hampel, *Menschensohn und historischer Jesus* 246-342.

the content of Zechariah 9-14, where the good shepherd, the Messiah, will die (13:7; 12:10). The formulation in Mk 8:31 that "the Son of Man was destined ... to be rejected by the elders" is also significant. This formulation is reminiscent of Zech 11:4-14's belief that the good shepherd will be rejected by the people. Moreover, this passage explains Jesus' hard saying to Peter in Mk 8:33. So even though we cannot conclude that the exact formulations in Mk 8:31; 9:31; 10:33-34 stem directly from Jesus, their content (especially in Mk 8:31) is compatible with the message of Zechariah 9-14 and can be regarded as original.

If it is difficult to regard Mk 8:31; 9:31; 10:33-34 as authentic sayings of Jesus, the case of Mk 10:45 is far more interesting. It contains a saying of Jesus which in terms of content corresponds to the above three logia: "For the Son of Man himself came not to be served but to serve, and to give his life as a ransom for many."[21] However, the formulations in this logia are not connected with the passion account and there is no reference to the resurrection. The content of Mk 10:45 runs parallel to the death of the messianic figure in Zechariah 9-14.[22] The idea of ransom is manifest in Zech 12:10-13:1 where the people confess that they are guilty of the death of the pierced one, a death which releases a fountain that will wash away sin and impurity. The fountain in Zech 13:1 was interpreted as a reference to the Christian baptism (see below).

Stuhlmacher emphasizes that the passive verb παραδίδοται in Jesus' logion on the death of the Son of Man (Mk 9:31) should be

---

[21]Hampel (*Menschensohn und historischer Jesus* 302-342) and many other scholars regard Mk 10:45 as an authentic logion of Jesus.

[22]Isa 43:3-4; Ps 49:8-9 and Prov 21:18 are often regarded as the Old Testament passages which lie behind the logion in Mk 10:45. See e.g. Hampel *Menschensohn und historischer Jesus* 326-333; W. Grimm & K. Dittert, *Deuterojesaja: Deutung - Wirkung - Gegenwart* (Calwer Bibelkommentare, Stuttgart 1990), 176-187; see also O. Betz's excursus in Grimm & Dittert, *Deuterojesaja: Deutung - Wirkung - Gegenwart* 425-434; P. Stuhlmacher, "Der messianische Gottesknecht," *JBT* 8 (1993) 131-154, esp. 144; R.E. Watts, "Jesus' Death, Isaiah 53, and Mark 10:45: A Crux Revisited," in: W.H. Bellinger & W.R. Farmer, *Jesus and the Suffering Servant: Isaiah 53 and Christian Origins* (Harrisburg: Trinity Press International 1998) 125-151.

"understood from the perspective of Isaiah 43:3-5 and 53:5-6, 11-12."[23] Even more important is Jesus' saying in Mk 14:21 which contains this same Greek verb and is also connected with the institution of Holy Communion. Its formulation is remarkable because there is a reference to the scriptures: "Yes, the Son of Man is going to his fate, *as the scriptures say* he will, but alas for that man by whom the Son of Man is betrayed (οὐαὶ δὲ τῷ ἀνθρώπῳ ἐκείνῳ δια οὗ ὁ υἱὸς τοῦ ἀνθρώπου παραδίδοται). Better for that man if he had never been born." Scholars seem to agree that there is no explicit biblical passage in the Old Testament which refers to the Son of Man being betrayed. Various solutions have been presented. For example, Gould states boldly that the Old Testament prophecy which is mentioned here is Isaiah 53.[24] The problem is that Isaiah 53 does not speak of the Son of Man. A common interpretation among scholars is that the reference is to Psalm 41, particularly verse 9 (and 2):[25]

> Even my close friend,
>> someone I trusted,
> one who shared my bread,
>> has lifted up his heel against me.

This solution can explain Jesus' reference to the man who betrays. The Septuagint text (LXX Ps 40:10) reads here that ὁ ἄνθρωπος τῆς εἰρήνης μου will betray. But nor does Psalm 41 clearly state that it is "the man" or "the Son of Man" who will be betrayed. The third solution

---

[23]Stuhlmacher, "Isaiah 53 in the Gospels and Acts" 150.

[24]E.P. Gould, *A Critical and Exegetical Commentary on the Gospel according to St. Mark* (Edinburgh: Clark 1921) 263.

[25]See, e.g., R. Pesch, *Das Markusevangelium II. Teil Kommentar zu Kap. 8,27-16,20* (HTKNT 2; Freiburg: Herder 1977) 345-353; J. Gnilka, *Das Evangelium nach Markus (Mk 8,27-16,20)* (EKK zum Neuen Testament II/2; Zürich: Benziger, Neukirchen-Vluyn: Neukirchener 1979) 238-239; J. Marcus, *Mark 8-16* (AB 27A, New Haven: Yale University Press 2009) 949-956

regards the reference to the scriptures as a common statement that prophecies predict such a fate for the Son of Man.[26] However, if our suggestion is correct (that Jesus integrated his Son of Man logia with the message of Zechariah 9-14), then Zech 11:4-14 could explain the reference to "the scriptures" in Mk 14:21. Zech 11:6 can be interpreted in different ways and, in particular, the MT can be read as meaning that "the Man" is betrayed:

καὶ ἰδοὺ ἐγὼ παραδίδωμι τοὺς ἀνθρώπους ἕκαστον εἰς χεῖρας τοῦ πλησίον αὐτοῦ καὶ εἰς χεῖρας βασιλέως αὐτοῦ
I shall deliver up the men every one into the hand of his neighbour, and into the hand of his king.

והנה אנכי ממציא את האדם איש ביד רעהו וביד מלכו
Look, I shall deliver up the Man, a man into the hands of his neighbor and to hands of his king

This text is interesting for several reasons. *First* of all we have the verb παραδίδωμι (LXX) which recurs in the sayings of Jesus. *Second*, the Hebrew text has the definite article before אדם, indicating that the reference may pertain to a particular Man.[27] If we assume that the Son of Man tradition and Zechariah 9-14 were intertwined in Jesus' teaching, then the Man in Zech 11:6 may well be the Son of Man. In that case, Mk 14:21 is reliant on the Hebrew text of Zech 11:6 and not the Greek, and we must assume an Hebrew or Aramaic quotation behind Jesus' saying. This is further evidence that the saying goes back to Jesus himself. *Third*, we have an expression איש ביד רעהו which closely reflects the content of Mark 14:21 according to which there is "one who betrays", i.e. Judas Iscariot. *Finally*, the last note "into the hands of his king" has no correspondence in the passion history according to the Gospel of Mark, but we can ask whether this particular reference could be one reason why

---

[26]C.S. Mann, *Mark* (AB 27, New York: Doubleday 1986) 568-569.

[27]Of course, grammatically this could be interpreted as referring to "the men" as in the LXX.

the passion history according to Luke emphasizes that Jesus was taken from the house of Pilate to the palace of Herod Antipas, i.e. Jesus was surrendered into the hands of his king. Of course, the "king" could also be assumed to refer to Pilate.

Assuming that Jesus identified himself with the messianic figure of Zechariah 9-14 and the Son of Man, Zech 11:6 could have prompted him reason to quote a biblical passage where one of his closest disciples would betray him. Through such a process of cross-referencing and integration Judas Iscariot became the typos of the betrayer in the Gospel. For example, in the Gospel of Matthew the thirty silver shekels mentioned in Zech 11:13 regarded as referring to the payment which Judas received from the priests (Mt 27:3-10).[28]

Logia in which Jesus speaks of the sufferings and death of the Son of Man are not to be found in Q. The reason must be sought in the fact that the composer of Q wanted to collect Jesus' teachings and parables rather than present the story of the passion. On the other hand, Mt 23:37-39 (par Lk 13:34-35), which is drawn from Q contains a reference to the coming prediction of the imminent death of Jesus.[29]

(3) The third theme in Zechariah 9-14 is that the Messiah will establish a universal kingdom (Zech 9:10), and the nations (who will first attack Jerusalem, Zech 12:1-8; 14:1-5) will come to Jerusalem to serve Yhwh at the Temple (Zech 14:16-19) – the Temple will be a holy place for all nations (Zech 14:21). Even this universal aspect of Zechariah 9-14 appears in Jesus' logia on the Son of Man.

Several logia in the Synoptic Gospels describe the eschatological coming of the Son of Man. These passages are traditio-historically linked with Daniel 7 and 1 Enoch 37-71. Nevertheless, they are also compatible with Zechariah 9-14 which describes the Messiah's universal empire

---

[28]We cannot exclude the possibility that Jesus' aristocratic opponents perceived his attempt to identify himself with the messianic figure of Zech 9:9-10. They may have acted ironically (on the basis of Zech 11:13) and given thirty shekels to Judas.

[29]See Goppelt *Theologie des Neuen Testaments* 235.

(Zech 9:10) and the hope that nations will submit to the power of God (Zech 12:1-8; 14:1-5). The nations will confess that the God of Israel is the one and only God and will worship him in the holy precincts of Jerusalem (Zech 14:9; 14:16-19, 21).

Kreplin has argued that all the sayings of the Son of Man who will come to judge the people in the eschatological age were fabricated by the Christians when they linked other Jesus' logia concerning the Son of Man with Dan 7:13-14. This may have occurred, according to Kreplin, during the Caligula crisis in 40 AD.[30] One argument which Kreplin has taken from Vielhauer is that "an eschatological expectation of the Son of Man would contradict Jesus' proclamation of the rule of God ... since we find no eschatological mediator figure in the expectation of the kingdom of God."[31] However, according to Kreplin Jesus presents himself "as the eschatological representative of God,"[32] and this could well parallel to the fact that Jesus did identify himself with the Son of Man of Dan 7:13-14. We have also seen that Jewish martyr theology contains the belief that the suffering and dying martyr is acting at the final judgment. According to Dan 12:1-3 the martyrs are *maśkîlîm* (Isa 52:13), who will play a major role at the last judgment (cf., Isa 53:11-12) and who "will shine like the brightness of the heavens, and those who lead many to righteousness, like the stars for ever and ever" (Dan 12:3). According to Wisdom 2-5, the righteous sufferer will finally have a glorious position in the Last Judgment when the ungodly realize that God is pleased in him: "The righteous man who has died will condemn the ungodly who are living, and youth that is quickly perfected will condemn the prolonged old age of the unrighteous man" (Wisd 4:16); "Then the righteous man will stand

---

[30]Kreplin, "The Self-Understanding of Jesus," 2485-2486, 2490-2491.

[31]Kreplin, "The Self-Understanding of Jesus," 2485-2486. See also P. Vielhauer, "Gottesreich und Menschensohn in der Verkündigung Jesu," in: idem, *Aufsätze zum Neuen Testament* (Tbü 31, Munich: Kaiser 1965) 55-91.

[32]See Kreplin, "The Self-Understanding of Jesus," 2496-2510; the quotation is from p. 2508.

with great confidence in the presence of those who have afflicted him, and those who make light of his labors. When they see him, they will be shaken with dreadful fear, and they will be amazed at his unexpected salvation" (Wisd 5:1-2). This being the case Jesus could well have combined his role as the suffering and dying Son of Man with the glorious coming of the Son of Man to the last judgement. Moreover, Zechariah 9-14 shows that a mediator will play an important role in the eschatological drama when Yhwh will become the King over the whole world (Zech 14:9) – at least we have good reason to assume that Jesus could have regarded himself as the mediator when he rode to Jerusalem and purged the Temple.[33]

Summing up our discussion so far, we may say that Zechariah 9-14 provide a good model for the understanding of the suffering of the Son of Man and his eschatological role as judge. A key text is Zech 12:10 which implies that God will take care of the pierced one, and the people who once rejected the pierced one will confess their guilt. The pierced one is not only a Messiah but also a martyr who will have a future in the salvation plans of God.

The importance of Zech 12:10 in early Christian theology becomes apparent in Peter's speech in Acts 2:14-41. Peter based his sermon on Zech 12:10-13:1. He argues that the Jerusalemites are responsible for the death of Jesus who is the pierced one in Zech 12:10. After hearing this message from Peter many confess their guilt as do the Jerusalemites in Zech 12:11-14. The confession prompts Peter to give them the promise (Acts 2:38):

---

[33] It is also worth noting that in the light of recent studies, there is no need to see any tension between the eschatological kingdom of God and the messianic expectations. See, e.g., Collins, *The Scepter and the Star*; A. Laato, *A Star Is Rising: The Historical Development of the Old Testament Royal Ideology and the Rise of the Jewish Messianic Expectations* (International Studies in Formative Christianity and Judaism, Atlanta: Scholars Press 1997).

> You must repent and every one of you must be baptized in the name of Jesus Christ for the forgiveness of your sins, and you will receive the gift of the Holy Spirit.

This promise is based on Zech 13:1: "When that day comes, a fountain will be opened for the House of David and the inhabitants of Jerusalem, to wash sin and impurity away." The fountain which washes away sin and impurity was interpreted as referring to baptism, where forgiveness was a central promise already in the proclamation of John the Baptist (Mk 1:4; see also 1 Cor 6:9-11; John 3:5).

When the meaning of Jesus's death was understood in the light of Zech 12:10 it brought to the fore also the close relationship between Jesus and Yhwh. Especially in Zech 11:13 and 12:10 Yhwh identifies himself with the fate of the Messiah who is first rejected by the people and then pierced by them. The mystery of salvation was that God himself was involved in the death of Jesus so that he reconciled the world with himself (2 Cor 5:18-21). This interpretation provided the impulse for high Christology. There is one God (*theos*) and one Lord (*kyrios*) and both acted in the creation and salvation of humankind (1 Cor 8:6). In Paul's theology the kyriology of Jesus was interpreted so as to glorify monotheism: "... and that every tongue should acknowledge Jesus Christ *as Kyrios to the glory of God the Father*" (Phil 2:11). This passage of the pre-Pauline hymn refers to Isa 45:21-25 which speaks of Yhwh as the only God who can save. I have translated this passage so that the concepts "salvation" and "righteousness" are emphasized:

> There is no other god but me, no saving God, no Saviour (*môšîaʿ*) but me! Turn to me and you sill be saved (*wᵉhiwwāšᵉʿû*), all you ends of the earth, for I am God, and there is no other. By my own self I swear it; what comes from my mouth is righteousness (*ṣᵉdāqâ*), it is an irrevocable word: All shall bend the knee to me, by me every tongue shall swear, saying: In Yhwh alone are righteousness (*ṣᵉdāqôt*) and strength, until all those who used to rage at him come to him in shame. In Yhwh the whole race of Israel finds righteous (or: become righteous, *yiṣdᵉqû*) and glory.

In the pre-Pauline Christological hymn in Phil 2:5-11, the monotheistic faith is glorified by the confession, "Jesus Christ is Kyrios." This confession glorifies the name of Yhwh according to Isa 45:21-25, because everyone must confess that only Yhwh can give righteousness. A similar universal monotheistic faith is emphasized in Zech 14:9 which says that Yhwh will be one and his name will be one.[34]

These parallels between the messianic figure of Zechariah 9-14 and the Son of Man logia enables us to argue that Jesus' self-understanding was based on the Book of Zechariah and his cryptic sayings about the Son of Man prepared his disciples to understand his final entrance to Jerusalem. The fact that in the early Church there was no Christological confession that Jesus is the Son of Man can be explained by the fact that at a very early stage, the Christological title "the Son of God" was developed from Dan 7:13-14 – which was seen as being parallel to Dan 3:25 (see sect. 3). The Qumran fragmentary text 4Q246 indicates that the Son of Man in Daniel 7 could be called the Son of God.[35] Therefore, the Son of God, rather than the Son of Man, was postulated in early Christological confession. This being the case, Paul's confession in Gal 4:4: "But when the set time had fully come, God sent his Son, born of a woman, born under the law" was based on the vision of the coming of the Son of Man in Daniel 7.

Every interpretation which allows one to speak of the messianic self-understanding of Jesus generates psychological questions regarding this self-concept. Was Jesus a madman? Was he some sort of an ancient

---

[34]See J. Thurén, "'Der Herr ist einer' in Neutestamentlicher Sicht," in: K.-J. Illman & J. Thurén (eds), *Der Herr ist einer, unserer gemeinsames Erbe* (Åbo: Åbo Akademi 1979) 98-121.

[35]See this text in E. Puech, "Fragment d'une Apocalypse en Araméen (4Q246 = pseudo-Dan^d) et le 'Royaume de Dieu," *RB* 99 (1992) 98-131; idem, "Notes sur le fragment d'apocalypse 4Q246 – 'Le fils de Dieu'," *RB* 101 (1994) 533-558; J.A. Fitzmyer, "4Q246: The 'Son of God' Document from Qumran," *Bib* 74 (1993) 153-174; Collins, *The Scepter and the Star* 154-172.

David Koresh who saw himself as the great messianic hero of his time and who therefore sought his own destruction? The problem is that scholarly approaches to understanding the proclamation and actions of Jesus have their limits. Suggesting that he identified himself with the Son of Man and the messianic figure of Zechariah 9-14 emphasizes the problems inherent in restricted theoretical models which lead to negative evaluations of Jesus' personality. On the other hand, a religious individual has other modes of argumentation for understanding Jesus' messianic self-knowledge. A believer could well regard Jesus as the Davidic Branch and emphasize simultaneously that he had nothing to do with the Branch Davidians in Waco Texas.

We have tried to demonstrate here that Jesus identified himself with the messianic figure in Zechariah 9-14 and used the Son of Man sayings to explain this connection. The idea of the suffering and dying Messiah was inextricably linked with the Jewish martyr theology which explains why, according to Jesus, the suffering and dying Son of Man can appear as the eschatological judge. Peter's speech at Pentecost illustrates that Zech 12:10-13:1 was understood by the first Christians as signifying that the death of Jesus was vicarious. The concept of the suffering and dying Messiah could then easily be transferred to Isaiah 53 which the New Testament interpreted in individual terms to refer to Jesus' vicarious death.[36] The universal consequences of this vicarious death were thus made visible by Isaiah 53 (see, e.g., 53:10-12).

---

[36]Note an important article: B. Janowski, "He Bore Our Sins: Isaiah 53 and the Drama of Taking Another's Place," in: B. Janowski & P. Stuhlmacher (eds), *The Suffering Servant: Isaiah 53 in Jewish and Christian Sources* (Grand Rapids: Eerdmans 2004) 48-74. Janowski discusses the modern intellectual problem of the concept *Stellvertretung* ("taking another's place") which since Kant's philosophy has been problematic.

The Interpretation of Isaiah 53 in the New Testament

While discussing the Christological interpretation of Isaiah 53 Melugin lays aside all historical questions – albeit without opposing them. He argues that the text creates its own world where the Christian interpretation may see fit to argue that Jesus' sufferings and death are those of the servant.[37] Hanson criticizes such an exegetical approach where all historical questions are disregarded.[38] In this study we have tried to answer this challenge. Indeed, there is no need to regard the Christian interpretation of Isaiah 53 in isolation from Jewish exegesis. We have argued that in order to evaluate the Christian interpretation of Isaiah 53 we cannot separate it from Jesus's messianic self-understanding, and this in turn cannot be separated from the Jewish martyr theology which in its own way is connected with the historical interpretation of Isaiah 53 in its literary context. Finally, the tradition of the suffering and dying figure behind Isaiah 53 is rooted in the dramatic end of Josiah at Megiddo.

The oldest textual material in the New Testament are the Letters of Paul. There are some passages in Paul's writings where he uses Semitic expressions (e.g., the kingdom of God) which indicate that they are older kerygmatic traditions (perhaps originating from Antioch) which he incorporated into his teaching and transmitted to his Greek-speaking audience. Scholars value these passages in Paul's letters because they reveal what the first Christians thought and learnt. When we study these

---

[37]R.F. Melugin, "On Reading Isaiah 53 as Christian Scripture," in: W.H. Bellinger & W.R. Farmer, *Jesus and the Suffering Servant: Isaiah 53 and Christian Origins* (Harrisburg: Trinity Press International 1998) 55-69. Similar ideas are presented also in D.J.A. Clines, *I, He, We, & They: A Literary Approach to Isaiah 53* (JSOTSS 1, Sheffield: Sheffield Academic Press 1983).

[38]See P.D. Hanson, "The World of the Servant of the Lord in Isaiah 40-55," in: W.H. Bellinger & W.R. Farmer, *Jesus and the Suffering Servant: Isaiah 53 and Christian Origins* (Harrisburg: Trinity Press International 1998) 9-23, esp. 9-11.

older traditions behind Paul's letters, we discover that Isaiah 53 plays a central role.

In 1 Cor 15:1-11 Paul presents central events of the salvation history in the Christian gospel which he has received (παραλαμβάνω) and handed on (παραδίδωμι) to the congregation in Corinth. The Greek expressions "receive" and "hand on" correspond well to those verbs in the tractate *Pirqe Avot* in the Mishnah: *qibbēl* and *māsar*. They are used to describe how Moses "received" the Torah at Sinai and "handed it on" to Joshua and so on until the first *Tannaim*.[39] Thus *Pirqe Avot* emphasizes that the correct interpretation of the Torah was delivered from Moses to the Tannaitic rabbis and was continued by later generations.

In 1 Cor 15:1-11 Paul emphasizes that there are four central messages in his gospel which he had received from tradition and which other apostles too proclaimed. All these four elements can be related to Isaiah 53:[40]

(1) "Christ died for our sins in accordance with the scriptures (ὅτι Χριστὸς ἀπέθανεν ὑπὲρ τῶν ἁμαρτιῶν ἡμῶν κατὰ τὰς γραφάς)", clearly indicates that the Old Testament contains one or several proof texts which predict the death of Jesus for our sins. It seems obvious that this text must be Isaiah 53.[41] There are several passages where the suffering and death of the Servant are attributed to "us" (Isa 53:4a, 5, 6b,

---

[39]Betz, "Jesus and Isaiah 53," 77. Concerning the oral tradition see further B. Gerhardsson, *Memory and Manuscript: Oral Tradition and Written Transmission in Rabbinic Judaism and Early Christianity* (Acta Seminarii Neotestamentici Upsaliensis 22; Lund: Gleerups 1961); idem, *The Reliability of the Gospel Tradition* (Peabody, Mass.: Hendrickson Publishers 2001); S. Byrskog, *Story as History – History as Story: the Gospel Tradition in the Context of Ancient Oral History* (WUNT 123; Tübingen: Mohr Siebeck 2000).

[40]Concerning this see Hofius, "The Fourth Servant Song in the New Testament Letters," 163-188, esp. 177 n. 57.

[41]See, e.g., Jeremias, *The Servant of God*, 89; Hofius "The Fourth Servant Song in the New Testament Letters," 118-121.

186

8b, 11b, 12b-c). Even though the preposition ὑπέρ is not used in the Septuagint[42] it is reasonable to assume that the Christian kerygma was formulated with the aid of the Hebrew (and Aramaic) texts and then translated into Greek.[43] In this way it is easy to comprehend why the preposition ὑπέρ became so important in the New Testament passages which emphasizes the vicarious death of Jesus. In this context we should consider that in the Letter of Clement (from the end of the first century AD) chapter 16 quotes Isaiah 53 in almost the same words as the Septuagint but reads in Isa 53:6 the preposition ὑπέρ: καὶ κύριος παρέδωκεν αὐτὸν ὑπὲρ τῶν ἁμαρτῶν ἡμῶν.[44] This indicates that Clement probably follows an early Christian kerygmatic tradition which was formulated with the aid of the Hebrew text.

(2) "... that he was buried" (ἐτάφη) means in this context that he really died. Isaiah 53 describes the death of the Servant (most explicitly in Isa 53:8: "For he was cut off from the land of the living") and his burial in Isa 53:9a: "He was assigned a grave with the wicked, and with the rich in his death."

---

[42]See D.P. Bailey, "Concepts of Stellvertretung in the Interpretation of Isaiah 53," in: W.H. Bellinger & W.R. Farmer, *Jesus and the Suffering Servant: Isaiah 53 and Christian Origins* (Harrisburg: Trinity Press International 1998) 223-250, esp. 230-231.

[43]Note also our conclusion in section 4 that the Greek translation of the Septuagint is not as close to the vicarious suffering of the Servant as is the Masoretic text. See, in particular, D.A. Sapp "The LXX, 1QIsa, and MT Versions of Isaiah 53 and the Christian Doctrine of Atonement," in: W.H. Bellinger & W.R. Farmer (eds), *Jesus and the Suffering Servant: Isaiah 53 and Christian Origins* (Harrisburg: Trinity Press 1998) 170-192. Sapp notes (pp. 191-192): "The 'punch line' for the Christian gospel — the description of the Servant's divinely intended sacrificial death, his justification of the many, and allusions to his resurrection — occurs only in the Hebrew texts." To this same conclusion comes also Nyberg. See H.S. Nyberg, "Smärtornas man: En studie till Jes. 52,13-53,12," *SEÅ* 7 (1942) 5-82, esp. 6-33. This also explains why the Wisdom of Solomon 2-5 has interpreted Isaiah 53 so that the sufferings of the Servant do not benefit the ungodly (the "we" in Isa 53 has been interpreted as the godless).

[44]See the text in J.A. Fischer, *Die apostolischen Väter* (Schriften des Urchristentums. Erster Teil, Darmstadt: Wissenschaftliche Buchgesellschaft 1986) 44.

(3) "... that he was raised on the third day according to the Scriptures" (ἐγήγερται τῇ ἡμέρᾳ τῇ τρίτῃ κατὰ τὰς γραφάς). The resurrection of the Servant is implied in Isa 53:10b, 11a. In particular, if we read the verse 11a according to the Qumran and LXX tradition then the expression "see a light" implies that the Servant will live after his death. Even Isa 52:13 can be taken as an indication of the Servant's future life. The reception history of the word *maśkîl* in Isa 52:13 in Dan 12:1-3 confirms the idea of resurrection (see sect. 3). In a corresponding way, Wisdom 2-5 takes for granted that the suffering righteous Servant will rise from the dead (see sect. 4). These examples from early Jewish tradition indicate how Isaiah 53 was understood in antiquity and it is natural to assume that Christians could "see" a real resurrection therein.

(4) "... and that he appeared (ὤφθη) to Cephas, and then to the Twelve. After that, he appeared (ὤφθη) to more than five hundred of the brothers and sisters at the same time, most of whom are still living, though some have fallen asleep. Then he appeared (ὤφθη) to James, then to all the apostles, and last of all he appeared (ὤφθη) to me also, as to one abnormally born." The appearance of the Servant after his suffering and death is implied in Isa 52:15b where it is said the Servant will be seen by many. In Isa 53:1 too the question is posed to whom the arm of Yhwh will be revealed.[45]

The vicarious death of Jesus is expressed in 1 Cor 15:3 with the aid of the preposition ὑπέρ. This preposition recurs in another tradition which Paul has received and which he presents in his First Letter to Corinthians, namely "the words of the Holy Communion" (1 Cor 11:23-26). It is said of bread that it is the body of the Christ which is given "in your behalf" (ὑπὲρ ὑμῶν). Corresponding expressions with the preposition ὑπέρ are presented in the Gospels with references to the Holy Communion (Mk

---

[45]Cyprian in Test. II.4 speaks of the Christological title "the Arm of God" and uses Isa 53:1 as one of his proof texts.

14:24; Lk 22:19-20). In the Gospel of Matthew the preposition περί is used (Mt 26:28). There is no difficulty in connecting the vicarious suffering of the Servant in Isaiah 53 with the theological meaning of the Holy communion.[46]

The third tradition which Paul has received and which can be linked with Isaiah 53 is Rom 4:25: "who was handed over to death for our trespasses and was raised for our justification (ὃς παρεδόθη διὰ τὰ παραπτώματα ἡμῶν καὶ ἠγέρθη διὰ τὴν δικαίωσιν ἡμῶν)."[47] Behind this tradition looms Isa 53:12 (and probably also Isa 53:5). The translation of the Septuagint does not contain the word παραπτώματα, but 53:12 in particular is reminiscent of Rom 4:25:[48]

Isa 53:12   διὰ τὰς ἁμαρτίας αὐτῶν παρεδόθη
Isa 53:5   ἐτραυματίσθη διὰ τὰς ἀνομίας ἡμῶν καὶ μεμαλάκισται διὰ τὰς ἁμαρτίας ἡμῶν

Both Isa 53:5, 12 and Rom 4:25 use the preposition διά. The latter part of Rom 4:25 may be an interpretation of Isa 53:11. Jesus has arisen from the dead and can now make many righteous. In this case, the tradition in

---

[46]See Jeremias, *The Servant of God* 89; Stuhlmacher, "Isaiah 53 in the Gospels and Acts," 97; Hofius, "The Fourth Servant Song in the New Testament Letters," 118 n. 53.

[47]There are scholars, e.g., Hooker ("Did the use of Isaiah 53 to Interpret His Mission Begin with Jesus?" 101), who regards Rom 4:25 as Paul's own text. We have presented a view that the preposition ὑπέρ has belonged to early Christian tradition on the death of Jesus interpreted on the basis of Isaiah 53 (and through the Hebrew text). The meaning of the death of Jesus has been presented in the New Testament with the aid of different prepositions: ὑπέρ, διά and περί. Therefore, it is possible that the tradition behind Rom 4:25 adopted another preposition at an early stage. Note also C. Breytenbach, "The Septuagint version of Isaiah 53 and the early Christian formula 'he was delivered for our trespasses'," *NT* 51 (2009) 339-351.

[48]Rom 4:25 may also be an early Hebrew tradition based on Isaiah 53 which has been translated into the Greek. This could explain why the word παραπτώματα, which does not appear in the translation of the Septuagint, has been used.

Rom 4:25 must be based on the Hebrew expression *yaṣdîq ṣaddîq ʻabdî lārabbîm* which implies that the suffering servant of Yhwh will make many righteous. This will come to pass after the resurrection of the Servant.[49] Such an interpretation of Isa 53:11 cannot be derived from the Septuagint. Isa 53:11 has been translated δικαιῶσαι δίκαιον εὖ δουλεύοντα πολλοῖς, which means that the Hebrew text was understood to mean that God "makes righteous [= he does justice to] his righteous one who serves well many."[50]

A corresponding interpretation of Isaiah 53, according to which the death of Jesus took place "for ourselves (ὑπὲρ ἡμῶν)" and the resurrection thereafter for our righteousness, appears in 2 Cor 5:21: "For our sake he made him to be sin who knew no sin, so that in him we might become the righteousness of God (τὸν μὴ γνόντα ἁμαρτίαν ὑπὲρ ἡμῶν ἁμαρτίαν ἐποίησεν, ἵνα ἡμεῖς γενώμεθα δικαιοσύνη θεοῦ ἐν αὐτῷ)."

2 Cor 5:14-21 is an important text containing similar atonement theology which is also used in the Second and Fourth Books of Maccabees. In this passage Paul uses the verb καταλλάσσω. The meaning of this verb is "reconcile". God's saving actions in Christ enabled reconciliation between the Holy God and the sinful world. In 2 Cor 5:14-21 reconciliation is possible because of the death of Christ, the Son of God – a parallel to the death of martyrs in 2 Macc 7:32-38. As a scapegoat Christ has taken upon himself the sin of the world (2 Cor 5:21) and eliminated this evil through his death. This atonement is a precondition for reconciliation as Paul writes: "So we are ambassadors for Christ, since God is making his appeal through us; we entreat you on

---

[49]Hofius "The Fourth Servant Song in the New Testament Letters," 121-122. It is possible that in early Christian tradition the reading of the Septuagint and 1QIsaª was followed, according to which the servant "will see light" after his death. In the Masoretic text this expression "sees light" is missing even though the idea of resurrection is presented.

[50]See more closely Sapp "The LXX, 1QIsa, and MT Versions of Isaiah 53," 173-176.

190

behalf of Christ, be reconciled to God (καταλλάγητε τῷ θεῷ)." Paul's exhortation means that the atonement has already taken place and the message of salvation is valid in Christ for everyone who wants to be reconciled to God. An additional text in Paul's letters where reconciliation and the atonement which Jesus made are connected is Rom 5:10-11:[51]

> For if while we were enemies, we were reconciled to God through the death of his Son (κατηλλάγημεν τῷ θεῷ διὰ τοῦ θανάτου τοῦ υἱοῦ αὐτοῦ), much more surely, having been reconciled, will we be saved by his life (πολλῷ μᾶλλον καταλλαγέντες σωθησόμεθα ἐν τῇ ζωῇ αὐτοῦ). But more than that, we even boast in God through our Lord Jesus Christ, through whom we have now received reconciliation (δι' οὗ νῦν τὴν καταλλαγὴν ἐλάβομεν).

Even these verses indicate that the reconciliation is based on the vicarious and atoning death of Jesus. Before these verses Paul refers several times to Jesus' sacrificial death (Rom 5:6, 8-9). The reconciliation which God effected through the death of Jesus is also manifest in Col 1:18-22 and Eph 2:14-16.[52] In Paul's theology the reconciliation between God and the whole world is based on the vicarious death of Jesus. This implies that the death of Jesus was understood as the decisive and final expiation of the sins of the world. The message of the gospel is based on this atonement.

We have seen that older traditions (based on Isaiah 53) which Paul quotes in his letters often give a theological explanation of the death of Jesus with the aid of a prepositional expression, ὑπὲρ ἡμῶν etc. The corresponding prepositions are πέρι and διά. This prompts us to suggest that the so-called ὑπέρ-formula and its parallels explaining the death of

---

[51]See the excellent analysis of the atonement theology of Paul in J. Thurén, *Sovituspaikka ja sovinto: Uuden testamentin käännössehdotuksen tarkastelua* (Kirkon tutkimuskeskus. Sarja B 65, Tampere: Raamattutalo 1991) 35-37, 47-49, 52-54.

[52]See Thurén, *Sovituspaikka ja sovinto* 59-71.

Jesus in the New Testament originate from Isaiah 53. In what follows I have listed the expressions in the New Testament where the death of Jesus is explained with these prepositions:

- The expression (παρ)έδωκεν ἑαυτόν ὑπέρ ("he gave himself on the behalf of [us etc]") frequently occurs in the New Testament: Gal 1:4; 2:20; Eph 5:2, 25; 1 Tim 2:6; Tit 2:14.
- Other ὑπέρ expressions appear in John 6:51; 2 Cor 5:14 (cf., also 1 Cor 1:13); Hebr 10:12; 1 Peter 2:21.
- The preposition πέρι can be found in e.g. 1 Peter 3:18; 1 John 2:2.
- The preposition διά concerning the theological meaning of the death of Jesus can be found also in 1 Cor 8:11.

The Christological hymn which is also an older tradition on which Paul draws in Phil 2:6-11 originates from Isaiah 53.[53] The Christ is here described as the pre-existent Lord who "takes the form of a slave (μορφὴν δούλου λαβών)" and "becomes obedient to the point of death (ὑπήκοος μέχρι θανάτου)." It is easy to see how the content of this Christological hymn follows the fate of the Suffering servant in Isaiah 53: after humiliation and death there will be a new glorious life for the Servant. Phil 2:6-11 is an interesting text because it justifies the parenesis which exhorts Christians to following the footsteps of their Master. This being the case, Isaiah 53 also has collective features in the New Testament. Beside Phil 2:6-11, also 1 Peter 2:21-25 reuses the formulations of Isaiah 53 and exhorts the Christians to follow Jesus to suffering and even to death. Such a use of Isaiah 53 in pareneses is easy

---

[53]E. Lohmeyer (*Kyrios Jesus: Eine Untersuchung zu Phil. 2, 5-11* [Sitzungsberichte der Heidelberger Akademie der Wissenschaften, Philosophisch-historische Klasse; 1927/28, Abh. 4; Heidelberg : C. Winter 1928]) first argued that in Phil 2:6-11, Paul quotes an older Christological hymn. This opinion has won acceptance among scholars.

to understand against the background of the early Jewish interpretive traditions which applied it chiefly to the sufferings of the righteous.[54]

Finally, we must return to Mk 10:45 (par Mt 20:28) because scholars have discussed whether these sayings – which we regard as going back to Jesus – are related to Isaiah 53:

> For the Son of Man came not to be served but to serve, and to give his life a ransom for many (καὶ δοῦναι τὴν ψυχὴν αὐτοῦ λύτρον ἀντὶ πολλῶν).

The argument that Jesus' saying is related to Isaiah 53 rests on the ground that Mk 10:45 is reminiscent of an old Christian tradition, Rom 4:25, which resembles the vocabulary in Isaiah 53.[55] The Greek λύτρον refers to the Hebrew kōper. The Old Testament texts which contain this word and which in the terms of content are parallel to Mk 10:45 are Isa 43:3-4, Ps 49:8-9 and Prov 21:18. Although the Septuagint version of Isa 43:3-4 translates the Hebrew kōper with ἄλλαγμα, the meaning is the same as λύτρον or ἀντίλυτρον. Otherwise the content of Isa 43:4 is a close parallel to Mk 10:45: καὶ δώσω ἀνθρώπους πολλοὺς ὑπὲρ σοῦ καὶ ἄρχοντας ὑπὲρ τῆς κεφαλῆς σου ("I give people in return for you, nations in exchange for your life"). While we can say that the content of Isaiah 53 is also suitable as background of Mk 10:45, there are no clear terminological parallels between these texts. This being the case, Hooker argued that the language of Mk 10:45 cannot be inferred from Isaiah 53.[56] But, for example, Betz and Watts consider that the content

---

[54]Cf., our conclusions in sect. 5.

[55]See, e.g., Stuhlmacher "Der messianische Gottesknecht," 144; "Isaiah 53 in the Gospels and Acts," 151-152; Hampel *Menschensohn und historischer Jesus* 302-342; Grimm & Dittert *Deuterojesaja* 144.

[56]Hooker, "Did the use of Isaiah 53 to Interpret His Mission Begin with Jesus?" 94-95. In his dissertation *Jesus and the Servant* (London 1959), Hooker argued that the synoptic traditions do not contain enough evidence that the historical Jesus would have

of Isaiah 53 looms behind Mk 10:45 even though its language mainly originates from Isa 43:3-4.[57] This being the case, we cannot give any decisive answer to the possible relationship between Isaiah 53 and Mk 10:45.

Conclusions

The evidence in this section shows that Isaiah 53 was not a specific messianic text for Jesus. We have argued that the Jewish martyr theology and the messianic texts in Zechariah 9-14 were important to Jesus. In this respect Isaiah 53 was understood by him as an expression of martyr theology which encompassed his self-understanding. On the other hand, we concluded that the concept of the Servant of Yhwh was not important to Jesus, neither was the idea of the suffering Messiah in the New Testament was primarily rooted in Isaiah 53. Rather, this principle is connected with Jesus' symbolic actions as related to Zechariah 9-14. However, we have seen that the early Christian kerygma was formulated soon after the Easter with the aid of Isaiah 53, which explains the use of the expression παῖς θεοῦ in the early Christian liturgy.

Although Jesus never identified himself with the Servant of Yhwh, the first Christians began to call him παῖς θεοῦ (*'ebed Yhwh*). At the beginning of Acts (Acts 3:13, 26; 4:27, 30) there are many liturgical texts where Jesus is called παῖς θεοῦ ("the servant of God"). This title originates from the Servant texts in Isaiah 40-55. Even in the texts of the Apostolic Fathers, this Christological title is often used (1 Klem 59:2-4; Mart. Pol 14:1; the Eucharistic prayers of the Didache 9-10), and also in

---

understood his task in conjunction with Isaiah 53. It seems to me that Hooker's thesis has a point. Jesus did not connect his speech about his suffering and death so much to Isaiah 53 as to Zechariah 9-14. The writers of the Gospels and early Christian theology emphasize Isaiah 53.

[57]Betz, "Jesus and Isaiah 53," 83-87; Watts, "Jesus' Death, Isaiah 53, and Mark 10:45," 125-151.

prayers as a liturgical formula "through Jesus, your servant (διὰ Ἰησοῦ τοῦ παιδός σου)." This evidence indicates that the Christological title "the Servant of God" was used in early Christian liturgy.[58]

Finally, it may be established that the typical Jewish collective interpretation of Isaiah 53 is attested also in the New Testament. Isaiah 53 could be used as a parenetic text so that Christians are exhorted to walk in the footsteps of Jesus who followed the way described in Isaiah 53 (see 1 Peter 2:18-25; Phil 2:5-11).[59]

---

[58]See Jeremias, *Servant of God* 85; Goppelt, *Theologie des Neuen Testaments* 345; Stuhlmacher, "Isaiah 53 in the Gospels and Acts," 156-157.

[59]For this see Jeremias, *Servant of God* 97-99.

8 Isaiah 53 in Patristic Evidence

Human Suffering and Divine Control

The article of Christoph Markschies is a good starting-point for this section.[1] He presents the hypothesis that the interpretation of Isaiah 53 was twofold in patristic literature. In the early phase, two models can be discerned: "exemplary" and "Christological." The first model was used in parenesis (e.g., 1 Clemens 16) and in Christian martyr theology (e.g., the account of the martyrs of Lyons included by Eusebios in his *Eccl Hist* V.1,3-2,7). But this model was later deprecated when Isaiah 53 came to be regarded as an important Christological text. Markschies perceives a development in the Christological model. In the early patristic period (Justin Martyr) the interpretation of Isaiah 53 was emphasized so that Jesus is the Servant of the Lord who was forsaken by God. However, this portrayal of the absolute God-forsakenness of Christ was later modified "with reference to the steadily growing Hellenistic influence of the axiom of God's impassibility or *apatheia* (ἀπάθεια)."[2] This development led to a distinction between the human and divine natures of Christ as can be seen when the interpretations of Origen, Eusebios and Hilary of Poitiers are examined. Suffering pertained to Christ's human nature and impassibility to his divinity. The chief theologian to take this step toward the impassibility axiom was Origen who opposed Celsus's criticism. Celsus took it for granted that God cannot suffer, and this philosophical statement began to modify Christology and the theories concerning the

---

[1]C. Markschies, "Jesus Christ as a Man before God: Two Interpretive Models for Isaiah 53 in the Patristic Literature and Their Development," in: B. Janowski & P. Stuhlmacher (eds), *The Suffering Servant: Isaiah 53 in Jewish and Christian Sources* (Grand Rapids: Eerdmans 2004) 225-320.

[2]Markschies, "Jesus Christ as a Man before God" 231.

sufferings and death of Christ. Markschies writes: "As a result of the impassibility axiom, the absolute God-forsakenness and weakness of Christ in Getshemane are explained away as an event of the body insignificant for the divine Logos, even though Origen adds that this body was sinless (with Isa. 53:9), despite all temptations (*c. Cels.* 1.69)."[3]

Markschies evaluates the impact of the impassibility axiom in the interpretation of Isaiah 53 in negative terms: "At this point the Christological development had distanced itself from the text, and one gets the impression that despite all the positive achievements of ancient Church Christology – which would be foolish to deny – it also had its deficits."[4] He concludes his article by voicing a warning concerning the development of interpretation: "In Eusebius's historical-theological interpretation and in Hilary's docetic interpretation – as well as in other problematic trends in the Christian exegesis of this text during the first centuries – one can see that a true interpretation, even *the* true interpretation, of a text does not protect against bitter errors in individual details. (And the docetic error is one of the most bitter errors of Christian theology.)"[5]

This evaluation of the patristic exegesis on Isaiah 53 provides an interesting emphasis of the influence of the development of Christology on the theological reflections of the suffering and death of Jesus. Nevertheless, it seems to me that Markschies has not adequately considered the different theological aspects of the suffering and death of Jesus which are already visible in the New Testament. The problem can be illustrated with Markschies's treatment of Origen's answer to Celsus. Celsus criticizes the Christian doctrine that Jesus was passive and did not help himself (*Contra Cels* II.59). Origen replied that Christ suffered of

---

[3]Markschies, "Jesus Christ as a Man before God" 292.

[4]Markschies, "Jesus Christ as a Man before God" 319.

[5]Markschies, "Jesus Christ as a Man before God" 319.

his own free will. Markschies characterizes Origen's answer to Celsus as follows: "Even if Christ was helpless, it was only in indifferent and corporeal matters; but Origen believes he was not in fact helpless but in control of his destiny. However, Origen's interpretation of Isaiah 52:13-53:12 is not based on the New Testament witness to Christ alone, but also on a two-part hermeneutic divided into a pneumatic and somatic understanding, in which the philosophical picture of God, above all the axiom of impassibility, plays a central role."[6] However, if we read Origen's own text, he writes *expressis verbis* that he can adduce proof from the Gospel (*Contra Cels* II.59):[7]

He imagines also that both the earthquake and the darkness were an invention; but regarding these, we have in the preceding pages, made our defence, according to our ability, adducing the testimony of Phlegon, who relates that these events took place at the time when our Saviour suffered. And he goes on to say, that "Jesus, while alive, was of no assistance to himself (οὐκ ἐπήρκεσεν ἑαυτῷ), but that he arose after death, and exhibited the marks of his punishment, and showed how his hands had been pierced by nails." We ask him what he means by the expression, "was of no assistance to himself?" For if he means it to refer to want of virtue, we reply that He was of very great assistance. For He neither uttered nor committed anything that was improper, but was truly *"led as a sheep to the slaughter, and was dumb as a lamb before the shearer"*[Isa 53:7]; and the Gospel testifies that 'He opened not His mouth' [Mt 26:62-63]. But if Celsus applies the expression to things indifferent and corporeal, (meaning that in such Jesus could render no help to Himself,) we say that we have proved from the Gospels that He went voluntarily to encounter His sufferings (ἀπεδείξαμεν ἐκ τῶν εὐαγγελίων ὅτι ἑκὼν ἐπὶ ταῦτ ἐλήλυθεν). Speaking next of the statements in the Gospels, that after His resurrection He showed the marks of His punishment, and how His hands had been pierced, he asks, "Who beheld this?" And discrediting the narrative of Mary Magdalene, who is related to have seen

---

[6]Markschies, "Jesus Christ as a Man before God" 290-291.

[7]Concerning the texts of Origen's Contra Celsum see the edition of M. Robert, *Origène: Contra Celse Tome I* (SC 132; Paris: Les Éditions du Cerf 1967) 422-425. The English translation is from ANF. But see also H. Chadwick, *Origen: Contra Celsum Translated With an Introduction & Notes* (Cambridge: University Press 1953).

Him, he replies, "A half-frantic woman, as you state." And because she is not the only one who is recorded to have seen the Saviour after His resurrection, but others also are mentioned, this Jew of Celsus calumniates these statements also in adding, "And some one else of those engaged in the same system of deception!"

Origen refers here to the Gospel according to which Jesus fulfilled Isa 53:7 when he was silent and did not answer his persecutors. Origen also quotes a Gospel passage bearing witness that Jesus voluntarily accepted his sufferings. He does not mention which passage he has in mind, but John 10:14-18 is a strong possibility: "I am the good shepherd; I know my sheep and my sheep know me – just as the Father knows me and I know the Father – and I lay down my life for the sheep. I have other sheep that are not of this sheep pen. I must bring them also. They too will listen to my voice, and there shall be one flock and one shepherd. The reason my Father loves me is that I lay down my life—only to take it up again. *No one takes it from me, but I lay it down of my own accord. I have authority to lay it down and authority to take it up again.* This command I received from my Father." Indeed, Origen interprets John 10:18 (in italics above) in his *Commentary on the Gospel of John* (VI.35 [§ 273-275]) as follows:[8]

If we enquire further into the significance of Jesus being pointed out by John, when he says, "This is the Lamb of God which takes away the sin of the world," we may take our stand at the dispensation of the bodily advent of the Son of God in human life (τὴν οἰκονομίαν τῆς σωματικῆς τοῦ υἱοῦ τοῦ θεοῦ εἰς τὸν τῶν ἀνθρώπων βίον), and in that case we shall conceive the lamb to be no other than the man. For the man "was led like a sheep to the slaughter, and as a lamb, dumb before his shearers," [Isa 53:7] saying, "I was as like a gentle lamb led to the slaughter" [Jer 11:19]. Hence, too, in the Apocalypse a lamb is seen, standing as if slain. This slain lamb has been made, according to certain hidden reasons, a purification of the whole world, for which, according to the Father's love to man, He submitted to death,

---

[8]See the text in C. Blanc, *Origene: Commentaire sur Saint Jean Tome II* (SC 157; Paris: Les Éditions du Cerf 1970) 336-339.

purchasing us back by His own blood from him who had got us into his power, sold under sin. And He who led this lamb to the slaughter was God in man (ὁ δὲ προσαγαγὼν τοῦτον τὸν ἀμνὸν ἐπὶ τὴν θυσίαν ὁ ἐν τῷ ἀνθρώπῳ ἦν θεός), the great High-Priest, as he shows by the words [John 10:18]: "No one takes My life away from Me, but I lay it down of Myself. I have power to lay it down, and I have power to take it again."

Origen combines the interpretation of Isa 53:7 which was discussed in *Contra Cels* II.59 with the word of Jesus in John 10:18, and we may well imagine that this particular passage was in his mind when he wrote to Celsus that he can prove that Jesus voluntarily gave his life. Origen's Christology emphasizes the incarnation of the Son of God in human life in order to save mankind (cf., the word οἰκονομία in the quotation). In John 10 the reference is to the Shepherd who is willing to sacrifice his life. Origen connects this sacrifice with Isa 53:7 but at the same time emphasizes that God (the Shepherd or the Great High Priest) was in the human being (lamb) and led him to death.[9] This being the case, Origen based his criticism against Celsus on the New Testament text when he refutes the view that Jesus was impotent (so could not have the option to avoid torture and death).

The Gospel of John is not alone here. Matthew, who has preserved a tradition according to which Jesus quoted Psalm 22:1 (a neat parallel to Markschies's concept "absolute God-forsakenness") while hanging on the cross, also reported the following words to Peter in Gethsemane (Mt 26:52-54): "Put your sword back in its place, for all who draw the sword will die by the sword. Do you think I cannot call on my Father, and he will at once put at my disposal more than twelve

---

[9] See this dichotomy in Origen's Christology in A. Grillmeier, *Christ in Christian Tradition Volume One: From the Apostolic Age to Chalcedon (451)* (Atlanta: John Knox 1975) 138-148. Grillmeier writes (p. 144): "Thus in Christ there is a twofold rule, that of the Son of God and that of the man Christ." The corporeality of Christ means concealment of Godhead (pp. 145-146): "In the manhood of Christ the fullness of the Godhead is present, even if hidden in the kenosis." Phil 2:5-8 is an important New Testament passage for this *kenosis* as becomes apparent in *Contra Celsum* IV.15-16.

legions of angels? But how then would the Scriptures be fulfilled that say it must happen in this way?" It is clear that in the Gospel of Matthew Jesus is depicted as one who is willing to suffer at the hands of men and dies for mankind. He had an option to avoid his fate but he left everything in the hands of God.

Apostle Paul presents the suffering and death of Jesus in a similar way. He has chosen to become a man and die on behalf of humanity (Phil 2:6-8): "Who, being in very nature God, did not consider equality with God something to be used to his own advantage; rather, he made himself nothing by taking the very nature of a servant, being made in human likeness. And being found in appearance as a man, he humbled himself by becoming obedient to death – even death on a cross!" It is worth noting that Origen, Eusebios and Cyril of Alexandria *expressis verbis* connect Phil 2:6-8 to the interpretation of Isaiah 53.

Origen writes concerning Celsus's misinterpretations that the divinity of Christ is not directly open to all because it is hidden from human eyes. A key-text for Origen is Phil 2:5-8 which he associates with Isa 53:7 (*Contra Celsum* IV.15-16):[10]

> And with respect to His having descended among men, He was "previously in the form of God" [Phil 2:6]; and through benevolence, "divested Himself" (ἑαυτὸν ἐκένωσεν) [Phil 2:7], that He might be capable of being received by men. But He did not, I imagine, undergo any change from good to evil, for "He did no sin" [1 Peter 2:22]; nor from virtue to vice, for "He knew no sin" [2 Cor 5:21]. Nor did He pass from happiness to misery, but He humbled Himself (ἑαυτὸν μὲν ἐταπείνωσεν) [Phil 2:8], and nevertheless was blessed, even when His humiliation was undergone in order to benefit our race. Nor was there any change in Him from best to worst, for how can goodness and benevolence be of the worst? Is it befitting to say of the physician, who looks on dreadful sights and handles unsightly objects in order to cure the sufferers, that he passes from good to evil, or from virtue to vice, or from happiness to misery? And yet the physician, in looking on dreadful sights and

---

[10]See the text in M. Borret, *Origène: Contra Celse Tome II* (SC 136; Paris: Les Éditions du Cerf 1968) 218-223.

handling unsightly objects, does not wholly escape the possibility of being involved in the same fate. But He who heals the wounds of our souls, through the word of God that is in Him, is Himself incapable of admitting any wickedness. But if the immortal God – the Word – by assuming a mortal body and a human soul (σῶμα θνητὸν καὶ ψυχὴν ἀνθρωπίνην ἀναλαβὼν ὁ ἀθάνατος θεὸς λόγος), appears to Celsus to undergo a change and transformation, let him learn that the Word, still remaining essentially the Word, suffers none of those things which are suffered by the body or the soul (ὁ λόγος τῇ οὐσίᾳ μένων λόγος οὐδὲν μὲν πάσχει ὧν πάσχει τὸ σῶμα ἢ ἡ ψυχή); but, condescending occasionally to (the weakness of) him who is unable to look upon the splendours and brilliancy of Deity, He becomes as it were flesh, speaking with a literal voice, until he who has received Him in such a form is able, through being elevated in some slight degree by the teaching of the Word, to gaze upon what is, so to speak, His real and pre-eminent appearance.

For there are different appearances, as it were, of the Word, according as He shows Himself to each one of those who come to His doctrine; and this in a manner corresponding to the condition of him who is just becoming a disciple, or of him who has made a little progress, or of him who has advanced further, or of him who has already nearly attained to virtue, or who has even already attained it. And hence it is not the case, as Celsus and those like him would have it, that our God was transformed, and ascending the lofty mountain, showed that His real appearance was something different, and far more excellent than what those who remained below, and were unable to follow Him on high, beheld. For those below did not possess eyes capable of seeing the transformation of the Word into His glorious and more divine condition. But with difficulty were they able to receive Him as He was; so that it might be said of Him by those who were unable to behold His more excellent nature: "We saw Him, and He had no form nor comeliness; but His form was mean, and inferior to that of the sons of men" [Isa 53:2-3]. And let these remarks be an answer to the suppositions of Celsus, who does not understand the changes or transformations of Jesus, as related in the histories, nor His mortal and immortal nature.

Origen writes that human beings have different ability to understand the divinity of Jesus. Thus the passage is a neat example of Origen's Christology which emphasizes Christ "as mediator of the mystical union of the soul with the hidden God, as mediator between church and God, and all this from the viewpoint of the union in knowledge and in love."[11] Phil 2:6-8 combined with Isa 52:2-3 enable Origen to emphasize that divinity is hidden in Christ. The human being can see the divine glory in Christ but it presupposes humility of which Celsus had no knowledge.

Eusebios begins his commentary on Isa 52:13 by associating it with Phil 2:8-9 and writes that "the present prophecy is clearly expressing the very same thing."[12] The expression μέχρι θανάτου ("unto death") in Phil 2:8 Eusebios refers to Isa 53:3-4, 7-8 and comments: "So when his humiliation and his death were presented in this fashion, the prophetic spirit was first predicting his posthumous exaltation and giving priority to the happy outcome rather than to the suffering which preceded it."[13] Eusebios comments that Aquila translated the Hebrew 'ebed with δοῦλος, the same word which is also used in Phil 2:7. Then Eusebios continues: "But this servant and child of God was filled with all wisdom and knowledge [Lk 2:40] and contained the Word of God in himself. Therefore it is said, 'He will gain understanding', but also 'he will be exalted and glorified and lifted up.' All of this was fulfilled concerning the humanity of our Savior because of its union with God the Word."

Eusebios's interpretation of incarnation has sometimes been criticized as unduly didactic.[14] However, Isa 52:13-53:12 is one of the passages in his commentary on Isaiah where emphasis of incarnation is clearly laid on atonement theology. Jesus became a man in order to save mankind. It is worth noting how Hollerich characterizes Eusebios's interpretation in these cases: "But there are also instances where Eusebius expounds an understanding of Christ's death as expiatory

---

[11]Grillmeier, *Christ in Christian Tradition* 141.

[12]See Eusebios's Commentary on Isa 52:13-53:12 in J. Ziegler, *Eusebius Werke Neunter Band: Der Jesajakommentar* (Berlin: Akademie Verlag 1975) 332-339.

[13]See the translation in R.L. Wilken, *Isaiah Interpreted by Early Christian and Medieval Commentators* (Grand Rapids: Eerdmans 2007) 422.

[14]See, e.g., J.N.D. Kelly, *Early Christian Doctrines* (London: Black 1993) 225.

sacrifice and redemption from the power of Satan. Such language was deeply rooted in catechesis, the liturgy, and the New Testament itself, all of which treated Isaiah as a central inspiration for reflecting on Christ's Passion, Death, and Resurrection. Eusebius could hardly escape its influence. Where the Commentary on Isaiah is concerned, there is scant evidence for an imbalance between a didactic-revelatory theology of Incarnation and a redemptive, atoning theology of the Cross."[15]

Cyril of Alexandria also begins his interpretation of Isa 52:13-53:12 by connecting it to Phil 2:6-8.[16] While Cyril's Christology paves the way to Chalcedon's doctrine of two natures human and divine combined in one person Jesus Christ, his interpretation of the Suffering Servant still takes its starting-point in solid New Testament background. As far as I know there is no earlier example where the combination of Isa 53 and Phil 2:6-8 is made so directly as in Origen's work *Contra Celsum*, and in the commentaries of Eusebios and Cyril of Alexandria. However, there is one possible case which should be mentioned here. In his *Dial* 134 Justin refers to Phil 2:8 and, according to Bailey, even Isa 53:11 (LXX) may have influenced the text: "... and Christ served, even to the slavery of the cross, for the various and many-formed races of mankind, acquiring them by the blood and mystery of the cross."[17]

Origen's emphasis on the difference between the human and the divine nature of Christ then became representative in Christian interpretations. Theodoret of Cyrus sheds valuable light inasmuch as in his Commentary on the Book of Isaiah he carefully formulates the

---

[15]M.J. Hollerich, *Eusebius of Caesarea's* Commentary on Isaiah: *Christian Exegesis in the Age of Constantine* (Oxford: Clarendon 1999) 64-65.

[16]See the text in PG 70:1164D-89C and parts of its translation in Wilken, *Isaiah Interpreted by Early Christian and Medieval Commentators* 416-421.

[17]D.P. Bailey, "'Our Suffering and Crucified Messiah' (Dial. 111.2): Justin Martyr's Allusions to Isaiah 53 in His Dialogue with Trypho with Special Reference to the New Edition of M. Marcovich," in: B. Janowski & P. Stuhlmacher (eds), *The Suffering Servant: Isaiah 53 in Jewish and Christian Sources* (Grand Rapids: Eerdmans 2004) 324-417, esp. 387-388.

suffering of the Servant of the Lord so that the idea of two personae (πρόσωπον) in Jesus Christ is avoided:[18]

Then he describes the kinds of scorn and dishonor: *He was a man of suffering*. He has revealed the nature which endured the passion: it was his body that was nailed to the cross, whereas his divinity made the passion his own (τὸ σῶμα γὰρ τῷ σταυρῷ προσηλώθη, ἡ δὲ θεότης ᾠκειοῦτο τὸ πάθος). *And acquainted with the bearing of sickness.* This again was mentioned concerning the function of his humanity (κατὰ τὸ ἀνθρώπινον): for to give proof of courage and to demonstrate a philosophical bearing are not characteristic of divine, but of human nature (οὐ θείας φύσεως ἀλλ ἀνθρωπείας). *For his face is turned from us: he was dishonored and not esteemed.* Of this passage, the three [Aquila, Symmachos and Theodotion] have given the following interpretation: "And as if there had been a withdrawal of his face, far from him, he was accounted for nothing and accorded no esteem" (καὶ ὡς ἀποκρυβὴ προσώπου ἀπ αὐτοῦ, ἐξουδενωμένος καὶ οὐκ ἐλογίσθη αὐτός). In other words: He had hidden his divine power since he had voluntarily accepted his passion (ἀπέκρυψε τὴν θείαν ἐνέργειαν, γνώμη τὸ πάθος δεξάμενος) and did not seek vengeance upon those who had crucified him; for when he was crucified, he said: "Father, forgive them, they do not know what they do" [Lk 23:24].

Theodoret wrote his commentary after the Council of Ephesus (431) which had established the doctrine of Cyril of Alexandria – which later found its more detailed expressions at the Synod of Chalcedon (451). Cyril's doctrine can be summarized in three points as presented by Grillmeier:[19]

(1) The ὑποστάσεις or φύσεις of Christ may not be divided after the union.[20]

---

[18]See the text in J.-N. Guinot, *Theodoret de Cyr: Commentaire sur Isaïe Tome III* (SC 315, Paris: Les Éditions du Cerf 1984) 148-151; see also the translation in J. Manley, *Isaiah Through the Ages* (Menlo Park: Monastery Book 1995) 785-786.

[19]See Grillmeier, *Christ in Christian Tradition* 482.

[20]Cyril adopted the Apollinarian *mia physis* formula which led him to use it as referring to "individual" or "existent substance".

(2) The ἰδιώματα may not be divided between two persons or two hypostases (or two independent *physeis*), but they must all refer to a single person, to the μία ὑπόστασις (φύσις) τοῦ θεοῦ λόγου σεσαρκωμένη.
(3) The Logos is united καθ ὑπόστασιν to the flesh which he has taken.

Theodoret's interpretation of the Greek word πρόσωπον in Isa 53:3 as rendered by Aquila, Symmachos and Theodotion is interesting. The term had been adopted as a central Christological term signifying "person". It is identical with ὑπόστασις.[21] Theodoret has taken the term πρόσωπον not as an indication of the divine person of the Logos, the Son of God, but as a reference to "divine power" which Jesus had hidden.[22] His suffering was realized in his human body (σῶμα) or nature (φύσις) while at the same time – because after the incarnation the Logos is united with human flesh – even the divinity must have suffered in its own way.

This evidence from the New Testament and patristic literature indicates that the suffering and death of Jesus were regarded from two different viewpoints from the beginning. One aspect is martyr theology which emphasizes the helplessness of Jesus faced with torture and pain. Another aspect concentrates on Jesus' messianic self-understanding when he seeks to fulfil the divine salvation plan. We argued in sect. 7 that this self-understanding is historically rooted in Jesus's application of the prophecies in Zechariach 9-14 to himself. In particular, two texts,

---

[21] See Grillmeier, *Christ in Christian Tradition Volume One* 489.

[22] Grillmeier (*Christ in Christian Tradition Volume One* 492) notes that *prosopon* means for Theodoret "the visible and tangible representation of the unity of God and man in Christ." Grillmeier also refers to Theodoret's interpretation of 2 Cor 4:6: "The 'in the countenance of Jesus Christ' (ἐν προσώπῳ Ἰησοῦ Χριστοῦ) has this meaning: as the divine nature is invisible, it becomes visible in its inwardness through the manhood that is taken, for this is illuminated with divine light and sends out lightnings." This is a neat parallel to understand Theodoret's interpretation of Isaiah 53. Apparently Theodoret is also dependent on the Pauline idea of kenosis (Phil 2:6-8). So Manley, *Isaiah Through the Ages* 786 n. 9.

Zech 11:13 and 12:10, were important in early Christological discussions which emphasize the close relationship between God and the suffering and dying Christ. The balance between the martyr theology and the messianic self-understanding of Jesus varied both in the New Testament and in the patristic literature. Even though we cannot agree with details of Marschies's analysis it contains an important point. It shows that both theological aspects are needed to describe the salvation event of the Christian kerygma. The description of the death of Jesus in the context of martyr theology is necessary to emphasize the absolute God-forsakenness – something which can be deprecated, even forgotten in Christian theology when the whole event was seen solely from the aspect of the divine salvation plan where Jesus controls and rules the course of events.[23]

In this section I have chosen another viewpoint in order to present the interpretation of Isaiah 53 in patristic literature. My aim is to demonstrate the different literary contexts and theological frameworks in which Isaiah 53 has been used in the patristic literature. The emphasis is on the early period which – I think – laid down the main lines of such use. Needless to say, the material is so extensive that it is impossible to consider all references to Isaiah 53 in patristic literature.

Isaiah 53 and Catechetical Teaching before Baptism

In section 7 we observed that Isaiah 53 looms behind 1 Cor 15:3-8 where Paul presents essential details of the Christian kerygma. These details are then included in the baptismal credo which indicates their centrality.[24] We can demonstrate that Isaiah 53 played an important role in the

---

[23]Cf., the dialogue between Virgin Mary and Jesus on the Cross. See this text in L. Gambero, *Mary and the Fathers of the Church: The Blessed Virgin Mary in Patristic Thought* (San Fransisco: Ignatius Press 1999) 333-337.

[24]See J.N.D. Kelly, *Early Christian Creeds* (Essex: Longman 1991) 30-61.

catechetical teaching which leads to baptism. A good New Testament background for this is Acts 8 where Philip proclaims the gospel to the eunuch of the Ethiopian queen on the basis of Isaiah 53 after which the eunuch was baptized.

The earliest post-biblical example of the connection between baptismal ritual and Isaiah 53 is the Letter of Barnabas. The letter was written about 130 AD and deals with the relationship between Judaism and Christianity.[25] It contains a passage where Isa 53:5,7 is used to present God's plan for salvation. The passage from Isaiah is interpreted as referring to the vicarious death of Jesus Christ through which purification (baptism) is achieved (Barn 5:1-3):[26]

> For to this end the Lord endured to deliver up His flesh to corruption, that we might be sanctified through the remission of sins (ἵνα τῇ ἀφέσει τῶν ἁμαρτιῶν ἁγνισθῶμεν), which is effected by the blood of His sprinkling (ὅ ἐστιν ἐν τῷ αἵματι τοῦ ῥαντίσματος αὐτοῦ)[27]. For it is written concerning Him, partly with reference to Israel, and partly to us (γέγραπται γὰρ περὶ αὐτοῦ ἃ μὲν πρὸς τὸν Ἰσραήλ, ἃ δὲ πρὸς ἡμᾶς) and [the Scripture] says thus: "He was wounded for our transgressions, and bruised for our iniquities (ἐτραυματίσθη διὰ τὰς ἀνομίας ἡμῶν καὶ

---

[25] Concerning the date of the letter see R. Hvalvik, *The Struggle for Scripture and Covenant: The Purpose of the Epistle of Barnabas and Jewish-Christian Competition in the Second Century* (Oslo: Det teologiske Menighetsfakultet 1994) 18-37.

[26] For the Greek text of the Letter of Barnabas see K. Wengst, *Didache (Apostellehre) Barnabasbrief Zweiter Klemensbrief Schrift an Diognet* (Schriften des Urchristentums Zweiter Teil; Darmstadt: Wissenschaftliche Buchgesellschaft 1984) and for the Greek translation, in the Ante-Nicene Fathers.

[27] In Wengst's edition, the reading of Codex Hierosolymitanus and the Latin version is followed: ὅ ἐστιν ἐν τῷ ῥαντίσματι αὐτου τοῦ αἵματος. However, the reading of Sinaiticus – which I follow here – is Semitism and can be regarded as *lectio difficilior*. Concerning this see Bailey's note in Markschies's article "Jesus Christ as a Man before God: Two Interpretive Models for Isaiah 53" 240 n. 50. Note, however, that Bailey gives the reading of Sinaiticus as grammatically wrong: ὅ ἐστιν ἐν τῷ αἵματος τοῦ ῥαντίσματος αὐτοῦ.

208

μεμαλάκισται διὰ τὰς ἁμαρτίας ἡμῶν)²⁸: with His blood we are healed (τῷ αἵματι αὐτοῦ ἡμεῖς ἰάθημεν)²⁹. He was brought as a sheep to the slaughter, and as a lamb which is dumb before its shearer (ὡς πρόβατον ἐπὶ σφαγὴν ἤχθη καὶ ὡς ἀμνὸς ἐναντίον τοῦ κείραντος αὐτὸν ἄφωνος)³⁰." Therefore we ought to be deeply grateful to the Lord, because He has both made known to us things that are past, and has given us wisdom concerning things present, and has not left us without understanding in regard to things which are to come.

The text is central in the letter and it presents the message of salvation.³¹ Barn 5:1-3 contains two linguistic details which explicitly refer to baptism. *First,* the remission of sins is related to the baptismal ritual where the sins are removed and the righteous sanctified (see, e.g., 1 Cor 6:9-11). *Second,* the blood of his sprinkling can be connected with the prophecy of baptism in Ezek 36:25 (καὶ ῥανῶ ἐφ᾽ ὑμᾶς ὕδωρ καθαρόν καὶ καθαρισθήσεσθε ἀπὸ πασῶν τῶν ἀκαθαρσιῶν ὑμῶν καὶ ἀπὸ πάντων τῶν εἰδώλων ὑμῶν καὶ καθαριῶ ὑμᾶς) and its application in Hebr 12:17 (προσερχώμεθα μετὰ ἀληθινῆς καρδίας ἐν πληροφορίᾳ πίστεως ῥεραντισμένοι τὰς καρδίας ἀπὸ

---

²⁸This passage is identical with the Septuagint translation in Isa 53:5.

²⁹This is almost identical with the LXX reading in Isa 53:5: τῷ μώλωπι αὐτοῦ ἡμεῖς ἰάθημεν. Probably the reading "blood" has been taken in the letter of Barnabas because the blood of Christ is so central in the New Testament and because the blood is a good correspondence to μώλωπι.

³⁰This is almost identical with the LXX reading in Isa 53:7: ὡς πρόβατον ἐπὶ σφαγὴν ἤχθη καὶ ὡς ἀμνὸς ἐναντίον τοῦ κείροντος αὐτὸν ἄφωνος.

³¹Hvalvik (*The Struggle for Scripture and Covenant* 153) regards the passage Barn 5:1-14 as the main point in the letter: "Christ came in flesh and suffered 1) 'that we might be purified by the forgiveness of our sins' (... 5:1) and 2) 'that he might fill out the total of the sins of those who had driven his prophets to death' (... 5:11). That this is the main point for Barnabas, is sustained by the fact that the same two features are repeated in 14:5: 'He was revealed in order that both *they* might attain the fullness of their sins and we might receive the covenant through the Lord Jesus, the heir to it ... who was prepared for this purpose, to appear and redeem from darkness our hearts ...'"

συνειδήσεως πονηρᾶς καὶ λελουσμένοι τὸ σῶμα ὕδατι καθαρῷ). Thus Barn 5:1-3 presents an essential catechetic message connected with the baptismal ritual, and scriptural proof is sought from Isaiah 53. The text supports the conclusion that the atonement death of the Servant was seen as an essential detail in the Christian kerygma which was taught before baptism.

One important detail in Barn 5:1 is the expression "the blood of his sprinkling" which is a Semitism. It is possible that the writer of the Letter of Barnabas has the Hebrew formulation of Isa 52:15 in mind: כן יזה גוים רבים. The verb יַזֶּה has been translated in Aquila and Theodotion with the Greek verb ῥαντισει, and the writer of the letter apparently knew of this possibility of interpreting Isaiah 53 (against the LXX reading).[32] Another interesting detail is that the promise of salvation in Isaiah 53 is given not only to Israel ("my people" in Isa 53:8) but also to "us" which may have been taken to refer to the peoples (i.e. *rabbîm* in Isa 52:15).

The Letter of Barnabas also contains another important early Christian tradition of baptismal ritual. In Barn 18-20 there is a teaching about "two ways." This section of the letter is almost identical with Didache 1-6 which *expressis verbis* contains instructions which should be given to catechumens before their baptism.

Additional support for the view that Isaiah 53 was an important catechumenal text can be obtained from the texts of Justin Martyr and Irenaeus. Concerning Justin, I discussed his interpretation of Isaiah 53

---

[32]Concerning the readings of Aquila and Theodotion see F. Field, *Origenis Hexaplorum Quae Supersunt; Sive Veterum Interpretum Graecorum in Totum Vetus Testamentum Fragmenta* (Oxford: Clarendon 1867) 533; H. Hegermann, *Jesaja 53 in Hexapla, Targum und Peschitta* (Gütersloh: Mohn 1954) 33, 45 and the tablet at the end of the book.

210

already in the first volume of Studies in Rewritten Bible.[33] The most significant presentation of Isaiah 53 in Justin's writings is to be found in *Dial* 13 where he quotes Isa 52:10-54:6 as a proof text for Christian baptism.[34] Justin introduces the proof text Isa 52:10-54:6 at the point where Trypho formulates the question why Christians do not need to consider the whole mosaic Torah (*Dial* 10). Justin begins by arguing that there are prophecies about the new covenant in the Old Testament (in particular Jer 31:31-34), and that Christians live according to this new covenant and not according to the Mosaic covenant which pertains only to Jews (*Dial* 11).[35] This new covenant is then connected with Isa 55:3-5

---

[33] A. Laato, "Isaiah 53 and the Biblical Exegesis of Justin Martyr," in: A.Laato & J. Van Ruiten (eds), *Rewritten Bible Reconsidered: Proceedings of the Conference in Karkku, Finland August 24-26 2006* (SRB 1, Winona Lake: Eisenbrauns; Turku: Åbo Akademi University 2008) 215-229; see also Bailey, "'Our Suffering and Crucified Messiah'" 324-417. I was aware of that Janowski's and Stuhlmacher edited study on Isaiah 53 was translated to English when I wrote my article. But I simply assumed that it was a translation. I did not know that Bailey had written his own contribution not attested in the German edition from 1996.

[34] See the texts of Justin Martyr in E.J. Goodspeed (ed.), *Die ältesten Apologeten. Texte mit kurzen Einleitungen* (Göttingen: Vandenhoeck & Ruprecht 1984); M. Marcovich (ed.), *Iustini Martyris Apologiae pro christianis*. Berlin: de Gruyter 1994; idem, *Iustini Martyris Dialogus cum Tryphone*. Berlin: de Gruyter 1997. The translations are from Ante-Nicene Fathers. See also *St. Justin Martyr: Dialogue with Trypho*. Transl. by Thomas B. Falls; rev. and with a new introduction by Thomas P. Halton; ed. by Michael Slusser. Washington: Catholic University of America Press 2003.

[35] On Justin's way to use the Old Testament and testimonies to argue for Christian kerygma see O. Skarsaune, *The Proof from Prophecy. A Study in Justin Martyr's Proof-Text Tradition: Text-Type, Provenance, Theological Profile* (SupNT 56, Leiden: Brill 1987); idem, "The Development of Scriptural Interpretation in the Second and Third Centuries – except Clement and Origen," in: M. Saebø (ed.), *Hebrew Bible Old Testament. The History of Its Interpretation I/1: Antiquity* (Göttingen: Vandenhoeck & Ruprecht 1996) 373-442. Christians' will to connect the kerygma intimately to the Old Testament texts from the first beginning led to many conflicts between Jews and Christians. Justin's *Dialogue* is a good source to understand this early confrontation. I have dealt with this problem in an article: A. Laato, "Justin Martyr Encounters Judaism," in: A. Laato & P. Lindqvist (eds), *Encounters of the Children of Abraham from Ancient to Modern Times* (STCA 1, Leiden: Brill 2010) 97-123.

which predicts a new era in the world when God will manifest the mercies of David (*Dial* 12). This Isaianic text is important because it appears just before the quotation of Isa 52:10-54:6 in *Dial* 13 and then recurs in *Dial* 14. Thus Isa 55:3-5 forms an inclusion to the quotation of Isa 52:10-54:6. The text of Isa 55:3-5 is quoted in non-LXX form in *Dial* 12 while it is a part of the LXX-text Isa 55:3-13 in *Dial* 14. This is an indication that Isa 55:3-5 was a proof-text which Justin had taken from an earlier Christian testimony.[36]

When Isa 55:3-5 is connected with the idea of the new covenant predicted in Jer 31:31-34 it is easier to understand why Isa 52:10-54:6 serves as an important proof-text for the new covenant in general and Christian baptism in particular. After all, baptism was an initiation ritual through which one could become a member of the new covenant. An introduction to the quotation of Isa 52:10-54:6 reads as follows (*Dial* 13):

> For Isaiah did not send you to a bath, there **to wash away murder and other sins**, which not even all the water of the sea were sufficient to purge; but, as might have been expected, this was that saving bath of the olden time which followed those who repented, and who no longer **were purified** by the blood of goats and of sheep, or by the ashes of an heifer, or by the offerings of fine flour, but **by faith through the blood of Christ, and through His death, who died for this very reason**, as Isaiah himself said, when he spake thus ...

After quoting Isa 52:10-54:6 Justin continues to describe Christian baptism (*Dial* 14):

> By reason, therefore, of **this laver of repentance and knowledge of God**, which has been ordained on account of the transgression of God's people, as Isaiah cries, we have believed, and testify that that **very baptism which he announced is alone able to purify** those who have repented; and this is the water of life.

---

[36]So Skarsaune, *Proof from Prophecy* 63-65.

212

Thus Isaiah 53 is intimately connected with the baptismal ritual by Justin.[37] Justin's Dialogue supports our claim that Isaiah 53 was regarded as a *locus classicus* in the Old Testament, which enabled the presentation of the Christian kerygma.

For Irenaeus the Book of Isaiah was the "fifth" Gospel.[38] This is well demonstrated in *Adv Haer* IV.23 where he interprets Jesus's saying in John 4:35-38. He argues that the apostles were able to use the sayings of the patriarchs and prophets "so that posterity, possessing the fear of God, might easily accept the advent of Christ, having been instructed by the prophets" (*Adv Haer* IV.23.1).[39] He then presents three essential passages from the Book of Prophets as examples. They are Isa 7:14 in Matthew 1, Isa 61:1 in Luke 4 and Isaiah 53 in Acts 8. This being the case, it was, according to Irenaeus, possible to present the Christian kerygma by interpreting prophecies from the Book of Isaiah. In particular, Irenaeus's discussion concerning Isaiah 53 is instructive (*Adv Haer* IV.23.2):[40]

> For this reason, also, Philip the Apostle, when he had discovered the eunuch of the Ethiopians' queen reading these words which had been written: 'He was led as a sheep to the slaughter; and as a lamb is dumb before the shearer, so He opened not His mouth: in His humiliation His judgment was taken away' [Acts 8:27; Isa 53:7]; and all the rest which the prophet proceeded to relate in regard

---

[37]The connection to baptismal ritual has also been presented in D.J. Bingham, "Justin and Isaiah 53," *Vigiliae Christianae* 54,3 (2000) 248-261, esp. 253-259; see further my detailed analysis in "Isaiah 53 and the Biblical Exegesis of Justin Martyr" 219-223.

[38]Cf., the following study: J.F.A. Sawyer, *The Fifth Gospel: Isaiah in the History of Christianity* (Cambridge: Cambridge University Press 1996).

[39]Elsewhere Irenaeus emphasizes that the Word of God, i.e. Jesus Christ, stands behind both covenants in the Old and New Testament (see, e.g., *Adv Haer* IV.9.1): "But one and the same householder produced both covenants, the Word of God, our Lord Jesus Christ, who spoke with both Abraham and Moses, and who has restored us anew to liberty, and has multiplied that grace which is from Himself."

[40]See the text of Irenaeus in A. Rousseau, *Irénée de Lyon: Contre les Hérésies Livre IV* (SC 100, Paris: Les Éditions du Cerf 1965) 694-699.

to His passion and His coming in the flesh, and how He was dishonoured by those who did not believe Him (τὰ λοιπὰ ὅσα περὶ τοῦ πάθους αὐτοῦ καὶ τῆς ἐνσάρκου παρουσίας καὶ πῶς ἠτιμάσθη ὑπὸ τῶν μὴ πιστευόντων αὐτῷ); easily persuaded him to believe in Him, that He was Christ Jesus, who was crucified under Pontius Pilate, and suffered whatsoever the prophet had predicted, and that He was the Son of God, who gives eternal life to men. And immediately when [Philip] had baptized him, he departed from him. For nothing else [but baptism] was wanting to him who had been already instructed by the prophets: he was not ignorant of God the Father, nor of the rules as to the [proper] manner of life, but was merely ignorant of the advent of the Son of God (ἀλλὰ μόνην τὴν παρουσίαν ἠγνόει τοῦ υἱοῦ τοῦ θεοῦ), which, when he had become acquainted with, in a short space of time, he went on his way rejoicing, to be the herald in Ethiopia of Christ's advent (τῆς τοῦ χριστοῦ παρουσίας). Therefore Philip had no great labour to go through with regard to this man, because he was already prepared in the fear of God by the prophets. For this reason, too, did the apostles, collecting the sheep which had perished of the house of Israel, and discoursing to them from the Scriptures, prove that this crucified Jesus was the Christ, the Son of the living God (ἐδείκνυον Ιησοῦν τὸν σταυρωθέντα τοῦτον εἶναι τὸν χριστὸν τὸν υἱὸν τοῦ θεοῦ τοῦ ζῶντος); and they persuaded a great multitude, who, however, [already] possessed the fear of God. And there were, in one day, baptized three, and four, and five thousand men [Acts 2:41; 4:4].

In this passage Irenaeus gives a precise witness of the mission strategy toward those people who know the Old Testament scriptures. He writes that the only thing which is needed is the confession that the crucified Jesus was the Messiah and the Son of God promised in the prophetic writings. This fittingly parallels Paul's proclamation of the gospel (Acts 17:2-3): "As was his custom, Paul went into the synagogue, and on three Sabbath days he reasoned with them from the Scriptures, explaining and proving that the Messiah had to suffer and rise from the dead. 'This Jesus I am proclaiming to you is the Messiah', he said." It is highly possible that the passage of the Scripture which Paul used in his preaching was Isaiah 53.[41]

Another significant element of Irenaeus' passage is his emphasis on the role of baptism which was followed by the proclamation of the gospel according to Isaiah 53. It is easy to believe that Isaiah 53 was used when catechumens were instructed and prepared for baptism.

In his *The Demonstrations of the Apostolic Preaching* Irenaeus explains how Isaiah 53 can serve to present the Christian message of salvation.[42] It is extant only in Armenian but Eusebios assesses it (*Eccl Hist* V.26) under the title: εἰς ἐπίδειξιν τοῦ ἀποστολικοῦ κηρύγματος. The book summarises essential biblical argumentation which was used to adduce Christian doctrines from biblical passages, in particular the Old Testament.

The book was written to Marcianus who was a Christian. It is described by Irenaeus himself as "a manual of essentials" (*Dem* 1). It may be regarded as a summary of Irenaeus's earlier larger work *Adversus Haereses*. Marcianus apparently knew that work because Irenaeus refers to it at the end of his book (*Dem* 99) under the title "Exposure and Overthrow of Knowledge Falsely So-called."

In *Dem* 66-70 Irenaeus presents the salvation plan of God which envisages the recapitulation of the whole universe through his Son. The Greek term *anakefalaiosis* (Lat. *recapitulatio*) was a rhetorical term, the aim of which was to sum up the main *points* (*caput*, "title") in a speech. Irenaeus adopted this term from the theology of *Corpus Paulinum* (Eph

---

[41]Cf., our conclusion in sect. 7 that Isaiah 53 looms behind 1 Cor 15:4-11.

[42]See the text in A. Rousseau, *Irénée de Lyon: Démonstration de la Prédication Apostolique* (SC 406, Paris: Les Éditions du Cerf 1995). The English translation of Demonstrations made by J. Armitage Robinson is in I.M. MacKenzie, *Irenaeus's Demonstration of the Apostolic Preaching: A Theological Commentary and Translation* (Aldershot: Ashgate 2002).

1:10)[43] and used it to describe Jesus' mission to collect all the saved in the Christian congregation through the orthodox faith in Father, Son and Holy Spirit and then in eschatological time through the resurrection (*Adv Haer* I.10.1):[44]

> The Church, though dispersed throughout the whole world, even to the ends of the earth, has received from the apostles and their disciples this faith: [She believes] **in one God, the Father Almighty**, Maker of heaven, and earth, and the sea, and all things that are in them; and **in one Christ Jesus, the Son of God**, who became incarnate for our salvation; and **in the Holy Spirit**, who proclaimed through the prophets the dispensations of God, and the advents, and the birth from a virgin, and the passion, and the resurrection from the dead, and the ascension into heaven in the flesh of the beloved Christ Jesus, our Lord, and His [future] manifestation from heaven in the glory of the Father 'to gather all things in one [Eph 1:10], and to raise up anew all flesh of the whole human race, in order that to Christ Jesus, our Lord, and God, and Saviour, and King, according to the will of the invisible Father,' 'every knee should bow, of things in heaven, and things in earth, and things under the earth, and that every tongue should confess' [Phil 2:10-11] to Him, and that He should execute just judgment towards all; that He may send 'spiritual wickednesses' [Eph 6:12], and the angels who transgressed and became apostates, together with the ungodly, and unrighteous, and wicked, and profane among men, into everlasting fire; but may, in the exercise of His grace, confer immortality on the righteous, and holy, and those who have kept His

---

[43]Irenaeus criticizes the Gnostic way to interpret Eph 1:10 (*Adv Haer* I.3.4). Concerning Irenaeus's recapitulation theory see E. Osborn, *Irenaeus of Lyons* (Cambridge: Cambridge University Press 2001) 97–140. Osborn distinguishes at least 11 different ideas in Irenaus's recapitulation (pp. 97–98). A.D. Alès ("La doctrine de la récapitulation en S. Irénée," [*RSR* 6 (1916) 185–211]) distinguishes between the logic and cosmic recapitulation theories. According to the logical theory, the starting- and end-points are related. The cosmic theory, again, emphasizes the idea presented in Eph 1:10: Christ will unite. See further C. Smith, "Chiliasm and Recapitulation in the Theology of Ireneus," *VC* 48 (1994) 313-331, esp. 321-329. According to Smith, "recapitulation itself is ... an insistence on the essential harmony of the true soteriological task that of bringing humanity from its Edenic state of infancy to the true maturity of God-likeness" (p. 329).

[44]See the text in A. Rousseau, *Irénée de Lyon: Contre les Hérésies Livre I* (SC 264, Paris: Les Éditions du Cerf 1979) 154-161.

commandments, and have persevered in His love, some from the beginning [of their Christian course], and others from [the date of] their repentance, and may surround them with everlasting glory.

Irenaeus emphasizes that the whole salvation plan has been revealed already by the prophets (*Dem* 66):[45] "So then, that the Son of God should be born, and in what manner born, and where He was to be born, and that Christ is the one eternal King the prophets thus declared. And again they told beforehand concerning Him how, sprung from mankind, He should heal those whom He healed, and raise the dead whom He raised, and be hated and despised and undergo sufferings and be put to death and crucified, even as He was hated and despised and put to death." After this Irenaeus observes that the healing of mankind and universe by the Son of God as well as the suffering and death of the Son of God on behalf of mankind are both foretold in Isaiah 53. The passage is so important to understand the role of Isaiah 53 in Irenaeus's theology that it is worth quoting here (*Dem* 67-70, all quotations from Isaiah 53 are set in italics):

> 67 At this point let us speak of His healings. Isaiah says thus: *He took our infirmities and bare our sicknesses* [Isa 53:4]. That is to say, He shall take, and shall bear. For there are passages in which the Spirit of God through the prophets recounts things that are to be as having taken place.[46] For that which with God is essayed and conceived of as determined to take place, is reckoned as having already taken place: and the Spirit, regarding and seeing the time in which the issues of the prophecy are fulfilled, utters the words (accordingly). And concerning the kind of healing, thus will He make mention, saying: 'In that day shall the deaf hear the words of the book, and in darkness and in me the eyes of the blind shall see' [Isa 29:18]. And the same says again: 'Be strong, ye weak hands and feeble and trembling knees: be comforted, ye that

---

[45]See the text of *Dem* 66-70 in Rousseau, *Démonstration de la Prédication Apostolique* 176-185.

[46]In *Adv Haer* IV.33.11 Irenaeus actually had rendered Isa 53:4 in the future tense (assuming that the Latin translation is right): *Ipse infirmitates nostras accipiet et langores portabit.* See this text in Rousseau, *Irénée de Lyon: Contre les Hérésies Livre IV* 832.

are of a fearful mind. Be strong, fear not. Behold, our God will recompense judgment: He will come and save us. Then shall the eyes of the blind be opened, and the ears of the deaf shall hear: then shall the lame man leap as an hart, and the tongue of the stammerers shall be plain' [Isa 35:4-6]. And concerning the dead, that they shall be raised, he says thus: 'The dead shall be raised, and they that are in the tombs shall be raised' [Isa 26:19]. And in bringing these things to pass He shall be believed to be the Son of God.

68 And that He shall be despised and tormented and in the end put to death, Isaiah says thus, *Behold, my son shall understand*[47], *and shall be exalted and glorified greatly. Even as many shall be astonished at thee, so without glory shall thy form be from men. And many races shall be astonished, and kings shall shut their mouths: for they to whom it was not declared concerning him shall see, and they who have not heard shall consider. Lord, who hath believed our report? And to whom hath the arm of the Lord been revealed? We declared before him as a child, as a root in a dry ground: and there is to him no form nor glory: and we saw him, and he had no form nor beauty: and his form was without honor, meaner than that of other seen: a man in chastisement, and acquainted with the bearing of pain; for his face was turned away, he was dishonored and made of no account. He beareth our sins, and for our sakes endureth pain: and we accounted him to be in pain and chastisement and affliction. But he was wounded for our iniquities, and was tormented for our sins. The discipline of our peace (was) upon him; by his stripes we were healed.* By these words it is declared that He was tormented; as also David says 'And I was tormented'. Now David was never tormented, but Christ (was), when the command was given that He should be crucified. And again by Isaiah His Word says: 'I gave my back to scourging, and my cheeks to smiting: and my face I turned not away from the shame of spitting.' And Jeremiah the prophet says the same, thus: 'He shall give his cheek to the smiter: he shall be filled with reproaches.' All these things Christ suffered.

69. Now what follows in Isaiah is this: *By his stripes we were healed. All we like sheep went astray: a man in his way went astray: and the Lord delivered him up to our sins.* It is manifest therefore that by the will of the Father these things occurred to Him for the sake of our salvation. Then he says: *And he by*

---

[47]Robinson notes in his translation that the Armenian text reads here the passive ("be understood"); but he notes that doubtless the LXX συνήσει should be followed here (the difference is only in the final letter).

reason of his suffering opened not (his) mouth: as a sheep to the slaughter was he brought, as a lamb dumb before the shearer. Behold how he declares His voluntary coming to death. And when the prophet says: *In the humiliation his judgment was taken away,* he signifies the appearance of His humiliation: according to the form of the abasement was the taking away of judgment. And the taking away of judgment is for some unto salvation, and to some unto the torments of perdition. For there is a taking away for a person, and also from a person. So also with the judgment—those for whom it is taken away have it unto the torments of their perdition: but those from whom it is taken away are saved by it. Now those took away to themselves the judgment who crucified Him, and when they had done this to Him believed not on Him: for through that judgment which was taken away by them they shall be destroyed with torments. And from them that believe on Him the judgment is taken away, and they are no longer under it. And the judgment is that which by fire will be the destruction of the unbelievers at the end of the world.

70 Then he says: *His generation who shall declare?* This was said to warn us, lest on account of His enemies and the outrage of His sufferings we should despise Him as a mean and contemptible man. For He who endured all this has an undeclarable generation; for by generation He means descent; (for) He who is His Father is undeclarable and unspeakable. Know therefore that such descent was His who endured these sufferings; and despise Him not because of the sufferings which for thy sake He of purpose endured, but fear Him because of His descent.

In this long quotation Irenaeus combines healing and the salvation of the cosmos. Isaiah 53 is a proof text for both events. Isa 50:6-7 is also included. By following Mt 8:17 Irenaeus interprets Isa 53:4 so that the whole cosmos will be delivered from the yoke of sin and death to the ultimate freedom granted by God. Healing means understanding the message of the prophetic writings and hearkening to the Gospel (Isa 29:18), freedom from the powers of illness and evil (Isa 35:4-6) and resurrection from death (Isa 26:19). Irenaeus finds proof texts in the Book of Isaiah for all three themes indicating once again that this prophetic work is for him the fifth Gospel. A similar idea is presented in *Adv Haer* IV.33.11 where references to Isaiah 26 and 35 can be found:[48]

> Those, again, who declare that at His coming "the lame man shall leap as an hart, and the tongue of the dumb shall [speak] plainly, and the eyes of the blind shall be opened, and the ears of the deaf shall hear" [Isa 35:5-6], and that "the hands which hang down, and the feeble knees, shall be strengthened" [Isa 35:3], and that "the dead which are in the grave shall arise" [Isa 26:19], and that He Himself "shall take [upon Him] our weaknesses, and bear our sorrows" [Isa 53:4; Mt 8:17] — [all these] proclaimed those works of healing which were accomplished by Him.

The text in *Dem* 66-70 fittingly illustrates how the passive and active obedience of Jesus Christ are combined here.[49] On the one hand, Jesus is ready passively to accept the fate destined for him by his Father: "... by the will of the Father these things occurred to Him for the sake of our salvation." On the other, by his own free will he undertakes to suffer in order to save mankind. This is manifest in Isa 53:7, according to Irenaeus: "Behold how he declares His voluntary coming to death." Irenaeus's text is a salutary corrective to Markschies's thesis on "absolute God-forsakenness" which was superseded more and more by Christological statements according to which Jesus had his suffering and death under control. We have no Hellenization here but Irenaeus simply follows the New Testament presentations where both passive and active obedience are already emphasized.

In *Dem* 70 Isa 53:8 is quoted and serves as a warning to "us" i.e. everybody should consider carefully who is this Suffering Servant whose generation cannot be declared – this refers to the virginal birth. Isa 53:8 was an important proof text for Jesus' virginal birth as, for example, can be seen in Justin's *Dialogue* (43; 97) and Irenaeus's *Adversus Haereses* (II.28.5; III.19.2).

---

[48] See the text in Rousseau, *Irénée de Lyon: Contre les Hérésies Livre IV* 824-833.

[49] Concerning the passive and active obedience of Jesus in *Dem* 69 see MacKenzie, *Irenaeus's Demonstration of the Apostolic Preaching* 198-199.

Our survey so far has conveyed a neat picture of how Isaiah 53 was an important theological text in the early Church. There is every sign that Isaiah 53 was used in a missionary context. It contained essential details of Christian kerygma. Therefore, I disagree with the conclusions which Markschies reached from the statistic analyses. He noted that there are 317 references to Isa 52:13-53:12 in the first three volumes of *Biblia Patristica* (corresponding to the period from the end of the first century to the end of the second century) and the corresponding number in the case of the Johannine Prologue is 1444. From these statistics he concludes that Isaiah 53 is "not completely unimportant."[50] If we are correct in believing that Isaiah 53 underlies 1 Cor 15 and that Isaiah 53 was an important proof text in catechetical instruction, then the regular use of the baptismal ritual emphasizes its role. For example, the Catechetical Lecture 13 of Cyril of Jerusalem is based on Isaiah 53. It begins with words taken from Isa 53:1, 7: "Who has believed our report? And to whom is the arm of the Lord revealed?...He is brought as a lamb to the slaughter ..." The following quotations illustrate how Isaiah 53 (in italics) and even Isa 50:6-7 were used in Cyril's Catechetical Lecture 13:[51]

13.13. But the High-priest having questioned Him, and heard the truth, is angry; and the wicked officer of wicked men smites Him; and the countenance, which had shone as the sun, endured to be smitten by lawless hands. Others also come and spit on the face of Him, who by spittle had healed the man who was blind from his birth. 'Do ye thus requite the Lord? This people is foolish and unwise' [Deut 32:6]. And the Prophet greatly wondering, says, '*Lord, who has believed our report?*' [Isa 53:1] For the thing is incredible, that God, the Son of God, and '*the Arm of the Lord*' [Isa 53:1], should suffer such things. But that they who are being saved may not disbelieve, the Holy Ghost writes before, in the person of Christ, who says, (for He who then spoke these things, was afterward Himself an actor in them,) 'I gave My back to the scourges'; (for Pilate, when he had scourged Him, delivered Him to be crucified ;) '*and*

---

[50]Markschies, "Jesus Christ as a Man before God" 228.

[51]See the text in PG 33.

My cheeks to smitings; and My face I turned not away from the shame of spittings' [Isa 50:6]; saying, as it were, 'Though knowing before that they will smite Me, I did not even turn My cheek aside; for how should I have nerved My disciples against death for truth's sake, had I Myself dreaded this?' I said. 'He that loves his life shall lose it' [John 12:25]: if I had loved My life, how was I to teach without practising what I taught? First then, being Himself God, He endured to suffer these things at the hands of men; that after this, we men, when we suffer such things at the hands of men for His sake, might not be ashamed. You see that of these things also the prophets have clearly written beforehand. Many, however, of the Scripture testimonies I pass by for want of time, as I said before; for if one should exactly search out all, not one of the things concerning Christ would be left without witness.

13.30: Concerning the robbers who were crucified with Him, it is written, *'And He was numbered with the transgressors'* [Isa 53:12]. Both of them were before this transgressors, but one was so no longer. For the one was a transgressor to the end, stubborn against salvation; who, though his hands were fastened, smote with blasphemy by his tongue. When the Jews passing by wagged their heads, mocking the Crucified, and fulfilling what was written, When they looked on Me, they shook their heads , he also reviled with them. But the other abused the reviler; and it was to him the end of life and the beginning of restoration; the surrender of his soul a first share in salvation. And after rebuking the other, he says, Lord, remember me ; for with You is my account. Heed not this man, for the eyes of his understanding are blinded; but remember me. I say not, remember my works, for of these I am afraid. Every man has a feeling for his fellow-traveller; I am travelling with You towards death; remember me, Your fellow-wayfarer. I say not, Remember me now, but, when You come in Your kingdom.

13.34: 'The Sun was darkened, because of the Sun of Righteousness' [Mal 3:20 (=4:2)]. Rocks were rent, because of the spiritual Rock. Tombs were opened, and the dead arose, because of Him who 'was free among the dead ; He sent forth His prisoners out of the pit wherein is no water' [Zech 9:11]. Be not then ashamed of the Crucified, but be also bold to say, *'He bears our sins, and endures grief for us, and with His stripes we are healed'* [Isa 53:4-5]. Let us not be unthankful to our Benefactor. And again; for the transgression of my people was He led to death; and I will give the wicked for His burial, and the rich for His death. Therefore Paul says plainly, that 'Christ died for our sins according to the Scriptures, and that He was buried, and that He has risen again the third day according to the Scriptures' [1 Cor 15:3-4].

A significant detail is reported in 13.34 where Cyril connects Paul's tradition about the Christian kerygma in 1 Cor 15:3-4 with Isaiah 53. It is also worth noting that Lecture 14 on the resurrection of Jesus begins with a quotation from 1 Cor 15:1-4. This being the case as late as the end of the 4th Century AD Isaiah 53 plays a decisive role in catechetical lectures. We may only imagine how often Isaiah 53 was read and interpreted on these occasions. This evidence give us reason to say that Isaiah 53 was a central text in the Early Church. It was an essential text in cathecetical teaching when the meaning of the death of Jesus was discussed.

Isaiah 53 and Parenesis to Christians

At the end of the first century AD Clement wrote his First Letter to the Corinthians. In chapter 16 he uses Isa 53:1-12 and Ps 22:6-8 whcn he presents Christ as an example of humility, and exhorts Christians to follow his example.[52] The text of Isaiah 53 which Clement quotes here is on many points identical with the LXX tradition. I have marked some important differences from the Greek text:[53]

> For Christ is of those who are humble-minded, and not of those who exalt themselves over His flock. Our Lord Jesus Christ, the Sceptre of the majesty of God, did not come in the pomp of pride or arrogance, although He might have done so, but in a lowly condition, as the Holy Spirit had declared regarding Him. For He says, *"Lord, who hath believed our report, and to whom is the arm of the Lord revealed? We have declared [our message] in His presence* (ἀνηγγείλαμεν ἐναντίον αὐτου): *He is, as it were, a child, and like a root in thirsty ground* (ὡς παιδίον ὡς ῥίζα ἐν γῇ διψώσῃ); *He has no form nor glory, yea, we saw Him, and He had no form nor comeliness; but His form was without eminence, yea, deficient in comparison with the [ordinary] form of men. He is a man exposed to stripes and suffering,*

---

[52] See Markschies, "Jesus Christ as a Man before God" 234-241.

[53] The translation is from the *Ante-Nicene Fathers*. Fort the Greek text see Wengst, *Didache (Apostellehre) Barnabasbrief Zweiter Klemensbrief Schrift an Diognet.*

and acquainted with the endurance of grief: for His countenance was turned away; He was despised, and not esteemed. He bears our iniquities, and is in sorrow for our sakes; yet we supposed that [on His own account] He was exposed to labour, and stripes, and affliction. But He was wounded for our transgressions, and bruised for our iniquities. The chastisement of our peace was upon Him, and by His stripes we were healed. All we, like sheep, have gone astray; [every] man has wandered in his own way; and the Lord has delivered Him up for our sins (καὶ κύριος παρέδωκεν αὐτὸν ὑπὲρ τῶν ἁμαρτιῶν ἡμῶν), *while He in the midst of His sufferings openeth not His mouth. He was brought as a sheep to the slaughter, and as a lamb before her shearer is dumb, so He openeth not His mouth. In His humiliation His judgment was taken away; who shall declare His generation? for His life is taken from the earth. For the transgressions of my people was He brought down to death* (ἥκει εἰς θάνατον). *And I will give the wicked for His sepulchre, and the rich for His death, because He did no iniquity, neither was guile found in His mouth. And the Lord is pleased to purify Him by stripes. If ye make an offering for sin, your soul shall see a long-lived seed. And the Lord is pleased to relieve Him of the affliction of His soul, to show Him light, and to form Him with understanding, to justify the Just One who ministereth well to many; and the Himself shall carry their sins. On this account He shall inherit many, and shall divide the spoil of the strong; because His soul was delivered to death, and He was reckoned among the transgressors, and He bare the sins of many, and for their sins was He delivered.*" And again He saith, "I am a worm, and no man; a reproach of men, and despised of the people. All that see Me have derided Me; they have spoken with their lips; they have wagged their head, [saying] He hoped in God, let Him deliver Him, let Him save Him, since He delighteth in Him." Ye see, beloved, what is the example which has been given us; for if the Lord thus humbled Himself, what shall we do who have through Him come under the yoke of His grace?

Clement's usage of Isa 53:1-12 is reminiscent of that in 1 Peter 2:18-25 and Phil 2:5-11. These passages show how Isaiah 53 was understood in early Christianity as a text which concerned every Christian who wanted to imitate Jesus Christ in his life. A significant deviation from the translation of the LXX consists in the use of the preposition ὑπέρ when Clement speaks of servant's sufferings on our behalf. It was probably based on an early Christian tradition where the translation of Isaiah 53 had been checked with the Hebrew text.[54]

The Apostolic Constitutions continue to use Isaiah 53 in parenesis. In particular, the text is invoked to exhort bishops to take good care of the Christian congregation (*Apost Const* II.4.25):[55]

> For you imitate Christ the Lord (μιμηταὶ γάρ ἐστε χριστοῦ τοῦ κυρίου); and as He "bare the sins of us all upon the tree" [1 Pet 2:24] at His crucifixion, the innocent for those who deserved punishment, so also you ought to make the sins of the people your own (οὕτως καὶ ὑμᾶς τοῦ λαοῦ τὰς ἁμαρτίας ἐξιδιοποιεῖσθαι χρή). For concerning our Saviour it is said in Isaiah, "He bears our sins, and is afflicted for us" [Isa 53:4]. And again: "He bare the sins of many, and was delivered for our offences" [Isa 53:12]. As, therefore, you are patterns (σκόποι) for others, so have you Christ for your pattern (σκόπον). As, therefore, He is concerned for all, so be you for the laity under you. For do not thou imagine that the office of a bishop is an easy or light burden. As, therefore, you bear the weight, so have you a right to partake of the fruits before others, and to impart to those that are in want, as being to give an account to Him, who without bias will examine your accounts.

The text is a part of the longer passage which deals with the tithes and first-fruits which should be given to bishops who will then distribute them to the needy. The quotation reveals that the parenetical text of 1 Peter 2:18-25 was the key text which inspired the writer to apply Isaiah 53 to bishops. Jesus is described as he who has fulfilled Isaiah 53 and Christians are exhorted to follow his example. Another text from the same letter, 1 Peter 5:1-4, enjoins elders or bishops to take care of the flock of God and in it the sufferings of Christ are presented as exemplary: "To the elders (πρεσβυτέρους) among you, I appeal as a fellow elder

---

[54]See further sect. 7.

[55]See the text in F.X. Funk, *Didascalia et Constitutiones Apostolorum Volumen I* (Paderborn: Schoeningh 1905) 97-99; M. Metzger, *Les Constitutions Apostoliques Tome I* (SC 320, Paris: Les Éditions du Cerf 1985) 232-233.

and a witness of Christ's sufferings who also will share in the glory to be revealed: Be shepherds of God's flock that is under your care, watching (ἐπισκοποῦντες) over them – not because you must, but because you are willing, as God wants you to be; not pursuing dishonest gain, but eager to serve; not lording it over those entrusted to you, but being examples to the flock. And when the Chief Shepherd appears, you will receive the crown of glory that will never fade away." Another text in the Apostolic Constitutions which uses Isaiah 53 for parenesis is *Apost Const* III.19. It deals with the task of deacons:[56]

> Let the deacons be in all things unspotted, as the bishop himself is to be, only more active; in number according to the largeness of the Church, that they may minister to the infirm as workmen that are not ashamed. And let the deaconess be diligent in taking care of the women; but both of them ready to carry messages, to travel about, to minister, and to serve, as spake Isaiah concerning the Lord, saying: "To justify the righteous, who serves many faithfully" (δικαιῶσαι δίκαιον εὖ δουλεύοντα πολλοῖς) [Isa 53:11].[57] Let every one therefore know his proper place, and discharge it diligently with one consent, with one mind, as knowing the reward of their ministration; but let them not be ashamed to minister to those that are in want, as even our "Lord Jesus Christ came not to be ministered unto, but to minister and to give His life a ransom for many" [Mt 20:28]. So therefore ought they also to do, and not to scruple it, if they should be obliged to lay down their life for a brother. For the Lord and our Saviour Jesus Christ did not scruple to "lay down His life," as Himself says, "for His friends" [John 15:13]. If, therefore, the Lord of heaven and earth underwent all His sufferings for us, how then do you make a difficulty to minister to such as are in want, who ought to imitate Him who underwent servitude, and want, and stripes, and the cross for us (μιμηταὶ ὀφείλοντες αὐτοῦ εἶναι τοῦ καὶ δουλείαν καὶ ἔνδειαν καὶ πληγὰς καὶ σταυρὸν δι ἡμᾶς ὑπομείναντος)? We ought therefore also to serve the brethren, in imitation of Christ (δουλεύειν τοῖς ἀδελφοῖς ὡς χριστοῦ μιμητάς). For says He: "He that will be great among you, let him be your minister (διάκονος); and he that will be first

---

[56]See the text in Funk, *Didascalia et Constitutiones Apostolorum Volumen I* 212-217.

[57]Isa 53:11 is here read according to the Septuagint.

among you, let him be your servant (δοῦλος)" [Mt 20:26-27]. For so did He really, and not in word only, fulfil the prediction of, "serving many faithfully" (εὖ δουλεύειν πολλοῖς) [Isa 53:11].

The passage quotes the Septuagint version of Isa 53:11 according to which the Servant serves many faithfully. This enables the writer to connect Isa 53:11 with the sayings of Jesus which emphasizes servitude. In particular, Mt 20:26-27 is an important text because it contains the words *diakonos* referring to the deacon and *doulos* referring to the Servant (Isa 53:11).

Isaiah 53 and Christian Martyr Theology

We have already seen that the Letter of Barnabas uses Isaiah 53 as a proof text about the suffering and death of Jesus Christ and relates its content to the baptismal ritual. In addition, Isa 50:6-9 too is interpreted in Barn 5:14-6:2 as a prophecy about the sufferings of Jesus. In this passage the Christians are exhorted to follow their Master in sufferings.[58] The idea is developed in Barn 7 which is a typological interpretation of the Day of Atonement and the two goats which are mentioned in Leviticus 16 and mYoma 6. Concerning the goat which should be sent to the wilderness the writer quotes an unknown (Jewish or Christian) source which says: "And all of you spit upon it, and pierce it, and encircle its head with scarlet wool, and thus let it be driven into the wilderness." This passage is then interpreted in Barn 7:11. Even though this verse does not contain any clear quotation from Isaiah 53, there is nevertheless reason to believe that the writer continued the interpretation which he formulated in Barn 5 concerning Isa 53:5, 7. He writes that even Christians had to suffer like their Master:

---

[58]Hvalvik (*The Struggle for Scripture and Covenant* 187-194) argues that Barn 5:1-8:7 is a section where proofs are presented concerning Christ's suffering and the two peoples.

But why is it that they place the wool in the midst of thorns? It is a type (τύπος ἐστίν) of Jesus set before the view of the Church. "They place the wool among thorns" means that any one who wishes to bear it away may find it necessary to suffer much (πολλὰ παθεῖν), because the thorn is formidable, and thus obtain it only as the result of suffering. Thus also, says He, "Those who wish to behold Me, and lay hold of My kingdom, must through tribulation and suffering obtain Me (ὀφείλουσιν θλιβέντες καὶ παθόντες λαβεῖν με)."

Thus the Letter of Barnabas argues that Christians must be prepared to become martyrs for the sake of Christ. We have two other texts from the first centuries where Christian martyrs are depicted with the aid of Isaiah 53.

The first text is the Martyrdom of Polycarp. In the prayer of Polycarp (chapter 14) Jesus is called the Servant of Lord ("your Servant"). According to Wolff, this title does not originate directly from Isaiah 53. He insists that the prayer of Polycarp is not written with reference to Isaiah 53 but rather to the Holy Communion.[59] I have my doubts as to whether this view can hold. After all we saw in sect. 3 that Isaiah 53 played a major role in developing Jewish martyr theology. The evidence in sect. 7 shows that Isaiah 53 was used for parenesis and this usage has continued in patristic literature. This being so, we can re-examine the case. In the introduction to the prayer of Polycarp he is presented as following the footsteps of his Master when he is ready to offer his life for the name of Jesus Christ:[60]

> They did not nail him then, but simply bound him. And he, placing his hands behind him, and being bound like a distinguished ram (κριὸς ἐπίσημος)

---

[59]H.W. Wolff, *Jesaja 53 im Urchristentum. Mit einer Einführung von Peter Stuhlmacher* (Giessen: Brunnen 1984) 115-116.

[60]For the Greek text of the Martyrdom of Polycarp, see P.T. Camelot, *Ignace d'Antioche, Polycarpe de Smyrne: Lettres, Martyr de Polycarpe* (SC 10, Paris: Les Éditions du Cerf 1998) 211-239. The English translations are from the Ante-Nicene Fathers.

228

[taken] out of a great flock for sacrifice, and prepared to be an acceptable burnt-offering (ὁλοκαύτωμα δεκτόν) unto God, looked up to heaven, and said ...

The fact that Polycarp is called a male sheep, i.e., "a distinguished ram," does not exclude the perception of Isaiah 53 and its verse 7 behind the text. The fact that this ram will become "an acceptable burnt-offering" can easily be connected with Isaiah 53. There the lamb is led to slaughter and the Lord is asked to accept the sacrifice (Isa 53:10). The prayer of Polycarp makes this relationship to Isaiah 53 even clearer:

O Lord God Almighty, the Father of thy beloved and blessed Servant (παιδός σου) Jesus Christ, by whom we have received the knowledge of Thee (περὶ σοῦ ἐπίγνωσιν εἰλήφαμεν), the God of angels and powers, and of every creature, and of the whole race of the righteous who live before thee, I give Thee thanks that Thou hast counted me, worthy of this day and this hour, that I should have a part in the number of Thy martyrs, in the cup of thy Christ (ἐν τῷ ποτερίῳ τοῦ Χριστοῦ), to the resurrection of eternal life, both of soul and body, through the incorruption [imparted] by the Holy Ghost. Among whom may I be accepted this day before Thee as a fat and acceptable sacrifice (ἐν θυσίᾳ πίονι καὶ προσδεκτῇ), according as Thou, the ever-truthful God, hast fore-ordained (προητοίμασας), hast revealed beforehand to me, and now hast fulfilled. Wherefore also I praise Thee for all things, I bless Thee, I glorify Thee, along with the everlasting and heavenly High Priest (διὰ τοῦ αἰωνίου καὶ ἐπουρανίου ἀρχιερέως) Jesus Christ, Thy beloved Servant (σου παιδός) with whom, to Thee, and the Holy Ghost, be glory both now and to all coming ages. Amen.

Not only does this prayer call Jesus "your Servant" (referring to the Father) but it includes other motifs which appear in Isaiah 53. *First* of all the martyr death of Polycarp is presented as "a fat and acceptable sacrifice" which is fore-ordained and then also revealed to him (as reported in the text). That the text mentions the cup of the Christ, a reference to Mk 10:38; Mt 20:22; 26:39, may link the prayer to the Eucharist (so Wolff) but this detail does not contradict the content of Isaiah 53. That the fate of Polycarp, the successor of Jesus is *fore-*

ordained may imply that Isaiah 53 served as a proof text for the sufferings of the Christians (cf., 1 Thess 3:4). The text refers to Jesus as the High Priest which reflects Jesus' priestly ministry in sacrificing Polycarp to the "Lord God Almighty, the Father". *Second*, the text refers to the hope of resurrection which pertains to the martyr which brings to mind Isa 53:11-12. *Third*, Polycarp says in his prayer that through Jesus Christ the Christians have received "the knowledge of God." This can be associated with the idea in Isa 53:10 according to which the Servant of the Lord gives knowledge which saves many.

Another important martyr text which contains references to Isaiah 53 is the account of the martyrs of Lyons which Eusebios has preserved in his *Eccl Hist* V.1.3-2.7.[61] The Christian martyrs are called "the servants of Christ" (δοῦλοι Χριστοῦ, 1.3) who must suffer and die and who in this respect are zealous to imitate Christ (2.2): "They were so zealous and imitators of Christ (ζηλωταὶ καὶ μιμηταὶ Χριστοῦ) 'who being in the form of God, counted it not a prize to be on an equality with God' (Phil 2:5)." Reference is made to the Christological hymn in Phil 2:5-11 which in turn is connected with the parenetic use of Isaiah 53 (as in 1 Peter 2:18-25). The Christians are exhorted to walk in the way of the Servant described in Isaiah 53. Even the torture of the martyrs of Lyons is depicted with the words of Isaiah 53 (*Eccl Hist* V 1.23) where it is said of Sanctus that "his body was a witness of his sufferings, being one complete wound and bruise, drawn out of shape, and altogether unlike a human form" (ὅλον τραῦμα καὶ μώλωψ καὶ συνεσπασμένον ἀποβεβληκὸς τὴν ἀνθρώπειον ἔξωθεν μορφήν). The wording and image are obviously borrowed from Isa 52:14-15; 53:2-5.[62] The text connects the death of the Christian martyrs with the idea of sacrifice to God (e.g., 1.40, 56) as in the Martyrdom of Polycarp.

---

[61]Concerning the Greek text of Eusebius see G. Bardy, *Eusèbe de Césarée: Histoire Ecclésiastique Livres V-VII* (SC 41, Paris: Les Éditions du Cerf 1955). For the English translation, see the *Ante-Nicene Fathers*.

[62]See also Wolff, *Jesaja 53 im Urchristentum* 116-117.

Isaiah 53 and the Christian Self-definition in Contrast to Judaism

Early patristic evidence shows that the interpretation of Isaiah 53 was instituted as a Christian manifesto against the more powerful Jewish party.[63] The best examples are Justin's works, in particular his *Dialogue with Trypho*.[64] Skarsaune has shown that beside the LXX-translations, Justin often uses other Greek versions which probably originate from an early Christian collection of testimonies. This is, in particular, the case with Isa 53:12 which is quoted twice in the First Apology 50-51. In 1 Apol 50:2 Justin introduces Isaiah 53 and quotes verse 53:12 in non-LXX translation:

ἀνθ ὧν παρέδωκαν εἰς θάνατον τὴν ψυχὴν αὐτοῦ καὶ μετὰ τῶν ἀνόμων ἐλογίσθη αὐτὸς ἁμαρτίας πολλῶν εἴληφε καὶ τοῖς ἀνόμοις ἐξιλάσεται
Because they delivered His soul unto death, and He was numbered with the transgressors, He has borne the sin of many, and shall make atonement for the transgressors.

Later in 1 Apol 51:5 he quotes Isa 53:12 according to its LXX-version. Skarsaune argues that the quotation in 1 Apol 50:2 is a Christian revision of the LXX text. The expression καὶ μετὰ τῶν ἀνόμων ἐλογίσθη appears in Lk 22:37 from which it was probably taken. The verb ἐξιλάσκειν which may be rendering of the Hebrew verb יפגיע (hiph.) in the context of Isaiah 53[65] emphasizes the expiatory suffering of the servant and comes close to the New Testament account of the atonement

---

[63]It is important to recognize that both Justin and Meliton wrote their texts at a time when Christians were persecuted and had socially insecure positions as Jews.

[64]Concerning the Greek text, see Goodspeed, *Die ältesten Apologeten*; M. Marcovich, *Iustini Martyris Dialogus cum Tryphone*. See the English translation in the *Ante-Nicene Fathers* and in Falls, *St. Justin Martyr. Dialogue with Trypho*.

[65]There are parallels between Leviticus 16 and Isaiah 53.

by the death of Jesus. According to Skarsaune, Justin "prefixed [this text] to the long quotation as a fitting summary of the whole Isaiah chapter."[66] The fact that the Greek version of the biblical passage was controlled by the Hebrew text indicates a tendency to define Christianity in relation to Judaism. Origen's Hexapla is a good example of this interest.[67] Even earlier Meliton, bishop of Sardes, collated his testimonies with the help of the Hebrew text as reported by Eusebios (*Eccl Hist* IV.26.12-14):

> But in the Extracts made by him the same writer gives at the beginning of the introduction a catalogue of the acknowledged books of the Old Testament, which it is necessary to quote at this point. He writes as follows: "Melito to his brother Onesimus, greeting: Since you have often, in your zeal for the word, expressed a wish to have extracts made from the Law and the Prophets concerning the Saviour and concerning our entire faith, and has also desired to have an accurate statement of the ancient book, as regards their number and their order, I have endeavored to perform the task, knowing your zeal for the faith, and your desire to gain information in regard to the word, and knowing that you, in your yearning after God, esteem these things above all else, struggling to attain eternal salvation. Accordingly when I went East and came to the place where these things were preached and done, I learned accurately the books of the Old Testament, and send them to you as written below. Their names are as follows: Of Moses, five books: Genesis, Exodus, Numbers, Leviticus, Deuteronomy; Jesus Nave, Judges, Ruth; of Kings, four books; of Chronicles, two; the Psalms of David, the Proverbs of Solomon, Wisdom also, Ecclesiastes, Song of Songs, Job; of Prophets, Isaiah, Jeremiah; of the twelve prophets, one book ; Daniel, Ezekiel, Esdras. From which also I have made the extracts, dividing them into six books." Such are the words of Melito.

---

[66]Skarsaune, *The Proof from Prophecy* 62-63, the quotation is from p. 63. See also E.F. Osborn, *Justin Martyr* (Beiträge zur historischen Theologie 47, Tübingen: Mohr Siebeck 1973) 111-119.

[67]For the role of the Hebrew Bible in the biblical exegesis of Origen, see N. De Lange, *Origen and the Jews: Studies in Jewish-Christian Relations in Third-Century Palestine* (University of Cambridge Oriental Publications 25; Cambridge: Cambridge University Press 1978) 49-61.

232

Isaiah 53 became an important proof text for Christians to explain that there are two different advents of the Messiah in the Hebrew Bible. At the end of *Dial* 14 Justin introduces these concepts, "the first advent of Christ (ἡ πρώτη παρουσία τοῦ χριστοῦ)" and "his second advent (ἡ δευτέρα παρουσία τοῦ χριστοῦ)".[68] Even though these ideas are deeply rooted in the New Testament gospel it is reasonable to assume that these concepts were directed against the counterargument of the Jewish party that the life of Jesus Christ does not correspond to the messianic expectations prevalent in the Hebrew Bible.[69] This is well documented in Trypho's question at the beginning of chapter 32:

> These and such like Scriptures, sir, compel us to wait for Him who, as Son of Man, receives from the Ancient of Days the everlasting kingdom. But this so-called Christ of yours was dishonourable and inglorious, so much so that the last curse contained in the law of God fell on him, for he was crucified (ἄτιμος καὶ ἄδοξος γέγονεν, ὡς καὶ τῇ ἐσχάτῃ κατάρᾳ τῇ ἐν τῷ νόμῳ τοῦ θεοῦ περιπεσεῖν· ἐσταυρώθη γάρ).

Trypho's argument is a typical Jewish answer to the Christian exegesis. Justin confronts it by referring to Isaiah 53 which was regarded as an important proof text in the Hebrew Bible to argue that the Messiah was "dishonourable and inglorious". In his answer Justin shows how the concepts of the first and the second advent of the Messiah are related to Isaiah 53 and to Zech 12:10-13:

---

[68]See further Osborn *Justin Martyr* 187-192.

[69]Tertullian used it in his work *Against Jews* (chap. 14). He even writes that Marcion follows the opinion of Jews who "to this day deny that their Christ has come, because He has not appeared in majesty, while they ignore the fact that He was to come also in lowliness" and argues against him that the Old Testament speaks about two different advents of the Messiah (*Contra Marcion* III.7). See the text in R. Braun, *Tertullien: Contre Marcion Tome III* (SC 399, Paris: Les Éditions du Cerf 1994) 84-93. Irenaeus also speaks about this concept of the two advents of the Messiah (*Adv Haer* IV.33.1,11).

If, sirs, it were not said by the Scriptures which I have already quoted, that (1) "His form was inglorious", and (2) "His generation not declared", and that (3) "for His death the rich would suffer death", and (4) "with His stripes we should be healed", and that (5) "He would be led away like a sheep"; and if I had not explained that there would be *two advents of His* (δύο παρουσίας αὐτοῦ) – one in which He was pierced by you; a second, when "you shall know Him whom you have pierced, and your tribes shall mourn, each tribe by itself, the women apart, and the men apart" – then I must have been speaking dubious and obscure things.

In particular, Zech 12:10-13 is a crucial text for Justin because it can be interpreted to signify that in his first advent the Messiah was pierced, and that later in the eschatological period (a clear reference to the war at the end of time can be found in Zech 12:1-9) the Jewish people will recognize this. Isaiah 53 in its turn is compatible with the mention of the pierced one in Zech 12:10.

In the Dialogue, Justin uses Isaiah 53 in order to define the Christian messianic position against that of the Jews. In fact, Isaiah 53 opens the whole dialogue. Justin quotes Isa 52:10-54:6 in chapter 13 and later selects different verses from it in order to explain to Trypho the central message of Christianity. Beside Isaiah 53 Justin quotes Isa 51:4-5 (*Dial* 11), Isa 55:3-5 (*Dial* 14), and Isa 58:1-11 (*Dial* 15). Thus the whole of Isaiah 51-55 and its immediate context Isa 58:1-11 are vital evidence of the Christian message in Justin's dialogue. According to Justin, Isa 51:4-5 together with Jer 31:31-34 show that the new law and covenant has been given to Christians and the fundamental content of this covenant or new law is the message presented in Isaiah 53.

Justin's long quotation Isa 52:10-54:6 is probably justified by the fact that according to Isa 52:10, "the Lord shall make bare *His holy arm* in the eyes of all the nations, and all the nations and the ends of the earth shall see the salvation of God" and Isa 53:1, in its turn, posed the question: "Lord, who hath believed our report? and to whom is *the arm of the Lord* revealed?" This shows that the holy arm of the Lord will be revealed to the nations while at the same time not all (i.e. Jews) believe in the message of the suffering Servant. In a similar way, Isa 52:15

234

emphasizes that many *nations* will hear the message of the suffering Servant confirming that the holy arm of the Lord has been accepted among the *nations* (Isa 52:10). In Isa 54:3, too, this universal scope of the message of Isaiah 53 is manifest. The *Dialogue with Trypho* 12-15 is a good example of how the verses from Isaiah 53 were not read in an atomistic way, but rather the broader context of the passage in the Book of Isaiah is considered.

Justin gives an overall interpretation of Isaiah 53 on the life of Jesus. Verse 53:8, which in the LXX renders τὴν γενεὰν αὐτοῦ τίς διηγήσεται, "who shall declare his generation?" is interpreted by Justin as referring to the mystic birth of Jesus which is not understood by humans (*Dial* 76.2; see also *Dial* 43.3; 63.2; 68.4). The expression ἀνομίαν γὰρ οὐκ ἐποίησεν, οὐδὲ δόλον τῷ στόματι in Isa 53:9 instructs Justin that Jesus Christ was sinless (*Dial* 102.7). The burial of Jesus is evident from the expression δώσω τοὺς πλουσίους ἀντὶ τοῦ θανάτου αὐτοῦ in Isa 53:9, and the resurrection in Isa 53:11-12.

Justin's exegesis is an interesting example of an attempt to interpret Isaiah 53 against the wider context of the Book of Isaiah. Justin refers to many other texts in the Hebrew Bible which speak of the sufferings of the Messiah (in particular, Psalm 22 in *Dial* 97-106).

In subsequent centuries, and after the turn of the Constantine era, the self-definition of Christianity toward the more powerful Judaism was superseded by overall criticism of the Jewish people because of its disbelief. A good example of this tendency can be seen in Athanasios's work *Incarnation*. Athanasios argues that the Scriptures used by Jews themselves show that the Messiah had to suffer (*Incarnation* 33):[70]

> These things being so, and the Resurrection of His body and the victory gained over death by the Saviour being clearly proved, come now let us put to rebuke both the disbelief of the Jews and the scoffing of the Gentiles (καὶ τὴν

[70]Concerning the Greek text of Incarnation 33-34, see C. Kannengiesser, *Sur L'Incarnation du Verbe* (SC 199, Paris: Les Éditions du Cerf 2000) 382-389.

ἀπιστίαν τῶν Ἰουδαίων καὶ τὴν τῶν Ἑλλήνων χλεύην διελέγξωμεν). For these, perhaps, are the points where Jews express incredulity, while Gentiles laugh, finding fault with the unseemliness of the Cross, and of the Word of God becoming man (τὸ ἀπρεπὲς τοῦ σταυροῦ καὶ τῆς ἐνανθρωπήσεως τοῦ θεοῦ λόγου διασύροντες). But our argument shall not delay to grapple with both especially as the proofs at our command against them are clear as day. For Jews in their incredulity may be refuted from the Scriptures, which even they themselves read; for this text and that, and, in a word, the whole inspired Scripture, cries aloud concerning these things, as even its express words abundantly show.

After citing many Old Testament passages as proof of Jesus's birth and life, Athanasios quotes a long passage from Isaiah 53 which he interprets in terms of the suffering and death of the Messiah (*Incarnation* 34):

Nor is even His death passed over in silence: on the contrary, it is referred to in the divine Scriptures, even exceeding clearly. For to the end that none should err for want of instruction in the actual events, they feared not to mention even the cause of His death—that He suffers it not for His own sake, but for the immortality and salvation of all, and the counsels of the Jews against Him and the indignities offered Him at their hands. 2. They say then: "*A man in stripes, and knowing how to bear weakness, for his face is turned away: he was dishonoured and held in no account. He bears our sins, and is in pain on our account; and we reckoned him to be in labour, and in stripes, and in ill-usage; but he was wounded for our sins, and made weak for our wickedness. The chastisement of our peace was upon him, and by his stripes we were healed.*" O marvel at the loving-kindness of the Word, that for our sakes He is dishonoured, that we may be brought to honour. "*For all we,*" it says, "*like sheep had gone astray; man had erred in his way; and the Lord delivered him for our sins; and he opens not his mouth, because he has been evilly entreated. As a sheep was he brought to the slaughter, and as a lamb dumb before his shearer, so opens he not his mouth: in his abasement his judgment was taken away.*" 3. Then lest any should from His suffering conceive Him to be a common man, Holy Writ anticipates the surmises of man, and declares the power (which worked) for Him , and the difference of His nature compared with ourselves, saying: "*But who shall declare his generation? For his life is taken away from the earth. From the wickedness of the people was he brought to death. And I will give the wicked instead of his burial, and the rich instead of his death; for he did no wickedness, neither was guile found in his mouth. And the Lord will cleanse him from his stripes.*"

The anti-Jewish tendency becomes even clearer in Christian commentaries after the Constantine era. Thus, for example, Cyril of Alexandria writes concerning Isa 52:14 that heathens have heard the message of salvation while Jews have rejected it:[71] "Those who do not perceive his glory have remained faithless and foolish, judging him without glory and honor. They call him a Samaritan, a glutton and drunkard, born of fornication, a sinner." While interpreting the central passage of passion Cyril implemented his anti-Jewish stance: "Our Lord, Jesus Christ, endured the cross, despising the shame [Heb 12:2], became obedient to the Father unto death [Phil 2:8], and bore the Jews' impiety, in order that he might take away the sin of the world [John 1:29] ..."

In a similar way, the interpretation of Theodoret of Cyrus contains anti-Jewish statements. Isa 53:1 is for Theodoret an expression of "the incredulity of the Jews":[72] "... but these Jews, although they often had to listen to us [prophets], and had experience of his power, had continued in disbelief and denial." The we-group in Isa 53:4 are Jews who think that the Servant "endured these sufferings because of his own sins." In the interpretation of Isa 53:9 Theodoret follows the reading of Aquila, Symmachos and Theodotion who translate "and he will give the wicked" instead of "I will give" and then continues: "The very One who has endured these sufferings will hand them over to the Roman war. He has called the Pharisees, the scribes and the chief priests 'rich' and similarly, it is these again he has called 'wicked', for they appropriated for themselves the benefits of all."[73]

In later Jewish-Christian dialogues (Athanasius and Zacchaeus, Simon and Theophilus, Timothy and Aquila) Isaiah 53 plays a central

---

[71]See the translation of Cyril's text in Wilken, *Isaiah Interpreted by Early Christian and Medieval Commentators* 416-421.

[72]See the translations of Theodoret of Cyrus in Manley, *Isaiah Through Ages* 780-794.

[73]So even Eusebios.

role. It is a proof text which shows that the Messiah must suffer in his first advent.[74]

Thus we can detect a tendency in the Christian interpretation where Isaiah 53 was first used as a proof text for the suffering, death and resurrection of Jesus, the aim of which was to exhort the Jewish party to believe in the gospel. Gradually anti-Jewish elements were baked into the interpretation of Isaiah 53 and in the Christian commentaries of the 5th century AD there is already a detailed reference to the disbelief of the Jews and their punishment in the Roman wars.[75]

Isaiah 53 and Christian Self-definition against Paganism

Another early trend in the Christian self-definition sought to confront paganism. One of the earliest examples is Origen's work *Contra Celsum*.[76] In Book II.54-55 Origen gives a long account of how Jews have been interpreted in Isaiah 53. The reason for this discussion is the reproach of Celsus – which we have already discussed. According to Origen, Celsus "reproaches the Saviour because of His sufferings (ὀνειδίζει τῷ σωτῆρι ἐπὶ τῷ πάθει), saying that 'He received no assistance from the Father, or was unable to aid Himself' (μὴ βοηθηθέντι ὑπὸ τοῦ πατρὸς ἢ μὴ δυνηθέντι ἑαυτῷ βοηθῆσαι)." Celsus' argument is that if Jesus Christ was divine he would have had

---

[74]See these texts and the use of Isaiah 53 (through index) in W. Varner, *Ancient Jewish-Christian Dialogues: Athanasius and Zacchaeus, Simon and Theophilus, Timothy and Aquila* (Lewiston: The Edwin Mellen Press 2004); see also W. Varner, "In the Wake of Trypho: Jewish-Christian Dialogues in the Third to the Sixth Centuries," *EQ* 80 (2008) 219-236.

[75]The Bar Kochba war was used already by Justin Martyr as an exhortation to the Jewish party to listen to the Christian message. But there is a clear difference in the tone. Justin Martyr wrote at a time when the Christians were always under threat of persecutions, while these later commentators formulated their opinions at a time when the Christian religion had become official in the Roman/Byzantine empire.

[76]See the text edition of M. Borret (SC 132, 136 and 147) and the translation in Ante-Nicene Fathers.

power to help himself or receive help from his Father. Origen's answer to this is that Christ's "sufferings were the subject of prophecy, along with the cause of them" and he even gives a theological explanation for this suffering: "because it was for the benefit of mankind that He should die on their account, and should suffer stripes because of His condemnation (ὅτι χρήσιμον ἦν ἀνθρώποις τὸ ἐκεῖνον ὑπὲρ αὐτῶν ἀποθανεῖν καὶ μώλοπα τὸν ἐπὶ τῷ καταδεδικάσθαι παθεῖν)". The proof text for the sufferings of the Messiah is Isa 52:13-53:8 which Origen quotes according to the LXX version, which contains only a few minor differences from Ziegler's edition. Origen reads the words καὶ μετεωρισθήσεται in 52:13, according to the Hebrew text as did Aquila, Symmachus and Theodotion. He follows the enigmatic reading in Isa 53:1: ἀνηγγείλαμεν ὡς παιδίον ἐναντίον αὐτοῦ, which is identical with that in Clement's quotation mentioned above, and which was established early in the manuscript tradition. These minor differences from the LXX version do not influence the meaning of the text. Origen emphasizes that Isaiah 53 predicts that the Christ "would be seen in a form which is deemed dishonourable among men (εἶδος ἄτιμον ἐν ἀνθρώποις φαινόμενον ἔχων ὀφθήσεται)." Origen closes his quotation in 53:8 which neatly ends the sufferings of the servant by reporting how he was taken away from the land of living.

In this context, Origen also presents important information about the way in which some Jews in antiquity interpreted Isaiah 53. According to Origen (*Contra Celsum* II.54-55), Jews proposed a collective interpretation which later became popular in Judaism when Rashi established it about 800 years later (see sect. 11). I quote the whole text in English translation (I have set in bold the Jewish way to interpret Isaiah 53 and in italics all references to the biblical passages):

> Now I remember that, on one occasion, at a disputation held with certain Jews, who were reckoned wise men, I quoted these prophecies; to which my Jewish opponent replied, that **these predictions bore reference to the whole people, regarded as one individual, and as being in a state of dispersion and suffering, in order that many proselytes might be gained, on account of**

the dispersion of the Jews among numerous heathen nations (ταῦτα πεπροφητεῦσθαι ὡς περὶ ἑνὸς τοῦ ὅλου λαοῦ, καὶ γενομένου ἐν τῇ διασπορᾷ καὶ πληγέντος, ἵνα πολλοὶ προσήλυτοι γένωνται τῇ προφάσει τοῦ ἐπεσπάρθαι Ἰουδαίους τοῖς λοιποῖς ἔθνεσι). And in this way he explained the words, *"Thy form shall be of no reputation among men"*; and then, *"They to whom no message was sent respecting him shall see"*; and the expression, *"A man under suffering* (ἄνθρωπος ἐν πλεγῇ ὤν)"[77] Many arguments were employed on that occasion during the discussion to prove that these predictions regarding one particular person were not rightly applied by them to the whole nation. And I asked to what character the expression would be appropriate, *"This man bears our sins, and suffers pain on our behalf"*; and this, *"But He was wounded for our sins, and bruised for our iniquities"*; and to whom the expression properly belonged, *"By His stripes were we healed."* For it is manifest that it is they (whether belonging to the Jewish nation or converts from the Gentiles) who had been sinners, and had been healed by the Saviour's sufferings (σαφῶς γὰρ οἱ ἐν ταῖς ἁμαρτίας γενόμενοι καὶ ἰαθέντες ἐκ τοῦ τὸν σωτῆρα πεπονθέναι, εἴτε ἀπὸ τοῦ λαοῦ ἐκείνου εἴτε καὶ οἱ ἀπὸ τῶν ἐθνῶν), who use such language in the writings of the prophet who foresaw these events, and who, under the influence of the Holy Spirit, applied these words to a person. But we seemed to press them hardest with the expression (μάλιστα δε ἐδόξαμεν θλίβειν ἀπὸ τῆς φασκούσης λέξεως), *"Because of the iniquities of My people was He led away unto death."* For if the people, according to them, are the subject of the prophecy, how is the man said to be led away to death because of the iniquities of the people of God, unless he be a different person from that people of God (εἰ γὰρ ὁ λαὸς κατα ἐκείνους εἰσὶν οἱ προφητευόμενοι, πῶς ἀπο τῶν ἀνομιῶν τοῦ λαοῦ τοῦ θεοῦ λέγεται ἦχθαι εἰς θάνατον οὗτος, εἰ μὴ ἕτερος ὢν παρὰ τὸν λαὸν τοῦ θεοῦ)? And who is this person save Jesus Christ, by whose stripes they who believe on Him are healed, when *He had spoiled the principalities and powers (that were over us), and had made a show of them openly on His cross?*[78] At another time we may explain the several parts of the prophecy,

---

[77]This is not a quotation from Isaiah 53 but Origen's summary of the content of the passage: "A man of sufferings."

[78]This text in cursive, i.e. ἀπεδυσαμένου τὰς ἐν ἡμῖν ἀρχὰς καὶ ἐξουσίας καὶ παρρησίᾳ δειγματίσαντος αὐτὰς ἐν τῷ ξύλῳ has allusions to Col 2:15:

leaving none of them unexamined. But these matters have been treated at greater length, necessarily as I think, on account of the language of the Jew, as quoted in the work of Celsus.

This Jewish interpretation followed the LXX-translation, and such a collective tendency may have been established when the interpretation of the suffering righteous (e.g. in Wisdom 2-5) was modified to concern the whole people.

In Origen's view, the expression in Isa 53:8 which in the LXX version renders ἀπὸ τῶν ἀνομιῶν τοῦ λαοῦ μου ἤχθη εἰς θάνατον was the most difficult passage for the Jewish parts to solve. Of course, this may be a correct evaluation if the discussion between Origen and Jews (living in Alexandria) was based on the Greek text. But we have already seen that the Masoretic tradition followed by Aquila, Symmachus and Theodotion interprets the text so that the Servant is referred to by the masculine plural suffix לָמוֹ. If this is true, then we may assume that Origen's account perhaps did not tell the whole truth. The text in Isa 53:8 according to LXX is plain, but Origen seems to know that this text is difficult to interpret in the singular and that three other Greek translations have interpreted it in the plural.[79] This being the case, Origen presented his Christian audience – who knew mainly LXX – with a straightforward interpretation.

Isaiah 53 and Christian Self-definition against Heresies

Isaiah 53 with its very concrete language of suffering was also an effective text against various heresies which the first Christians confronted. The basic concept in the orthodox Christian doctrine was that the high Christology is compatible with the description of the suffering

---

ἀπεκδυσάμενος τὰς ἀρχὰς καὶ τὰς ἐξουσίας ἐδειγμάτισεν ἐν παρρησίᾳ, θριαμβεύσας αὐτοὺς ἐν αὐτῷ.

[79] See Origen's Hexapla in 534-535. *Origenis Hexaplorum Tomus II.*

and dying Servant in Isaiah 53. Jesus is the Son of God who became a man, suffered, died, was buried but then also rose again. As is well-known, such a combination of high Christology, implying that Jesus was divine, and his torture on Via Dolorosa created many intellectual problems among philosophically oriented minds. Here I shall give some examples and their rebuttal in Christian literature.

Docetism was an attempt to avoid the idea that the Son of God really did suffer and die. One of the most effective texts in the Old Testament which was used to refute docetic views on the suffering and death of the Son of God was Psalm 22. Bailey observed that the language which Justin uses in *Dial* 99.2, *Dial* 100.2 and *Dial* 103.8 (while interpreting mainly Psalm 22) is anti-docetic:[80]

> *Dial* 99.2: But lest any one should say, He did not know then that He had to suffer, He adds immediately in the Psalm: 'And it is not for want of understanding in me.' Even as there was no ignorance on God's part when He asked Adam where he was, or asked Cain where Abel was; but [it was done] to convince each what kind of man he was, and in order that through the record [of Scripture] we might have a knowledge of all: so likewise Christ declared that ignorance was not on His side, but on theirs, who thought that He was not the Christ, but fancied they would put Him to death, and that He, like some common mortal, would remain in Hades.

> *Dial* 100.2: Accordingly He revealed to us all that we have perceived by His grace out of the Scriptures, so that we know Him to be the first-begotten of God, and to be before all creatures; likewise to be the Son of the patriarchs, since He assumed flesh by the Virgin of their family, and submitted to become a man without comeliness, dishonoured, and subject to suffering (ἄνθρωπος ἀειδής καὶ ἄτιμος καὶ παθητός).

> *Dial* 103.8: His heart and also His bones trembling; His heart being like wax melting in His belly: in order that we may perceive that the Father wished His Son really to undergo such sufferings for our sakes (ἐν τοιύτοις πάθεσιν

---

[80]Bailey, "'Our Suffering and Crucified Messiah'" 409-415.

242

ἀληθῶς γεγονέναι δι᾿ ἡμᾶς), and may not say that He, being the Son of God, did not feel (οὐκ ἀντελαμβάνετο) what was happening to Him and inflicted on Him. Further, the expression, 'My strength is dried up like a potsherd, and my tongue has cleaved to my throat,' was a prediction, as I previously remarked, of that silence, when He who convicted all your teachers of being unwise returned no answer at all.

Bailey has suggested that, in particular, the language of *Dial* 100.2 was influenced by Isaiah 53. In his article he deals with all the passages in the Dialogue where παθητός occurs and concludes that this very term is closely related to Isaiah 53. The strongest link is Dial 89.3 where Justin connects the term with Isa 53:8d: ἀπὸ τῶν ἀνομιῶν τοῦ λαοῦ μου ἤχθη εἰς θάνατον and other passages in Isaiah 53:[81]

If Christ was not to suffer (εἰ μὲν μὴ ἔμελλε πάσχειν ὁ Χριστός), and the prophets had not foretold that He would be led to death on account of the sins of the people, and be dishonoured and scourged, and reckoned among the transgressors, and as a sheep be led to the slaughter, whose generation, the prophet says, no man can declare, then you would have good cause to wonder. But if these are to be characteristic of Him and mark Him out to all, how is it possible for us to do anything else than believe in Him most confidently? And will not as many as have understood the writings of the prophets, whenever they hear merely that He was crucified, say that this is He and no other?

Beside the word παθητός Bailey goes through other similar terms ἄτιμος, ἀειδής and ἄδοξος and concludes that these combine in a network which mentions the suffering and death of the Messiah (i.e. his first *parousia*) as described in Isaiah 53 among others in contrast to the second coming of the Messiah in glory as reported in Daniel 7 among others.[82]

---

[81]See Bailey, "'Our Suffering and Crucified Messiah'" 348.

[82]Bailey, "'Our Suffering and Crucified Messiah'.

Gnostic Heresies are refuted in Irenaeus' comprehensive book "A refutation and subversion of Knowledge falsely so called" (*Hist Eccl* V.7) better known by its shorter title "Against Heresies" (*Adversus Haereses*) where he presents the orthodox Christian doctrine. Irenaeus often cites Isaiah 53 to emphasize that Jesus is the true man and God who was sent into the world by the Father, the Creator of the world, in order to save mankind (*Adv Haer* IV.20.2). Irenaeus uses Isa 53:8 to illustrates that Jesus is the Logos whose origin is from Father (*Adv Haer* II.28.5): "As for the prophet, he declares respecting Him, 'Who shall describe His generation?' [Isa 53:8] But you pretend to set forth His generation from the Father, and you transfer the production of the word of men which takes place by means of a tongue to the Word of God, and thus are righteously exposed by your own selves as knowing neither things human nor divine." In *Adv Haer* III.19.2 Irenaeus explains the phrase in Isa 53:8 with other biblical references showing that the incarnation of the Son of God and the salvation of the humankind are closely related to each other:

> But that He had, beyond all others, in Himself that pre-eminent birth which is from the Most High Father, and also experienced that pre-eminent generation which is from the Virgin [Isa 7:14], the divine Scriptures do in both respects testify of Him: also, that He was a man without comeliness, and liable to suffering [Isa 53:2]; that He sat upon the foal of an ass [Zech 9:9]; that He received for drink, vinegar and gall; that He was despised among the people, and humbled Himself even to death and that He is the holy Lord, the Wonderful, the Counsellor, the Beautiful in appearance, and the Mighty God [Isa 9:6], coming on the clouds as the Judge of all men [Dan 7:13]; — all these things did the Scriptures prophesy of Him.

The incarnation of the Logos was necessary in order that the human flesh can be saved. Therefore, the Logos or the Son of God became flesh in order to save mankind (*Adv Haer* V.14).

In *Adv Haer* III.12 Irenaeus deals with the content of the proclamation of the apostles. In the case of Philip he brings to the fore once again the episode of the eunuch of the Ethiopian queen (Acts 8). The eunuch who had become convinced that Jesus is the suffering

Servant of the Lord described in Isaiah 53, was baptized and was ready to confess (Act 8:37): "I believe Jesus Christ to be the Son of God." Irenaeus continues (*Adv Haer* III.12.8): "This man was also sent into the regions of Ethiopia, to preach what he had himself believed, that there was one God preached by the prophets, but that the Son of this [God] had already made [His] appearance in human nature (*secundum hominem*), and had been led as a sheep to the slaughter; and all the other statements which the prophets made regarding Him." Therefore, the essential Christian doctrine is that the one and same God is behind both testaments. This belief enables all to see that the salvation plan of God was fulfilled in the death of the Son of God as predicted by prophets, in Isaiah 53 *inter alios* (*Adv Haer* IV.33.12).

One of the Gnostic heretics mentioned by Irenaeus in his work is **Marcion** (*Adv Haer* I.27). A more detailed refutation of Marcion's belief system was proposed by Tertullian in his study "Against Marcion" (*Adversus Marcionem*). Like Irenaeus, Tertullian also argues that the suffering, death and resurrection of Jesus were predicted in the Old Testament prophecies. Tertullian speaks of two comings of the Messiah, Isaiah 53 being one key text proving that the first coming of the Messiah must be humble. The Messiah is forced to suffer and die. Isa 53:8 indicates the miraculous incarnation of the Messiah (*Adv Marc* III.7). *Adv Marc* III.19 is an illuminating text where Tertullian uses Isaiah 57:2 and Isaiah 53 to prove to Marcion that Jesus had to suffer, die, be buried and rise again:[83]

> Besides, if he should be unwilling to allow that the death of my Christ was predicted, his confusion must be the greater if he announces that his own Christ indeed died, whom he denies to have had a nativity, while denying that my Christ is mortal, though he allows Him to be capable of birth. However, I will show him the death, and burial, and resurrection of my Christ all indicated in a single sentence of Isaiah, who says, 'His sepulture was removed from the

---

[83]See the text in Braun, *Tertullien: Contre Marcion Tome III* 170-171.

midst of them' (*sepultura eius sublata de medio est*)[84]. Now there could have been no sepulture without death, and no removal of sepulture except by resurrection. Then, finally, he added: 'Therefore He shall have many for his inheritance, and He shall divide the spoil of the many, because He poured out His soul unto death' [Isa 53:12]. For there is here set forth the cause of this favour to Him, even that it was to recompense Him for His suffering of death. It was equally shown that He was to obtain this recompense for His death, was certainly to obtain it after His death by means of the resurrection.

Tertullian frequently refers to Isaiah 53 in order to show (against Marcion) that Jesus was humiliated in order to save mankind (III.17), he had to suffer and die for the salvation of mankind (Isa 53:5; IV.21), that Jesus was silent before Herod Antipas and did not open his mouth (Isa 53:7; IV.42), that the Passover was a fitting time for his death because he was the Lamb of God to be slaughtered (Isa 53:7; IV.40). In addition, Tertullian emphasizes the healing motif of Isaiah 53 as does Irenaeus (through Mt 8:17; IV.8-10).

---

[84]This reading is the Old Latin version of Isa 57:2 based on the LXX (ἡ ταφὴ αὐτοῦ ἦρται ἐκ τοῦ μέσου). See *Vetus Latina 12 (Pars II): Esaias* (ed. R. Gryson) 1397-1398. The Old Latin version reads *sepultura* also in Isa 53:8 (see p. 1323 in Gryson's edition) and it is apparently this connotation which led Tertullian to combine Isa 57:2 and Isaiah 53 with each other.

246

Finally, Isaiah 53 was often cited when various *"heretical"*[85] Christological views were opposed. Tertullian used Isaiah 53 when he answered Praxeas who was a monarchian and who believed in the unity of the Godhead and did not recognize any distinction between the persons of the Father, the Son and the Holy Spirit. Tertullian refers to Isa 53:1-2 and states that here the prophet Isaiah speaks to the Father respecting the Son (*Adv Prax* 11). In particular, Tertullian argues that the Arm of the Lord in Isa 53:1 is Christ (*Adv Prax* 13): "But I find in

---

[85]I have set quotation marks round the word "heretical" here because on many occasions it is relative to say which dogmatic view differed from traditional orthodox views. For example, Nestorius's Christological views are difficult to stamp with the word "heretical". For this see S. Brock, "The Christology of the Church in the East in the Synods of the Fifth to Early Seventh Centuries: Preliminary Considerations and Materials," in: G.D. Dragas (ed), *Aksum - Thyateira: A Festschrift for Archbishop Methodios of Thyateira and Great Britian* (London: Thyateira House 1985) 125-142. See the Nestorian Christology in the document "The Jewel" written by Mar Abd Yeshua in G.P.Badger, *The Nestorians and Their Rituals Volume 2* (1852) 380-422. Note, in particular, how the ideas of Cyril of Alexandria are dealt with (p. 398): "Cyril maintained that we ought to call the Virgin 'Mother of God,' and wrote twelve Sentences excommunicating all who should, in any way, draw a distinction between the divinity and humanity of Christ after the union. Nestorius replied to these Sentences, and showed that they were erroneous, and with respect to the appellation 'Mother of God,' he argued that it did not exist either in the writings of the Prophets or Apostles. The Prophets prophesied of Christ to come, and the Apostles preached of that same Christ, predicted by the Prophets as coming into the world, that this was He Who was born of Mary. Now, were we to use the expression 'Mother of Man' only, we should be like Paul of Samosata, and Photinus of Galatia, who said of our Lord that He was but a mere man like one of the prophets, and on this account they were excommunicated; so if we use the bare expression 'Mother of God,' we become like Simon and Menander, who say that God did not take a body from Mary; but that His life and actions were in appearance only and not real, and on that account they also were excommunicated. But we call the Virgin 'Mother of Christ,' the name used by Prophets and Apostles, and which denotes the union generally. Cyril, in the Sentences which he drew up, and in which he excommunicated all who shall distinguish between the divinity and humanity of Christ, virtually excommunicates the Holy Scriptures, since the Apostles and Prophets do distinguish between the natures of the Person respecting Whom the dispute is, and from these the holy Fathers learnt to confess of Christ, that He is perfect God and perfect Man, the Likeness of God and the likeness of a servant, the Son of David and the Son of the Highest, flesh and Word."

Scripture the name Lord also applied to them Both: 'The Lord said unto my Lord, Sit on my right hand' [Ps 110:1]. And Isaiah says this: 'Lord, who has believed our report, and to whom is the arm of the Lord revealed?' [Isa 53:1] Now he would most certainly have said Your Arm, if he had not wished us to understand that the Father is Lord, and the Son also is Lord." The principal aspect of Isaiah 53 to show that Son and Father are two different persons is the fact that the Son was forsaken by the Father upon the cross. Tertullian uses both Psalm 22 and Isaiah 53 to illustrate this (*Adv Prax* 30):

> However, if you persist in pushing your views further, I shall find means of answering you with greater stringency, and of meeting you with the exclamation of the Lord Himself, so as to challenge you with the question, What is your inquiry and reasoning about that? You have Him exclaiming in the midst of His passion: 'My God, my God, why have You forsaken me?' [Ps 22:1; Mt 27:46] Either, then, the Son suffered, being 'forsaken' by the Father, and the Father consequently suffered nothing, inasmuch as He forsook the Son; or else, if it was the Father who suffered, then to what God was it that He addressed His cry? But this was the voice of flesh and soul, that is to say, of man— not of the Word and Spirit, that is to say, not of God; and it was uttered so as to prove the impassibility of God, who 'forsook' His Son, so far as He handed over His human substance to the suffering of death. This verity the apostle also perceived, when he writes to this effect: 'If the Father spared not His own Son' [Rom 8:32]. This did Isaiah before him likewise perceive, when he declared: 'And the Lord has delivered Him up for our offenses' (*Et dominus eum tradidit pro delictis nostris*)[86] [Isa 53:6]. In this manner He 'forsook' Him, in not sparing Him; 'forsook' Him, in delivering Him up. In all other respects the Father did not forsake the Son, for it was into His Father's hands that the Son commended His spirit.

---

[86]See *Vetus Latina* in Gryson's edition p. 1301.

Isaiah 53 and Passover

The Servant is described as a helpless lamb prepared to be slaughtered (Isa 53:7): "... he was led like a lamb to the slaughter, and as a sheep before its shearers is silent, so he did not open his mouth." This note combined with the historical fact that Jesus was crucified during the Passover festival prompted the typological interpretation: Jesus was a Passover lamb who was sacrificed. It is easy to see that such a typology from the sacrificial milieu came to hand because the same imagery was used in Jewish martyr theology from the Maccabean period onwards. This connection is visible already in the New Testament. Paul writes to the congregation at Corinth (1 Cor 5:6-8):

> Your boasting is not good. Do you not know that a little yeast leavens the whole batch of dough? Get rid of the old yeast, so that you may be a new unleavened batch—as you really are. For *Christ, our Passover lamb, has been sacrificed.* Therefore let us keep the Festival, not with the old bread leavened with malice and wickedness, but with the unleavened bread of sincerity and truth.

The text bears a clear allusion to the Passover Festival and the typological identification between Jesus Christ and Passover Lamb is taken for granted without any explanation – a feature which indicates that this typological interpretation was known to the Corinthians. It seems reasonable to assume that this interpretation was an essential part of catechetical lectures as becomes clear from the teaching of Cyril of Jerusalem. His Lecture 13 begins with reference to Isa 53:1, 7, and Christ is identified with the Passover lamb at the outset (13.3):

> Let us then not be ashamed of the Cross of our Saviour, but rather glory in it. For the word of the Cross is unto Jews a stumbling-block, and unto Gentiles foolishness, but to us salvation: and to them that are perishing it is foolishness, but unto us which are being saved it is the power of God. For it was not a mere man who died for us, as I said before, but the Son of God, God made man. Further; if the lamb under Moses drove the destroyer [Ex 12:23] far away, did not much rather the Lamb of God, which takes away the sin of the world [John

1:29], deliver us from our sins? The blood of a silly sheep gave salvation; and shall not the Blood of the Only-begotten much rather save? If any disbelieve the power of the Crucified, let him ask the devils; if any believe not words, let him believe what he sees. Many have been crucified throughout the world, but by none of these are the devils scared; but when they see even the Sign of the Cross of Christ, who was crucified for us, they shudder. For those men died for their own sins, but Christ for the sins of others; for He did no sin, neither was guile found in His mouth. It is not Peter who says this, for then we might suspect that he was partial to his Teacher; but it is Esaias who says it, who was not indeed present with Him in the flesh, but in the Spirit foresaw His coming in the flesh. Yet why now bring the Prophet only as a witness? Take for a witness Pilate himself, who gave sentence upon Him, saying, I find no fault in this Man [Lk 23:14] and when he gave Him up, and had washed his hands, he said, I am innocent of the blood of this just person [Mt 27:24]. There is yet another witness of the sinlessness of Jesus—the robber, the first man admitted into Paradise; who rebuked his fellow, and said, "We receive the due reward of our deeds; but this man has done nothing amiss ; for we were present, both you and I, at His judgment."

Cyril refers to the Gospel of John where John the Baptist says of Jesus that he is the lamb who will take away the sin of the world. According to the Gospel of John, Jesus died at the time when the Passover lamb was sacrificed in the Temple thus indicating even more strongly the association.

In patristic literature the connection between Jesus and the Passover lamb is often emphasized in association with Isaiah 53. One of the best examples is Meliton's *Peri Pascha* (= *PP*). The text is a homily on the exodus of the Hebrews as is clearly attested at the beginning (*PP* 1):[87] "The Scripture about the Hebrew Exodus has been read (ἡ μὲν γραφὴ τῆς ἑβραικῆς ἐξόδου ἀνέγνωσται) and the words of the mystery have been explained (διασεσάφηται)[88] as to how the sheep was

---

[87]H.M. Knapp,"Melito's Use of Scripture in *Peri Pascha*: Second-Century Typology," *Vigiliae Christianae* 54 (2000) 343-374.

[88]Concerning different translations of the verb διασεσάφηται see Knapp, "Melito's Use of Scripture" 345.

sacrificed and the people were saved." Then the text goes on to speak of the Passover lamb and its sacrifice with clear reference to Isaiah 53:7:

> The law is old, but the gospel is new; the type was for a time, but grace is forever. The sheep was corruptible, but the Lord is incorruptible, who was crushed as a lamb, but who was resurrected as God. For although "*he was led to sacrifice as a sheep*" (ὡς πρόβατον εἰς σφαγὴν ἤχθη), yet he was not a sheep; and although he was as a *lamb without voice*, yet indeed he was not a lamb. The one was the model; the other was found to be the finished product.

The Greek text quoted above is from the Septuagint (Isa 53:7) and the expression "a lamb without voice" must also refer to Isa 53:7 where it is said that "as a sheep before its shearers is silent, so he did not open his mouth." Indeed, the whole verse Isa 53:7 is quoted in *PP* 64, but not in total agreement with the Septuagint.[89] There are also many other references and allusions to Isaiah 53 according to the index of O. Perler who has edited the text.[90] Another important passage is *PP* 66 where it is said that the incarnation of the Son of God was a precondition to the salvation of humankind. Even though no clear parallels to the vocabulary of Isaiah 53 can be found, the content is a nice parallel to the Lamb of God (Isa 53:7) who must suffer and die:

> When this one came from heaven to earth for the sake of the one who suffers, and had clothed himself with that very one through the womb of a virgin, and having come forth as man, he accepted the sufferings of the sufferer through his body which was capable of suffering (ἀπεδέξατο τὰ τοῦ πάσχοντος

---

[89]Because Meliton wrote a major work of testimonies known by Eusebios as *Extracts* (*Hist Eccl* IV.26), it is possible that Old Testament passages quoted in *PP* 61-64 and 72 are from these testimonies. See R. Kraft, "Barnabas' Isaiah Text and Melito's Paschal Homily," *JBL* 80 (1961) 371-373; J. Kugel, *Early Biblical Interpretation* (Library of Early Christianity 3; Philadelphia: Westminster Press 1986); Knapp, "Melito's Use of Scriptures" 358.

[90]O. Perler, *Méliton de Sardes Sur La Pâque et Fragments* (SC 123; Paris: Les Éditions du Cerf 1966) 251.

πάθη διὰ τοῦ παθεῖν δυναμένου σώματος καὶ κατέλυσεν τὰ τῆς σαρκὸς πάθη). And he destroyed those human sufferings by his spirit which was incapable of dying. He killed death which had put man to death.

Meliton's *Peri Pascha* is a text where confrontation with Judaism is acute. We cannot speak of full-blown anti-Judaism in Meliton's case. After all, there is reason to believe that the Jewish population in Sardes or its vicinity was dominant and Christians had to struggle for their existence.[91] Meliton's homily is also a good example of a Christian self-definition. The Christian Easter is confronted with the Jewish Passover festival, and Isaiah 53:7 is one key passage which enabled Meliton to compare these two festivals with each other.

Tertullian is another early witness who uses Isaiah 53:7 to allude to the Passover festival (*Adv Marc* IV.40): "In like manner does He also know the very time it behoved Him to suffer, since the law prefigures His passion. Accordingly, of all the festal days of the Jews He chose the Passover. In this Moses had declared that there was a sacred mystery: 'It is the Lord's Passover' [Lev 23:5]. How earnestly, therefore, does He manifest the bent of His soul: 'With desire I have desired to eat this Passover with you before I suffer' [Lk 22:15]. What a destroyer of the law was this, who actually longed to keep its Passover! Could it be that He was so fond of Jewish lamb? But was it not because He had to be 'led like a lamb to the slaughter; and because, as a sheep before her shearers is dumb, so was He not to open His mouth' [Isa 53:7]." Origen also uses Isaiah 53:7 and connects it to the words of John the Baptist (John 1:29)

---

[91]A.T. Kraabel, "Melito the Bishop and the Synagogue at Sardis: Text and Context," in: D.G. Mitten, J.G. Pedley, J.A. Scott (eds.), *Studies Presented to George M.A. Hanfmann* (Mainz: Philipp von Zabern 1971) 77-85; E.M. Smallwood, *The Jews under Roman Rule: From Pompey to Diocletian* (Leiden: Brill 1976) 508-509; H. Remus, "Justin Martyr's Argument with Judaism," in: S.G. Wilson (ed.), *Anti-Judaism in Early Christianity. Volume 2: Separation and Polemic* (Waterloo: Wilfrid Laurier University Press 1986) 59-80, esp. 72-73; P. Trebilco, *Jewish Communities in Asia Minor* (SNTS MS 69, Cambridge: Cambridge University 1991); concerning Sardis see esp. index in Trebilco's study.

according to which Jesus is the Lamb of God (Commentary on John VI.35).

Isaiah 53 and Psalm 45

In patristic literature Psalm 45 has often been connected with the interpretation of Isaiah 53. While Isaiah 53 speaks of the sufferings of the Servant, Psalm 45 in its turn says of the King: "You are the most excellent of men." This connection is remarkable because in Medieval Jewish anti-Christian exegesis the Christian interpretation of Isaiah 53 was criticized because it applied both Isaiah 53 and Psalm 45 to Jesus (see further sect. 12). The earliest example of the connection between Isaiah 53 and Psalm 45 may originate already in Irenaeus. Irenaeus (*Adv Haer* III.19.2) writes:[92]

> For this reason [it is, said], "Who shall declare His generation?" [Isa 53:8] since "He is a man, and who shall recognise Him?" [Jer 17:9] But he to whom the Father which is in heaven has revealed Him, [Mt 16:16] knows Him, so that he understands that He who "was not born either by the will of the flesh, or by the will of man" [John 1:13], is the Son of man, this is Christ, the Son of the living God. For I have shown from the Scriptures, that no one of the sons of Adam is as to everything, and absolutely, called God, or named Lord. But that He is Himself in His own right, beyond all men who ever lived, God, and Lord, and King Eternal, and the Incarnate Word, proclaimed by all the prophets, the apostles, and by the Spirit Himself, may be seen by all who have attained to even a small portion of the truth. Now, the Scriptures would not have testified these things of Him, if, like others, He had been a mere man. But that He had, beyond all others, in Himself that pre-eminent birth which is from the Most High Father, and also experienced that pre-eminent generation which is from the Virgin, [Isa 7:14] the divine Scriptures do in both respects testify of Him: also, that "He was a man without comeliness, and liable to suffering" [Isa 53:2]; that He sat upon the foal of an ass [Zech 9:9]; that He received for drink, vinegar and gall; that He was despised among the people, and humbled Himself even to death and that He is the holy Lord, the Wonderful, the

---

[92]See the text in Rousseau, *Irénée de Lyon: Contre les Hérésies Livre III* 374-379.

Counsellor, *the Beautiful in appearance*, and the Mighty God [Isa 9:6], coming on the clouds as the Judge of all men [Dan 7:13] — all these things did the Scriptures prophesy of Him.

The expression "beautiful in appearance" may be an allusion to Ps 45:3 as one editor of the text, Rousseau, has suggested. In any case, the passage is an example of how Jesus Christ is described with the Old Testament passages – some of which glorify him and others depict him as suffering and under torture. Another early patristic text where Psalm 45 is related to Isaiah 53 is Tertullian's study against Marcion (*Adv Marc* III.17):[93]

> Let us compare with Scripture the rest of His dispensation. Whatever that poor despised body may be, because it was an object of touch and sight, it shall be my Christ, be He inglorious, be He ignoble, be He dishonoured; for such was it announced that He should be, both in bodily condition and aspect. Isaiah comes to our help again: "We have announced (His way) before Him", says he; "He is like a servant, like a root in a dry ground; He has no form nor comeliness; we saw Him, and He had neither form nor beauty; but His form was despised, marred above all men" [Isa 53:1-2]. Similarly the Father addressed the Son just before: "Inasmuch as many will be astonished at You, so also will Your beauty be without glory from men" [Isa 52:14]. For although, in David's words, "He is fairer than the children of men" [Ps 45:2], yet it is in that figurative state of spiritual grace, when He is girded with the sword of the Spirit, which is verily His form, and beauty, and glory. According to the same prophet, however, He is in bodily condition "a very worm, and no man; a reproach of men, and an outcast of the people" [Ps 22]. But no internal quality of such a kind does He announce as belonging to Him. In Him dwelt the fullness of the Spirit; therefore I acknowledge Him to be "the rod of the stem of Jesse." His blooming flower shall be my Christ, upon whom has rested, according to Isaiah, "the spirit of wisdom and understanding, the spirit of counsel and might, the spirit of knowledge and of piety, and of the fear of the Lord" [Isa 11:1-2]. Now to no man, except Christ, would the diversity of spiritual proofs suitably apply. He is indeed like a flower for the Spirit's grace, reckoned indeed of the stem of Jesse, but thence to derive His descent through

---

[93] See the text in Braun, *Tertullien: Contre Marcion Tome III*. The translation is from *Ante-Nicene Fathers*.

Mary. Now I purposely demand of you, whether you grant to Him the destination of all this humiliation, and suffering, and tranquillity, from which He will be the Christ of Isaiah, – a man of sorrows, and acquainted with grief, who was led as a sheep to the slaughter, and who, like a lamb before the shearer, opened not His mouth; who did not struggle nor cry, nor was His voice heard in the street who broke not the bruised reed – that is, the shattered faith of the Jews – nor quenched the smoking flax – that is, the freshly-kindled ardour of the Gentiles. He can be none other than the Man who was foretold. It is right that His conduct be investigated according to the rule of Scripture, distinguishable as it is unless I am mistaken, by the twofold operation of preaching and of miracle. But the treatment of both these topics I shall so arrange as to postpone, to the chapter wherein I have determined to discuss the actual gospel of Marcion, the consideration of His wonderful doctrines and miracles – with a view, however, to our present purpose. Let us here, then, in general terms complete the subject which we had entered upon, by indicating, as we pass on, how Christ was fore-announced by Isaiah as a preacher: "For who is there among you," says he, "that fears the Lord, that obeys the voice of His Son?" [Isa 50:10] And likewise as a healer: "For," says he, "He has taken away our infirmities, and carried our sorrows" [Isa 53:4].

For Tertullian Psalm 45 is illustration of Jesus' spiritual beauty. However, in a subsequent Christian interpretation tradition Psalm 45 came to play another role. It was interpreted as referring to the divinity of Jesus. The first example of this is Origen who refutes Celsus's statement that the God cannot physically possess an ugly form (*Contra Celsum* VI.75):

To the preceding remarks he adds the following: "Since a divine Spirit inhabited the body (of Jesus), it must certainly have been different from that of other beings, in respect of grandeur, or beauty, or strength, or voice, or impressiveness, or persuasiveness. For it is impossible that He, to whom was imparted some divine quality beyond other beings, should not differ from others; whereas this person did not differ in any respect from another, but was, as they report, little, and ill-favoured, and ignoble." Now it is evident by these words, that when Celsus wishes to bring a charge against Jesus, he adduces the sacred writings, as one who believed them to be writings apparently fitted to afford a handle for a charge against Him; but wherever, in the same writings, statements would appear to be made opposed to those charges which are adduced, he pretends not even to know them! There are, indeed, admitted to be recorded some statements respecting the body of Jesus having been "ill-favoured"; not, however, "ignoble", as has been stated, nor is there any certain evidence that he was "little". The language of Isaiah runs as follows, who prophesied regarding Him that He would come and visit the multitude, not in comeliness of form, nor in any surpassing beauty: "Lord, who has believed our report, and to whom was the arm of the Lord revealed? He made announcement before Him, as a child, as a root in a thirsty ground. He has no form nor glory, and we beheld Him, and He had no form nor beauty; but His form was without honour, and inferior to that of the sons of men." These passages, then, Celsus listened to, because he thought they were of use to him in bringing a charge against Jesus; but he paid no attention to the words of the forty-fifth Psalm, and why it is then said, "Gird Your sword upon Your thigh, O most mighty, with Your comeliness and beauty; and continue, and prosper, and reign."

Chrysostom continues this description of the divine and human form of Jesus. Like Origen he emphasizes that the divine beauty of Jesus did not fade during his sufferings (*Homilies on the Gospel of Matthew* 27.2):[94]

> For not by any means in working wonders only was He wonderful, but even when merely showing Himself, He was full of great grace; and to declare this the prophet said, "Fair in beauty beyond the children of men." And if Esaias says, "He has no form nor comeliness," he affirms it either in comparison of the glory of His Godhead, which surpasses all utterance and description; or as declaring what took place at His passion, and the dishonor which He underwent at the season of the cross, and the mean estate which throughout His life He exemplified in all respects.

Another aspect of the sufferings of Jesus is taken up in Jerome's interpretation where he refers to natural circumstances at the time of Jesus' death which bear witness to Jesus' beauty (*Commentary on Isaiah* 14.21-22):[95]

---

[94]The translation is from *Nicene and Post-Nicene Fathers.*

[95]See the translation in M.W. Elliott, *Isaiah 40-66* (Ancient Christian Commentary on Scripture Old Testament XI, Downers Grove: InterVarsity Press 2007) 161-162.

He did not have a beauty or glory. His form was base and lacking before [humanity], or as the Hebrew has it, despised and least among people... How then can it be said in the psalms, 'Gird your side with your sword, O most powerful, with your beauty and fairness'? This puzzle can be easily solved. He was despised and base when he hung on the cross and was made for us a curse and carried out sins and said to the Father, 'God, my God, why have you forsaken me?' But he was glorious and fair in appearance when, at his passion, the earth trembled, rocks were split and the elements were terrified at the sun's fleeing and the eternal night.

Cyril of Alexandria again follow Origen's line and established the view in the Church that Psalm 45 testifies to the beauty of the divine nature of Jesus, and Isaiah 53 the passion of the human nature of Jesus (Commentary on Isaiah 5.1.53.2):[96]

For human things are in every way small and cheap and worthless compared with the divine and highest eminence and outshining beauty of [his human] nature (physis). For it is said, "He is fair in beauty among the sons of men." And [Isaiah 53:2] adds to this description: "He is more rejected than all men," that is, his appearance (form) is more rejected, as if to say: Among men of distinction some are seen as distinguished by their fine radiant appearance. But Emmanuel was not among them. Rather, his appearance was reduced to a lowly and despised level.

The first Church Father, as far as I know, who combined Isaiah 53 and Psalm 45 in his criticism of the Jews is Gregory of Nazianzus (*Theological Oration* 29.19):[97]

For He Whom you now treat with contempt was once above you. He Who is now Man was once the Uncompounded. What He was He continued to be; what He was not He took to Himself. In the beginning He was, uncaused; for what is the Cause of God? But afterwards for a cause He was born. And that cause was that you might be saved, who insult Him and despise His Godhead, because of this, that He took upon Him your denser nature, having converse

---

[96]See the translation in Elliott, *Isaiah 40-66* xxviii.

[97]The translation is from *Nicene and Post-Nicene Fathers.*

with Flesh by means of Mind. While His inferior Nature, the Humanity, became God, because it was united to God, and became One Person because the Higher Nature prevailed in order that I too might be made God so far as He is made Man. He was born — but He had been begotten: He was born of a woman — but she was a Virgin. The first is human, the second Divine. In His Human nature He had no Father, but also in His Divine Nature no Mother. Both these belong to Godhead. He dwelt in the womb — but He was recognized by the Prophet, himself still in the womb, leaping before the Word, for Whose sake He came into being. He was wrapped in swaddling clothes [Lk 2:41] — but He took off the swathing bands of the grave by His rising again. He was laid in a manger — but He was glorified by Angels, and proclaimed by a star, and worshipped by the Magi. Why are you offended by that which is presented to your sight, because you will not look at that which is presented to your mind? He was driven into exile into Egypt — but He drove away the Egyptian idols. He had no form nor comeliness in the eyes of the Jews [Isa 53:2] — but to David He is fairer than the children of men [Ps 45:2]. And on the Mountain He was bright as the lightning, and became more luminous than the sun [Mt 17:2], initiating us into the mystery of the future.

This mode of combining two different descriptions of the Messiah – one depicting him under torture and suffering, another emphasizing his beauty – produced an intellectual problem which the Jewish party formulated in their anti-Christian writings during the Middle Ages. This dichotomy was probably known to Jews through various discourses. At least Psalm 45 (together with Isaiah 53) was been used in early disputations.[98]

Conclusions

Our survey of the patristic evidence has shown that Isaiah 53 was a crucial theological text in the early Church. It played a central role in catechumenical teaching. It provided a suitable starting-point to present the Christian kerygma as indicated in the account in Acts 8. Already in the New Testament the Christian kerygma was formulated with the help

---

[98]See these texts in Varner, *Ancient Jewish-Christian Dialogues*.

of Isaiah 53 (1 Cor 15:1-11) which rendered it easy to present the atonement theology connected with the death of Jesus. Furthermore, Isaiah 53 has been used in many different theological contexts: it has been a parenetic text for Christians to follow in the footsteps of the their Master Jesus who served others. It has also been used in Christian martyr theology. The text proved suitable for Christian self-identification against Judaism and paganism. With its aid the Christian theologians have refuted different Christological heresies.

9 Perspectives on Isaiah 53 in Rabbinical Writings

The use of Isaiah 53 in the rabbinical writings has often been considered to determine whether or not the passage has been interpreted as referring to the Messiah. This topic has been a challenge in Jewish-Christian relations since the Barcelona disputation in 1263 and the conclusion of Raymundus Martini's magnificent opus *Pugio fidei* (1278) where he refers to the rabbinical sources which recount the suffering and death of the Messiah.[1] The point at issue in this chapter pertains to the messianic interpretation of Isaiah 53 in the rabbinical context. Some preliminary remarks on the Messiah in the rabbinical writings are therefore needed.

The Messiah in the Rabbinical Literature

The Messiah does not play a major role in the rabbinical writings, nor do they contain standard messianic expectations as Jacob Neusner has

---

[1]One of the most significant topics in the Barcelona disputation concerned the suffering Messiah and, in particular, the interpretation of Isaiah 53. The fact that after the disputation Nahmanides was compelled to write an analysis of the messianic interpretation of Isaiah 53 among rabbis shows its importance. See R. Chazan, *Barcelona and Beyond: The Disputation of 1263 and Its Aftermath* (Berkeley: University of California 1992) 158-171; concerning Nahmanides interpretation of Isaiah 53 see C. Chavel, *Kitvei Rabbenu Moshe ben Nahman. 2 Volumes* (Jerusalem: Mossad Harav Kook 1971) I:322-326. See also A. Neubauer, *The Fifty-Third Chapter of Isaiah According to the Jewish Interpreters. I: Texts* (Varda Books 2005) 75-81 and translation in A. Neubauer & S. Driver, *The "Suffering Servant" of Isaiah According to the Jewish Interpreters Translated by S.R. Driver and A. Neubauer* (Eugene: Wipf and Stock 1999) 78-85. We shall deal with the Barcelona disputation and *Pugio fidei* more thoroughly in sect. 11.

convincingly shown in his study *Messiah in Context*.[2] Therefore any attempt to present a rabbinical messianic doctrine fails.[3] In order to illustrate his thesis Neusner uses a neat image of stones which were not used in a building project:[4]

> Judaism as we know it contains numerous allusions to a Messiah and references to what he will do. But so far as we examine the original canon of the ancient rabbis, framed over the second through seventh centuries, we find these inherited facts either reformed and reshaped for use in an essentially nonmessianic and ahistorical system, or left like rubble after a building has been completed: stones that might have been used, but were not. So Judaism as we know it presents no well-crafted doctrine of the Messiah, and thus its eschatology is framed within the methods of an essentially ahistorical teleology.

After scrutiny of references to Isaiah 53 and other passages relevant to the sufferings of the Messiah in rabbinical writings I would evaluate the situation along similar lines. There are few references to Isaiah 53 and only a fraction of them refer to the Messiah. This being the case there is no *prima facie* assumption that we shall find any consistent perspective on Isaiah 53 in rabbinical writings.

---

[2]J. Neusner, *Messiah in Context: Israel's History and Destiny in Formative Judaism* (The Foundations of Judaism: Method, Teleology, Doctrine 2; Philadelphia: Fortress Press, 1984).

[3]Neusner criticized *expressis verbis* J. Klausner's and G. Scholem's constructions for rabbinical messianism (Neusner, *Messiah in Context* 227): "Klausner and Scholem provide portraits of a composite that, in fact, never existed in any one book, time, or place, or in the imagination of any social group, except an imagined 'Israel' or a made-up 'Judaism'." Neusner refers to the following works: J. Klausner, *The Messianic Idea in Israel from Its Beginning to the Completion of the Mishnah* (New York: Macmillan 1955); G. Scholem, *The Messianic Idea in Judaism and Other Essays on Jewish Spirituality* (New York: Schocken Books 1971) and, in particular, its article "Toward an Understanding of the Messianic Idea in Judaism."

[4]Neusner, *Messiah in Context* ix.

Rabbinical documents contain some references to the suffering (and/or dying) Messiah and Isaiah 53 or Zechariah 12 are quoted therein.[5] We shall deal with the different texts and, in particular, interpret them in their own literary contexts.

Messiah ben Joseph

The earliest rabbinical document which mentions the sufferings of the Messiah is the Talmud Jerushalmi, and its tractate Sukka (5:2). The key-text used in this passage is Zech 12:12 and the lamentations there described. The passage in the Talmud Jerushalmi deals with the question of how men and women were separated in the area of the women's court by building the construction of a gallery so that women can look on from above and the men from below:[6]

> Whence did they learn this rule? From a teaching of the Torah: "The land shall mourn, each family by itself; the family of the house of David by itself, and their wives by themselves; the family of the house of Nathan by itself, and their

---

[5]See the rabbinical texts which have been discussed in the following works: A. Wünsche, Die Leiden des Messias (Leipzig: Fues's Verlag 1870); A. Neubauer, *The Fifty-Third Chapter of Isaiah According to the Jewish Interpreters. I : Texts* (Varda Books 2005) 6-9 and translations in A. Neubauer & S. Driver, *The "Suffering Servant" of Isaiah According to the Jewish Interpreters Translated by S.R. Driver and A. Neubauer* (Eugene: Wipf and Stock 1999) 7-11; P. Billerbeck, *Kommentar zum Neuen Testament aus Talmud und Midrasch von Hermann L. Strack und Paul Billerbeck Vol I-V* (Munich: Oskar Beck 1922-1928) I:481-485; H.A. Fischel, "Die deutero-jesajanischen Gottesknechtlieder in der juedischen Auslegung," *HUCA* 18 (1943/44) 53-76; K. Hruby, "Die rabbinische Exegese messianischer Schriftstellen," *Judaica* 21 (1965) 100-22; H. Haag, *Der Gottesknecht bei Deuterojesaja* (EdF 233, Darmstadt: Wissenschaftliche Buchgesellschaft 1985) 36-47; M. Pickup, "The Emergence of the Suffering Messiah in Rabbinic Literature," in: J. Neusner (ed), *Approaches to Ancient Judaism. New Series Vol 11* (South Florida Studies in the History of Judaism 154), Atlanta 1997, 143-62.

[6]The English translation here is taken from J. Neusner, *Talmud of the Land of Israel: A Preliminary Translation and Explanation* (Chicago: The University of Chicago Press 1988).

262

wives by themselves." [There were] two Amoras. One said, "This refers to a lamentation for the Messiah (זה הספידו של משיח)." The other said, "This refers to a lamentation for the evil impulse (יצר הרע)." He who said, "This refers to a lamentation for the Messiah": now if at a time at which they are mourning, you have said, "The men must be by themselves and the women by themselves," when they are rejoicing, is it not an argument *a fortiori*! He who said, "This refers to a lamentation for the evil impulse": now if at a time at which they are not subject to the evil impulse, you have said, "The men must be by themselves and the women by themselves," when they are subject to the evil impulse, is it not an argument *a fortiori*!

The purpose of this passage is not to present a messianic concept but to expound the halakhic rule concerning the separation of men and women during services at the time of Sukkoth. Reference is made to two rabbis from the Amoraic period who interpret Zech 12:12 subjectively. The first associates the passage with "the lamentation made on the Messiah" and the second to the mourning for "an evil inclination". Both utterances are then discussed to determine whether it is possible to formulate a general rule that men and women should be separated when religious rituals are performed. As the text shows it is possible to use the *qal wa-chomer* argument (לא כל שכן) in such a case. Because the transmitter of the tradition in y.Sukkah 5:2 is not minded to discuss messianic expectations the text gives no details about what kind of sufferings the Messiah must endure, nor can we know for sure whether the reference pertains to Messiah ben David or to Messiah ben Joseph. The parallel tradition in b.Sukkah 52a from a later period indicates that Messiah ben Joseph (or Ephraim) is meant. Mitchell argued that the Babylonian Talmud has preserved an early Tannaitic saying of Dosa ben Harkinas who maintains that "the lamentation for the Messiah" refers to the Messiah ben Joseph.[7]

Mitchell postulates that Mishnaic Hebrew was not a spoken language during the time of the Amoraic rabbis so that the two separate opinions concerning the lamentation in Zech 12:12 formulated in Hebrew

---

[7]D.C. Mitchell, "Rabbi Dosa and the Rabbis Differ: Messiah ben Joseph in the Babylonian Talmud," *RBJ* 8.1 (2005) 77-90.

in bSukkah 52b, one from Rabbi Dosa ("The cause is the slaying of Messiah the son of Joseph") and the second of other rabbis ("The cause is the slaying of the evil inclination"), must originate from the Tannaitic period. These opinions were transmitted in Hebrew and quoted by Amoraic rabbis. This perspective on the tradition of the Babylonian Talmud gives Mitchell reason to allege that the word *amoraim* in jSukkah 5:2 should be rendered more generally "interpreters" or "opinions".[8] Mitchell translates the passage as follows (the words in italics are written in Aramaic):[9]

> And the land will mourn, family by family apart (Zech 12:12). *There are two opinions. One says*: this mourning is for Messiah; *and the other says*: this mourning is for the evil inclination.

Mitchell's thesis challenges the common date of the concept of the Messiah ben Josef which is assigned to the post-Bar-Kochba period. It is worth noting that Mitchell's date is based on the information in the Babylonian Talmud although the name of Dosa ben Harkinas is omitted in the Talmud Jerushalmi which refers to this saying anonymously. In another article he challenges the popular view among scholars that Messiah ben Joseph's death has no atoning power.[10] While Mitchell has shown that the idea of atonement was connected with the death of Messiah ben Joseph long before the 16th century Isaiah Horowitz (a view put forward by Klausner), he failed to prove that the idea goes back to the

---

[8]Mitchell's opinion receives support from S.G. Wald's article "Baraita, Baraitot," *Encyclopaedia Judaica* 3:124-128.

[9]Mitchell, "Rabbi Dosa" 82. Mitchell criticizes Klausner's dating of the concept of Messiah ben Joseph to the time after Bar Kochba. See J. Klausner, *The Messianic Idea in Israel* 487-492. J. Heinemann ("The Messiah of Ephraim and the Premature Exodus of the Tribe of Ephraim," *HTR* 8 [1975] 1-15) argues that even though the concept of the Messiah of Joseph may be old the idea of his slaying was developed after the war of Bar Kochba.

[10]D.C. Mitchell, "Messiah ben Joseph: A Sacrifice of Atonement for Israel," *RRJ* 10 (2007) 77-94.

Talmudic writings. I can follow his arguments from Horowitz back to Saadiah but then I found his theory wanting. One of his main arguments is that Pesiqta Rabbati 36-37 refers to the atoning death of Messiah ben Joseph. However, PesR states *expressis verbis* that the "Ephraim Messiah, my righteousness" belongs to the house of David as becomes clear from Piska 36 § 6: "During the seven-year period when the son of David will appear iron beams will be brought and loaded upon his neck until the Messiah's being is bent low. Then he will cry and weep, and his voice will rise up to the very height of heaven and he will say to God: Master of the universe, how much can my strength endure?"[11] A little later Psalm 22 is said to be applied to the son of David (Braude's translation): "During the ordeal of the son of David, the Holy One, blessed be He, will say to him: Ephraim, My true Messiah, long ago, ever since the six days of creation, thou didst take this ordeal upon thyself. At this moment, thy pain is like my pain." Another problem in Mitchell's interpretation arises from his statement that the Messiah will die in PesR 36-37. However, there is no suggestion that such will occur, as we shall see later in sect. 10. Therefore, it seems to me that Mitchell's interpretation of Pesiqta Rabbati is not convincing. Inasmuch as Pesiqta Rabbati is a significant link between Saadiah and the Talmud Mitchell's theory fails to prove its point.

Neither the Talmud Jerushalmi nor the Babylonian Talmud explain the significance of the death of Messiah ben Joseph. It is impossible to determine whether or not the Messiah will suffer or die vicariously. It is true that the context of Zech 12:10 enables us to speculate that the death may have something to do with atonement because Zech 13:1 states that the inhabitants of Jerusalem and the House of David will have an open fountain which "cleanse them from sin and impurity." However, we must be aware of overestimating the biblical context in such cases. We have seen that the vicarious element in Isaiah

---

[11]Concerning the interpretation of Pesiqta Rabbati see further sect. 10.

53 has often been deprecated in interpretations (e.g., LXX, Wisdom 2-5, Targum Jonathan).

The passage in b.sukkah 52a distinguishes between the fates of Messiah ben Joseph and Messiah ben David in the coming eschatological battle. The former will die in the battle when Israel goes to war against its enemies (cf., the context of Zechariah 12) while the latter requests God to save his life:[12]

> Our Rabbis taught, The Holy One, blessed be He, will say to the Messiah, the son of David (May he reveal himself speedily in our days!), "Ask of me anything, and I will give it to you," as it is said, *"I will tell of the decree ... this day I have begotten you, ask of me and I will give the nations for your inheritance."* But when he will see that the Messiah the son of Joseph is slain, he will say to Him, "Lord of the Universe, I ask of You only the gift of life." "As to life", He would answer to him, "Your father David has already prophesied this concerning you", as it is said, *"He asked life of you, you gave it him [even length of days for ever and ever]."*

This tradition consists of the dialogue between God and Messiah ben David. God's starting-point is to execute the great expectations written in Psalm 2, whereby the Davidic Messiah will rule over all nations. Messiah ben David, who has experienced the death of Messiah ben Joseph, asks God to save his life. God's answer is based on Psalm 21:5 which promises eternal life to Messiah ben David. This detail, which is included as a brief observation in the middle of an halakic discussion, indicates the fundamental difference between the fates of Messiah ben Joseph and Messiah ben David. Messiah ben David does not die. This is precisely the conclusion which Nahmanides presents to Pablo Christiani

---

[12]The translations of the Babylonian Talmud are according to Soncino Talmud.

in the Barcelona disputation in 1263. According to his own report *Vikuach* he had said:[13]

> I said to him, "It is true that our Teachers, may their memory be for a blessing, in the Aggadic books, interpret the passage as referring to the Messiah (דורשים אותו על משיח). But they never said that the Messiah would be slain by the hand of his enemies. You will never find in any book of the literature of Israel, either in the Talmud or the Aggadic books, that the Messiah, son of David, would ever be slain, or that he would be betrayed into the hands of his enemies, or that he would be buried among the wicked, for even your Messiah, whom you made for yourselves, was not buried among the wicked. If you like, I will give you an excellent and detailed explanation of the passage in Isaiah. There is nothing there about the Messiah's being slain as happened with your Messiah." But hey did not want to hear it.

Isaiah 53 and Messiah ben David

An early midrash which predates the Babylonian Talmud, and which contains a messianic interpretation of Isaiah 53 is Ruth Rabbah. Ruth R 5:6 interprets Ruth 2:14. This contains five allegorical explanations and then a literal interpretation concerning Boas. The five allegorical interpretations refer to the Messiah and his four types in the Hebrew Bible: David, Solomon, Hezekiah and Manasseh. All these four kings (1) must suffer and (2) lose their kingship for a time, but all (3) will be reinstated on their thrones. In every case these events are justified by a text in the Hebrew Bible. In the case of the Messiah the reference is to Isa 53:5 when the text recounts his sufferings, to Zech 14:2 when it mentions about his temporary dethronement, and to Isa 11:4 when it describes the restoration of the Messiah:[14]

---

[13]See the text in Chavel, *Kitvei Rabbenu Moshe ben Nahman* I:302-320 and the translation from H. Maccoby, *Judaism on Trial. Jewish-Christian Disputations in the Middle Ages* (London: The Littman Library of Jewish Civilization 1993) 102-150, esp. 112-113.

[14]The translation is from *Midrash Rabbah: Ruth* (Translated by L. Rabinowitz, London: The Soncino Press 1983).

The fifth interpretation makes it refer to the Messiah. COME HITHER: approach to royal state. AND EAT OF THE BREAD refers to the bread of royalty; AND DIP THY MORSEL IN THE VINEGAR refers to his sufferings, as it is said, *But he was wounded because of our transgressions* (Isa 53, 5). AND SHE SAT BESIDE THE REAPERS, for he will be deprived of his sovereignty for a time, as it is said, *For I will gather all nations against Jerusalem to battle; and the city shall be taken* (Zech 14, 2). AND THEY REACHED HER PARCHED CORN, means that he will be restored to his throne, as it is said, *And he shall smite the land with the rod of his mouth* (Isa 11,4). R. Berekiah said in the name of R. Levi: The future Redeemer will be like the former Redeemer. Just as the former Redeemer revealed himself and later was hidden from them – and how long was he hidden? Three months, as it is said, *And they met Moses and Aaron* (Ex 5, 20) – so the future Redeemer will be revealed to them, and then be hidden from them. And how long will he be hidden? R, Tanhuma, in the name of the Rabbis, said: Forty-five days, as it is said, *And from the time that the continual burnt-offering shall be taken away ... there shall be a thousand two hundred and ninety days. Happy is he that waiteth, and cometh to the thousand three hundred and five and thirty days* (Dan 12, 11-12). What are these extra days? R. Isaac b. Kazarta said on behalf of R. Jonah: These are the forty-five days during which Israel shall pluck saltwort and eat it, as it is said, *They pluck saltwort with wormwood* (Job 30, 4). Where will he lead them? From the land of Israel to the wilderness of Judah, as it is said, *Behold, I will allure her, and bring her into the wilderness* (Hos 2, 16); while some say to the wilderness of Sihon and Og, as it is said, *I will yet again make thee to dwell in tents, as in the days of the appointed season* (Hos 12, 10). He who believes in him will live, and he who does not believe will depart to the Gentile nations and they will put him to death. R. Isaac b. Marion said: Finally the Holy One, blessed be He, will reveal Himself to them, and He will rain down manna upon them, *And there is nothing new under the sun* (Qoh 1, 9).

How should we interpret the sufferings of the Messiah? The literary structure of Ruth Rabbah indicates clearly that Isa 53:5 is not regarded as an account of the real death of the Messiah but rather of his temporary sufferings. The parallels to the sufferings of the Messiah in Ruth Rabbah are the sufferings of his prototypes: God rebuked David (Ps 6:2) and David was forced to flee from his son Absalom; Solomon was deposed when an angel in his likeness descended from Heaven and took his throne; Hezekiah was ill and near to death and his sovereignty was taken from him at the time of Sennacherib's invasion; Manasseh was deposed by the Assyrian king and by the will of God because of his many sins. Thus the sufferings of the Messiah and his concealment cannot in any way refer to his death. Neusner writes on this messianic passage in the Midrash Ruth:[15]

> The Messiah-doctrine of Rabbinic Judaism encompasses the pattern of the Messiah's own suffering. The Messiah lives out the fate of Israel. Israel got the Land, lost the land, suffered, and was, and again would be, restored to the Land. So too the Messiah, embodied by David, came to the throne, lost the throne, suffered, but was restored to the throne.

The Messiah will lose his throne for a time when the enemy army will invade Jerusalem and conquer it (Zech 14:2). In Ruth R 5:6 it is discussed how many days the power of the Messiah will be hidden. From Dan 12:11-12 and the numbers 1335 and 1290 the conclusion is reached that the Messiah will lose his sovereignty for 45 days but after this time he will be reinstated. Nowhere in the text is reference made to the fact that the Messiah will die vicariously for the sins of the people, atoning for them. This interpretation of Isaiah 53 in Ruth R 5:6 is parallel to b.Sukkah 52a according to which Messiah ben David will encounter tribulation after the death of Messiah ben Joseph but not die. Thus the "sufferings" of the Messiah and the "deprivation of his sovereignty" must be dated at the time of the final war. The enemy will have the upper hand at first (Zech 14:2) but then the Messiah ben David will finally smite his enemy, the proof text for this destruction being Isa 11:4. In this context it should be mentioned that rabbi Alexandri interprets Isa 11:2-3 as referring to the sufferings of the Messiah (bSanh 93b): "R. Alexandri said: This teaches that he loaded him with good deeds and suffering as a mill [is laden]." "As a millstone" (כריחיים) is a word-play from the word "shall make him of understanding" (והריחו) in Isa 11:3.

---

[15]J. Neusner, *A Theological Commentary to the Midrash, Volume 6: Ruth Rabbah and Esther Rabbah I* (Studies in Ancient Judaism, Lanham: University Press of America 2001) 49.

The period of 45 days is illustrated with many biblical passages all of which depict the deep distress of Israel when the Messiah is hidden from them. The end of the quotation reveals that this period will be the time of testing. There are Jews who will not believe in God, depart to the Gentiles and be put to death by them. This "death" should probably be interpreted as signifying that the Jews in question will convert to Christianity and die spiritually.

Before we deal with the interpretation of Isaiah 53 in the Babylonian Talmud we must take a stand concerning the text in Sifra Leviticus: *Wajjiqra Dibura Dehoba Parasha* 12 to which we referred already in sect. 5. As is there stated the logion has two different versions, the one presented in the rabbinical tradition which was printed in the Vienna edition from 1545 and the other found in Raymundus Martini's *Pugio Fidei* (1278, Folio 674-675; pages 866-867 in Carpzov's edition). According to the logion preserved in *Pugio Fidei,* the Messiah will suffer on the behalf of the sins of the peoples and expiate them by annulling the destruction caused by Adam. I provide this translation in the form whereby all phrases attested in Sifra are given in *italics.* In addition I have placed in parentheses some phrases which occur in Sifra but are not attested in *Pugio Fidei* in order to indicate differences in the text. A case which requires a special note is indicated in bold type:[16]

> *R. Yosé* the Galilean *said,* Come forth and learn the righteousness of the King Messiah and *the reward of the righteous ones* [in the coming time] *from the first man who was commanded only concerning a single commandment*[17]*, involving merely refraining from a given action, and he violated that*

---

[16]The English translation is based on Driver & Neubauer, *Suffering Servant of Isaiah* 10-11 but I have modified it for this particular comparative purpose.

[17]Sifra reads על מצוה אחת while *Pugio Fidei* reads the same phrase without על.

commandment: consider how many deaths were exacted for **him and**[18] his
generations and for all generations to the end of all generations. Which
attribute is the greater, the attribute of goodness, or the attribute of
vengeance? He answered, The attribute of goodness is the greater, and the
attribute of vengeance is the less;[19] how much more, then, will the King
Messiah, who endures affliction and pains for the transgressors (as it is written,
"He was wounded") justify all generations and this is what is meant when it is
said, "And the Lord made the iniquity of us all meet upon him."

The passage under discussion is a classical example of those "quotations"
in *Pugio Fidei* which many scholars regard as Christian interpolations.
Interestingly, Wünsche in his *Die Leiden des Messias* gives the *Pugio
Fidei* text as representing the text in Sifra.[20] But as we observed in sect.
5, Jeremias changed his mind concerning the authenticity of this passage
in *Pugio Fidei*. One who energetically rejects this authenticity is Schiller-
Szinessy. He comments that the words שכרן של צדיקים "have no
meaning if ... the merit of the Messiah is higher than the keeping of
negative commandments" – a statement which seems to be a conclusion
from the *Pugio Fidei* "quotation."[21] Schiller-Szinessy's evaluation of
Pugio Fidei must be read cautiously because he failed in several respects
to reach a fair judgment of Martini's work. This has been demonstrated

---

[18]*Pugio Fidei* translates here: "*vide quot mortes decrete sunt illi, generationibus ejus
...*" and postulates the Hebrew text which reads לו ולדורריו. This reading can be found
in Sifra. However, the Hebrew text given in *Pugio Fidei* has only לדורריו.

[19]From this point onwards the texts in *Pugio Fidei* and Sifra diverge. Sifra continues:
"Now see how many deaths were exacted for him and his generations and for all
generations to the end of all generations. The trait of bestowing benefit is greater: one
who merely refrains from consuming sacrificial meat that has been subjected to an
improper intention on the part of the officiating priest and from meat that is left over
[beyond the time allotted to eat it], who afflicts himself on the Day of Atonement, how
much the more so that such a one, and his generations, and all generations to the end of
all generations, will receive merit!"

[20]A. Wünsche, *Die Leiden des Messias* (Leipzig: Fues's Verlag 1870) 65-66.

[21]See S.M. Schiller-Szinessy, "The Pugio Fidei," *Cambridge Journal of Philosophy*
16 (1888) 131-152, esp. 139-141.

convincingly by Neubauer who observes that many readings in *Pugio Fidei* which are accused as being forgeries in fact can now be found in the Prague Manuscripts of Moshe Ha-Darshan.[22] The question is whether Martini himself invented his sources or whether he drew on manuscripts which contained variations. I am inclined to believe that he took a reading from Sifra which he renders in *Pugio Fidei*. But this is not to say that all his readings originate from Jewish believers. After all there were converts who may well have interpolated passages into Jewish manuscripts. As far as the above quotation from *Pugio Fidei* is concerned Lieberman regards it as a Christian interpolation but notes that the attribute of Jose, i.e. Galilaeus, given by Martini in his quotation can now be attested in the Jewish manuscript Codex Rome which contains a dating from the year 1073.[23] We can sum up our discussion and conclude that even though Martini cannot be accused of fabricating forgeries – a recourse which would certainly be unwise because Jewish exegetes would have recognized them – there is no evidence that the specific passage in Sifra was originally Jewish. Therefore, we must exclude it from our discussion here.

The Babylonian Talmud contains no passage in which Isaiah 53 was associated with the fate of Messiah ben Joseph. On the other hand, Isaiah 53 was once used to describe Messiah ben David. In the tractate Sanhedrin different names of the Messiah are listed and the long list includes a name which is rooted in Isa 53:4 (b.Sanh 98b):

---

[22]See A. Neubauer, "Jewish Controversy and the 'Pugio Fidei'," *The Expositor* 38 (1888) 81-105; 39 (1889) 179-197. Concerning the reliability of Martini's quotations from sources known to him see also S. Lieberman, "Raymund Martini and His Alleged Forgeries," *Historia Judaica* 5 (1943) 87-102; R. Harvey, *Raymundus Martini and the Pugio Fidei: The Life and Work of a Medieval Controversialist* (Diss. London 1991).

[23]Lieberman, "Raymund Martini and His Alleged Forgeries," 101-102.

272

His name is "the leper scholar" (חיוורא דבי רבי שמו) as it is written, '*Surely he has borne our griefs and carried our sorrows: yet we did esteem him a leper (nāgûaʿ), smitten of God, and afflicted'* (Isa 53:4).

The word *nāgûaʿ* ("stricken") in Isa 53:4 can be interpreted in the light of Lev 13:45 as referring to the human being who has been smitten by disease, leper. This does not mean that the Messiah was stricken by leprosy because b.Sanh 98a give us a more detailed description. According to this passage Messiah will be found among the lepers and the ailing:[24]

R. Joshua b.Levi met Elijah standing by the entrance of R. Simeon b. Yohai's tomb. He asked him: 'Have I a portion in the world to come?' He replied, 'If this Master desires it.' R. Joshua b. Levi said, 'I saw two, but heard the voice of a third.' He then asked him, 'When will the Messiah come?' – 'Go and ask him himself,' was his reply, 'Where is he sitting?' – 'At the entrance.' 'And by what sign may I recognise him?' – 'He is sitting among the poor lepers: all of them untie [them] all at once, and rebandage them together, whereas he unties and rebandages each separately, [before treating the next], thinking, should I be wanted, [it being time for my appearance as the Messiah] I must not be delayed [through having to bandage a number of sores].' So he went to him and greeted him, saying, 'Peace upon thee, Master and Teacher.' 'Peace upon thee, O son of Levi,' he replied. 'When wilt thou come Master?' asked he, 'To-day', was his answer. On his returning to Elijah, the latter enquired, 'What did he say to thee?' – 'Peace upon thee, O son of Levi,' he answered. Thereupon he [Elijah] observed, 'He thereby assured thee and thy father of [a portion in] the world to come.' 'He spoke falsely to me,' he rejoined, 'stating that he would come to-day, but has not.' He [Elijah] answered him, 'This is what he said to thee, *To-day, if ye will hear his voice.*'

The passages in b.Sanh 98a-b belong to the larger structure of b.Sanh 96b-99a which Neusner analyzed in his study.[25] Neusner outlines five central themes in the messianic expectations which become manifest in this passage:

---

[24]Translation according to the Soncino Talmud.

[25]Neusner, *Messiah in Context* 168-178.

1. Troubles preceding the appearance of the Messianic age.
2. Calculations of the time of the coming of the Messiah.
3. The history of the world divided into three periods: desolation (without the Torah), the time of the Torah and the time of the Messiah.
4. The Messiah will be sent to a generation worthy of it, i.e., which repent because of its righteousness or because of lamentable conditions.
5. The Messiah is the son of David.

Neusner concludes that this passage in the Sanhedrin on the whole clearly shows that "the matter of the Messiah remained subordinated: 'If you do this or that, the Messiah will come.' Thus the Messiah myth supplied the uniform apodosis of diverse protases, the fixed teleology for the variety of ineluctable demands of the system as a whole."[26] When the discussion between Rabbi Joshua ben Levi, Elijah and the Messiah is read in this wider context it becomes clear that the coming of the Messiah is dependent on how Israel repents. The reference to Psalm 95:7 ("Today if you will obey") illustrates this well. Against this background the role of the Messiah as one who cares for the sick and the lepers shows every Jew of how to show mercy and good will toward his neighbour. Thus the Messiah who wishes to help these people will finally be identified as one of them so that his name will be Leper. In a certain sense the idea corresponds to the picture which the Synoptic Gospels convey about Jesus who was the friend of sinners and the poor and then Isa 53:4 was applied to him (see Mt 8:16-17): "When evening came, many who were demon-possessed were brought to him, and he drove out the spirits with a word and healed all the sick. This was to fulfill what was spoken through the prophet Isaiah: 'He took up our infirmities and bore our diseases'." It is clear that we cannot conclude on the basis of the Messiah's name Leper as delivered from Isa 53:4 that Messiah ben David

---

[26]Neusner, *Messiah in Context* 177.

274

would die for the sins of the people. The only relevant conclusion is that he is the one who helps the poor and sick. It is worth noting that in his letter to Yemenite Jews, Maimonides refers to a certain false Messiah. Some Jews had begun to regard a man who had been healed of his illness, leprosy, as the Messiah. Maimonides discussed how the word *nāgûa'* in Isa 53:4 was applied to this man. This letter is strong evidence of how the noun "leper" and Isa 53:4 had been understood in a rabbinical context:[27]

> The king then said to all the Jews of his kingdom: "Let your scholars go out to meet this multitude and ascertain whether their pretension is true and he is unmistakably your Expected One. If so, we shall conclude peace with you under any conditions you may prefer. But if it is dissimulation, then I shall wage war against them." When the sages met these Jews, the latter declared: "We belong to the children of the district beyond the River." Then they asked them: "Who instigated you to make this uprising?" Whereupon they replied: "This man here, one of the descendants of David, whom we know to be pious and virtuous. This man, whom we knew to be a leper at night, arose the following morning healthy and sound." They believed that leprosy was one of the characteristics of the Messiah, for which they found an allusion to the verse: "stricken, smitten of God, and afflicted," (Isaiah 53:4), that is by leprosy. Whereupon the sages explained to them that this interpretation was incorrect, and that he lacked even one of the characteristics of the Messiah, let alone all of them. Furthermore they advised them as follows: "O, brethren, you are still near your native country and have the possibility of returning thither. If you remain in this land you will not only perish, but also undermine the teachings of Moses, by misleading people to believe that the Messiah has appeared and has been vanquished, whereas you have neither a prophet in your midst, nor an omen betokening his oncoming." Thereupon they were persuaded by these arguments. The Sultan turned over to them so and so many thousand of dinars by way of hospitality in order that they should leave his country. But after they had returned home, he had a change of heart with respect to the Jews upon whom he imposed a fine for his expenditures. He ordered them to make a special mark on their garments, the writing of the word "cursed," and to attach one iron bar in the back and one in the front. Ever since

---

[27]See this letter of Maimonides in I. Twersky, *A Maimonides Reader* (Springfield: Behrman House 1972) 458-459.

then the communities of Khorasan and Ispahan experienced the tribulations of the Diaspora. This episode we have learned from oral reports.

According to b.Pesh 54a the name of the Messiah was established before creation. This belief later gave rise to the concept that the Messiah has pre-existence. This pre-existence is apparently implied already in bSanh 98a-b. In his pre-existence the Messiah participates in the sufferings of the poor so that when he finally appears he will be found among the poor and sick. The idea of the pre-existence and the sufferings of the Messiah is further developed in Pesikta Rabbati and Zohar (sect. 10).

Isaiah 53 and Moses

We have seen that the Babylonian Talmud interprets Isaiah 53 messianically not, however, so that the Messiah would die to expiate the sins of the people. References to Isaiah 53 in the Babylonian Talmud are not confined to the Messiah. In the tractate b.Sotah 14a Isaiah 53 is quoted to refer to Moses:

> R. Simlai expounded: Why did Moses our teacher yearn to enter the land of Israel? Did he want to eat of its fruits or satisfy himself from its bounty? But thus spake Moses, 'Many precepts were commanded to Israel which can only be fulfilled in the land of Israel. I wish to enter the land so that they may all be fulfilled by me.' The Holy One, blessed be He, said to him, 'Is it only to receive the reward [for obeying the commandments] that thou seekest? I ascribe it to thee as if thou didst perform them': as it is said, *Therefore will I divide him a portion with the great, and he shall divide the spoil with the strong; because he poured out his soul unto death, and was numbered with transgressors; yet he bare the sins of many , and made intercession for the transgressors.* 'Therefore will I divide him a portion with the great' – it is possible [to think that this portion will be] with the [great of] later generations and not former generations; therefore there is a text to declare, '*And he shall divide with the strong*' i.e. with Abraham, Isaac and Jacob who were strong in Torah and the commandments. '*Because he poured out his soul unto death*' – because he surrendered himself to die, as it is said, *And if not, blot me, I pray thee* etc. '*And was numbered with the transgressors*' – because he was numbered with them who were condemned to die in the wilderness. '*Yet he*

bare the sins of many' – because he secured atonement for the making of the Golden Calf. *'And made intercession of transgressors'* – because he begged for mercy on behalf of the sinners in Israel that they should turn in penitence; and the word *pegi'ah* [intercession] means nothing else than prayer, as it is said, *Therefore pray not thou for this people, neither lift up cry nor prayer for them, neither make intercession to Me.*

Moses' willingness to be a mediator between God and the sinful people is described with the aid of the suffering servant (Isa 53:12). This interpretation contains some characteristic features indicating how Isaiah 53 can be understood without emphasizing that the person identified as Servant would die.

First, the Servant will divide a portion with the great and strong. This refers to the coming generations (= "the great ones") and to the patriarchs Abraham, Isaac and Jacob (= "the strong ones"). It is not clear from this passage what is meant by the coming generations. However, another passage in Sifre Deuteronomy concerning Deut 33:21 (§ 355) sheds some light on this point:[28]

Another interpretation [of the phrase, 'where the heads of the people come']: This teaches that Moses is destined to enter in at the head of every single association [formed for Torah-study], at the head of the association formed for the study of Scripture, at the head of the association formed for the study of the Mishnah, at the head of the association formed for the study of Talmud. He receives the reward that is coming to each such group, and so it is said, *'Therefore I shall divide him a portion among the great, and he shall divide the spoil with the mighty'* (Isa 53:12).

---

[28]See the Hebrew text in L. Finkelstein, *Siphre ad Deuteronomium* (Berlin: Jüdischer Kulturbund in Deutschland 1939) 418. The English translation is from J. Neusner, *Sifre to Deuteronomy: An Analytical Translation Volume Two: Pisqaot One Hundred Forty-Four through Three Hundred Fifty Seven* (Brown Judaic Studies 101, Atlanta: Scholars Press 1987) 443-444. See further H. Bietenhard, *Der tannaitische Midrash Sifre Deuteronomium Übersetzt und erklärt von Hans Bietenhard mit einem Beitrag von Henrik Ljungman* (Judaica et Christiana 8, Bern: Peter Lang 1984) 872-873.

Second, the death of the servant ("Because he poured out his soul unto death" Isa 53:12) was seen to conform to Moses' request that God will blot his name from the book of life so that the Israelites will be saved (Ex 32:31-32). This willingness to die is an interpretive perspective on Isaiah 53 which later, in medieval times, became characteristic of Jewish interpretations (see sect. 11).

Third, the expression "He was numbered with the transgressors" in Isa 53:12 was seen as parallelling the fate of Moses when he died with the sinful Israelites in the wilderness. Moses was never allowed to cross the River of Jordan and enter the Land of Canaan. He had to suffer the consequences of the sins of his people.

Fourth, the expression "He bore the sins of many" in Isa 53:12 was used to justify how Moses secured atonement for the Israelites after their worship of the golden calf. The expression does not refer to the atoning death of Moses but his willingness to seek atonement for his people. In a similar way, the expression "He made intercession for the transgressor" (Isa 53:12) was associated with Moses' prayers for the sinful people.

This being the case, Moses is depicted in b.Sotah 14a as the suffering servant of Yhwh who must bear the consequences of the sins of the people and seek atonement for them. He is ready to die for the sins of the people and finally he is compelled to bear the consequences of these sins, i.e. he could not enter the Land of Canaan (Ex 33-34). Nevertheless, he did not die for the sins of the people like Jesus in the New Testament. There is no atonement death.

Isaiah 53 and Righteous Sufferers

In the rabbinical literature Isaiah 53 has also been interpreted as referring to the sufferings of the (righteous) Israelites. The only interpretation of Isaiah 53 in Talmud Jerushalmi is y.Shek 5:1 where the verse Isa 53:12 is applied to Rabbi Akiba who died as martyr:

It is written: *'Therefore I will divide him a portion with the great, and he shall divide the spoil with the strong; because he poured out his soul to death, and was numbered with the transgressors; yet he bore the sin of many, and made intercession for the transgressors.* This refers to Rabbi Akiba who organized the learning, halakha-laws and haggada-stories (שהתקין מדרש הלכות והגדות).

This application of Isaiah 53 is in line with the early Jewish traditions where the passage was used to refer to the sufferings and death of the martyr (see sect. 3). It is interesting that Isa 53:12 was applied to Akiba because the verse refers to the resurrection and new life of the servant. Apparently the transmitters of this tradition argued that Akiba will live among the coming generations through his Torah studies and his compilations of rabbinical traditions. Akiba and his school are regarded as teachers and compilers of the Mishnah.[29]

Moreover, the Talmud Jerushalmi includes another early rabbinical text where Isaiah 53 is interpreted. Genesis Rabbah belongs to the early midrashim which probably date from the 5th century AD.[30] GenR 20:10 deals with the recovery of a sick person. The text lists various signs of recovery, every sign being justified by one biblical proof text: sneezing (Job 41:10), sweating (Gen 3:19); sleeping (Job 3:13), dreaming (Jes 38:16) and ejaculation (Jes 53:10: "He shall see seed and prolong his days").[31] The fact that Isa 53:10 was used as a proof text for the recovery of a sick person is strong evidence that in the Jewish

---

[29]G. Stemberger, *Introduction to the Talmud and Midrash* (Minneapolis: Fortress 1991) 138-141.

[30]According to Stemberger (*Introduction* 276-283) Genesis Rabbah used a version of the Talmud Jerushalmi which was not identical with the known text. All rabbis and historical events mentioned in GenR require a date no later than the 5th century. Therefore GenR may be from about the same time as Talmud Jerushalmi.

[31]This tradition is also preserved in *Pesikta de-Rab Kahana* 19.5. See W.G. Braude & I.J. Kapstein, *Pesikta de-Rab Kahana: R. Kahana's Compilation of Discourses for Sabbaths and Festal Days* (Philadelphia: Jewish Publication Society of America 1975) 328.

interpretive tradition, Isaiah 53 was regarded as containing an accurate description of a sufferer.

The discussion in b.Ber 5a is based on the Rabbinical idea that sufferings can expiate sins. The text is related to the interpretation voiced in Prov 3:12: "For whom the Lord loves He corrects":

> Raba, in the name of Rabbi Sahorah, in the name of R. Huna says: If the Holy One, blessed be He, is pleased with a man, he crushes him with painful suffering. For it is said, *And the Lord was pleased with [him, hence] he crushed him with disease.* Now, you might think that this is so even if he did not accept them [sufferings] with love. Therefore it is said[32]: *To see if his soul would offer itself in restitution.*[33] Even as the trespass-offering must be brought by consent [of the sacrificer], so also the suffering must be endured with consent.[34] And if he did accept them, what is his reward? *He will see his seed, prolong his days.* And more than that, his knowledge [of the Torah] will endure with him. For it is said: *The purpose of the Lord will prosper in his hand.*

The passage exhorts a person who is in distress to examine himself and see whether his situation is caused by his sins. If not, then he must ask if he has neglected the study of the Torah. The passage indicates that God can through sufferings lead the believer to study the Torah. However, if the person does not see himself as guilty of the neglect of Torah studies he can be sure that his sufferings are caused by the love of God as it is formulated in Prov 3:12. This passage of the Talmud indicates that the old Jewish interpretive tradition according to which Isaiah 53 refers to the sufferings of the righteous person was transmitted in rabbinical circles. The crux is that the sufferer should accept his fate because it is

---

[32]The expression "scriptures states (תלמוד לומר)" is used to reject an opinion with the aid of a text or several texts from the Hebrew Bible as in this passage of the Talmud.

[33]The Hebrew text is difficult but the context reveals that Isa 53:10 has been interpreted in this way in the passage of the Talmud.

[34]The Hebrew expression מה אשם לדעת אף יסורין לדעת contains a comparison (*heqqeš*) מה and אף, "as" and "so also". In the Rabbinical Hebrew the expression לדעת means also "acceptance" i.e. that which one knows and accepts.

promised in Isa 53:10 that he will benefit thereby. There is no reference to vicarious and atoning suffering as in the Jewish martyr theology. The reward is given to the sufferer after his testing comes to an end, and in this respect b.Ber 5a comes closer to the interpretation of Isaiah 53 in Wisdom 2-5.

Conclusions

This survey of the early texts in the rabbinical literature indicates that Isaiah 53 has been regarded as referring to those who suffer. Among these sufferers even Moses and the Messiah can be found. However, there is no example in the rabbinical writings that Isaiah 53 was interpreted in the same way as in the New Testament, viz. as referring to the Messiah who must die to expiate the sins of the people. This proves that we must distinguish between the messianic (Jewish), and the messianic (Christian) interpretation of Isaiah 53. The messianic interpretation of Isaiah 53 in the New Testament differs markedly from the messianic interpretation in the rabbinical tradition. This was already apparent when we studied Targum Jonathan in sect. 6. We can conclude this section by referring to the view of Nahmanides in his *Vikuach* (referred above) that the messianic interpretation of Isaiah 53 in Jewish haggadot does not imply a concept of Messiah who would suffer and die vicariously and atone for the sins of the people.

10 Pesiqta Rabbati and the Sufferings of the Messiah

The Messiah as A Suffering Figure

There is only one short reference to Isaiah 53 in Pesiqta Rabbati but the concept of the suffering Messiah is crucial in several of its homilies. What makes the homilies in Pesiqta Rabbati highly interesting is the fact that a similar concept of the suffering Messiah was articulated in the Jewish-Christian disputation at Barcelona 1263 when the interpretation of Isaiah 53 was discussed.

Pesiqta Rabbati is a collection of sermons which were composed for special feast days and Sabbaths.[1] The manuscript evidence shows that "the Pesiqta Rabbati homilies are not clearly defined writings which possess a singular redactional identity."[2] This is also reason why Ulmer produced a synoptic edition where manuscripts are presented in parallel columns. Because the redactional identities of Pesiqta Rabbati are manifold "the search for one *Urtext* is futile."[3] Therefore, it is essential to recognize which form of Pesiqta Rabbati we read when we refer to its text. There are four main textual witnesses which differ substantially from each other: 1) the Parma manuscript, 2) the Casanata and Dropsie manuscripts, 3) the Cambridge and Budapest fragments and 4) the *editio*

---

[1] The Hebrew text is now available in Rivka Ulmer (ed), *A Synoptic Edition of Pesiqta Rabbati Based upon All Extant Manuscripts and the Editio Principes. Volumes 1-3* (South Florida Studies in the History of Judaism 155, 200; Atlanta: Scholars Press 1997, 1999; and Studies in Judaism; Lanham: University Press of America 2002).

[2] Ulmer, *A Synoptic Edition* 1:xxvii.

[3] Ulmer, *A Synoptic Edition* 1:xliii. It is worth noting that the so-called Frankfurt project under the leadership of Arnold Goldberg has a different agenda from the synoptic edition. In this project, many doctoral dissertations were produced in which different editing systems were followed.

princeps (printed in Prague in 1653 or 1656) together with the Jewish Theological Seminary Manuscript 8195.[4]

By reason of the redactional varieties it is difficult to date the different forms of this collection. The *editio princeps* contains an interesting date in the first chapter (Piska 1): "Behold how long a time since the House of our life was destroyed! It is already a week of years, already a cycle of seven weeks of years, already seven hundred and seventy-seven years. (And at this writing it is one thousand one hundred and fifty-one years)."[5] There is a comment that the 777 years from the destruction of the Temple have already passed, and now when the text is written, 1151 years have elapsed. These chronological details give us reason to suppose that the year 847 AD was significant for the compilation of this sermon collection and that another editor revised it in 1221 AD when the *editio princeps* was issued.[6] However, scholars do not regard these chronological details as final because the earliest manuscripts (Parma from 1270; Casanata from 1387 or later; Dropsie from 1531) do not contain these chronologies.[7] This being the case the question of the date of Pesiqta Rabbati or its parts is open for different proposals.[8] We can surely conclude that the date 1221 AD cannot

---

[4]Ulmer, *A Synoptic Edition* 1:xxviii-xliv; G. Stemberger, *Introduction to the Talmud and Midrash* (Second Printing, Minneapolis: Fortress Press 1996) 296-302.

[5]See the text in Ulmer, *A Synoptic Edition* 1:2 and the English translation in W. Braude (ed), *Pesikta Rabbati. Discourses for Feasts, Fasts and Special Sabbaths. Translated from the Hebrew. Two Volumes* (Yale Judaica Series 18:1-2, New Haven 1968) 39.

[6]It has also been discussed whether reference is made to the destruction of the First or the Second Temple. It seems to me that the only relevant possibility would be the destruction of the Second Temple. See the discussion of date in Braude, *Pesikta Rabbati* 20-26; Stemberger, *Talmud and Midrash* 299-302.

[7]See *Pesiqta Rabbati* Piska 1, §4 as well as Ulmer's comments in that work pp. xv-xxvii.

[8]See, e.g., discussion in W. Braude (ed), *Pesikta Rabbati.* 20-26, 39; Ulmer, *A Synoptic Edition* 1:xv-xxviii; M. Pickup, 'The Emergence of the Suffering Messiah in Rabbinic Literature'.

correspond to the date of origin of Pesiqta Rabbati because already Rashi (1040-1105) knew this collection of sermons.[9] Therefore every sermon in Pesiqta Rabbati must be dated on its own merits.[10] This is well illustrated in the Frankfurt project when several studies on Pesiqta Rabbati were written.[11]

Pesiqta Rabbati contains four important homilies which describe the sufferings of the Messiah (Piskot 31, 34, 36 and 37).[12] However, there is only one short reference to Isaiah 53 in these four homilies: Piska 34 § 4.[13] The *editio princeps* here has כצאן תעינו which is an identical reading with Isa 53:6. The Parma manuscript contains a longer quotation and there reference is made *expressis verbis* to the Book of Isaiah:

> Then the righteous men of generation will stand up and remove their tefillin, lay them upon the ground and say to Him: "Master of the universe, we have not acted rightly all these years – *like sheep we have gone astray each of us has turned to our own way* (כצאן תעינו איש לדרכו פנינו)."

---

[9]See Braude, *Pesikta Rabbati* 20-21; Ulmer, *A Synoptic Edition* 1:xvii-xviii.

[10]An illustrative example is the dating of Piska 8. See the discussion in J. Schwartz, "Gallus, Julian and Anti-Christian Polemic in Pesikta Rabbati," *TZ* 46 (1990) 1-19.

[11]See K.E. Grözinger, *Ich bin der Herr, dein Gott! Eine rabbinische Homilie zum Ersten Gebot (PesR 20)* (FJS 2, Bern: Herbert Lang 1976); A. Goldberg, *Ich komme und wohne in deiner Mitte: Eine rabbinische Homilie zu Sacharja 2,14 (PesR 35)* (FJS 3; Frankfurt a.M.: Selbstverlag der Gesellschaft zur Förderung Judaistischer Studien 1977); idem, *Erlösung durch Leiden: Drei rabbinische Homilien über die Trauernden Zions und den leidenden Messias Efraim (PesR 34, 36, 37)* (FJS 4; Frankfurt a.M.: Selbstverlag der Gesellschaft zur Förderung Judaistischer Studien 1978); H. Hahn, *Wallfahrt und Auferstehung zur messianischen Zeit: Eine rabbinische Homilie zum Neumond-Shabbat (PesR 1)* (FJS 5; Frankfurt a.M.: Selbstverlag der Gesellschaft zur Förderung Judaistischer Studien 1979); B.A.A. Kern, *Tröstet, tröstet mein Volk! Zwei rabbinische Homilien zu Jesaja 40,1 (PesR 30 und PesR 29/30)* (FJS 7; Frankfurt a.M.: Selbstverlag der Gesellschaft zur Förderung Judaistischer Studien 1986).

[12]Braude's translation divides the parts of Piskot differently from Ulmer. I cite Pesiqta Rabbati according to the Hebrew text in Ulmer's synopsis, i.e. references are made to Piska X, § Y.

[13]Goldberg (see, e.g., *Erlösung durch Leiden* 278-279) discusses the possibility that Isaiah 53 may loom behind some formulations, but these allusions are uncertain.

According to Piska 34, in the eschatological time to come the righteous Jews will confess that they "have not acted rightly" in mocking the mourners for Zion. This group of "mourners for Zion" is derived from Isa 61:3 – and the term refers to the group of Jews who put their trust in the prophetic promises and expected that the coming glory of Zion and the appearance of the Messiah will occur in the immediate future.[14] This group lived in conflict with surrounding Jewish religious circles. Many mocked them, even those who took the Torah and its stipulations seriously.[15] In Piska 34 the righteous will recognize their error and then identify themselves with the group of "we" in Isaiah 53 who confess their guilt. Therefore the suffering Servant in Piska 34 cannot be identified primarily with the Messiah but rather with the mourners for Zion. However, Goldberg writes that even the Messiah can be included here:[16]

> Ob die Gerechten die Trauernden Zions oder den leidenden Messias nicht erkannten, von dem ja in Jes 53 die Rede ist, das kann man dem Text nicht entnehmen. Wahrscheinlich sind beide gemeint, denn für die Predigt gehören die Trauernden und der leidende Messias zusammen, sind doch die Trauernden die, die dem Leidenden gleichen.

In Piska 34 § 8 – which according to Goldberg is textually difficult – the mourners of Zion wait for the Messiah who has taken sufferings on

---

[14]In scholarly discussion "the mourners for Zion" has been tentatively identified with different groups, Karaim, among others. However, Goldberg (*Erlösung durch Leiden* 131-144) has rightly noted that the theme is old and is connected with mourning for the destruction of the Temple (see, e.g., t.Sot 15:11-13; t.BB 2:17).

[15]That those who follow the stipulations of the Torah have also mocked the Messiah becomes clear from Piska 34 § 7 where God promises to them reward for their obedience to Torah notwithstanding that they have failed to respect the mourners of Zion.

[16]Goldberg, *Erlösung durch Leiden* 84

himself before he appears to the world.[17] Thus the mourners follow in the footsteps of the Messiah. They must all suffer until the beginning of the messianic era. Piska 34 § 7 promises that the messianic era will benefit many Jews because of "the merits of the Messiah (בזכות משיח)" – the Messiah who is ready to suffer as Piska 34 § 9 states, interpreting Zech 9:9:

> *Afflicted, and he is riding upon an ass* describes the Messiah. And why is he called *afflicted*? Because he was afflicted during all his years in the house of chastisements (בבית האיסורין) while transgressors in Israel laughed at him.

This detail in Piska 34 raises the question of whether the reference is to a real historical messianic candidate who was held in prison. The problem is the expression בית האיסורין "the house of chastisements" which does not need to mean "prison" here, but rather can be taken metaphorically.[18] As we shall see, other details in Piskot 31, 34, 36-37 indicate that the Messiah is suffering in his pre-existence, that this "prison" can be understood metaphorically as referring to a heavenly house. In order to obtain a better picture of the sufferings of the Messiah we must first consult other Piskot.

In Piska 36 § 4 there is a heavenly vision where the Messiah confers with the Holy One and expresses his willingness to accept sufferings for the salvation of Israel and the resurrection of the dead. Messiah says to the Holy One:[19]

---

[17]Goldberg, *Erlösung durch Leiden* 110: "Die Verwendung des Perfekts sollte kaum einen Zweifel daran lassen, dass all dies schon geschehen ist, so wie ja auch die Bedrängnis der Trauernden gegenwärtig zu sein scheint. Aber die Verwendung der Tempora ist in der PesR so eigen, dass sichere Schlüsse daraus nicht möglich sind."

[18]See the discussion in Goldberg, *Erlösung durch Leiden* 109-117.

[19]The Parma manuscript and the *editio princeps* contain almost similar text, but only the Parma manuscript mentions the generation of Adam. Cf., Braude's translation on his p. 679; and Goldberger's (*Erlösung durch Leiden*) on p. 150.

> Master of universe, with joy in my soul and gladness in my heart I take this suffering upon myself, provided that not one person in Israel will perish; that not only those who are alive will be saved in my days, but that also those who are dead, who died from the days of Adam up to the time of redemption; and that not only these will be saved in my days, but also those who died as abortions; and that not only these will be saved in my days, but also those whom You thought to create but were not created. Such are the things I desire, and for these I am ready to take upon myself [whatever You decree].

The theological concept of the sufferings of the Messiah before his appearance in the world is based on the rabbinical view that the Messiah was part of the divine plan before the creation (bPes 54a; see also bNed 39a; GenR 1:4): "Seven things were created before the world was created: Torah, repentance, the Garden of Eden, Gehinnom, the Throne of Glory, the Temple and the Name of the Messiah." This idea is developed in the homilies of Pesiqta Rabbati. For example, Piska 33 § 31 states *expressis verbis* that the Messiah was born before creation:[20]

> You find that at the very beginning of the creation of the world, the king Messiah had already come into being (נולד מלך המשיח), for he existed in God's thought even before the world was created[21].

The proof text for the view that the Messiah existed already before the creation is Gen 1:2 which speaks of the Spirit of God hovering on the level of the sea. This spirit is connected with the spirit of the Messiah in Isa 11:2 (Piska 33 § 33). This tradition is parallel to the utterance of R. Shimon ben Laqish in GenR 2:4: "*The Spirit of God hovered*: this alludes to the Messiah, as you read, *And the spirit of the Lord shall rest upon him* (Isa 11:2).*"*Another important proof text is Gen 1:4, according to which God formed the light at the beginning of the creation. Piska 36 § 2 states that God "contemplated the Messiah and his works before the world was created and put the Messiah and his generation (למשיח ולדורו) under his

---

[20]Both the Parma manuscript and the *editio princeps* have substantially the same text.

[21]שעלה במהשבה עד שלא נברא העולם.

throne."[22] Goldberg writes that the text is corrupt here because both the Parma manuscript and the *editio princeps* lack the object.[23] However, the preposition *le* can be used in the biblical and Rabbinic Hebrew as expressing the object.[24] This being the case the text simply states that both the Messiah and his generation are put under the throne of God.

The idea of the Messiah who is hidden has an interesting parallel to the Son of Man who is also pre-existent and hidden. The idea is most clearly formulated in the First Book of Enoch. 1 Enoch 46:1-3; 48:4-6 and 62:7-9 speak of the Son of Man who is "hidden before" the Lord. 1 Enoch 62:7 says that "the Most High has preserved him in the presence of his might and revealed him to the elect." There is a similar observation in Pesiqta Rabbati where the Messiah has been born and hidden but revealed to the mourners of Zion. There is no need to suppose that 1 Enoch underlies this rabbinical tradition. A similar concept can be discerned in Daniel 7. Indeed, the Son of Man in Daniel 7 has been identified with the Messiah in bSanh 98a where Rabbi Alexander gives two alternatives: "If they will be righteous [the Messiah will come] *on the clouds of heaven* (Dan 7:13); if they will not be righteous, [he will come] as *a poor man riding upon an ass* (Zech 9:9)." The Son of Man is a pre-existent figure in Daniel 7, and verses 9-10 refer to the heavenly thrones. This being the case, Daniel 7 contains three important elements which appear in Pesiqta Rabbati Piska 34: 1) the idea of the pre-existence of the Messiah; 2) the reference to the divine throne(s); 3) the future vision which will be realized in the world when the messianic kingdom comes to pass.

---

[22]The *Editio princeps* adds the word "glory" for the throne: "under the throne of his glory."

[23]Goldberg, *Erlösung durch Leiden* 148 n. 3: "... in beiden Texten fehlt das Objekt." Goldberg translates (p. 148): "... und er verbarg (das Licht) für den Messias [und] seine Generation unter seinem Thron <der Herrlichkeit>."

[24]See M.P. Fernández, *An Introductory Grammar of Rabbinic Hebrew* (Leiden: Brill 1997) 163.

It is worth noting that the Book of Daniel also speaks of the seven-year period which plays an important role in the description of the sufferings of the Messiah. After the Messiah has asked how long his suffering will last he receives the following answer (Piska 36 § 4):[25]

> Upon your life and the life of My head, it is a period of seven years which I have decreed for you. But if your soul is sad at the prospect of your suffering, I shall at this moment banish these sinful souls.

The Messiah may avoid suffering but he is willing to suffer in order to save many. A possible reference to Daniel 7 may also be found in Piska 36 § 8 which mentions the wars between Persia, Arabia and Edom – which neatly reflects the content of the Book of Daniel which describes major struggles before the advent of the kingdom of God.[26]

The sufferings of the Messiah in his pre-existent life are intensified during the final seven-year period before his appearance in the world. Later in the same Piska 36 § 6 we read:

> During the seven-year period when the son of David will appear[27] iron beams will be brought and loaded upon his neck until the Messiah's stature (קומתו)[28] is bent low. Then he will cry and weep, and his voice will rise up to the very

---

[25]The Parma manuscript and the *editio princeps* have almost the same Hebrew text.

[26]It is worth noting that B.J. Bamberger ("A Messianic Document of the Seventh Century," *HUCA* 15 [1940] 425-431) argues that the struggles between these three powers Persia, Arabia and Edom (Byzantium) indicate that the Midrash was "composed during the period of about five years when Persia and Arabia were both world powers" (p. 428), i.e., during the period 632-637 AD.

[27]The Hebrew ... שבוע שבן דוד בא מביאין uses participle forms here and apparently indicates the durative aspect of the Messiah's suffering during the seven-year period.

[28]Braude translates here with "body" but the context indicates that the Messiah has not yet appeared in the world because later in Piska 36 § 7 the congregation says: "A day is appointed for me when my king will reveal himself for my sake." The basic meaning of קוֹמָה is "height, stature, man's height". It is clear that the Messiah has been seen in the vision in a bodily form. I have translated here "stature."

height of heaven and he will say to God: Master of the universe, how much can
my strength endure?

The text goes on to say how the Messiah will suffer like God. His pain
is like the pain of God who has suffered since the destruction of his
Temple. The Piska refers to Ps 22:16 and the sufferings of the Messiah.
All these sufferings will still take place before the appearance of the
Messiah in the world. When he finally enters the world he will be a
strong and powerful king as stated in Piska 36 § 9:

> When the king Messiah appears, he will come stand on the roof of the Temple
> and will make a proclamation to Israel, saying: Meek ones, the day of your
> redemption is come.

There has been discussion of whether Pesiqta Rabbati borrowed the
concept of the suffering Messiah from Christianity. If several elements
were borrowed, then the whole theological concept is markedly different.
In Christianity the pre-existent Son of God became a real man, then
suffered and died for the sins of the world, while in Pesiqta Rabbati the
Messiah is suffering in his pre-existent "life" and waiting until God will
allow him to enter into the world to help his people to victory. This
fundamental difference between the Christian and Jewish concept of the
Messiah became evident in the Barcelona disputation 1263.

Nahmanides reports that Pablo Christiani quoted an Aggadah
which says that the Messiah will accept sufferings on behalf of Israel.
The text where the Messiah is speaking and which is quoted by
Nahmanides runs as follows:[29]

> I accept the sufferings (יסורין) on condition that the resurrection of the dead
> shall take place in my days; and not only for those who die in my era, but also
> for all those who have died from Adam onwards. And not only for those who

---

[29]The Hebrew text can be found in M. Chavel, *Kitvei Moses ben Nahman* (Jerusalem:
Mossad Harav Kook 1973) Vol 1:303-319, esp. 312. The English translation is from H.
Maccoby, *Judaism on Trial. Jewish-Christian Disputations in the Middle Ages*
(London: The Littman Library of Jewish Civilization 1993) 123.

died natural deaths, but also for those who were thrown into the sea and drowned, or who were eaten by wolves and other wild animals.

Such an Aggadah has not been preserved in any rabbinical writing. M. Cohen thinks that Pablo Christiani's Aggadah as recorded in Nahmanides' rapport may be a compilation of "several Midrashim, such as those based on Isa. 52:2 (see *Yalqut Shime'oni* II, 475), the idea of the Holy Spirit bringing resurrection ('Avodah Zarah, 20b) and the concept of the Messiah's revelation at the time of resurrection recorded in the Zohar I, 110b."[30] However, if Pablo had compiled his own midrash it is unlikely that Nahmanides would have quoted it without commenting that such a midrash *de facto* did not exist. After all Nahmanides introduces this passage in his *Vikuach* as follows: "He then cited further an Aggadah which says about the Messiah that he prays for Israel that God may pardon them for their sins and accepted on himself sufferings, but said before God." Therefore, Nahmanides would have stated in his own report whether such an Aggadah could not be found in rabbinical writings because he once writes that Pablo could not find a text which he sought in a book: "They brought the book which he had asked for, and he searched it but could not find what he had said was there." This being the case, it is reasonable to assume that Nahmanides refers to a Jewish midrash which is now lost but which has parallels in other rabbinical writings e.g., in Pesiqta Rabbati Piska 36 § 4 which we have quoted above.

The content of Piska 36 § 4 in Pesiqta Rabbati and Nahmanides' midrash are parallel to each other but there is only one striking linguistic similarity:

---

[30]M.A. Cohen, "Reflections on the Text and Context of the Disputation of Barcelona," *HUCA* 35 (1964) 157-192, esp. p. 178 n. 85.

אלא על כל המתים שמתו מאדם הראשון ועד הנה (Nahmanides' midrash)
אלא אף מתים שמתו מאדם הראשון עד עכשיו (the text in the manuscript
of Parma)

This linguistic parallel shows that these two texts are in some way
connected traditio-historically. It is also worthy of note that Hulsius in
his *Theologia Judaica*[31] quotes a Pesiqta source which contains another
parallel to the midrashim in Nahmanides' *Vikuach* and Pesiqta Rabbati
Piska 36 § 4:[32]

> The Holy One brought forth the soul of the Messiah, and said to him: 'Are you
> willing to be created and to redeem my sons after 6000 years?' He replied, 'I
> am.' God replied, 'If so, you must take upon yourself chastisements (ייסורין)
> in order to wipe away their iniquity, as it is written, *Surely our sickness he has
> carried*.' The Messiah answered, 'I will take them upon me gladly (בשמחה).'

This text presupposes the dialogue between God and the Messiah during
the time of creation.[33] Reference is made to the eschatological time after
6000 years, indicating that the conservation must have taken place during
creation. The Messiah accepts to suffer in his pre-existent life. So even
in this parallel Isaiah 53 is connected with the idea of the sufferings of
the Messiah in his pre-existence.

Two additional parallels to these midrashim have been presented:
Yalqut Shimoni § 499 and the midrash of Moses ha-Darshan quoted in

---

[31]See W. Horbury (edited and revised), Samuel Krauss, *The Jewish-Christian
Controversy from the Earliest Times to 1789. Volume I: History* (Tübingen: Mohr
1995) 205.

[32]See the text in S.R. Driver & A. Neubauer, *The Suffering Servant of Isaiah
According to the Jewish Interpreters I Texts* (Varda Books 2005) 9 and *II Translations*
(Varda Books 2005) 11.

[33]We have argued that this presupposition of the existence of the Messiah is derived
from the early belief that the name of the Messiah was established from the beginning
before the creation.

Pugio Fidei which Raymundus Martini (with his research team) compiled in 1278 AD.[34]

In *Pugio Fidei* 416 the passage renders the text from the Commentary on Genesis by Moshe ha-Darshan as follows. The Messiah will say to the Holy One who asks whether he is willing to submit a heavy yoke:[35]

> Said the Messiah, Lord of the world: "I accept it joyfully, and will endure these chastisements, upon condition that you will give life again to those who die in my days, and to those who died from the time of the first man until now; and that you will save in my days not these only, but those also whom wolves and lions have devoured, and who have been swallowed up in waters and rivers; and not only these, but such also as were born out of due time; nor again these only, but those also whom you thought to create but who were not created." The Holy One replied: "I will do so." And forthwith the Messiah accepted the chastisements of love, as it is written: "He was oppressed, and he was afflicted."

Raymundus Martini presents five texts from Moshe ha-Darshan's Commentary on Genesis which speak of the Messiah and where reference is made to Isaiah 53.[36] These texts enable us to evaluate how

---

[34]Goldberg, *Erlösung durch Leiden* 260-263; H.-G. Mutius, *Die Christlich-Jüdische Zwangsdisputation zu Barcelona* (Judentum und Umwelt 5, Frankfurt: Lang 1978) 177-182.

[35]*Pugio Fidei* II.11 § 16 (folio 333, pages 416-417 in Carpzov's edition from 1667). An English translations of Moshe ha-Darshan's texts in *Pugio Fidei* can be found in Driver & Neubauer, *The Suffering Servant of Isaiah* 33-35.

[36] I. M. Ta-Shma ("Moses ha-Darshan," *EJ* 14:556-557) notes: "For many years the *Genesis Rabbah* by Moses ha-Darshan, frequently quoted by Raymond Martini in his polemic work *Pugio Fidei*, constituted a unique problem. No book of that name was known to scholars in previous centuries. Isaac Abrabanel, for one, stated in his *Yeshu'ot Meshiho* that he did not know of such a book and suspected it to be a forgery. Only recently has it become evident that the early authorities did indeed know a midrashic anthology by Moses ha-Darshan, or at least one emanating from his school, and that this extensive anthology was the basis of the Midrash called Genesis Rabbati, which was apparently adapted and abridged from the work of Moses."

Moshe ha-Darshan interpreted the Messiah's sufferings. It is clear from the quoted passage that a similar idea appears in Pesiqta Rabbati and other Jewish sources cited above and, therefore, we have no *prima facie* reason to think that Raymundus Martini's text is a forgery.[37] The immediate context of the quoted passage indicates that the reference is to the pre-existence of the Messiah. He and his generation were hidden

---

[37]Scholars have discussed in which respect Raymundus Martini's quotations can be regarded as reliable. When we compare the quotations of Moshe ha-Darshan given in *Pugio Fidei* (= PF, references to page numbers according to Carpzov's edition) with the edition of C. Albeck (*Midrash Bereshit Rabbati* [Jerusalem Mekize Nirdamim 1940]) the following remarks can be made. PF 346 and Moshe 244 have the same text (both refer to Isa 11:3). Both PF 349 and Moshe 130-31 contain utterances in the name of Shamuel ben Nahman where the birth of the Messiah and the destruction of the Temple are chronologically connected; both even refer to Isa 66:7. PF 350-51 and Moshe 131 contain practically the same text, as is the case also in PF 377 and Moshe 71. PF 379 and Moshe 88 refer to Psalm 105 and comment on it in the same way. PF 385-86 and Moshe 136-37 are almost identical even though there are some parts which are not parallel with each other. PF 407 and Moshe 81 have an identical phrase even though the passages are not otherwise parallel. Both PF 416-17 and Moshe 4 refer to Ps 36:10 and interpret it so that the light is the Messiah. Otherwise texts do not parallel well with each other. PF 419 is not presented in Moshe 22, but it is noted *expressis verbis* in PF 416 that this is a "Glossa" in Moshe ha-Darshan's text. PF 468 is not attested in Moshe 145. PF 535-36 and Moshe 97 contain a reference to Isa 53:5 even though the text is only partly identical. The text given in PF 862 parallels to that in PF 535 and even there a reference to Isa 53:5 can be found. PF 538 and Moshe 185 are partly parallel with each other; both refer to Mic 2:13. The text in PF 880 is parallel to that in PF 538. PF 562 (indicating that the text is "Glossa") and Moshe 37 do not have identical texts but both refer to Ps 90:4. PF 563-64 and Moshe 24 partly overlap. PF 643-644 and Moshe 236 do not parallel but Moshe's text is remarkably short in Gen 49:8 and the question is whether the text has been shortened here. PF 714-15 and Moshe 93 have substantially the same text as is the case in PF 728-29 and Moshe 92. Both PF 767 and Moshe 239 contain messianic interpretation of Gen 49:10. PF 759 and 769 have no clear parallels in Moshe's text. PF 771-72 and Moshe 102-03 have substantially the same text. Major sections of PF 842 and Moshe 239 parallel with each other as is the case with PF 850 and Moshe 239. PF 937-38 and Moshe 29-30 contain a long parallel text. At the end of the PF quotation there is no parallel in Moshe's text. PF 956-957 contains a text which has no clear parallel in Moshe 175. See further Albeck's introduction pp. 5-6 and S. Lieberman, "Raymund Martini and His Alleged Forgeries," *Historia Judaica* 5 (1943) 87-102, esp. 87-92. This evidence gives us reason to believe that Raymundus Martini aimed to mention rabbinical texts available to him.

294

underneath the throne of God. Then there is a dialogue between Satan and the Lord and finally between the Messiah and God which concludes with the Messiah's consent to take the yoke of sufferings on himself in order to save many. All this indicates that the Messiah accepts the heavy yoke of sufferings in his pre-existent life. Therefore, Martini's quotation too makes it clear that the Messiah will not suffer when he appears but is doing so in his pre-existent life, although Martini tries to use this quotation to argue that the rabbinical writings present a Christian-like soteriology.

Martini's reasoning emerges when he interprets Moshe Ha-Darshan's quotation on Gen 24:67.[38] The Hebrew text quoted in *Pugio Fidei* clearly uses perfect tenses:

זה מלך המשיח שהיה בדורון של רשעים

But Martini translates this in the future tense: "*Hic est Rex Messias qvi erit in generatione impiorum.*" Thus he interprets the whole passage as referring to the coming eschatological time when the Messiah will appear and suffer. On the other hand, Moshe Ha-Darshan refers to the time when the Messiah was willing to accept the yoke of sufferings (in his pre-existent life).

In Piska 37 the Messiah is speaking with three patriarchs. The patriarchs say (Piska 37 § 2): "Ephraim, our true Messiah, even though we are your forebears, you are greater than we because you did suffer for the iniquities of our children ... for the sake of Israel you did become a laughingstock and a derision among the nations of the earth ..."[39] The Messiah answers: "O Patriarchs, all that I have done, I have done only for your sake and for the sake of your children, for your glory and for the glory of your children, that they benefit from that goodness which the

---

[38]*Pugio Fidei* III.16 § 29 (folio 671, p. 862 in Carpzov's edition).

[39]Concerning the idea that the Messiah is greater than the patriarchs see Goldberg, *Erlösung durch Leiden* 278-288.

Holy One, blessed be He, will bestow in abundance upon them – upon Israel." The reference is to the past event and can easily be reconciled with the view that the Messiah suffered in his pre-existent life.

In Piska 37 § 4 the passage of Jer 31:20 is interpreted. The central question is why there are two references to "mercy". The answer given is that the first mercy refers to "the time when he was shut (שהיה חבוש) up in the house of chastisements (בבית האיסורין)."[40] During this period the nations of the earth can mock and deride the Messiah. The second mercy refers to the time when the Messiah "comes forth (שהיה יוצא) out of the house of chastisements." Even this is expressed in the perfect which Goldberg has translated in the past tense.[41] In his interpretation Goldberg observes that the content of the Piska is unclear but he gives the following proposal:[42]

> Versucht man die Abfolge zu rekonstruieren, mit allem Vorbehalt des Irrtums, dann ergibt sich hier etwa folgender Ablauf: Da der Messias sich (zunächst wohl nur Israel?) offenbart, wird er nicht erkannt und gefangengesetzt. Nach einer Leidenzeit gelangt es wieder zur Freiheit, und nun beginnt der Kampf der Völker gegen ihn, ein Kampf, den, wie es scheint, nicht der Messias zur Befreiung Israels beginnt. Dies ist gewiss der "Krieg Gogs und Magogs".

I suggest another interpretation. The Messiah is suffering in his pre-existence and imprisoned in the house of chastisements while the people and the ungodly from Israel are mocking and deriding all Jews waiting

---

[40]Braude translates this in the future tense but the perfect tense makes the translation difficult here. For example, Goldberg (*Erlösung durch Leiden* 269) translates "da er im Gefängnis <gebunden> war."

[41]Note, however, what Goldberg (*Erlösung durch Leiden* 110) writes concerning the use of the perfect in Pesiqta Rabbati: "Aber die Verwendung der Tempora ist in der PesR so eigen, dass sichere Schlüsse daraus nicht möglich sind."

[42]Goldberg, *Erlösung durch Leiden* 293.

for him.[43] This mockery is interpreted figuratively so that the Messiah himself is derided. A similar idea prevailed in Christianity according to which Jesus Christ himself attended his oppressed servants and supported them. The second mercy mentioned in Piska 37 § 4 implies that a decisive change in the divine world has taken place and the Messiah will soon appear to help his people.

Abraham Ibn Ezra provides support for our conclusion that the sufferings of the Messiah pertain to his pre-existence before he appears as a victorious king. Ibn Ezra notes briefly such a belief among Jews by writing: "Many believe that Messiah is meant by this expression, because our ancient teachers said that Messiah was born on the day on which the temple was destroyed, that he was, as it were, bound in chains (והוא אסור בזיקי)."[44] This note should be taken so that the Messiah was regarded as living and suffering on the behalf of the people in his pre-existent life (before his appearance in the world).

In Pesiqta Rabbati the Messiah is called Ephraim but the name does not confirm that the messiah will be Messiah ben Joseph (or ben Ephraim) who, according to the rabbinical interpretation, would die and to whom Zech 12:10 has been applied (b.Sukkah 52a). Ephraim as the name of the Messiah appears in three Piskot 34, 36 and 37. Piska 34 § 8 contains a quotation from Jer 31:9 which refers to the Messiah riding upon an ass in Zech 9:9-10: "They shall come with weeping, and with supplications will I lead them; I will cause them to walk by rivers of waters, in a straight way wherein they shall not stumble; for I become a father to Israel, and Ephraim is My first-born."

---

[43]Cf., M. Zobel, *Gottes Gesalbter: Der Messias und die messianische Zeit in Talmud und Midrash* (Berlin: Schocken & Jüdischer Buchverlag 1938) 153-157; E. Fascher, *Jesaja 53 in christlicher und jüdischer Sicht* (Aufsätze und Verträge zur Theologie und Religionswissenschaft 4; Berlin: Evangelische Verlagsanstalt 1958) 30-33.

[44]M. Friedländer, *The Commentary of Ibn Ezra on Isaiah* (New York: Philipp Feldheim 1873) 240 (the Hebrew text on p. 90).

The passage from Jeremiah says that Ephraim is the first-born of God. That the name of Messiah is Ephraim accords with the idea that the Messiah was created by God before all other creation. He is – as Proverbs 8:22-31 says of the Wisdom of God – the first-born before all others. Another passage which calls the Messiah "Ephraim" is Piska 36 § 3. In that context Psalm 89:23-24, 26 are used to speak about his relationship to God – something which fits Piska 36 § 6 where the Messiah is called "ben David."[45] It is also worthy of note that in Ps 89:28 David (and his sons) are called the first-born of God which is the title given to Ephraim in Jer 31:9. Piska 37 § 2-5, 8 interprets Isa 61:10 in the light of Jer 31:13 and calls the Messiah "*Ephraim Messiah Zidqēnû* (or *Zidqî*)." Again it is easy to see that in the context of Jer 31:13 reference is made to "Ephraim, my first-born" (Jer 31:9) and "Ephraim, my beloved son" (Jer 31:20). On the other hand, the title *Zidqēnû* pertains to Jer 23:5-6; 33:14-15 where the reference is clearly to the Davidic Messiah. This being the case, there are no grounds to connect the Messiah of Pesiqta Rabbati with Messiah ben Joseph even though he is called Ephraim.

There are two other references to the Servant of Isaiah 40-55. Isa 49:8-13 has been interpreted as the Messiah in Piska 31 § 26-27, and Isa 42:1-4 in Piska 36 § 5.

In Piska 31, where Isa 49:8-13 has been interpreted messianically, the rhetorical question is posed why the lament of Zion in Isa 49:14 is preceded by Isa 49:8-13 which speaks of the dialogue between God and the Messiah and, in particular, the creation of the Messiah as the verb *we'eṣṣarkā* ("I have formed you") indicates. The answer given is that this dialogue took place in the heavenly stage when the Messiah was already created (during the time of creation) and when he expressed his willingness to take chastisements upon himself (Piska 31 §26-27):[46]

---

[45]See Goldberg, *Erlösung durch Leiden* 170.

[46]See the Hebrew text in *Pesiqta Rabbati*, 755-756.

298

God is standing and talking with the king Messiah and says (to him): "*And I will form you* (ואצרך)", as though the Messiah did not yet exist[47]. How then explain the words "*And I will form you*"? Our Masters answered: One could recite endlessly the chastisements the Messiah is afflicted with in every generation in keeping with the sins of the generation, but when the Messiah is no longer afflicted then God will say to him: "I shall make him strong again and he will no longer have to suffer" and this is meaning for the words "*And I will form you and give you for a covenant of the people*".

This neatly summarizes the messianic view in Pesiqta Rabbati. According to this text, the pre-existent Messiah must suffer in every generation for the sins of the people before he comes into the world. When the Messiah appears in the world he will be made strong again and his sufferings will be ended. So even though the sufferings of the Messiah have become an essential part of the Jewish messianology they are not associated with the Messiah's life in the world but rather his pre-existence. Such a view is contrasted to the Christian belief according to which the Son of God became flesh in order to suffer and die for the sins of the people. According to the Christian view, the appearance of the Messiah in this world involves the beginning of sufferings, while according to Pesikta Rabbati, the coming of the Messiah into the world coincides with the end of his sufferings.

Thus we may conclude that Pesiqta Rabbati contains a view that the Messiah and his generation are known by God and hidden under his throne of glory. Before his appearance the Messiah must suffer and this suffering will be intensified during the last seven years. During this time the Messiah must bear all the iniquities of Israel and this suffering is described in Piska 36 §6 and Piska 37 §4 with the words of Psalm 22. Even though this may resemble the Christian tradition there is one essential difference. According to Pesiqta Rabbati, Psalm 22 describes the sufferings of the Messiah in his pre-existence. When the Messiah

---

[47]ועד עכשיו הוא להיבראות.

appears in the world he will destroy the enemies of Israel according to the words in Psalm 89 or Isaiah 11.

The influence from Christian theology is prominent when homilies in Pesiqta Rabbati emphasize that the sufferings of the Messiah have an important soteriological meaning. In Piska 36 God speaks with the Messiah and asks whether he is willing to bear all sufferings. The Messiah accepts and requests that he may thereby save all the children of Israel, even those who died as infants (Piska 36 §4). However, after hearing this Satan became nervous and began to struggle against the Messiah and his generation so that they never will be born into this world. Nevertheless, God guarantees that his plans will be realized. He will support the Messiah and his chosen one as it is written in Isa 42:1-4. According to Piska 36 §5, God says to the enemies of the Messiah and Israel:

> I would as soon cause every one of you to perish, consumed in flame by the firebrands with which you would be girded, but not one breathing creature of the Messiah's generation will I cause to perish.

This being the case, there is no reason to suppose that these influences from Christian theology would involve the acceptance of the Christian view of soteriology inherent in the atonement death of the Messiah. Rather the aim has been to give an alternative to the Christian interpretation. The Messiah will suffer before his coming into the world, but in his appearance he will be a victorious warrior. The messianic proclamation in Pesikta Rabbati apparently sought to answer the question of how Israel will receive comfort and forgiveness after the Temple has been destroyed. Christian messianic belief provided good concepts which in Pesikta Rabbati were modified and directed against the Christian witness about Jesus.[48]

---

[48]There are anti-Christian polemics in the homilies. See Braude, *Pesikta Rabbati* 11-12.

Isaiah 53 and the Zohar

The interpretation of the sufferings of the Messiah in Pesiqta Rabbati has interesting parallels in the Zohar, the pearl of the Jewish mystic literature.[49] I shall conclude this section with a brief survey of the way in which the Zohar understood Isaiah 53 because it supports our conclusion that the sufferings of the Messiah will take place in his pre-existent reality before his appearance in the world.[50]

---

[49] Scholars agree that the Zohar is a pseudepigraphon which was written in the name of Rabbi Simon bar Yohai who lived in Palestine during the second century AD. Zohar appeared in Spain in the 13th century by the Kabbalists who flourished there. Rabbi Moses de Leon published the Zohar and he is generally regarded as responsible for compilation of the traditions preserved in the Zohar and as its final writer sometimes between 1280 and 1286. Between 1275 and 1280 Moses de Leon wrote an earlier version of the Zohar, *Midrash ha-Neelam* (Secret Midrash), where Simeon bar Yohai was not yet the principal character. Apparently Moses de Leon had some earlier sources about Jewish mysticism (in particular *Sefer ha-Bahir*), and he had copied and modified some of these texts and been influenced by them. The texts of Zohar were imitated in Kabbalistic circles and in the turn of the 14th and 15th centuries there appeared two important works, *Tikkunei Zohar* and *Raya Mehemna* (Faithful Shepherd). The latter is incorporated in the three-parts-edition of the Zohar, while *Tikkunei Zohar* has been printed as a separate fourth volume. The fifth part of the Zohar consists of those texts which appeared in Safed in Israel from the 16th century (Safed was then the centre of Kabbalism) and which are not included in the first three volumes. This fifth part is known as *Zohar Hadash* (New Zohar). See G. Scholem, *Major Trends in Jewish Mysticism* (New York: Schocken Books 1941); D.C. Matt, *Zohar: The Book of Enlightenment. Translation and Introduction* (New York: Paulist Press 1983), 3-15; L. Fine, "Kabbalistic Texts," in: B.W. Holtz (ed), *Back to the Sources. Reading the Classic Jewish Texts* (New York: Touchstone 1984) 304-359, esp. 305-314; A. Green, "Introduction," in D.C. Matt, *The Zohar: Pritzker Edition* (Stanford CA.: Stanford University Press 2001) XXXI-LXXXI. In particular M. Idel (*Kabbalah. New Perspectives* [New Haven: Yale University Press 1989]) has emphasized that behind Zohar there are earlier traditions.

[50] There is no critical edition of the Zohar available, and the printed volume (Mantua edition [1558-1560] with variant readings in Cremona edition [1559-1560]) does not represent the best readings in manuscripts. It is even plausible to assume that there never existed any complete Zohar before these editions but the texts were circulated in sections and booklets. I have consulted *Soncino Zohar* (The CD-Rom Judaic Classics Library); *Gershom Scholem's annotated Zohar Volumes 1-6* (Jerusalem Magness Press

In the Zohar Isaiah 53 is an important text which explains why the sufferings of the righteous ones belong to the salvation plan of God.[51] The basic theological view on these sufferings can be read in Zohar III, 217b-218b. It states that when God "wishes to give cure to the world (למיהב אסוותא לעלמא)[52] he punishes one of the righteous among them with disease and misfortune, and through him all are healed[53]". A key text in the Hebrew Bible which is used in support of this is Isa 53:5: "He was wounded because of our transgressions, he was crushed because of our iniquities ... and with his stripes we are healed."[54] Through the sufferings of the righteous ones the secret plan of God can be realized in

---

1992); Matt's Aramaic version available in http://www.sup.org/zohar/ and even M. Berg (ed), *The Zohar 1-23 with The Sulam Commentary by Rav Yehuda Ashlag* (New York : Kabbalah Centre International, 2003). A good translation but not yet completed for the whole Zohar is C.D. Matt, *The Zohar: Pritzker Edition. Volumes 1-5* (Stanford CA.: Stanford University Press 2004-2009). Very useful is also I. Tishby, *The Wisdom of the Zohar. An Anthology of Texts. Volumes 1-3* (Oxford: Oxford University Press 1989).

[51]The theological strength of the Zohar was important for Judaism. The philosophical tradition was confronted with dynamic religiosity, the danger being that religion would become more or less religious theory. It was important to receive a new mystic viewpoint which could be used to preserve the dynamic nature of Judaism. The texts of the Zohar pierce deeply into the questions of life and existence and justify why it is important to keep the Torah and live according to its laws. The Torah is given to Jews in order that they could achieve a mystic relation to Creator and the Savior of Israel. This mystic relationship can be achieved to God even though His true substance, Ein-Sof, "without end", cannot be achieved. But God has revealed himself through ten *sefirot*. These *sefirot* emanated from God and human being can through them achieve contact and understand some aspects of the substance of God. It can be said that this view was also partly a protest against the philosophical theology of Maimonides which was based on the idea of the divine transcendence. See A. Green, "Introduction," in D.C. Matt, *The Zohar: Pritzker Edition* (Stanford CA.: Stanford University Press 2001) XXXI-LXXXI; idem, *A Guide to the Zohar* (Stanford CA.: Stanford University Press 2003).

[52]The Aramean word אֲסוּתָא means "cure" (the plural form אַסְוָותָא). The idea is that the world is sick and God will cure it through sufferings of the righteous.

[53]ובגיניה יהיב אסוותא לכלא

[54]See Tishby, *The Wisdom of the Zohar* 1494-1496, esp. 1495.

the world. A similar interpretation of Isa 53:5 can be found in Zohar III, 231a, where it is said that God "desires atonement for the sins of the world (לכפרא חובין דעלמא)", and therefore strikes the righteous according to Isa 53:5.[55]

According to Zohar I,140a, God tests the righteous as he once tested Abraham. In the interpretation of Gen 22:1 the verb *nissāh* ("test") prompts the idea that it means "raise up a standard (*nēs*)" which is the theme in Isa 62:10. Thus the testing of the righteous will render the greatness of God visible throughout the world. This same passage of the Zohar also discusses how according to Isa 53:10 ("It pleases Yhwh to crush him by disease") God gives sufferings to the body of the righteous so that his soul will understand better the will of God and His plan. The body is connected with this world while the soul is able to attain the world above. Through sufferings "the body is broken" but "the soul becomes dominant" and sees God.[56] Isa 53:10 is mentioned also in Zohar II,244b and in this passage the text is interpreted so that God will purify the righteous to prepare him for the coming world. It is emphasized that sufferings do not come "from the other side" (מסטרא אחרא)[57] but are called "the chastisements of love (יסורין דאהבה)".[58] This evidence shows that the Zohar interprets Isaiah 53 from the viewpoint of individual piety. God purifies his own and makes them ready to understand the secret world of God and go thither.

---

[55]Tishby, *The Wisdom of the Zohar* 1298-1302, esp. 1300. Tishby translates here "desires atonement for the sins of *the people*."

[56]Tishby, *The Wisdom of the Zohar* 1483-1487, esp. 1485; Matt, *The Zohar: Pritzker Edition* 2:277.

[57]The concept *sitra ahra* in the Zohar refers to the evil forces which emanate from sefirot but in an unbalanced way so that the divine judgment (*gevurah*) is not tempered by divine love (*hesed*). As Green ("Introduction" L) puts it: "The demonic is born of an imbalance within the divine, flowing ultimately from the same source as all else, the single source of being."

[58]Tishby, *The Wisdom of the Zohar* 475-482, esp. 481-482.

Zohar III,124a-126a (*Raya Mehemna*) contains an interesting midrash on the exile of Moses. Moses' soul is seen as being incarnate in the teachings of the rabbis who interpret the Torah. Thus Moses shares the rabbis' fate. Moses also suffers with these rabbis when they encounter persecution – apparently by the Christian Church. The midrash applies Isa 53:5 to Moses: "he was wounded because of our transgression." Furthermore, the exile of Moses in the lives of rabbis is compared with his living in the grave, the reference being to Isa 53:9. Moses is forced to live under oppression in the grave and he exhorts Elijah to come soon in order that he will be released from his distress.[59] Such an interpretation is a close parallel to our reading of the sufferings of the Messiah in Pesiqta Rabbati. Like Moses so also the Messiah is living with God and suffering because he identifies himself with the fate of the suffering Jews in the world.

An even closer parallel to the concept of the suffering Messiah in Pesiqta Rabbati can be found in Zohar II,212a which speaks *expressis verbis* about the Messiah and his sufferings by referring to Isaiah 53. According to this passage many souls come to the Messiah and tell him of the tribulation of Jews in the world. The Messiah begins to weep on behalf of these sufferers and even for those who do not want to live according to the will of the Creator. The weeping of the Messiah is related to Isa 53:5. Then the Messiah goes to the garden of Eden where a room called the "Hall of sufferers (היכלא דבני מרעין)" is found. In this Hall he proclaims that he is ready to bear the sins of the people so that his people can overcome their distress:

> And were it not that he (= the Messiah) eases[60] the burden from Israel, taking it on himself, no one could endure the sufferings meted out to Israel on account

---

[59]Tishby *The Wisdom of the Zohar* 1147-1154.

[60]The Aramean verb קיל (Af) can mean "make light", "treat with contempt" and even "curse".

of their neglect of the Torah.[61] So Scripture says: *Surely our diseases he did bear* (Isa 53:4).

Such a midrashic interpretation in the Zohar is developed from the discussion of how illnesses and sufferings (מרעין ויסורין) can be eliminated according to Moses' instructions when the Temple no longer exists. The answer states that it is now the task of the Messiah to eliminate illnesses and sufferings. By opening their eyes to see a new heavenly drama where the Messiah in his pre-existence is already acting on the behalf of Israel the Zohar gives comfort to the oppressed Jews. They are not alone because their Messiah is with them. It seems clear that the Zohar is influenced by the Christian theology which has emphasized the role of Jesus Christ among his suffering disciples.[62] However, there are essential differences: the Messiah suffers in his pre-existence by relieving the sufferings of his people but he does not die for the sins of the world. When he appears in the world he will be victorious not the suffering and dying Messiah.

Conclusions

In this section we have seen a new means of modifying the interpretation of Isaiah 53 when the passage is seen as referring to the sufferings of the Messiah – something which was manifest already in Targum Jonathan. Both Pesikta Rabbati and the Zohar emphasize the sufferings of the Messiah in his pre-existent "life". It may well be that the concept of the Messiah's sufferings was borrowed from Christian theology but it was

---

[61]לא הוי בר נש דיכיל למסבל יסוריהון דישראל על עונשי דאורייתא. The English translation of the Soncino edition of the Zohar translates "in expiation on account of their neglect of the Torah". The clarifying words "in expiation" can be understood from the context where the rituals of the Temple are referred to.

[62]Concerning the Christian influence in Zohar note also Y. Liebes, *Studies in Zohar* (SUNY Series in Judaica: Hermeneutics, Mysticism, and Religion, Albany, N.Y.: State University of New York Press 1993).

understood in a different light. The Messiah will suffer in his pre-existence but he will appear to the world as the victorious Messiah.[63]

---

[63]It would be interesting to consider how the concept of the suffering Messiah can be related to the view of the messianic Chabad Lubavitch movement. After all many members of the Chabad movement are prepared to proclaim that the late Rabbi Menachem Mendel Schneerson is the Messiah. His death was interpreted as a part of his messianic sufferings before he will come again to this world. This movement has received much criticism because it is thought to be unduly influenced by the Christian messianic programme. See the criticism of Chabad's messianic view in D. Berger, *The Rebbe, the Messiah, and the Scandal of Orthodox Indifference* (London: The Littman Library of Jewish Civilization 2001). I am not convinced that the criticism is justified. Concerning the messianic view of Chabad Lubavitch see N. Rosengård, *We Want Moshiach NOW! Understanding the Messianic Message in the Jewish Chabad-Lubavitch Movement* (Turku: Åbo Akademis förlag 2009).

11 Medieval Jewish Interpretations of Isaiah 53

The medieval Jewish interpretation of the Hebrew Bible was based on new trends in philosophy and philology which influenced all three Abrahamic religions.[1] Islamic dialectical theology (*kalam*) emphasized the dual basis of rationality and Scripture. These two complement each other. Linguistic, poetic and philosophical ideas constituted new impulses in exegesis. One reason why these new interpretive methods were adopted was the challenge of Karaism which rejected the rabbinical tradition altogether. The origin of Karaism has been connected with the name Anan ben David in the middle of the 8th century AD. However, historically, the formation of this Jewish sect is more complicated, and recent scholarship dates it to the 9th and 10th centuries.[2] In particular, Karaism challenged the rabbinical interpretive method *derash* and adapted the new philosophically and philologically oriented literal (*peshat*) method to the interpretation of the Hebrew Bible.[3] Criticism of the midrashim and their validity forced the rabbinical sages to defend

---

[1]A good presentation of medieval Jewish philosophy may be found in C. Sirat, *A History of Jewish Philosophy in the Middle Ages* (Cambridge: Cambridge University Press 1995).

[2]Concerning the origin of the Karaite Judaism and its history see F. Astren, *Karaite Judaism and Historical Understanding* (Columbia: University of South Carolina Press 2004).

[3]Concerning the *peshat* and *derash* in rabbinical exegesis see D. Weiss Halivni, *Peshat and Derash: Plain and Applied Meaning in Rabbinical Exegesis* (New York: Oxford University Press 1991). He notes (pp. 19-20) that the Karaite exegesis challenged the rabbinical exegesis which resulted in a new understanding of the *peshat*. In rabbinical writings *peshat* means mainly "contextual exegesis" (52-88) while in the Middle Ages the new understanding of the term "literal meaning" was introduced. See further E.L. Greenstein, "Medieval Bible Commentaries," in: B.W. Holtz, *Back to the Sources: Reading the Classic Jewish Texts* (New York: Simon & Schuster 1992) 213-260. He emphasizes that the *peshat* method was developed by Saadiah and his disciples to encounter the growth of Karaite exegesis (p. 224).

their interpretations and traditions. We may say that Karaism compelled rabbinical Judaism to emerge from its reticent circle. In exclusive rabbinical academies sophisticated traditions had been developed with the help of peculiar interpretive methods. These methods were applied mainly to confirm that halakhah rules were in conjunction with the Torah of Moses. In its confrontation with Karaism rabbinical Judaism was forced to argue in a new way for its self-understanding. We can detect a new argumentation which stated that the rabbinical belief system could also be defended by means of philosophical starting-points and appropriate linguistic interpretive methods.[4]

The aim of this section is to explain how new philosophical and philological trends in the medieval Jewish exegesis influenced also the interpretation of Isaiah 53. Saadiah Gaon was one of the first advocates of the new linguistic and historical methods. Other important interpreters were Rashi, Abraham Ibn Ezra and David Kimhi. Moreover, rabbinical Judaism eventually had to confront another challenge: the Christian mission strategy where diverse rabbinical midrashic interpretations were used to convince the Jewish party of the validity of the Christian interpretations.[5] This new missionary strategy was introduced at the Barcelona disputation in 1263 and received its full-blown articulation in

---

[4]It should be emphasized that the medieval Jewish philosophy assumed its special nature because of the background of the Hebrew Bible and rabbinic literature. Concerning this see D. Shatz, "The Biblical and Rabbinic Background to Medieval Jewish Philosophy," in: D.H. Frank & O. Leaman (eds), *The Cambridge Companion to Medieval Jewish Philosophy* (Cambridge: Cambridge University Library 2003) 16-37.

[5]For this new challenge see J. Cohen, "Scholarship and Intolerance in the Nedieval Academy: The Study of Evaluation of Judaism in European Christendom," in: J. Cohen (ed), *Essential Papers on Judaism and Christianity in Conflict: From Late Antiquity to Reformation* (New York: New York University Press 1991) 310-341; idem, "Christian Theology and Anti-Jewish Violence in the Middle Ages: Connections and Disjunctions," in: A. Sapir Abulafia (ed), *Religious Violence between Christians and Jews: Medieval Roots, Modern Perspectives* (New York: Palgrave 2002) 44-60; D.L. Lasker, "Jewish-Christian Polemics at the Turning Point: Jewish Evidence from the Twelfth Century," *HTR* 89 (1996) 172-201.

the famous *Pugio Fidei* (1278) written by Raymundus Martini. Thus rabbinical Judaism encountered two different challenges concerning the rabbinical midrashim: their refutation by Karaim and their misuse by Christians.

Saadiah Gaon

The confrontation of rabbinical Judaism and Karaism was highlighted in the literary works of the Jewish genius Saadiah ben Joseph Al-Fayyūmī (892-942). Saadiah was a native of Egypt and spoke Arabic as his mother tongue. His principal work was written in Arabic, *Al-Amānāt Wa-l-I'tiqādāt* (The Book of Beliefs and Opinion). Judah Ibn Tibbon translated this work into Hebrew in 1100's (*Sefer Emunot we-De'ot*) and it was copied for centuries among Jews until it was published for the first time in Constantinople in 1562.[6] In his main work Saadiah defends the Jewish belief as it was formulated in the rabbinical tradition. His main rhetorical strategy was to avoid referring to rabbinical writings as far as possible because he sought to show that the rabbinical theology can be inferred from the Hebrew Bible by means of philological and philosophical methods.

---

[6]Rav Sa'adya Gaon, *Sefer Emunut ve'Deot: First Edition, Constantinople 1562* (Reprint; Jerusalem: Makor Publishing 1972). A good English translation is available in Saadia Gaon, *The Book of Beliefs and Opinions* (translated by S. Rosenblatt; New Haven: Yale University Press 1976). It is worth noting that this main work of Saadiah does not contain any reference to Isaiah 53 even though suffering of the righteous (Job) is an important theme in Treatise V.3. The problem of theodicy is dealt with in Saadiah's work on Job. See Sa'adia ben Joseph, *The Book of Theodicy: Translation and Commentary on the Book of Job* (translated from the Arabic with a philosphic comment by L. E. Goodman; Yale Judaica Series 25; New Haven: Yale University Press 1988). But this study does not deal with the interpretation of Isaiah 53 either. There are only two references to Isa 53:11. The first reference (p. 125) deals with discipline and instruction of the righteous one without any further eloboration. The second (p. 208) reference is an example of philology in Job 7:4.

Saadiah became the leader of the Jewish Academy in Sura which was situated in Babylonia, and thus received his honorary title, Gaon.[7] He is the first well-known Jewish sage who used new interpretive methods: philology, linguistics, rethorics, and philosophy to understand the Hebrew Bible and defend the validity of the Rabbinical heritage. These new methods were adopted from Muhammedan theologies (so-called *mutakallimun*).[8] In his writings Saadiah demonstrated how these new interpretive methods can be used to defend the rabbinical heritage. Abraham Ibn Ezra glorifies Saadiah as being the first to advance scholarship. The new philosophical tradition established by Saadiah in the rabbinical tradition reached its zenith in the production of Moses Maimonides[9] and in medieval Jewish biblical exegesis.

Saadiah's biblical interpretation was based on a literal understanding of the text by using grammatical, historical and philosophical arguments but he could also apply homiletic techniques and polemics (against Karaites) in order to bring interpretation in tune with rabbinic tradition.[10] By adducing grammatical and historical

---

[7]See the biographical details in H. Malter, *Saadia Gaon: His Life and Works* (Hildesheim: Olms 1978).

[8]S. Stroumsa, "Saadya and Jewish *kalam*," in: D.H. Frank & O. Leaman (eds), *The Cambridge Companion to Medieval Jewish Philosophy* (Cambridge: Cambridge University Library 2003) 71-90; see also Sirat, *A History of Jewish Philosophy in the Middle Ages* 18-37.

[9]The most important works of Maimonides were *Mishneh Torah* (the interpretation of the Torah) and *Dalālat al-Hā'irīn* written in Arabic and translated in 1204 by Samuel Ibn Tibbon for the Hebrew *Moreh ha-Nevukîm* (Guide to perplexed). In this later work the most important questions of the medieval Jewish philosophical heritage can be discerned: (1) God and his attributes. God is transcendent and, therefore, cannot be approached by human reason. (2) God takes care of this world. (3) Creation of the world which becomes a problem in Maimonides' philosophy because God is transcendent. (4) Prophecy. (5) Human knowledge. See Sirat, *A History of Jewish Philosophy in the Middle Ages* 157-203.

[10]H.W. Basser, "Exegesis of Scripture, Medieval Rabbinic," in: J. Neusner, A.J. Avery-Beck, W.S. Green (eds), *The Encyclopaedia of Judaism Volume I* (Leiden: Brill) 266-280, esp. 267.

arguments Saadiah created a new interesting approach to the understanding of Isaiah 53. He sought literal and historical parallels between Isaiah 53 and the Book of Jeremiah and concluded that the suffering Servant was the prophet Jeremiah himself.

The Cairo Geniza writings included Saadiah's interpretation of Isaiah 53. Even though the text does not contain Saadiah's name its editor, Alobaidi, comes to this conclusion when he compares Saadiah's interpretation with the criticism of this interpretation found in Karaite Jefet ben Eli's text on Isaiah 53.[11] It emerges from Jefet ben Eli's text that Saadiah interpreted Isaiah 53 as referring to the prophet Jeremiah. Moreover, Alobaidi overlooked a further argument that Abraham Ibn Ezra presents five details supporting Saadiah's Jeremiah-interpretation.[12] All five details mentioned by Ibn Ezra can be found in the text edited by Alobaidi.[13] *First*, Ibn Ezra states that Isa 52:15 refers to the prophet's powerful word.[14] *Second*, Isa 53:2 was interpreted by Saadiah as a reference to the young Jeremiah (cf., Jer 1:6-7).[15] *Third*, according to Jer

---

[11]J. Alobaidi, *The Messiah in Isaiah 53: The Commentaries of Saadia Gaon, Salmon ben Yeruham and Yefet ben Eli on Is 52:13-53:12. Edition and translation* (Bern: Lang 1998) 12-17.

[12]These ideas I presented already in A. Laato, "Isaiah 53 in Jewish Perspective: Four Misunderstandings in Christian Exegesis," in: J. Svanberg, A. Holmberg & N.G. Holm (eds), *Kritisk läsning och ärliga ord: Vänskrift till Siv Illman* (Religionsvetenskapliga skrifter 71, Åbo: Åbo Akademi 2007) 127-141.

[13]See the interpretation of Isaiah 53 in Ibn Ezra's commentary on the Book of Isaiah in M. Friedländer, *The Commentary of Ibn Ezra on Isaiah Vol. I Translation of the Commentary* (New York: Philipp Feldheim 1873) 239-247; and the Hebrew text in M. Friedländer, *Pirush Rabbenu Abraham Eben Ezra al Jesa`ya* (New York: Feldheim 1873) 90-93. Note also that the English translation of Neubauer and Driver is reprinted in S. Schreiner, "Isaiah 53 in the Sefer Hizzuk Emunah ('Faith Strengthened') of Rabbi Isaac ben Abraham of Troki," in: B. Janowski & P. Stuhlmacher (eds), *The Suffering Servant: Isaiah 53 in Jewish and Christian Sources* (Grand Rapids: Eerdmans 2004) 418-461, esp. 452-456.

[14]See Alobaidi, *The Messiah in Isaiah 53*, 51.

[15]Alobaidi, *The Messiah in Isaiah 53*, 56-57.

18:20, the prophet was intercessor before God on behalf of the people and this corresponds to the way in which the suffering servant of Yhwh offers his life for his people (Isa 53:6,12).[16] *Fourth*, Isa 53:7 describes the servant as a lamb which will soon be sacrificed. This parallels the words of Jeremiah in Jer 11:19. Jeremiah tells how the men of his hometown planned to kill him and he was like a lamb ready for slaughtering.[17] *Fifth*, Isa 53:12 is, according to Saadiah, a reference to Jer 40:5, wherein Jeremiah received many gifts. There is no direct correspondence to this detail in Saadiah's text because its end is fragmentary. But it is reasonable to assume that even this reference is a part of Saadiah's interpretation. At the end of the text Saadiah writes that the expression of Isa 53:12 "and among the corrupted he was counted" corresponds to Jer 40:1 which states that Jeremiah was chained among the captives who were exiled. However, the text in the Book of Jeremiah goes on to record that the prophet was released and that he received gifts – which can be connected with the end of Isa 53:12 and we have reason to believe that Saadiah's interpretation – now lost – contained this detail.[18]

Saadiah's interpretation of Isaiah 53 is not confined only to Jeremiah. He writes that the suffering servant can be seen as reflecting in general terms the fates of the prophets, then argues that the text fits the life of Jeremiah. Saadiah's Jeremiah-interpretation, which is based on the meanings of the Hebrew words, could be paraphrased as follows:

> Despite of his youth (Jer 1:6) Jeremiah became wise in his task (*yaśkîl*, Isa 52:13). He was a great and important prophet (Isa 52:13; Jer 1:18), whose duty was to proclaim doom for many peoples (Isa 52:15; Jer 46-50). Jeremiah was called to prophesy when he was young (Isa 53:1-2; Jer 1) and had to suffer much in this task. The men of his own hometown attempted to kill him because his proclamation was not regarded as valid (Isa 53:3; Jer 12:6). Because of the word of God Jeremiah was forced to bear pain and sufferings (Isa 53:3-4; Jer

---

[16]Alobaidi, *The Messiah in Isaiah 53*, 59, 63.

[17]Alobaidi *The Messiah in Isaiah 53*, 59-60.

[18]Alobaidi *The Messiah in Isaiah 53*, 63-64.

15:18) and even the princes of Judah beat him (Jer 37:15). Thus he was forced to bear the sins of the people (Isa 53:5) but was willing to submit to this fate (Jer 18:20). The prophet's pain and sufferings are often depicted in the Book of Jeremiah (Jer 8:18; 4:19). The people were going astray like lambs and the prophet who wished to be God's messenger by proclaiming the word of God to them had to bear the consequences (Isa 53:6; Jer 1:17). The prophet became himself like a lamb and was on the point of being put to death (Isa 53:7; Jer 11:18-19). Finally, Jeremiah was captured and cast into prison but "from imprisonment and judgment he was taken away (*mē'ōṣer ûmimmišpāṭ luqqāḥ*)" from his distress and he became free again (Isa 53:8; Jer 39:13-14). None of his contemporaries defended this righteous prophet (Isa 53:8; Jer 5:1). Jeremiah had inner psychological pressure to proclaim the word of God even though at the same time he had to live among the ungodly and bear the consequences of his proclamation (Isa 53:9; Jer 20:9). The prophet came near to death (Jer 11:21). But it pleased God that Jeremiah executed his mission even though he was forced to suffer (Isa 53:10; Jer 7:5,7). Only thus could the prophet have seen his people's descendants (Isa 53:10; Jer 17:24-25); and God's good will was realized through his mission. Through his sufferings the prophet succeeded in leading many to repentance (Isa 53:11; Jer 20:18; here Saadiah refers to the responsibility of the prophet in Ezek 3:19, 21). The prophet must bear the sins of many because they hated him and sought to destroy him (Isa 53:11; Jer 20:2; 37:14-15 etc). Finally, God recompensed the prophet for all his sufferings and he could function as the messenger of God (Isa 53:12; Jer 15:19). Even though he was chained and counted among the corrupted his life was spared (Isa 53:12; Jer 38:2; 40:1). Jeremiah was willing to pray for the ungodly (Jer 18:20) even though God exhorted him not to pray for the people (Jer 7:16; 11:14; 14:11).

Saadiah's interpretation is an interesting attempt to find linguistic and thematic similarities between the fate of the Servant and that of Jeremiah. In many respects the argumentation resembles those modern interpretations where the suffering servant is identified with a prophet. In particular, scholars have often compared the suffering Servant with the portrayal of Jeremiah in the Hebrew Bible.

Saadiah's interpretation is a novelty in rabbinical Judaism, it is apparently based on new methodological reasoning. It is a literal method (*peshat*) which dominates the interpretation.[19] Apparently Saadiah knew that midrashim did not produce a coherent interpretation so that it was possible to seek a new alternative by using a literal method. Even though Saadiah succeeded in finding good linguistic and thematic parallels to the Book of Jeremiah his interpretation seems problematic. His contemporary the Karaite Yefet ben Eli criticizes Saadiah's interpretation in his own tractate on Isaiah 53:[20]

> Al-fayyumi, the rabbanite, for instance, erred in its [interpretation], since he applied it to the prophets and some sages. He leaned toward [the opinion] that this chapter have been said about Jeremiah. But his commentary is not worth the attention that we may give its refutation. In fact, the man practiced the business of commenting the Books of the prophets, according to a manner that he, himself invented. That is why no commentary of his is harmonious.

Yefet ben Eli's own interpretation emphasizes that Isaiah 53 speaks about the Messiah. He criticizes, anonymously, the Karaite Salmon ben Yeruham's contrived interpretation.[21] According to Salmon, every negative detail (i.e. details referring to suffering) in Isaiah 53 must be applied to the descendants of David who lived in the exile, while every positive expression (e.g., Isa 52:13 and 52:15) must be applied to the Messiah.[22] In this respect Salmon's interpretation is reminiscent of the Targum Jonathan translation of Isaiah 53 where every detail of suffering in the Masoretic text has not been related to the Messiah, rather reinterpreted to concern the exile of the people.

Yefet ben Eli emphasizes that the sufferings of the Messiah have theological implications. The principal detail is Isa 53:4 which Yefet interprets with the help of the Hebrew Bible so that Israel has always

---

[19] For this see M. Liber, *Rashi* (London: Mazin 1911) 109.

[20] Alobaidi, *The Messiah in Isaiah 53*, 141, 169.

[21] See this interpretation in Alobaidi, *The Messiah in Isaiah 53*, 65-123.

[22] Alobaidi, *The Messiah in Isaiah 53*, 170.

needed those who were ready to suffer for the sins of the people. Otherwise the people would have been executed by the divine wrath. Sufferers like the Servant in Isaiah 53 include Moses, Aaron, Samuel, David, Elijah and Elisa *et alii*. The prophet Ezekiel, too, was forced to bear the sins of the people (Ezek 4:4-6). Yefet refers to the expressions in Ezek 9:9 and Lam 4:6, according to which the sins of the people are so great that all would have been executed. This did not take place because the righteous ones were among the people and they were ready to suffer for the sake of all and thereby appease the wrath of God. When the exile of the Jews ends there is no other person who could mediate between God and the people but the Messiah himself. Thus the Messiah will become a vicarious sufferer. But in Yefet's interpretation the Messiah will not die in order to expiate the sins of the people. His vicarious sufferings correspond to those of the Jewish martyrs which can move the divine wrath away from the people so that God can be merciful (see sect. 3).[23] It is clear that in his messianic interpretation Yefet ben Eli did not support the Christian interpretation of the dying Messiah who would expiate the sins of the world by his death.

Rashi

New interpretive methods of *kalam* became influential also in Europe, first in Spain and then in Provence. Without question the most famous medieval Jewish interpreter of the Hebrew Bible was Rabbi Salomon ben Isaac, who is better known as Rashi (1040-1105).[24] Rashi established his position in the rabbinical tradition and his comments on the Hebrew Bible can be found on every page of rabbinical Bibles (*Miqraot Gedolot*) and Talmud-editions.

---

[23]Alobaidi, *The Messiah in Isaiah 53*, 176-178.

[24]For Rashi's life see Liber, *Rashi*; M.I. Gruber, *Rashi's Commentary on the Book of Psalms* (Leiden: Brill 2004) 1-10.

316

The Jewish grammarians in Spain had influenced Rashi and his school.[25] From this tradition he adopted the plain meaning (*peshat*) of the scriptures but was reluctant to exclude homiletical (*derash*) aspects. Another source of influence was Moses ha-Darshan's and Menahem ben Helbo's writings where grammar but also *peshat* interpretation were discussed.[26] Rashi often explains the relationship of the methods *peshat* and *derash* in his texts. An illustrative example is Gen 3:8:[27] "There are many aggadic Midrashim [on Scriptures] and our Rabbis have already collected them ... but I have only come for the sake of the plain sense of the verse, and such Aggadoth that explain the words of the text in a manner that fits in with them." Gelles analyzed Rashi's use of *peshat* and *derash* and concluded that they are complementary.[28] Rashi's great popularity can be explained from the fact that he never attempted to depart from thc flow of the rabbinical tradition but adopted it and

---

[25] In particular, Rashi used Menachem ben Saruq's and Dunash Ibn Labrat's philological and lexicographical investigations. For this see B.J. Gelles, *Peshat and Derash in the Exegesis of Rashi* (EJM 9, Leiden: Brill 1981) 26; see also Liber, *Rashi* 126-132.

[26] Liber, *Rashi* 110-111. Menahem ben Helbo's studies were known to Rashi mainly through his nephew Joseph Kara. Concerning the influence of Old French in Rashi's writings see M. Banitt, *Rashi: Interpreter of the Biblical Letter* (Tel Aviv: Chaim Rosenberg School of Jewish Studies 1985).

[27] See Gelles, *Peshat and Derash in the Exegesis of Rashi* 10 (whence the English translation is taken), 16, 116. The same passage has been emphasized in A. Grossman, "The School of Literal Jewish Exegesis in Northern France," in: M. Saebø, *Hebrew Bible / Old Testament: The History of Its Interpretation. Volume 1: From the Beginning to the Middle Ages (Until 1300). Part 2: The Middle Ages* (Göttingen: Vandenhoeck & Ruprecht 2000) 321-371, esp. 335.

[28] Gelles (*Peshat and Derash in the Exegesis of Rashi* 116) writes: "Peshat and Derash emerge not so much as conflicting forces but rather as the two ends of an exegetical spectrum, separated by intermediate shades of perception, including, no doubt an area of methodological indeterminacy."

deepened it by his *peshat* method.[29] In particular, Rashi carefully followed halakhic midrash in his commentaries.[30] Rashi never wrote any systematic presentation of his theology but only commented on the texts of the Hebrew Bible and the Talmud. From these interpretations it can be seen that according to Rashi, the Hebrew Bible describes the future from the salvation-historical perspective of God and from the prophetic perspective. In his messianic interpretations Rashi often follows the principles established in the rabbinical traditions. But sometimes he intentionally diverges from this rabbinical tradition, apparently because he wanted to oppose Christian interpretations.[31] A good example is Psalm 2, which in the rabbinical tradition has been interpreted as referring to the messianic age (e.g., b.Ber 7a). Rashi insists that the text must be interpreted "according to its basic meaning and for refutation of Christians (ולפי משמעו ולתשובת המינין)" as referring to King David against whom Philistines planned to war when they heard the Israelites had crowned him king (2 Sam 5:17).[32]

Rashi's interpretation of Isaiah 53 is based on careful exegetical examination. He comments at the beginning of his interpretation (on Isa

---

[29]Grossman ("The School of Literal Jewish Exegesis in Northern France" 336) favourably characterizes Rashi's exegesis: "Once Rashi had selected a suitable *midrash*, he was faced with the problem of its wording. Very frequently, he reworked the text as formulated by the Sages, omitting part of the talmudic argument, adding and omitting words and sometimes even changing the wording. At times, it seems, he did so in order to adapt the *midrash* to his own world view."

[30]See Gelles, *Peshat and Derash in the Exegesis of Rashi* 34-42 and Grossman, "The School of Literal Jewish Exegesis in Northern France" 326.

[31]J. Sarachek, *The Doctrine of the Messiah in Medieval Jewish Literature* (New York: Hermon Press 1932) 52-53. Gruber (*Rashi's Commentary on the Book of Psalms* 54-55) notes that "Rashi deliberately intended that his commentary would be the definitive Jewish counterpart to the Christian *Glossa ordinaria*."

[32]See Rashi's interpretation in M.I. Gruber, *Rashi's Commentary on Psalms 1-89* (South Florida studies in the history of Judaism 161, Atlanta: Scholars Press 1998) 1 (the Hebrew text is at the end of the edition) and 52-57; idem, *Rashi's Commentary on the Book of Psalms* 177-182 (Hebrew text on p. 811).

52:13) that the Servant must refer to Israel, or rather "the righteous ones among them" (צדיקים שבהם). He has apparently come to this conclusion from Isa 53:8 where he interprets the phrase מִפֶּשַׁע עַמִּי נֶגַע לָמוֹ as follows:

מפשע עמו בא הנגע הזה לצדיקים שבהם

"because of the transgression of his people this stroke (of exile) had fallen upon the righteous ones among them"

Rashi understands the suffix in לָמוֹ as plural 3 masc, and referring to the righteous ones among the people. Neubauer and Driver here translates "the stroke of exile" because of the context where Rashi has understood "the land of living" (ארץ חיים) as the Land of Israel. Apparently this translation is correct. Another argument for the Israel interpretation is the contextual exegesis. Rashi notes (on Isa 53:3) that the passage speaks of Israel "as one man" (כל ישראל כאיש אחד) and refers to Isa 44:1-2 where the expression עבדי יעקב has been used twice. An emphasis that the righteous ones among the people of Israel must suffer is proposed from the beginning of the interpretation. The "we"-group of the passage will confess after God has manifested his power and helped his people that "this people was ... a despised people" (העם הזה ... עם שפל היה מאד, on Isa 53:2).

   The "we"-group is identified with the nations. Even though Rashi did not say *expressis verbis* that the nations represent the Christian Church this must be his opinion. *First*, the "we"-group thinks it has a certain relation to the God of Israel so that it has a theological opinion of the sufferings of Israel (on Isa 53:4): "we thought that he was hated by God" (אנו היינו סבורים שהוא שנאוי למקום). *Second*, "we" oppresses Jews by forcing them to abandon God and choose idolatry – which they imagine to be a true worship (on Isa 53:9): "consenting to the worship of idols as though they had been God" (לקבל עליו עבדת זרה באלוה). *Third*, Rashi's interpretation of Isa 53:9 implies that Jews have been persecuted and even murdered by the nations – a comment which may echo the events in the First Crusade. This last point needs further discussion.

The massacre of Jews in the Rhineland cities took place during the First Crusade in 1096.[33] Scholars have discussed the way in which the First Crusade was directed against Jews. The recent consensus is that the crusader armies included troops who lacked clerical and military control which led to pillaging and devastation when they were on their way to the Holy Land. Chazan has devoted careful studies to the fate of European Jews during the First Crusade and concluded that there were very few instances of anti-Jewish actions among baronial armies, while violent measures against Jews were taken by the German crusaders.[34] The Hebrew sources indicate that the events of 1096 were a great shock to the Jews in the Rhineland and the existence of written documents shows that the events left traumatic traces in Jewish communities. The central question in our case is whether Rashi wrote about these events and whether his interpretation of Isaiah 53 is related to them.

Rashi died in 1105 and his major works were written already before 1096. However, his grandson Samuel ben Meir said that Rashi would have complemented his biblical commentaries if he had had the time.[35] This implies that, in principle, he would have modified his commentaries. A number of scholars are inclined to believe that Rashi's

---

[33]These events took place when German crusaders made their way to the Holy Land. See, e.g., S. Runciman, *The First Crusade* (Cambridge: Cambridge University Press 2007) 62-68.

[34]R. Chazan, *European Jewry and the First Crusade* (Berkeley: University of Californian Press 1996); idem, *God, Humanity, and History: The Hebrew First Crusade Narratives* (Berkeley: University of California Press 2000); idem, "The Anti-Jewish Violence of 1096: Perpetrators and Dynamics," in: A. Sapir Abulafia (ed), *Religious Violence between Christians and Jews: Medieval Roots, Modern Perspectives* (New York: Palgrave 2002) 21-43.

[35]This is indicated in M. Liber, *Rashi* (London: Mazin 1911) 125-126.

interpretation of Isa 53:9 contains a reference to the massacre of the Jews in the Rhineland.[36] Rashi's interpretation is as follows:

> He gave himself over whatever burial the wicked Gentiles might decree: for the Gentiles used to condemn the Israelites to be murdered and then buried like asses in the bellies of dogs. He agreed, then, to be buried according to the judgment of the wicked, refusing to deny the living God; and according to the judgment of the ruler he gave himself up to any form of death which had been decreed upon him, because he would not deny God by perpetrating violence and doing evil, like all the nations amongst whom he was a sojourner ...

Gentiles gave Jews alternatives, "death" or "conversion", and this accords with the situation during the First Crusade. In addition, burials in humiliating circumstances are often recorded in Jewish First Crusade sources.[37]

It is worth noting that Rashi's Israel-interpretation is no new phenomenon. Already in the Talmud and in the Second Temple Jewish sources the servant has been described as representing righteous sufferers among the people of Israel. The interesting point in Rashi's interpretation is his emphasis that sufferings have a meaning. In many places Rashi writes that sufferings are needed in order that Israel's exile will finally come to an end. On Isa 53:4 Rashi writes: "Israel suffered in order that by his sufferings atonement might be made for all other nations." A

---

[36]See the opinion of E.B. Pusey in the introduction of A. Neubauer & S. Driver, *The "Suffering Servant" of Isaiah According to the Jewish Interpreters Translated by S.R. Driver and A. Neubauer* (Eugene: Wipf and Stock 1999) xliv-xlvi. It is worth noting that Pusey characterizes Rashi's interpretation as "the prominent misinterpretation" (p. lx) indicating his own tendency. See further the discussion in C.R. North, *The Suffering Servant in Deutero-Isaiah: An Historical and Critical Study* (Oxford University Press1963) 17-20; H. Haag, *Der Gottesknecht bei Deuterojesaja* (EdF 233, Darmstadt: Wissenschaftliche Buchgesellschaft 1985) 51-58, and H. Sicherman & G.J. Gevaryahu, "Rashi and the First Crusade: Commentary, Liturgy, Legend," *Judaism* 48 (1999) 181-197.

[37]See the translation of the Hebrew sources in Chazan, *European Jewry and the First Crusade* 225-297 where it is frequently stated that Jews were buried naked. See further Sicherman & Gevaryahu, "Rashi and the First Crusade," 196 n. 17.

similar interpretation refers to Isa 53:5: "He was chastised in order that the whole world might have peace." The Servant will receive his credit and he will receive an inheritance with patriarchs who are the "great ones" in verse 12. Rashi ends his interpretation by emphasizing the sufferings of the Servant: "And in virtue of his sufferings – because through him the world received prosperity – he interceded for the transgressors." Through the servant God's goodness will be finally directed toward the whole world.

Rashi's interpretation emphasizes that the servant Israel has a positive task, to save all nations in the world. Rashi's collective interpretation, i.e. that the servant is Israel, became popular and was soon established in the medieval Jewish interpretive tradition.[38] However, his opinion that the Servant Israel suffers in order to establish peace for nations was not always accepted by exegetes as we shall see below.

Abraham Ibn Ezra

Abraham Ibn Ezra (1089-1164) was born in Spain (Tudela). He was forced to leave Muslim Spain in 1140. He moved to Italy and then wandered through different European countries. He wrote in Arabic but after having left Spain began to write in Hebrew and all his extant works survive in that language. Ibn Ezra's exegetical method is summarized in his introduction to the Pentateuch:[39]

---

[38]See the evidence in A. Neubauer & S. Driver, *The "Suffering Servant" of Isaiah According to the Jewish Interpreters Translated by S.R. Driver and A. Neubauer* (Eugene: Wipf and Stock 1999); J.E. Rembaum, "The Development of a Jewish Exegetical Tradition Regarding Isaiah 53," *HTR* 75 (1982) 289-311.

[39]See the translation in *Ibn Ezra's Commentary on the Pentateuch: Genesis* (Bereshit). Translated and Annotated by H.N. Strickman & A.M. Silver (New York: Menorah Publishing Company 1988) 1; see further U. Simon, "Abraham Ibn Ezra," in: M. Saebø, *Hebrew Bible / Old Testament: The History of Its Interpretation. Volume 1: From the Beginning to the Middle Ages (Until 1300). Part 2: The Middle Ages* (Göttingen: Vandenhoeck & Ruprecht 2000) 377-387, esp. 378.

> This *Sefer Hayyashar*, composed by Abraham the poet,
> is bound by ropes of grammar.
> The eyes of the intelligent will find it fit.
> All who take hold of it will be glad.

Simon refers to Ibn Ezra's commentary on Num 22:28 and notes that the word *yashar* ("straight") is synonymous for *peshat* interpretation. More than Rashi Ibn Ezra developed the *peshat* method and used it more consistently than did Rashi. He often voices his criticism of midrashim. This critical attitude toward midrashim was due to the development of philological, literal and historical interpretive methods but it may also be related to apologetics. Christian exegesis, with its emphasis on allegorical interpretation, could have been regarded as a good alternative to sophisticated rabbinic midrashim. The use of the *peshat* method could challenge all Christian allegories more effectually. At least Ibn Ezra – as did David Kimchi – used *peshat* method to criticize Christian exegesis. Simon notes, however, that Ibn Ezra respected rabbinic halakhah and did not recognize "the legitimacy of any *peshat* interpretation that contradicts halakhah."[40]

Abraham Ibn Ezra's commentary on the Book of Isaiah was composed in Lucca, Italy, in 1145.[41] The work contains sophisticated intellectual interpretations which may be characterized as a forerunner of modern exegesis.[42] This becomes apparent in his treatment of the latter part of the book, i.e. Isaiah 40-66. Ibn Ezra argues that the message of Isaiah 40-66, which concerns the return to Jerusalem, the rebuilding of the city and the Temple, and the proclamation about the victorious Cyrus were all

---

[40]Simon, "Abraham Ibn Ezra," 381.

[41]M. Friedländer, *Essays on the Writings of Abraham Ibn Ezra* (London: Truebner 1877) 164-165.

[42]So U. Simon, "Ibn Ezra between Medievalism and Modernism: The Case of Isaiah XL-LXVI," in: J.A. Emerton (ed), *Congress Volume: Salamanca 1983* (VTSup 36, Leiden: Brill 1985) 257-271.

irrelevant in the time of Hezekiah when the Assyrian crisis was acute. Therefore, he post-dated the latter part of the book to the time of the Babylonian exile. He notes in his commentary on the beginning of chapter 40 that even Moses Hakkohen ibn Chiquitilla postdated Isaiah 40-66 and that he himself has adopted a modified version of this opinion.[43]

In his commentary on Isaiah, Ibn Ezra received much inspiration from Ibn Chiquitilla. The latter's commentaries have not been preserved but Ibn Ezra quotes his texts about 80 times, and about 20 other references can be found in other sources. Simon characterizes Ibn Chiquitilla's exegesis as containing two methods: 1) "wild assumptions about supposed historical events for which there is no evidence outside the prophecy itself", and 2) "the interpretation of supernatural eschatological promises as mere metaphors in order to adjust them to the natural conditions of the near future."[44] Ibn Ezra followed Ibn Chiquitilla's method to seek contemporary applications from the time of Isaiah to the interpretations of the texts in the Book of Isaiah. However, his interpretation concerning Isaiah 40-66 differs markedly from that of Ibn Chiquitilla. While the latter seeks interpretation which historically matches the exodus from the Babylonian exile, Ibn Ezra states that "everything refers to the coming redemption from our present exile." Nevertheless, Ibn Ezra adds that some of the prophecies in Isaiah 40-66 refer to the Babylonian exile but "in the last section of the book all the prophecies surely refer to a period yet to come."[45] Simon has argued that

---

[43]Friedländer, *Commentary of Ibn Ezra on Isaiah* 169-171; see further Simon, "Abraham Ibn Ezra," 383.

[44]Simon, "Ibn Ezra between Medievalism and Modernism" 260.

[45]Concerning the incomplete clause כי כורש ששלח הגולה in his Commentary on Isa 40:1 and its text-critical problems see Simon, "Ibn Ezra between Medievalism and Modernism" 263 n. 17: "The minimal emendation would be the erasure of the dittographical *š* in *šeššālah* since it creates a meaningless incomplete subordinate clause." Friedländer (*The Commentary of Ibn Ezra on Isaiah* 170 n. 3) has another explanation.

324

Ibn Ezra sees the Babylonian exile as typology for the present exile, and the Book of Isaiah contains messianic promise of the present exile:[46]

> ... when Ibn Ezra writes in his explanation of xl 1 that henceforth "everything refers to our present exile", he presumably means to say that for the exiles in Babylon, too, the messianic promises were the heart of the prophet's message. And when he adds that "There are, it is true, also prophecies concerning the Babylonian exile; they have been included only in order to state that Cyrus released the exiles", he presumably means to say that the consolations for the time of the Second Temple are subordinate to the messianic promises, since they are cited only for the sake of analogy.

Ibn Chiquitilla's interpretation of Isaiah 53 has been preserved in Ibn Bal'am's commentary on the Book of Isaiah. According to this work Ibn Chiquitilla interpreted the passage as referring to Hezekiah.[47] Ibn Ezra's interpretation of Isaiah 53 is not easy to formulate. He begins his exegesis by refuting the Christian understanding of the passage. Then he goes on to say that "my servant means each individual belonging to Israel, and consequently God's servant, who is in exile." After that he notes that many Jewish commentators have interpreted the passage as referring to the Messiah but remarks that many passages like "despised and forlorn of men", "taken from prison and judgment", "made his grave with the wicked" and "will see seed, and prolong days" then have no meaning. He also mentions Saadiah Gaon's interpretation that the passage refers to the prophet Jeremiah and regards it as "attractive". Finally he returns to his opinion that the passage refers to each individual in Israel who is in the exile. He uses the argument of "the context" and

---

[46]Simon, "Ibn Ezra between Medievalism and Modernism," 265.

[47]M. Goshen-Gottstein, *R. Judah Ibn Bal'am's Commentary on Isaiah: The Arabic Original According to MS Firkowitch (Ebr-Arab I 1377) with a Hebrew Translation, Notes and Introduction* (Ramat Gan: Bar-Ilan University Press 1992) 216.

therefore refutes the interpretation concerning Jeremiah. However, at the end of his interpretation of Isaiah 53, Ibn Ezra observes:[48]

> I have now explained for you the whole Parashah: in my opinion the expression my servant (52:13; 53:11) denotes the same person who is the subject of 42:1; 49:3; 53:11, the same who says of himself, "I gave my back to the smiters" 50:6. In my commentary of chap. 40 I mentioned briefly the leading principle of my opinion, which considers all these Parashas as connected with each other.

Thus Ibn Ezra accepts the Israel interpretation but presents his own view that the passage refers to the prophet as an alternative. This is typical of medieval Jewish exegesis. Jewish interpreters delighted in giving alternative interpretations – apparently because the Talmud has taught them to accept two diverging opinions which, nevertheless, aim in the same direction and often emphasize the same halakhic position. At the beginning of his interpretation, Ibn Ezra often mentions *expressis verbis* two alternatives "individual" and "collective" interpretation. This can be seen when he explains Isa 53:2 ("The Israelite who is the servant of the Lord, or the whole nation of the Israelites") and 53:3 ("The servant of the Lord, or the whole nation of the Israelites"). But then he seems to concentrate on the collective interpretation and only at the end of his explanation returns to the possibility of interpreting the servant as an individual, i.e., the prophet. These two alternatives are also in focus in the interpretation of Isa 49:3. As Ibn Ezra says it: "You are an Israelite of whom I am proud" and "'You are Israel,' you are estimated in my eyes like all Israelites together" and then notes that "I prefer this latter explanation."[49] In the case of Isa 42:1 and 50:6 Ibn Ezra presents only

---

[48]See the translation in Neubauer & Driver *The "Suffering Servant" of Isaiah* 48; Friedländer, *The Commentary of Ibn Ezra on Isaiah* 246; Simon, "Ibn Ezra between Medievalism and Modernism" 270.

[49]Friedländer, *The Commentary of Ibn Ezra on Isaiah* 223 (the Hebrew text on p. 83).

"prophetic" interpretation.[50] We shall later in this section see that a similar double interpretation of Isaiah 53 was proposed by Nahmanides. He interpreted the passage as referring to Israel but gave also an alternative meaning to those Jews who regarded it as concerning the Messiah – as indicated in the rabbinical interpretation tradition (see sects. 9 and 10).

Let us now deal with Ibn Ezra's "Israel"-interpretation of Isaiah 53. Ibn Ezra identifies *rabbîm* with nations who regard Jews as disfigured and do not believe that "there could ever be deliverance for Israel" (שתהיה לישראל תשועה, on Isa 52:15). The argument that there will never be a deliverance for Jews is rooted in medieval Christian theological argumentation. The Christians argued that the coming of the Messiah is connected with the destruction of the temple (the key-text was Dan 9:24-27) and that the royal status of Judah will end when the Messiah comes (Gen 49:8-12).[51] Isaiah 53 is then taken by Ibn Ezra as an example of this theological hubris which will end when the time of vengeance comes to pass in the world. The verb *yazzeh* is taken as a meaning to "shed blood" and Ibn Ezra interprets it so that the blood of nations will be shed (on Isa 52:13-15).

---

[50]Friedländer, *The Commentary of Ibn Ezra on Isaiah* 186-187 (the Hebrew text on p. 70) and 229-230 (the Hebrew text on p. 86).

[51]Concerning the role of Dan 9:24-27 in medieval Jewish-Christian disputations and polemics see R. Chazan, "Daniel 9:24-27: Exegesis and Polemics," in: O. Limor & G.G. Stroumsa (eds), *Contra Iudaeos: Ancient and Medieval Polemics between Christians and Jews* (Texts and Studies in Medieval and Early Modern Judaism 10, Tübingen: Mohr Siebeck 1996) 143-159. In particular, it is worth noting that Saadiah interprets Dan 9:24-27 in a confrontation with Christianity. Concerning Gen 49:8-12 in ancient Jewish and Christian interpretations see A. Laato "Gen 49:8-12 and Its Interpretation In Antiquity – A Methodological Approach to Understanding of the Rewritten Bible" in: E. Koskenniemi & P. Lindqvist (eds), *Rewritten Biblical Figures* (SRB 3, Turku: ÅAU, Winona Lake: Eisenbrauns 2010) 1-26; and in Medieval Jewish writings see M. Gómez Aranda, "Jacob's Blessings in Medieval Jewish Exegesis," in: E. Koskenniemi & P. Lindqvist (eds), *Rewritten Biblical Figures* (Studies in Rewritten Bible 3, Winona Lake: Eisenbrauns & Åbo Akademi University 2010) 235-258.

The sufferings of the servant refer to the distress of the exile: "The expressions pains and sickness allude to the distress occasioned by exile." During the exile, the most dangerous threat for Jews is that they will lose their hope when they see how the nations will prosper. Ibn Ezra emphasizes that the crux is to understand the Torah aright. He criticizes nations "whose laws were altogether vanity, but they came upon Israel instead, whose law was a law of faithfulness" (on Isa 53:4). Verse 7 is understood so that a Jew "in the hour of his affliction never opens his mouth to speak." His only "care in this world is the service of God." The expression "He shall see his seed, he shall prolong his days" in verse 10 is interpreted by Ibn Ezra so that a Jew who has not considered the stipulations of the Torah will "put his soul before him the fear of the Lord" and "return to the Torah of God when the end, the advent of the Messiah, has taken place." At that time even the "nations are converted to the true religion" (ישובו הגוים לדת השם).

Ibn Ezra understands the Sufferings of Israel as meaning peace for the nations. Isa 53:5 is interpreted so that "all the time that Israel is in the humiliation of exile the nations will have peace." Ibn Ezra emphasizes that the exile of the servant means that his oppressors can have peace, i.e., through the servant's wounds the nations have been healed. But the destiny of the servant will be changed. He will be released from his exile and then the nations must pay for their deeds. However, in the interpretation of Isa 53:11-12 Ibn Ezra gives an alternative explanation: the Servant will give peace for the nations and pray for them so that Zech 14:16-19 will be realized. The nations will do pilgrimage to Jerusalem and serve the God of Israel. Thus Ibn Ezra even on this point gives two alternatives for the fate of nations in the coming messianic era. He prefers the view according to which the nations will be saved: "I approve of the latter explanation, since its correctness is evidenced by the words which follow" (i.e., verse 12).

Concerning Isa 53:12, Ibn Ezra refers to the common interpretation which can be seen already in Rashi's commentary: "All the interpreters say that this verse alludes metaphorically to those who

328

perished in defense of the Diviner Unity (המתים על ייחוד השם)." They can divide booty with *rabbîm*, i.e. prophets and *'atsûmîm* i.e. patriarchs. It seems that Ibn Ezra here, and probably also in his alternative view of the meaning of the sufferings of the Servant (derived out of Isa 53:11-12), is dependent on the interpretation of Rashi.

David Kimhi

Beside Rashi and Ibn Ezra, David Kimhi (acronym Radak [1160?-1235?]) was a third famous Jewish exegete whose writings have been transmitted in the rabbinical bibles, viz. *Miqraot Gedolot*. Radak was trained as philologist and exegete. His first work was *Mikhlol* which contained two parts "the grammatical portion (*Ḥelek ha-Dikduk*) which itself came to be known as the *Mikhlol* (Constantinople, 1532), and the lexicon (*Ḥelek ha-Inyan*) known independently as the *Sefer ha-Shorashim*."[52] His detailed linguistic analyses became a typical feature of his biblical interpretations. Beside his philological and grammatical analyses Kimhi emphasized the *peshat* method and considered the contexts of the biblical texts in his interpretations. Apparently he followed the "scientific" tradition established by earlier Jewish interpreters, including, in particular, Abraham Ibn Ezra. Kimhi was also known as an adherent of Maimonides' philosophy, and was active in Maimonidean controversy. Kimhi was no enthusiastic follower of rabbinical midrashim but practiced literal and contextual interpretation according to the *peshat* method. Talmage neatly summarizes:[53] "These then were technical criteria for Radak's critique of midrash: observance of the rules of grammar and stylistic principles and suitability to the context." But there are cases when literal interpretation can be unreasonable. In those cases midrashim provided a solution. Talmage

---

[52]F.E. Talmage, "David Kimhi," Encyclopaedia Judaica 12:155.

[53]F.E. Talmage, *David Kimhi: The Man and the Commentaries* (Cambridge MA: Harvard University Press 1975) 125.

writes that Radak demonstrated that "much of so called 'midrash' is to be considered *peshat*" and "the more Radak became the lord of *peshat*, the more was he the vassal of midrash".[54]

On the other hand, Kimhi's eagerness to use and develop the *peshat* method can also be related to the challenge of Christian allegorical interpretations. David's father, Joseph Kimhi, states in his famous *Sefer Berith* that a Jew can interpret all teachings and prophecies in the Hebrew Bible which Christians regard as Christological passages with the aid of the *peshat* method:[55]

> You have neither teachings nor prophecies which I cannot explain according to their plain sense and context (שלא אוכל לתרצם כפשטם ובמקראם).

David Kimhi often contradicts Christian interpretations in his commentaries and then uses grammatical, stylistic and contextual arguments.[56] At the end of his exegesis of Isaiah 53, Radak criticizes the Christian interpretation by presenting a grammatical problem (*lamô* in 53:8 has a plural suffix, not singular) and ridiculing Christology which Christians apply to Isaiah 53.[57] The question is, how much does this criticism originate in his father's polemics? Indeed, David Kimhi refers to his father's works at the beginning of his interpretation of Isaiah 53:

> I will now proceed to expound the Parashah as it is expounded by my father of blessed memory in the *Sefer ha-Galuy* and the *Sefer ha-Berith*, composed by him in answer to the heretics.

---

[54]Talmage, *David Kimhi: The Man and the Commentaries* 133 and 134.

[55]See F.E. Talmage, *The Book of the Covenant of Joseph Kimhi* (Toronto: The Pontificial Institute of Mediaeval Studies 1972) 39; the Hebrew text is in F.E. Talmage, *Sefer ha-berît ûvikûhe RaDaQ 'im hannazerôt* (Jerusalem: Bialik Institute 1974) 32.

[56]F.E. Talmage, "R. David Kimhi as Polemicist," *HUCA* 38 (1967) 213-235; Talmage, *David Kimhi: The Man and the Commentaries* 135-162.

[57]We shall discuss the Jewish characterization of the Christian interpretation in more detail in sect. 12.

Unfortunately, the fragmentary *Sefer ha-Berit* does not contain any reference to how Joseph Kimhi interpreted Isaiah 53.[58] Nevertheless, the criticism of Christology which Radak actualizes in the interpretation of Isaiah 53 is a current theme in *Sefer ha-Berith*.

Radak begins his interpretation by referring to the context of Isaiah 40-55 where "the captivity of Israel" is mentioned as "my servant" (Isa 41:8). Isa 52:13 refers to the exaltation of Israel, and Kimhi understands the multiple terms *yārûm, ûnissā'* and *wĕgābah* as stylistic reasons to emphasize the coming greatness of Israel. His interpretation is heavily dependent on Abraham Ibn Ezra's. He mentions ibn Ezra's comment that "they" in Isa 52:14 refers to "many nations" who despise Jews because of their present distress in the exile. The "we"-group in Isa 53:1-10 are nations who could never have believed that God will deliver Jews from the exile. The expressions "like a sucker" and "like a root" in Isa 53:2 describe how Jews will be saved from the distress of the exile. Radak emphasizes that "in front of him" (*lĕpānāyw*) means that "Israel was continually before God" even though its distress in the exile did not seem so to indicate.

Unlike Rashi (and Ibn Ezra) Radak did not see any vicarious atonement in the sufferings of the Jews for the nations. He establishes an interpretive axiom on the basis of Ezek 18:20: "the son shall not suffer for the iniquity of the father, nor the father for the iniquity of the son: *a fortiori*, therefore, one man cannot suffer for another man, or one people for another people" (on Isa 53:4). Radak explains such expressions as "carrying our sickness" psychologically:

---

[58]Concerning the fragmentary nature of *Sefer ha-Berit* see Talmage, *Joseph Kimhi: The Book of the Covenant* 18-26. Concerning the influence of Joseph Kimhi's work see further R. Chazan, "Joseph Kimhi's 'Sefer ha-Berit'; Pathbreaking Medieval Jewish Apologetics," *HTR* 85 (1992) 417-432; D. Börner-Klein, "Das Buch des Bundes: Josef Qimchis Diskussion zwischen einem Gläubigen und einem Ungläubigen," in: C. Thoma, G. Stemberger, J. Maier (eds), Judentum - Ausblicke und Einsichten: Festgabe fûr Kurt Schubert (Frankfurt a.M.: Lang 1993) 209-251.

Here the phrases put into the mouth of the Gentiles, such as 'he carried our sickness' etc., are merely the expression of their own thoughts; it is not asserted that Israel actually bore the iniquity of the Gentiles, but the latter only imagine it to be the case when they see, at the time of deliverance, that the faith which Israel adhered to was the true one, while that which they themselves had adhered to was the false; accordingly they say (Jer 16:19): 'Our fathers have inherited nothing but falsehood'.

One reason for Radak's reluctance to follow Rashi's interpretation of Israel's vicarious and atoning suffering in Isaiah 53 which could benefit nations was probably his deep personal frustration that Jews were oppressed by Islam in the East and Christianity in the West. He demanded divine justice and that meant punishment for those who had oppressed Jews. When the gentiles realize that God has saved the Jews they confess that "the sickness and pain which ought to have fallen upon us has fallen upon them, and they were our ransom and the price of our atonement (והם היו כופר וכפרה לנו)." Neubauer and Driver translate here "they are our ransom ..." but because Radak has already refuted the idea of vicarious and atoning suffering, he must have meant that the sufferings of the Jews meant peaceful life for gentiles until the time of vengeance when they will be punished and Israel will be saved. Therefore, the translation should be in the past tense.

Isa 53:6 is interpreted as a desperate confession of the nations when they realize that they have been like sheep who "had gone astray, while Israel had been in possession of the truth." The land of living in 53:8 is the land of Israel, and gentiles think that God has forsaken his people and uprooted it from their land. The confession of the "we" in 53:8, "for the transgression of my people" is explained so that every nation "will make this confession, saying that in consequence of their own transgression, and not Israel's, had the stroke fallen upon them." Thus "my people" does not refer to Israel but to every nation.

The persecutions of the Christians are taken up at several points of the interpretation. In 53:9 Radak explains how the servant, i.e the Jews, "gave himself voluntarily to death; they were ready to release him if he would renounce his own law and transfer his allegiance to theirs;

but rather than do this, he met a voluntary death." The plural form *môtāyw* in 53:9 is explained by Radak so that it refers to many deaths of Jews: "some were burnt, some were slain, and others were stoned – they gave themselves over to any form of death for the sake of the unity of the Godhead (יחוד השם)." Verse 53:10 gives the reason for the Jews' sufferings. The question is of divine mystery: God wanted to bruise his people which gentiles could not understand. Radak emphasizes that the servant "will receive a full reward for the misfortune he has endured" (on Isa 53:10).

Kimhi understood the text so that "the words of the gentiles cease" at Isa 53:10 and "those of God begin" in 53:11. Radak connects the expression "my righteous servant will by his knowledge make righteous many (nations)" with Isa 2:3: "He will teach us of his ways, and we will walk in his paths." That the servant "will bear the iniquities of the gentiles" means that "there will be peace and prosperity in the whole world, even for gentiles." An interesting interpretation is presented for 53:12. "The mighty" and "the strong" are Gog and Magog, and the verse reports the eschatological battles of Zechariah 12 and 14. Thus the final verse describes the reward which Israel will receive when "he poured out his soul to die." Radak explains once again the meaning of the sufferings of Israel. They are not to be understood vicariously. Israel had to bear the consequences of the evil actions of the gentiles: "Israel bore the consequences of the sin of many, i.e. of the gentiles when they sinned against him, and he bore the sufferings which their sin occasioned." During the time of the distress of the exiles the oppressed servant nevertheless followed the instruction of Jeremiah (Jer 29:7) and "continued interceding for the wicked who were transgressing against him, and sought blessings on their land from the Lord." Nevertheless, Radak leaves open the possibility that the reference may also be to the coming time of deliverance when the servant will intercede the gentiles and establish peace upon the world.

At the end of his interpretation Radak states that "our Rabbis" (in the Talmud) have interpreted Isaiah 53 as referring to Moses who according to Exodus 32-34 was ready to sacrifice himself on behalf of the people. Here Radak apparently refers to b.sotah 14a which we have already discussed in sect. 8.

Nahmanides and the Barcelona Disputation

Some years before Barcelona 1263 the Christian Church had undertaken a new aggressive mission strategy against Jews.[59] The Jewish convert Saul[60] who took a new Christian name Pablo Christiani had preached in Jewish synagogues by permission and order of King James I, and attempted to convince Jews that the rabbinical literature in fact confirms all elementary Christian doctrines about the Messiah. This new mission strategy was surprisingly new, and its basic viewpoints in many different modifications can be found even today.[61] What makes Barcelona 1263 so important for our study is the fact that during the disputation it was stressed that the rabbinical sources support the Christian view that Isaiah 53 refers to the Messiah who must suffer and die for the people of Israel.

---

[59]Good introductions to the Barcelona disputation are, e.g., H.-G. Mutius, *Die Christlich-Jüdische Zwangsdisputation zu Barcelona* (Judentum und Umwelt 5, Frankfurt am Main: Lang 1982) and R. Chazan, *Barcelona and Beyond. The Disputation of 1263 and Its Aftermath* (Berkeley: University of California 1992).

[60]We know very little about Saul. The most valuable source is Jacob bar Elijah's letter or Iggeret which is edited and published by J. Kobak, "Jacob ben Elia. 'Letter to the Apostate Saul'," *Jeschurun* 6 (1868) 1–34. Presentations of the main characters in the disputation can be found in R. Chazan, *Barcelona and Beyond*, 17-38; H. Maccoby, *Judaism on Trial. Jewish-Christian Disputations in the Middle Ages* (London: The Littman Library of Jewish Civilization 1993) 79-81.

[61]It is worth noting that the disputation in Paris ended with the burning of Jewish documents: Talmud editions and rabbinical writings. See this evolution in J. Cohen, *The Friars and the Jews: The Evolution of Medieval Anti-Judaism* (Ithaca: Cornell University Press 1982); idem, "Scholarship and Intolerance in the Medieval Academy: The Study of Evaluation of Judaism in European Christendom," in: J. Cohen (ed), *Essential Papers on Judaism and Christianity in Conflict: From Late Antiquity to Reformation* (New York: New York University Press 1991) 310-341.

Pablo's discussion partner in Barcelona was the famous rabbi from Gerona, Moses ben Nachman or Nahmanides (1194-1270).[62] There are two accounts of the Barcelona disputation: the shorter Christian in Latin, the author of which is unknown, and Nahmanides' (1194-1270) own account in Hebrew.[63] Scholars have discussed which of these two accounts is historically more accurate.[64] However, it seems clear that both the Jewish and the Christian party have written their account from their own restricted viewpoints and emphasized their own biased interests.[65] The disputation was composed so that the truth of the Christianity would outshine Judaism. Pablo Christiani submitted questions to Nahmanides concerning the Hebrew Bible and the rabbinical sources and the latter was forced to answer. According to both accounts there were four central issues in the disputation: (1) Arguments will be presented that the Messiah has already come. (2) The Messiah is both divine and human. (3) The Messiah must suffer and die, and on this subject Isaiah 53 and its interpretation was prominent. (4) Discussion of whether the Jews still possess the true Torah.

Pablo Christiani presented typical examples of *eisegesis* where some ideas of the rabbinical documents are taken out of their context and

---

[62]Concerning the life and works of Nahmanides see the articles in I. Twersky (ed), *Rabbi Moses Nachmanides (Ramban): Explorations in His Religious and Literary Virtuosity* (Cambridge MA: Harvard University Press 1983); D. Novak, *The Theology of Nahmanides Systematically Presented* (Brown Judaic Studies 271, Atlanta: Scholars Press 1992).

[63]Concerning the Latin text see Y. Baer (ed), "The Disputations of R. Yechiel of Paris and of Nachmanides" (Hebrew), *Tarbiz* 2 (1931) 172-187; R.I. Burns, "The Barcelona 'disputation' of 1263: Conversionism and Talmud in Jewish-Christian Relations," *Catholic Historical Review* 79 (1993) 488-495 and the text of Nahmanides's *Vichuah* in H. Chavel, *Kitvei Moses ben Nahman Vol 1* (Jerusalem: Mossad Harav Kook) 302-320. Good English translations can be found in Maccoby, *Judaism on Trial*. I follow Maccoby's translation. See also Maccoby's notes to the Hebrew text in pp. 76-78.

[64]See, e.g., M.A. Cohen, "Reflections on the Text and Context of the Disputation of Barcelona," *HUCA* 35 (1964) 157-192; Maccoby, *Judaism on Trial* 39-75.

[65]See Chazan, *Barcelona and Beyond* 1-16, 80-141.

compared with the Christian ideas. Apparently Pablo Christiani succeeded in causing confusion among the Jews, and the Christian argumentation to use the Rabbinical documents as supporting the Christian doctrines was regarded by Nahmanides as dangerous – even though today we would evaluate such an approach as perverse and tendentious. Therefore, Nahmanides after the disputation wrote not only his own report on the discussions (*Vikuach*) but also an interpretation of Isaiah 53 as well as an essay on redemption (*Ge'ullah*).

From Nahmanides' point of view the interpretation of Isaiah 53 was not a central issue in Judaism. In *Vikuach* Nahmanides emphasizes the central role of *Halakha* in Judaism. He rebukes Pablo by saying that "the trouble is that you do not understand Halakhic matters; you just know a little about Aggadic matters" (p. 107). Traditionally in Judaism Halakhah and Aggadah have been differentiated. Aggadic material contains more or less homiletical viewpoints which vary in rabbinical documents and indeed are at odds with each other.[66] Therefore, Nahmanides could answer Pablo that he does not believe in certain Aggadah. Nahmanides reported how Pablo "cried out, 'See how he denies the writings of the Jews'" (p. 110), and the Christian account is even more critical and tendentious by stating that "he [= Nahmanides] said publicly that he did not believe in the authorities which were cited against him, although they were in ancient, authoritative books of the Jews, because, as he said, they were sermons, in which their teachers, for

---

[66]See the discussion concerning the relationship of Halakhah and Aggadah in M. Fox, "Nahmanides on the Status of Aggadot: Perspectives on the Disputation at Barcelona, 1263," *JJS* 40 (1989) 95-109; R. Chazan, *Barcelona and Beyond* 142-157; Maccoby, *Judaism on Trial* 44. Nahmanides' attitude toward Aggadot can be compared with his reaction to Maimonidean controversy. In both cases Nahmanides chose a diplomatic stance avoiding unnecessary controversy. That such a "diplomatic insincerity" cannot be overemphasized has rightly been noted by B. Septimus ("'Open Rebuke and Concealed Love': Nahmanides and the Andalusia Tradition," in: I. Twersky [ed], *Rabbi Moses Nachmanides [Ramban]: Explorations in His Religious and Literary Virtuosity* [Cambridge MA: Harvard University Press 1983] 11-34). That all midrashic Aggadot were not regarded as authoritative was well established in the Andalusian tradition – even Rashi had some reservations.

336

the sake of exhorting the people, often lied" (p. 149). Nahmanides explains the role of Jewish books as follows (p. 115):

> Know that we Jews have three kinds of books: the first is the Bible, and we all believe in this with perfect faith; the second is called the Talmud, and it is an explication of the commandments of the Torah, for there are 613 commandments in the Torah, and every single one of them is explicated in the Talmud, and we believe in this explication of the commandments; and we have also a third book which is called the Midrash, which means 'Sermons' ... And as for this book, the Midrash, if anyone wants to believe in it, well and good, but if someone does not believe in it, there is no harm.

We have already in sect. 9 noted that according to Neusner's analysis, the role of the Messiah is not central in the Rabbinical writings. This is exactly the position of Nahmanides, and he formulates this opinion in his *Vikuach*: "The Messiah is not fundamental to our religion" (p. 119). In the same context Nahmanides also describes how he and other Jews had to suffer, and his formulations here indicate that he regards the sufferings of Jews as corresponding to those of the servant in Isaiah 53 (p. 119):

> When I serve (עובד) my Creator in your territory in exile and in affliction and servitude and reproach of the peoples who "reproach us continually", my reward is great[67]. For I am offering a sacrifice (עולה עושה) to God from my body, by which I shall be found more and more worthy of the life of the world to come.

Little later Nahmanides argues that the Christian doctrine is distasteful for every Jew because according to it (p. 120),

> ... the Creator of Heaven and earth resorted to the womb of a certain Jewess and grew there for nine months and was born as an infant, and afterwards grew up and was betrayed into the hands of his enemies who sentenced him to death and executed him, and that afterwards, as you say, he came to life and returned to his original place. The mind of a Jew, or any other person, cannot tolerate

---

[67]Cf., Isa 49:4-5.

this; and you speak your words entirely in vain, for this is the root of our controversy.

The crux of this disputation as far as our study is concerned is the question concerning the sufferings of the Messiah. The Christian account reports this discussion as follows:[68]

> ... he was asked whether the chapter of Isaiah 53, 'Lord, who would have believed ...' (which according to the Hebrews, begins at the end of chapter 52, where it says, 'Behold my servant will understand ...') speaks about the Messiah. He firmly asserted that it does not speak of the Messiah at all, but it was proved to him by many authorities from the Talmud, which speak of the passion of Christ and his death, which they understood of the Christ, and in it the death of Christ and his passion and burial and resurrection are plainly contained. He, however, compelled at length by the authorities, admitted that it is understood and explained in reference to Christ. From this it is plain that the Messiah had to suffer and die.

According to Nahmanides, Pablo Christiani also asked whether he believes that the passage which begins with Isa 52:13 pertains to the Messiah. Nahmanides replied that he interprets the passage as referring to Israel because the servant and Israel are identified in the context of Isa 41:8; 44:1. Pablo went on to report how the Aggadic texts in the Rabbinical literature interpreted Isaiah 53 in terms of the Messiah. When the Christian protocol reports that "it was proved to him [Nahmanides] by many authorities from the Talmud, which speak of the passion of Christ and his death,"[69] the term "Talmud" must be taken as a general

---

[68]See the Christian account in Baer, "The Disputations of R. Yechiel of Paris and of Nachmanides," 172-187 and the English translation in Maccoby, *Judaism on Trial* 147-150.

[69]See Baer's edition of the Latin text in "The Disputations of R. Yechiel of Paris and of Nachmanides" 185-187. The Latin text renders: *probatum fuit ei per multas auctoritates de Thalmut, que loquuntur de passione Christi ac morte.* The titles *Christus* and *Messias* are intimately interconnected in the Christian account, and the better word in this connection would have been *Messias,* but the tendentious Christian document wants to emphasize that rabbinical sources contain witness about Jesus Christ.

338

reference to rabbinical writings and the Targum.[70] Apparently
Nahmanides (and the Jewish party in the disputation) regarded this point
as a dangerous challenge. *Pugio Fidei* which Raymundus Martini
compiled later in 1278 indicates how carefully the Christian party had
read the rabbinical sources. *Pugio Fidei* contains many references to
rabbinical sources whereby it is argued that Isaiah 53 has been interpreted
among Jews in terms of the Messiah.[71] Nahmanides agreed with Pablo
that the messianic interpretation of Isaiah 53 received support from
Aggadic sources:

> It is true that our Teachers, may their memory be for a blessing, in the Aggadic
> books (בספרי ההגדות), interpret the passage of the Messiah.[72]

Nahmanides does not record which passages in the Rabbinical literature
were singled out but seems to refer to passages such as Midrash Ruth.[73]
Nevertheless, Nahmanides vehemently refutes the claim that the
Christian exegesis of Isaiah 53 is supported by rabbinical documents (p.
112-113):

> But they never said that the Messiah would be slain by the hand of his enemies.
> You will never find in any book of the literature of Israel, either in the Talmud
> or the Aggadic books, that the Messiah, son of David, would ever be slain, or
> that he would be betrayed into the hands of his enemies, or that he would be
> buried among the wicked, for even your Messiah, whom you made for

---

See the English translation in Macoby, *Judaism on Trial* 149.

[70]For this see von Mutius, *Die Christlich-Jüdische Zwangsdisputation zu Barcelona* 97-103.

[71]See Raymundi Martini, *Pugio Fidei Adversus Mauros et Judeos cum Observationibus Josephi de Voisin, et Introductione Jo. Benedicti Carpzovi* (Paris 1667) folios 655-679 where the passion of Christ is dealt with.

[72]דורשים אותו על משיח. Maccoby (*Judaism on Trial* 112) adds the word "allegorically" to his translation and this interpretation is based only on the verb *dāraš*.

[73]In Maccoby, *Judaism on Trial* reference is made to *Yalqut Isaiah*, 476 and *Tanhuma Toledot*, 14.

yourselves, was not buried among the wicked. If you like, I will give you an excellent and detailed explanation of the passage in Isaiah. There is nothing there about the Messiah's being slain as happened with your Messiah. But they did not want to hear it.

Here Nahmanides refers to his detailed interpretation of Isaiah 53 which he probably published only after the disputation in order to explain to his fellow Jews what form the Jewish messianic exegesis on Isaiah 53 would take.[74] It is possible that Nahmanides' treatise on Isaiah 53 was written to counter Pablo Christiani's argumentation during the disputation which caused much confusion among Jews. After all, many of them could have followed Rashi's interpretation and now they were reminded that Rabbinical writings allow of a messianic interpretation.

In his own interpretation of Isaiah 53 Nahmanides admits that in the rabbinical tradition (haggada) Isaiah 53 has been explained as referring to the Messiah, even though he prefers the interpretation "Israel" because the context implies that the servant is Israel (reference is made to Isa 41:8 and 49:3):[75]

"Indeed, my servant shall prosper." What is sure in this interpretation is that it refers to Israel in its entirety (הנכון בפרשה הזאת שהיא על ישראל כלו) as in the expression "Fear not, my servant Jacob" or "He said to me: 'You are my servant in whom I glory" and many similar passages. However, according to the view of the midrash that refers to it [Isaiah 53] interprets it in the terms of the Messiah (אבל על דעת המדרש המיחס אותם על משיח), we must interpret it according to those books.

Nahmanides gives a detailed alternative interpretation of Isaiah 53 in terms of the Messiah, but emphasizes that rabbis never taught that the Messiah would be killed (for the sins of the people). This is stated *expressis verbis* at the end of his exegesis:[76]

---

[74]See the Hebrew text in Chavel, *Kitvei Moses ben Nahman* Vol 1:321-326.

[75]See the text in Chavel, *Kitvei Moses ben Nahman* Vol 1:322.

[76]See the translation in Chazan, *Barcelona and Beyond* 161.

והנה לא נזכר בפרשה שינתן בידי שונאיו
ולא שיהרג ולא שיתלה על עץ
אלא שיראה זרע ויאריך ימים
וירום וינשא מלכותו בין הגוים
ומלכים עצומים יהיו לו לשלל

Behold, there is no reference in this passage to that he would be delivered into the hands of those who hate him, nor that he would be killed, nor that he would be crucified on a tree. Rather [the passage states] that he will see offspring and live a long life, that he will be exalted and that his kingdom will be raised among the nations, and that the mighty kings will become his booty.

Nahmanides connects *yaśkîl* in Isa 52:13 with Dan 12:9-10 and interprets the passage as referring to the Messiah who "will understand the end". The heart of the Messiah will be "lofty in the ways of the Lord" (2 Chr 17:6) and this same biblical reference is mentioned even in *Vikuach* when Nahmanides speaks of the Messiah who, according to the famous Midrash, is "higher than Abraham, more exalted than Moses, and loftier than the ministering angels." This midrash was quoted by Pablo Christiani in the disputation. Pablo attempted to use the midrash for Christological purposes. In his interpretation of Isaiah 53 Nahmanides gives a more detailed exegesis of this midrash: "The Messiah will do more than he (Abraham) did; he will proselytize many nations ... he will stir himself up against the kings of the whole world, so as to bring forth Israel from their hands, and to execute vengeance upon the Gentiles ... and wisdom will accompany this elevation of the Messiah, and his nearness to God." Daniel 7 is interpreted by Nahmanides so that the figure of the Son of Man is the Messiah and is obviously also loftier than the angels.

The sufferings of the Servant are explained by Nahmanides psychologically. The key text which illustrates these sufferings is Zech 9:9. The Messiah will appear in the form of a "despised" figure. He is "meek and riding upon an ass" and this will cause mockery among nations and kings (on Isa 52:14). On the other hand, the servant is "pained for the iniquities of Israel, which occasion his tarrying, and hold

him back from becoming king over his people" (on Isa 53:3). The crux
of Nahmanides' interpretation is that he identifies the "we"-group with
Jews. They are sinners who "during their exile apply all their attention to
the business of this world" (on Isa 53:4-6). The Messiah will arouse
repentance among his people.

Isa 53:7 is interpreted by referring to Zech 9:9. The Messiah will
first come "meek and riding upon an ass" and does not cease "to entreat
for Israel, saying to all the kings of the nations: 'Thus says the Lord, let
my people go that they may serve me'." The Messiah is ready to die in
order to fulfil his mission and, therefore, the prophet uses vivid pictures
in Isa 53:8-9 describing the "death" and "burial" of the Messiah. But
Nahmanides insists that these expressions in Isa 53:8-9 do not refer to the
actual death or burial of the Messiah. The sufferings are intended to make
the Messiah complete (on Isa 53:10): "his merit was imperfect, and so all
this befell him in order that it might become complete." Nahmanides
takes the Hebrew words אם תשים in Isa 53:10 as the words of God and
interprets the passage: "If he will only bear all this, and humble himself,
so as not to present complaints or impure thoughts concerning my
attributes (שלא יקרא תגר והרהור אחרי מדותי), I will then give him his
reward, measure for measure, that he may see seed." Nahmanides
probably refers here to the Christian mode of deriving Christological
doctrines from divine attributes – which he mentions at the end of his
Vikuach when he reports his discussion on the Trinity and the divine
attributes. Through his sufferings the Messiah "will accomplish the
redemption in which the Lord finds his pleasure, and will teach all the
gentiles to 'understand and know' the Lord."

Nahmanides' alternative, messianic interpretation of Isaiah 53 follows the
rabbinical tradition and diverges from the messianic interpretation in the
New Testament. In any case the confrontation in Barcelona illustrates
how problematic a passage Isaiah 53 is for the Jewish-Christian
encounter. Nahmanides follows Rashi's interpretation that the servant is

Israel but admits that the messianic interpretation is feasible in a Jewish context but that it must be considered in a specific light.[77]

Conclusions

M. Saebø characterizes the shift of the interpretive tendency of Isaiah 53:[78]

> Thus with an understanding of the servant of God in Deutero-Isaiah there clearly emerges *an interpretative tendency which moves from the individual to the collective* and which may be recognized already in the subsequent editing of the Massoretic text as well as in the oldest textual history of the Servant Songs.

This is indeed correct when we evaluate interpretations from Rashi onwards. However, we have seen that rabbinical writings and diverse interpretations before Rashi have many variations, the messianic understanding of the passage being the most important. The interpretation established by Rashi that the servant in Isaiah 53 is Israel[79] soon became popular in Judaism as evidenced by its acceptance by Ibn Ezra, Radak and Nahmanides.[80] Nevertheless, it is worth noting that even other explanations of Isaiah 53 were considered (the collective interpretation

---

[77]See further Chazan, *Barcelona and Beyond* 158-171, esp. 159. See further Sarachek *Doctrine of the Messiah* 170-171.

[78]M. Saebø, *On the Way to Canon: Creative Tradition History in the Old Testament* (JSOTSS 191, Sheffield: Sheffield Academic Press 1998) 267.

[79]It is worth noting that already Origen bears witness that Jews interpreted the servant in Isaiah 53 as referring to Israel. See sect. 8. In addition, von Mutius (*Die Christlich-Jüdische Zwangsdisputation* 92-96) refers to the recension of Otijot de-Rabbi Akiba where the servant has been interpreted in terms of Israelites who lived in the eschatological endtime.

[80]See the evidence of Israel interpretation in Neubauer & Driver, *The "Suffering Servant" of Isaiah*. See further Rembaum, "The Development of a Jewish Exegetical Tradition."

as noted by Origen; Ibn Ezra: the prophet himself; Radak: Moses; Nahmanides had to examine the messianic interpretation). One reason for the popularity of Rashi's interpretation was apparently the new exegetical method *peshat*, which emphasizes the literary exegesis of the text by considering the context. The context of Isaiah 40-55 mentions several times that the servant of Yhwh is Israel. The most obvious example is Isa 49:3 where this is said *expressis verbis*. Nevertheless, the messianic interpretation was not deprecated in the Jewish reception history of Isaiah 53 (e.g., Zohar).[81] This is the reason why Isaiah 53 even today is a key text in Jewish and Christian encounters.

---

[81]See these interpretations in Driver & Neubauer. In particular, it is worth noting that Rabbi Mosheh el-Sheikh wrote: "I may remark, then, that our Rabbis with one voice accept and affirm the opinion that the prophet is speaking of the King Messiah, and we shall ourselves also adhere to the same view" (p. 258). However, Mosheh el-Sheikh's interpretation considers even other dimensions in Isaiah 53. He, for example, takes up the interpretation that the servant is Moses, referring to b.Sotah 14b (see pp. 269-274).

12 The Christian Interpretation of Isaiah 53 in the Medieval Jewish Sources

Insofar we have seen in sect. 11 that Isaiah 53 was one of the most important Old Testament texts in the Jewish-Christian confrontation. This text has always been significant in Christianity from New Testament times onwards. It is the principal text in the Old Testament which has been considered to prophesy the suffering, the death and the resurrection of Jesus. This is the reason why Isaiah 53 became a key text in medieval disputations and polemical writings between Christianity and Judaism. In this section we shall deal with the medieval Jewish sources which refer to the Christian exegesis of Isaiah 53. The aim is to describe some representative examples of how the Jewish party presented the Christian interpretation, and how these presentations conveyed a biased picture.

Rabbi Jacob ben Reuben

The earliest example of the detailed criticism of the Christian interpretation of Isaiah 53 was presented by Jacob ben Reuben.[1] Almost everything we know about Jacob ben Reuben is that c. 1170 he wrote his *Milchamot Ha-Shem* which subsequently became an influential basic work in Judaism to refute Christian interpretations of the Hebrew Bible.[2] His work provided general arguments against Christian missionary attempts to convert Jews. There are different suggestions concerning the

---

[1]In his commentary on the Book of Isaiah, Abraham ibn Ezra refers briefly to the shortcomings of the Christian interpretation of Isaiah 53 (see sect. 11).

[2]The text has been edited by J. Rosenthal, *Milhamot ha-Shem* (Jerusalem: Mossad ha-Rav Kook 1963).

origin of this work; in southern France or in northern Spain.[3] The study was compiled according to four main topics:

Chap. 1 – philosophical introduction
Chap. 2-10 – refutation of Christian biblical testimonies which were used to argue for their Christological beliefs
Chap. 11 – critical questions around the Gospel of Matthew
Chap 12 – evidence that the Messiah has not yet come

Reuben's work is a dialogue between *meyached* ("the confessor of Unity") and *mekached* ("denier" of this unity). The title of *mekached* referring to the Christian is pejorative, and indicates that he denies the central belief in Judaism: the unity of God (Deut 6:4). Indeed, the writer characterizes the Christian doctrine in harsh terms: "It is known to every rational being that it is futile and pursuit of wind, so much so that the ear cannot hear it nor the eye see it."[4] Robert Chazan has attempted to demonstrate that Jacob ben Reuben would have given a respectful picture of the Christian opponent.[5] This is certainly not the right way to

---

[3]*Milchamot Ha-Shem* pp. 4-5 contains Jacob ben Reuben's own account of his exile in a place the name of which is uncertain. Two possibilities are Huesca, in northern Spain (so, e.g. C. de Valle, "Jacob ben Rubén de Huesca. Polemista. Su patria y su época." In: J. Maier [ed.], *Polémica Judeo-Christiana estudios* [Madrid: Aben Ezra Ediciones 1992] 59-65 [I have not seen the article]; R. Chazan, *Fashioning Jewish Identity in Medieval Western Christendom* [Cambridge: Cambridge University Press 2004] 99; idem, *The Jews of Medieval Western Christendom 1000-1500* [Cambridge: Cambridge University Press 2006] 100), or Gascony (so J. Rosenthal, *Milhamot ha-Shem*, ix). Southern France is suggested also in D. Berger, "Christian Heresy and Jewish Polemics in the 12. and 13. Century," *HTR* 68 (1975) 287-303, esp. 298; J.E. Rembaum, "The Influence of Sefer Nestor Hakomer on Medieval Jewish Polemics." *PAAJR* 45 (1978) 155-185, esp. 165.

[4]*Milchamot Ha-Shem* p. 4. (Chazan's translation)

[5]R. Chazan, "The Christian Position in Jacob Ben Reuben's Milchamot Ha-Shem." in: J. Neusner, E.S. Frerichs, N.M. Sarna (eds), *From Ancient Israel to Modern Judaism. Intellect in quest of understanding. Essays in honor of Marvin Fox. Vol 2: Judaism in the formative age: theology and literature. Judaism in the Middle Ages: the*

characterize Jacob ben Reuben's picture of the Christian antagonist. Even though we do not know what experience Jacob ben Reuben had of Christians and their theology, it can be demonstrated that he misunderstood Christology in many central points and it is hardly possible that such a Christology would have prevailed in the Christianity of France. Jacob ben Reuben struggled against a straw man because he was not trained in Christian theology and was therefore incapable of conveying a true picture of Christology. Similar problems arose among Christian writers who tried to understand Rabbinical writings from their own restricted principles. Nevertheless, it is possible that Jacob ben Reuben discussed Christian doctrinal views with poorly educated Christians who sought from their rationalistic viewpoints to argue for the relevance of Christianity. If this is so then Jacob ben Reuben's polemics may constitute an attempt to formulate Christology in terms which do not corroborate the classical Christian dogma.

 The aim of *Milchamot ha-Shem* was to be a pedagogic aid to Jews to confront the missionary activities undertaken by the Christian Church. *Meyached* characterizes the Christian by means of an allusion to Isa 6:9-10: "... our Creator has glazed his eyes that they not see and his heart that it not understand, so that his soul cleaved to its idolatry and his will and reason worshipped his sticks and stones (לעבוד את עציו ואת אבניו)."[6] Indeed, it is difficult to agree with Chazan who writes: "The relationship between the Christian and the Jew ... involves human warmth and intellectual respect."[7]

---

encounter with Christianity, the encounter with Scripture, philosophy and theology. Atlanta: Scholars Press 1989, 157-170.

[6]*Milchamot Ha-Shem* p. 4-5. (Chazan's translation)

[7]Chazan, "The Christian Position in Jacob Ben Reuben's Milchamot Ha-Shem" 161. It is worth noting that still in 2006 Chazan formulates (*The Jews of Medieval Western Christendom*, 100) the following terms: "The portrayal of Christian argumentation is detailed, and the Christian figure in the dialogue is hardly a straw man, easily dispatched. Rather, the exchanges are protracted, with the Christian defending his position repeatedly and vigorously." A more realistic description of the nature of the

Chazan also emphasizes that Jacob ben Reuben was familiar with the new rationalistic thinking of Anselm and attempted to summarize the essential rational arguments of Christian theology. However, Anselm's theological approach can hardly be defined as "rationalism" because his central formulation was *fides quaerens intellectum* ("faith seeking understanding of itself"). The purpose was not to develop rationalistic arguments in order to create belief, but rather, as Anselm puts it, first comes belief and only then an attempt to understand this belief with rationalistic arguments. Such rationalistic arguments are no longer objective but subjective, although derived from biblical texts and Christian traditions.[8] Indeed, Anselm's argumentation is based on Chalcedonian Christology which, in turn, is rooted in the biblical texts and the Second Temple Jewish understandings of certain key texts in the Hebrew Bible.[9]

---

medieval Jewish (as well as also Christian) polemical texts is given in D. Berger, "Mission to the Jews and Jewish-Christian Contacts in the Polemical Literature of the High Middle Ages," *American Historical Review* 91 (1986) 576-591.

[8] Anselm's *fides quaerens intellectum* should be understood as emphasizing that the Christian belief system has axioms which must be accepted before one can begin to argue rationalistically and make the belief system even more comprehensible.

[9] See J. Pelikan, *Jesus Through the Centuries* (New Haven and London: Yale University Press, 1985). Concerning the development of Christology see A. Grillmeier, *Christ in Christian Tradition Volume One: From the Apostolic Age to Chalcedon (451)* (Atlanta: John Knox 1975). In order to understand the development of Christology in the early Church it is important to grasp that it is rooted in Second Temple Jewish theology. One key text in the Hebrew Bible is the divine Wisdom in Proverbs 8. The relationship of the personified Wisdom to God is difficult to explain as a creation of God. The verb *qānâ* in Prov 8:22 should be interpreted as "acquire." not as "create," because the verb was so used in Proverbs: acquire a wise heart etc. This means that God adopted his divine Wisdom as co-worker before creation. Indeed, it would be difficult to understand that God would have created his personal Wisdom without his own wisdom. Such a mystical connection between God and his Wisdom in Proverbs 8 provides correct theological (mystical not philosophical) language for the first Christians to speculate about Christology. The Book of Wisdom goes on to describe the mysterious beginning of the divine Wisdom (Wisd 7:24-25). Genesis 1 was interpreted in Jewish texts before the Christian era so that the divine Wisdom (called *reshit* in Prov 8) assisted God in creation. The very beginning of Gen 1:1 could be translated "With

Let us now take some examples of how Jacob ben Reuben characterizes Christology in his work. It can be demonstrated that Jacob ben Reuben puts different classical Christological heresies in the mouth of his Christian antagonist, thereby indicating that there are in Jewish medieval criticism tendencies redolent of the Greek rationalistic attacks on Christology in the Early Church. In *Milchamot ha-Shem* pp. 7-8 the Christian antagonist defines the Trinitarian and Christological belief as follows:[10]

---

the Beginning God created the heavens and the earth". Consequently Gen 1:26 was understood so that God spoke with his divine Wisdom when creating the world. The whole Christological discussion was based on this divine mystery between God and his Wisdom. Concerning these early Jewish interpretations see J. Kugel, *Traditions of the Bible. A Guide to the Bible As It Was at the Start of the Common Era* (Cambridge MA.: Harvard University Press 1998) 44-53. I dealt with the problem of Christology in A. Laato, *Monotheism, the Trinity and Mysticism. A Semiotic Approach to Jewish-Christian Encounter* (Frankfurt am Main: Peter Lang 1999); "Interpreting the Hebrew Bible with Different Hermeneutical Models," in: S.-O. Back & M. Kankaanniemi (eds), *Voces Clamantium in Deserto: Essays in Honor of Kari Syreeni* (Studier I exegetik och judaistik utgivna av Teologiska fakulteten vid Åbo Akademi 11; Åbo: Åbo Akademi University 2012) 163-183, and in a Finnish study *Emmauksen tiellä. Miten ensimmäiset kristityt selittivät Vanhaa testamenttia* [On the Way to Emmaus. How the First Christians Interpreted the Old Testament] (Åbo: Åbo Akademi 2006) 26-80. The early Rabbinic theology did not developed the Second Temple Jewish concept of the divine Wisdom but rather opposed all forms of theology which came close to the idea of the two powers in heaven. For this see A. Segal, *Two Powers in Heaven. Early rabbinic reports about Christianity and Gnosticism* (Leiden: Brill 1977). This being the case, the real nature of Christology must always be related to these Second Temple Jewish theological concepts. When the Christological formulations were presented in philosophical language, the result was a paradox which emphasizes the above mentioned Jewish mystical language from the Second Temple period. This being the case the first Christian apologetics used formulations and images which appear in Proverbs 8 and Wisdom 7-9 such as "light from light" or "fire from fire" indicating how God (as substance) can appear in different persons. The early rabbinic literature did not adopt such mystical language while avoiding reference to two powers in heaven.

[10]Chazan deals with this text on p. 162 and characterizes the text as follows: "The Jewish author allows his Christian antagonist to emerge as a man of religious sensitivity and intelligence, with whose views to be sure the Jewish author disagrees." I disagree with Chazan.

I believe and acknowledge concerning him that he created (הוא היוצר) everything from nothing and was created (נוצר) for the redemption of his creatures at the time of his choosing. He created (הוא הבורא) all that has been created and was created (ונברא) in the form of flesh at the proper time as one of us, in order to save his creatures from descending to Hell, but not for his own sake, for he is in need of nothing ... ... I know that he brings into being and was brought into being (הוא המוליד והוא הנולד), that he is the father and the son, that he is the one who is designated by two and they became three[11], that trinity does not disrupt unity, and that unity does not contradict trinity ... ... I shall show you these things through the understanding of the intellect, for every man of understanding must believe truly in the worship of the Trinity. I shall bring you proofs from created things, so that you understand through them the greatness of the Creator. Through his wonders you shall comprehend and know some of his majesty.

In some points Jacob ben Reuben succeeded in formulating the classical Christology. For example "he brings into being and was brought into being (הוא המוליד והוא הנולד)" can be understood aright ("being born in flesh" against the unorthodox formulation "being created"). Another expression concerns the origin of the Holy Spirit from Father and Son: "he is the one who is designated by two and they became three" which follows the famous Western *filioque* addition and sounds correct in 12th century Western Europe. But there are many other instances where Jacob ben Reuben's formulations do not follow classical Christological statements from Nicea (325), Constantinople (381) and Chalcedon (451). The following details can be discerned:

1. The Christian speaks about Father and Son as one divine person. This being the case, Jacob ben Reuben allows the Christian to speak about God that he "created all that has been created and was created (נברא) in

---

[11]Chazan translates here "that he is the one who is designated as two and became three." The Hebrew expression שהוא האחד הנקרא בשם שנים והיו שנים והיו שלשה is an expression of how the Holy Spirit will be sent or designated by Father and Son.

the form of flesh." Later in *Milchamot ha-Shem* 154 Jacob ben Reuben articulates this idea more precisely:[12]

> You have said that God is one and this your messiah is His son who descended from heaven without separation from (בלי פירוד מן) the Father and Holy Spirit. In this son there were two natures (שני נהוגין)[13], the divine nature and the human nature, which were never separated. Now, when you say that the substance of the Son (קנין הבן)[14] descended to Mary's womb, tell me if the Father and Spirit attached themselves to him [in that descent], or he alone attached himself to her. If you say only the Son and Spirit attached themselves, then your statement that there are [two] natures in one substance[15], a divine nature and a human nature, is false because the nature of the Father is not at all in him. Now, if you say the messiah was of the substance of the Father, Son and Holy Spirit, part adhering and part not adhering, your words, i.e. that one part did not separate from another part, are false.

The passage indicates that the incarnation should concern the whole divinity. The argument is based on the philosophical monotheism that God is truly unified. As Rosenthal and Lasker observe, this argument was first proposed by Nestor Ha-Komer.[16] The argument does not consider the fact that the challenge of philosophical monotheism was met in the

---

[12]This text of Jacob ben Reuben and other parallels in Jewish polemics against Christianity are analyzed in D.J. Lasker, *Jewish Philosophical Polemics against Christianity in the Middle Ages* (New York: Ktav Publishing House 1977) 121-125.

[13]The word *nihug* – which usually means "custom" – is probably an unusual translation from the Arabic *ḍimar* ("nature"). Concerning this see D.J. Lasker & Sarah Stroumsa, *The Polemic of Nestor the Priest. Qissat Mujādalat al-Usquf and Sefer Nestor Ha-Komer*. Volume 1 (Jerusalem: Ben-Zvi Institute for the Study of Jewish Communities in the East 1996) 30.

[14]It may be surprising that the Hebrew word *qinyan* ("purchase, property, affirmation") has been used to denote substance. The reason is that the Arabic word *uqnūm* means person or hypostasis, but not substance. For this see Lasker, *Jewish Philosophical Polemics against Christianity* 216 n. 286; Lasker & Stroumsa, *The Polemic of Nestor the Priest Volumes 1* 30.

[15]נהוגים בקנין אחד.

[16]See the text in Lasker & Stroumsa, *The Polemic of Nestor the Priest*.

Christian Church during the first four centuries when Christology was developed. *First*, there is no distinction between "substance" and divine personae. The argument presented here implies that the whole Trinity would have been incarnate. However, in classical Christology there is a formulation that Father and Son are two distinct divine persons but *homousios* as far as substance (*ousia*) is concerned (the Nicene Creed). Thus we read in the Athanasian Creed: "neither confounding the Persons, nor dividing the Substance" and later "For like as we are compelled by the Christian verity to acknowledge every Person by Himself to be both God and Lord, so we are forbidden by the Catholic Religion, to say, there be three Gods, or three Lords." *Second*, according to Jacob ben Reuben, the substance and nature would be related to each other in a straightforward manner which is not typical of Christology. The Chalcedonian Christology speaks of the incarnation of the Son of God and his two natures which, however, remain distinct. The Chalcedonian Christology makes this important doctrinal statement in very sophisticated terms:

> Therefore, following the holy fathers, we all with one accord teach men to acknowledge one and the same Son, our Lord Jesus Christ, at once complete in Godhead and complete in manhood, truly God and truly man, consisting also of a reasonable soul and body, of one substance with the Father as regards his Godhead, and at the same time of one substance with us as regards his manhood; like us in all respects, apart from his sin; as regards his Godhead, begotten of the Father before the ages, but yet as regards his manhood begotten, for us men and for our salvation, of Mary the Virgin, the God-bearer; one and the same Christ, Son, Lord, Only-begotten, recognized in two natures, without confusion, without change, without division, without separation; the distinction of natures being in no way annulled by the union, but rather the characteristics of each nature being preserved and coming together to form one person and subsistence (*hypostasis*), not as parted or separated into two persons, but one and the same Son and Only-begotten God the Word, Lord Jesus Christ; even as the prophets from earliest times spoke of him, and our Lord Jesus Christ himself taught us, and the creed of the Fathers has handed down to us.

2. In the light of classical Christology the incarnation was not presented in terms of creation like the formulations used by Jacob ben Reuben in *Milchamot ha-Shem*: "was created in the form of flesh" and "was brought into being." The incarnation was formulated with the idea of "being born." Thus in the Athanasian Creed we read: "God, of the substance of the Father, begotten before the worlds; and Man, of the Substance of His Mother, born in the world" and "Who, although He be God and Man, yet He is not two, but one Christ; One, not by conversion of the Godhead into flesh, but by taking of the Manhood into God; One altogether; not by confusion of Substance, but by unity of Person."

It seems clear that Jacob ben Reuben makes his Christian antagonist formulate the incarnation in unchristian terms and then argues that it is ridiculous. Indeed, the Jewish partner in this dialogue comments as follows on the Christian doctrine of incarnation: "All the philosophers and men of reason ridicule you and ask concerning this [incarnation]. If the Creator, may he be blessed, was created [notice the same misunderstanding as above], tell me if he was created prior to his existence or subsequent to his existence?"[17] The real problem for Jacob ben Reuben is that he cannot understand the mystic background of Christology but attempts to comprehend it as a part of the discourse of philosophical monotheism.[18]

In this context it is also meaningful to consider the statement of the Jewish protagonist in *Milchamot ha-Shem* p. 9 who discusses the title "Son". He asks whether this title can be used of the Son before creation (אם נקרא בן קודם שנולד) and regards it as impossible. Nevertheless, classical Christology was based on the Old Testament texts where the pre-existence of the divine Wisdom or the Son of Man is presented (also

---

[17]*Milchamot ha-Shem* pp. 8-9 (Chazan's translation).

[18]We may even ask whether the idea of philosophical monotheism adopted in Islam and Judaism as a tool to understand their religious monotheism did justice to the essence of Judaism and Islam. Cf., P. Lapide & J. Moltmann, *Jüdischer Monotheismus – Christliche Trinitätslehre: Ein Gespräch* (Munich: Chr. Kaiser 1979).

called the Son of God in 4Q246 or identified with the Son of God in Psalm 2, in 1 Henoch, or 4 Ezra).

3. The Christian antagonist stipulates, according to Jacob ben Reuben, that God "is the father and the son, that he is the one who is designated by two and became three, that trinity does not disrupt unity, and that unity does not contradict trinity." This formulation is reminiscent of the Athanasian Creed which states: "And yet they are not three eternals, but one eternal. As also there are not three incomprehensibles, nor three uncreated, but one uncreated, and one incomprehensible." But even in that case it is essential to emphasize that the Creed distinguishes between person and substance: "For there is one Person of the Father, another of the Son, and another of the Holy Ghost. But the Godhead of the Father, of the Son, and of the Holy Ghost, is all one, the Glory equal, the Majesty co-eternal." In a similar way the Creed uses biblical ideas, e.g. that the Son emanates from Father as Wisdom from God in Proverbs 8 and Wisdom 7-9: " The Father is made of none, neither created, nor begotten. The Son is of the Father alone, not made, nor created, but begotten. The Holy Ghost is of the Father [and of the Son], neither made, nor created, nor begotten, but proceeding."

4. Finally, it is difficult to accept the Christian antagonist's emphasis as representing the classical Christian position when he argues that the mystery of the Trinity can be proved by rationalistic arguments: "I shall show you these things through the understanding of the intellect, for every man of understanding must believe truly in the worship of the Trinity." As stated above such argumentation did not represent Anselm's position either. Nevertheless, we must consider the possibility that the Christian discussion partners of Jacob ben Reuben may have attempted to present their position with such a philosophical approach.

In *Milchamot ha-Shem* pp. 12-13 Jacob ben Reuben allows his Jewish protagonist to formulate the following criticism of the Christian idea of the need for incarnation:

> Subsequent to creation, when all was created according to his will, how could one of his creatures bring him to the point of control, so that he could not save the rest of his creatures from his [Satan's] hands until he was born like one of us and turned himself over to him [Satan] on our behalf, so that he was crucified and they were saved? Indeed we have not even seen this salvation. For in the very same way that Satan killed the created beings, similarly he still kills them.

In fact the Jewish protagonist poses questions similar to those of Boso in Anselm's *Cur Deus homo* I:5.[19] Boso presents the following question to Anselm: "If this deliverance were said to be effected somehow by any other being than God (whether it were an angelic or a human being), the mind of man would receive it far more patiently. For God could have made some man without sin, not of a sinful substance, and not a descendant of any man, but just as he made Adam, and by this man it should seem that the work we speak of could have been done." Anselm answers that only God can save human beings but this must take place in earthly life, so that the incarnation is the only possibility.

There is an interesting possibility that the Christian antagonist in *Milchamot ha-Shem* may be Petrus Alfonsi who converted to Christianity in 1106 in Huesca and wrote his important work "Dialogue against the Jews". As noted above, it may well be that Jacob ben Reuben was also from Huesca and, therefore, probably knew Alfonsi's work. Alfonsi represents the so-called "attributist Trinitarian" doctrine, i.e. that the Trinity can be explained by adducing divine attributes. This Christology originates in the Eastern Church where the persons correspond to "essence" (= Father), "wisdom" (= Son) and "life" (= the Holy Spirit). It

---

[19]We remarked above that according to Chazan, Jacob ben Reuben probably knew Anselm's works perhaps even *Cur Deus Homo?* If so, he seemed to have accepted the opinion of Boso.

is clear that such Christology could have been presented in a way which would have been an easy target for the Jewish counterarguments. For example, in his version of the Barcelona disputation (*Vikuach*) Nahmanides allows Pablo Christiani to present Trinity as "Wisdom, will and power". Nahmanides argues that God has attributes and it is even possible to find more than three attributes so that it could be feasible to speak of Quaternity etc.[20] We can ask whether Nahmanides' account gives correct picture in this point. The classical attributist Christology would never speak of the Trinity without the divine "essence" or "substance". Therefore, even the Jewish convert Alfonsi explains the mystery of incarnation by comparing it with fire which is one substance but possesses both heat and light. Heat and light can exist without fire but fire never without heat and light. Therefore, the incarnation of the Son of God is possible without the incarnation of the whole Trinity.[21]

These preliminary remarks show that Jacob ben Reuben has a philosophic approach to the Christian doctrines and that, in fact, he allows his Christian antagonist to articulate several classical Christological heresies. Therefore, it is no wonder if similar anomalies also appear in Jacob ben Reuben's description of the Christian interpretation of Isaiah 53. According to Jacob ben Reuben, the Christian antagonist interprets Isaiah 53 as follows:

---

[20]See Nahmanides' account in Chaim Chavel (ed.), *Kitvei Rabbenu Moshe ben Nachman* (Two Volumes Jerusalem: Mossad Harav Kook 1971) Vol 1:302-320. A good translation can be found in H. Maccoby, *Judaism on Trial*. London: Associated University Press 1982, 97-146. See further R. Chazan, *Barcelona and Beyond. The Disputation of 1263 and Its Aftermath*. Berkeley: University of California Press 1992.

[21]See I.M. Resnick, *Petrus Alfonsi. Dialogue against the Jews*. (The Fathers of the Church. Mediaeval Continuation. Washington: The Catholic University of America Press 2006) 33-35, 185-195. The original Latin text is in J.P. Migne (ed.), *Patrologiae cursus completus series latina* Vol 157 (Paris 1844-64). See further B.P. Hurwitz, *Fidei Causa et Tui Amore: The Role of Petrus Aphonsi's Dialogues in the History of Jewish-Christian Debate* (Diss. Yale University 1983) esp. 56-69.

Isa 52:13-53:12. You have in these verses, from their first letter to their last, a proof as clear and patent as noon-day that what we assert concerning our Messiah is incontrovertible; there is no need then to say more, and explain how each separate verse reveals some mystery in his life, and declares plainly all the principal actions which he accomplished, or how not a single word fell to the ground of all the testimony which the prophet here presents.

This description does not give us a complete picture of how Isaiah 53 was interpreted by the denier of monotheism, but it reveals that in 12th century Christianity every detail in Isaiah 53 was regarded as fitting the life, death and resurrection of Jesus Christ. Indeed, when we read Petrus Alfonsi's "Dialogue Against the Jews", chapter 9 we find a detailed Christian interpretation of Isaiah 53. It is worth noting that Alfonsi's work was very influential and many copies have been preserved, indicating its popularity in Jewish-Christian dialogue. Therefore, it seems plausible that Jewish opponents knew this work or at least were familiar with its basic arguments which Christians adduced in debates. Alfonsi gives the following correspondences between Isaiah 53 and the life of Jesus Christ:[22]

Behold, my servant will understand, he will be exalted and extolled, and he will be especially high.
> Christ "was the servant of God and one of great understanding, and he was exalted and raised especially high over all the servants of God. His works were wondrous and stupendous, and he was never interested in glory."

As many have been astonished at you, so shall his visage be inglorious among men and his form among the sons of men ... He will sprinkle many nations.

---

[22]The translation of the following synopsis is from Resnick's translation (pp. 208-214). Alfonsi makes it clear that the text he interprets is the translation of the Vulgate, i.e. "Variant translation of the blessed Jerome".

The Lord Christ rained a great rain on the Israelite nation "when he came among them just as among his own and showed them his works and his mighty deeds. He sprinkled many other nations, however, when he watered them from afar, not with the presence of signs but with their hearing and report just as if with a dew, and he rendered all their foolish ones silent with wonder."

Kings will shut their mouth at him, for what was not told to them, they have seen; and what they have not heard, they have beheld.

"As it was told to the Jews about him, and they heard."

Who has believed our report? And to whom is the arm of the Lord revealed?

The things "will come to pass are so amazing, it will be difficult for anyone to judge that they should be believed – namely, that the arm of the Lord has to be revealed, that is, that his son has to be made incarnate and in this way visibly revealed to the world through the flesh that has been assumed."

And he will grow up just like a tender plant before him, and as a root out of thirsty ground.

"We see that from a thirsty ground ... neither a rod nor a root can be generated without moisture. For moisture is like the very sun's masculine sex. Christ, however, grew up like a root or a tender plant before the Lord from the dry earth, when God the Father begot him from the flesh of a virgin without a union with a man."

There is no beauty in him, nor comeliness, and we have seen him, there was no slightness in him, and we have desired him to be despised, the most strange of men.

"... to display his humility and contempt for worldly pomp."

A man of sorrows.

"... he was not free from the snares of the malevolent in infancy, or in childhood or adolescence, nor from hardship, so that it was of great report and well known that he is 'acquainted with infirmity'. For here by that 'infirmity' the prophet wanted nothing else to be understood than the afflictions and hardships that Christ endured in the world according to the flesh."

His look was, as it were, hidden and despised, whereupon we esteemed him not.

"The look of Christ, howver, was hidden, as it were, because the splendor of divinity hid itself under his flesh, and he was unwilling to resist those assailing him (although he could have), which is why he was despised and not esteemed."

Surely he has borne our infirmities and carried our sorrows.

"He himself endured the sorrows and punishments which were due our crimes."

And we have thought him, as it were, wounded and as one struck by God and afflicted.

"We thought that the blow, that is, that scourge and that striking and that beating, befell him on his own account, but this was never the case."

But he himself was wounded for our iniquities; he was bruised for our sins. The chastisement of our peace was upon him.

"He himself – as one compassionate and kind – sustained on our behalf the chastisement and correction that we had to suffer to have peace."

By his bruises we are healed.

"The bruises of the flails and of the wounds which he bore for us."

All we like sheep have gone astray, every one has turned aside into his own way.

"Sheep ... are simple, and the most senseless and wandering animals. And we erred just like senseless sheep, because we did not know him, who or what he was ... "Hardly anyone believed his teaching, but each one stayed on his old path."

And the Lord has placed upon him the iniquity of us all.

"The Lord forgives and washes away through him (that is, through the baptism that he gave) the original sin in which all are entangled."

He was oppressed and afflicted, and he did not open his mouth. He will be led like a sheep to the slaughter, and he will be silent as a lamb before his shearer, and he will not open his mouth.

"None of this needs an explanation; rather it is clear to all. For Christ, when he was led before Pilate and falsely accused, even beaten and cut with blows, remained silent before Pilate himself, who was interrogating him with several questions, and hardly replied with any word at all."

He was taken away from distress and judgment.

"... is said through 'endiadis', for he said 'from distress' and 'judgment' for 'from a distressed judgment.' And, certainly, we call a distressed judgment an unjust judgment. Assuredly, Christ was taken away from a distressed judgment, that is, he was seized because of a distressed and unjust judgment, although he had committed no crime."

Who shall declare his generation?

"Certainly he pronounced this with respect to his divine generation, which is indescribable and ineffable, and by this he revealed that he would be God."

He is cut off from the land of the living. For the wickedness of my people he was struck.

"... is the same as what he said above 'he himself was wounded for our iniquities'; 'he was bruised for our sins'."

And he shared his grave with the ungodly and his death with the rich.

"'With the ungodly' and 'with the rich' means one and the same thing. For certainly the rich of this world are almost all ungodly. There was, however, a custom among the Jews that the ungodly and those killed for their crime be buried apart from the community of other human beings. And Christ was crucified and died with the ungodly, that is, with thieves, and he was buried outside a common graveyard, although he committed no iniquitous deed and there was no deceit in his mouth."

The Lord was pleased to bruise him and to weaken him.

The Lord willed it so that is, to make him suffer.

If he lays down his soul for sin, he will see a seed.

"We know that in fact in ancient times Scriptures called a sacrifice that was performed for sin by the name of sin. This is why here, too, the prophet said: If, Lord, you will lay down his soul (that is, Christ's soul) for sin, that is, as sin's sacrifice. That is: if he will be sacrificed for our sin, he will see a seed, that is, he will have a great seed and many heirs. And through the sacrifice of his body and his death Christ saw a great seed and had many heirs, and time was extended, and the will of the Lord was fulfilled in him."

Because of the labor of his soul he will see and be filled.

"His soul will labor so much that it will be filled when it sees that labor, because it is so much; that is, it will appear to be too much ... Christ bore too many distresses and labors."

By his knowledge the just one will justify many.

"Through his knowledge the Lord, who is just one, will reveal him to many to be just. Christ, however, was just, and the Lord reveals him to many to be just."

He has carried their iniquities.

"... is the same as what he said above – 'Surely he has borne our infirmities and carried our sorrows'."

Therefore, said the Lord, I will make him to participate in many, and he will divide the spoils with the strong.

"And Christ participated in many because numerous people from among many nations believed in him. And he divided the spoils with the strong because, having divided the booty, as it were, he carried his portion away from the princes of hell, who had despoiled this world, when he snatched from there those who believed that he was the one who would come."

Because he has handed his soul over to death.
"Clearly this recalls the reason why he participated in many, namely, that for the world's redemption he endured death, owing to his exceedingly great piety."
And he was counted with the wicked.
"And just as we described, Christ was reckoned with the wicked because he was hung with thieves."
And he has borne the sins of many...
"... but not the sins of all, because he saved many but not all."
And he has prayed for the transgressors.
"Christ, however, prayed for the transgressors when he prayed for those who were crucifying him saying: 'Father, forgive them, for they know not what they do'."

Alfonsi ends his interpretation with an exhortation to his "alter ego" Moses: "Therefore, O Moses, both the time and all the other things that the prophets predicted concerning the Christ appeared in both word and deed in the one whom we believe him to have been. It is clear that in truth he has already come, and you should have no further doubt concerning this any longer."

This outline of Alfonsi's interpretation contains several emphases that Isaiah 53 is a clear-cut prophecy about the life, death and resurrection of Jesus Christ. Alfonsi characterizes Isaiah 53 to Moses as follows: "The hardness of your heart and that of those like you is not something new. Neither did you believe, moreover, when the prophets addressed you openly and without allegory, which is why it is not surprising that the words of my explanation seem absurd to you. Nevertheless, in order to cut short all your pretexts and objections, let me now show you the one extremely clear authority from Isaiah himself." In the light of Alfonsi's detailed interpretation and emphasis that Isaiah 53 is clear evidence about Jesus Christ it is well possible that Jacob ben Reuben knew a similar Christian argument concerning Isaiah 53 if not Alfonsi's own work.

After presenting a general description of Christian interpretation, Jacob ben Reuben mentions five problems to which the denier's viewpoints give rise.[23] The *first* (and also the *third*) problem concern the tension between this passage, Isaiah 53, and other texts which the denier applied to Jesus. While Isaiah 53 is adduced to testify that "his countenance and form are 'marred', or that he is despised and forlorn of men," another Christian proof text such as Ps 45:3 where "the Psalmists speaks of him as 'beautiful'" contradicts Isaiah 53.[24] This connection between Psalm 45 and Isaiah 53 is a common theme in patristic literature as we saw in sect. 8. And it is easy to perceive that Jacob ben Reuben's argument here is biased because the Christian writers used Isaiah 53 to describe Jesus in his *Via Dolorosa* at the same time as they maintained that Jesus was the Son of God and had a beauty of his own. Jacob ben Reuben later takes up the *third* problem where he states that expressions in Isaiah 53, "despised and forlorn of men", "man of pains and known of sickness", could be used only of the man "who suffered from severe sickness continually". Jacob ben Reuben who had also studied the New Testament emphasizes that no reference to such chronic sickness can be found.[25]

---

[23]See the English translation in A. Neubauer & S. Driver, *The "Suffering Servant" of Isaiah According to the Jewish Interpreters Translated by S.R. Driver and A. Neubauer* (Eugene: Wipf and Stock 1999) 57-60.

[24]Jacob ben Reuben also mentions that Christians used Jer 11:16 as a prophecy about Jesus.

[25]It is worth noting that the Jewish sages in Spain probably knew different polemical anti-Christian texts where the selections of the passages of the Gospels are criticized. One good example is the old Judeo-Arabic text *Qiṣṣat Mujādalat al-Usquf* (The Account of the Disputation of the Priest) which was later translated and revised into the Hebrew text *Sefer Nestor Ha-Komer* (The Book of Nestor the Priest) in Spain. This work contains many translations from the Christian Gospels and their polemical evaluations. See Lasker & Stroumsa, *The Polemic of Nestor the Priest*. Institute for the Study of Jewish Communities in the East 1996. It is worth noting that Jacob ben Reuben knew Nestor Ha-Komer since he gives a summary in his *Milchamot Ha-Shem* (p. 154) as far as the main problem in Christianity is concerned: "The following question is the question of Nestor the Priest before he returned to the Lord our God. He became

364

The *second* interpretive problem of the Christian understanding of Isaiah 53 concerns a Christological doctrine. The (Christian) denier "asserts that this your Messiah is God, and that all the essence of the Godhead resides in him (וכל ענין אלהות בו)". As already postulated, for example, Alfonsi's attributist Christology clearly emphasizes that it is impossible that "all the essence of the Godhead resides in him". After conveying an apparently erroneous picture of Christology, the Jewish protagonist poses a critical question to his Christian opponent concerning the claim that the Servant will be "exalted, lifted up, and lofty exceedingly":

> Who supposes that God could first of all be in a state of depression, affliction, and disfigurement, out of which he would afterwards raise himself, and be exalted above those who knew him?

Jacob ben Reuben's statement recalls the Christological heresy of Paul of Samosata according to whom Christ was consubstantial with the Father but not a distinct person in the Godhead. Therefore Jesus could be identified with God. The Godhead is present in Jesus just as human reason exists in a man. Such a Christological statement was condemned by the Christian Church, mainly because it does not take account of the *kenosis* theology of Philippians 2:6-11. As noted in sect. 8, the Church Fathers often interpreted Isaiah 53 in conjunction with Philippians 2:6-11.

The *fourth* problem in the Christian understanding of Isaiah 53 is that the Messiah who is God "was smitten by God". The Jewish protagonist asks: "God smites him and he is smitten by God: how then can it be said that he is himself God?". Again we encounter the problem of how the Jewish polemicist confronts a Christological statement which is not based on philosophical monotheism.

---

converted to Judaism because of this [question] ..." The question concerns the Christian explanation that God is One but nevertheless has a Son and even the Holy Spirit. See further D.J. Lasker, "Jewish-Christian Polemics in Transition: From the Lands of Ishmael to the Lands of Edom," in: B. Hary, J. Hayes & F. Astren (eds) *Judaism and Islam: Boundaries, Interaction, and Communication* (Leiden: Brill 2000) 53-65.

The *fifth* problem in Christian interpretation concerns the grammatical problem in Isa 53:8: the form in *lamô* is plural: "there was a stroke for them" indicating that the reference pertains to the people of Israel. This last argument is free from subjective evaluations of Christian doctrinal statements. In a corresponding way Jacob ben Reuben continues to maintain that the context of Isaiah 53 indicates that Israel is often referred to as "my servant".

Rabbi Joseph ben Nathan

In the mid-13th century, the members of the family of Nathan Official defended Judaism in mandatory disputations arranged by the Christian authorities. We are aware of many of these disputations because of the writings of the son of Nathan, Rabbi Joseph ben Natan.[26] His book *Yosef ha-Meqanne*, Joseph the Zealot, (also known as *Sefer ha-Nizzahon* which is a different work from *Nizzahon Vetus* edited by D. Berger or Yom-Tov Lipmann's *Nizzahon*) is the polemic which contains his father's arguments against Christianity. The book is arranged according to the order of the Hebrew Bible. The Christological arguments in each passage are first presented and then refuted.[27] Joseph ben Nathan also wrote an account of the famous Paris disputation in 1240.[28]

The interpretation of Isaiah 53 is one of the central biblical passages in *Yosef ha-Meqanne*. The Christian arguments are presented in

---

[26]See S. Krauss & W. Horbury, *The Jewish-Christian Controversy from the Earliest Times to 1789 Volume 1: History* (Tübingen: Mohr Siebeck 1995) 150-153.

[27]The text has been edited by J.M. Rosenthal, *Joseph ben Nathan Official, Sepher Joseph Hamekane* (Jerusalem: Mossad Harav Kook 1970).

[28]See Maccoby, *Judaism on Trial* 20-21. The text itself is very polemical – something which corresponds well to the nickname of Joseph ben Nathan: "the Zealous". Indeed, the text is difficult to translate into English because of its different literary devices. See the text in R. Margulies (ed.), *Sefer Wikuach Rabbenu Jehiel mi-Paris* (Lwow 1928) and its English paraphrase in Maccoby, *Judaism on Trial* 153-162.

detail and then refuted.[29] Joseph ben Nathan does not describe the Christian interpretation in detail, but rather concentrates on various broader lines of the Christian exegesis which together show the weaknesses of this "heretic" opinion.

1) Joseph ben Nathan begins his report by stating that "this Parashah is applied by the heretics to the Nazarene" and then goes on to tell the following story:

> A very learned apostate (מְשׁוּמָד) came once into the presence of the great R. Yoseph BeKhor-Shor: "How", he asked, "can you meet the evidence of this Parashah?" He replied, "O fool, your ears will hear that which you utter from your mouth: 'See, my servant will prosper'. The prophet calls him his 'servant', but if he is God, how could he be termed a servant?" At once the apostate rent his clothes and rolled himself in ashes and repented [of his apostasy].

The story is very illustrative and points to the simplicity of the argument which favors the Jewish interpretation of the passage in contrast to the Christian understanding. There is indirect reference to the incompatibility of the Christological statements that Jesus from Nazareth is God, yet can also be called the Servant of God.

2) In the second aspect of the Christian interpretation the passage reports the new acts of God which "had not been told them" previously:

> Then he speaks of their having seen what "had not been told them", i.e. the wondrous and mighty acts of the Deity; but do they possess no record of the Creation as told in Genesis, and of what God did to the generation of the deluge, and to the generation of the dispersion, to Pharaoh and the kings of

---

[29]Rosenthal, *Joseph ben Nathan Official, Sepher Joseph Hamekane* 79-82. The text is also given in A. Neubauer *The Fifty-Third Chapter of Isaiah According to the Jewish Interpreters. I: Texts* (Varda Books 2005) Vol 1:68-71; its translation is in A. Neubauer & S. Driver, *The "Suffering Servant" of Isaiah According to the Jewish Interpreters Translated by S.R. Driver and A. Neubauer* (Eugene: Wipf and Stock 1999) vol 2: 71-74.

Canaan, and the cleaving of the Reed Sea, and all the miracles and mighty acts which were achieved before the birth of the Nazarene?

This refers to the Christian idea presented in Alfonsi's interpretation, inter alia, according to which the passage describes the incarnation, sufferings, death and resurrection of Jesus Christ which were seen as being a surprise to Jews. Joseph ben Nathan turns this attempt to explain the passage into a question of whether the passage refers to the records of the Hebrew Bible concerning the creation, the flood, the exodus, the settlement etc. which took place long before the time of Jesus. Again Joseph ben Nathan does not directly attack any Christian doctrine but simply tries to show his fellow Jews how the passage could be otherwise understood. It pertains to God's salvation historical events in the Hebrew Bible and not to the new message about the crucified Messiah.

3) According to Joseph ben Nathan the expression מפשע עמי נגע למו was interpreted by the Christians as referring to the atonement of the sins committed by Adam and Eve:

> But did he meet death for any other cause but in order to wipe out the sin of our forefathers in having eaten of the tree of knowledge, for which all were going down into Gehenna? This being so, however, he ought rather to have written: 'For the transgression of Adam and Eve was he stricken' (מפשע אדם והוה נגע למו).

This description of the Christian interpretation of Isaiah 53 receives support from Alfonsi's text quoted above. Alfonsi observes that "for the wickedness of my people he was struck" has the same meaning as Isa 53:4-5, according to which the Servant "was wounded for our iniquities". The interpretation of the passage "the Lord has placed upon him the iniquity of us all" in Alfonsi's text is as follows: "The Lord forgives and washes away through him ... the original sin in which all are entangled." This being the case, the Jewish argument against the Christian view that Isaiah 53 pertains to the story of Genesis 3 seems historically valid.

368

It is also worth noting that Joseph ben Nathan seems to accept the view that, grammatically, למו can be read in the singular as referring to an individual because he formulates 'For the transgression of Adam and Eve was he (the Servant Jesus) stricken'. This does not mean that Joseph ben Nathan did not know that למו should be read in the plural. After all, he later explains the passage and there writes that it concerns the righteous ones: "... because of the transgression of my people this stroke was upon the just amongst them" (מפשע עמי הנגע הזה לצדיקים שלהם). It is not typical of Jewish writers to accept a singular reading for למו. We have seen that, for example, Abraham ibn Ezra writes *expressis verbis* that למו should read in the plural: בעבור מלת למו שהוא כמו להם, "As far as the word למו is concerned it should be read as להם."[30] A similar view is presented also by Rashi (see sect. 11).

4) The fourth point of the Christian interpretation to be considered by Joseph ben Nathan concerns the application of the passage "although he did no violence" to Jesus who, according to the heretic view, is regarded as God. Joseph ben Nathan asks ironically: "but if he is God, towards whom could he behave violently? Do not all belong to God? 'God is judge: he sets down one and raises up another' (Ps 75:8)."

Joseph ben Nathan gives a more or less accurate picture of the Christian interpretation of Isaiah 53 which he criticizes from his own Jewish viewpoints. There is no attempt to formulate complicated Christological statements and then criticize them as does Jacob ben Reuben. Rather, Joseph ben Nathan demonstrates to his Jewish readers that the overall Christian interpretation of Isaiah 53 makes no sense. There are accurate formulations of Christian interpretation which follow the views of Petrus Alfonsi.

---

[30]See M. Friedländer (ed), *The Commentary of Ibn Ezra on Isaiah* (New York: Philipp Feldheim, First Edition: 1873) 244. The Hebrew text can be found at the end of this volume from p. 92.

Nizzahon Vetus

This work is called *Nizzahon Vetus* (ie., "old", *Yashan*) in order to distinguish it from Yom-Tov Lipmann Mühlhausen's work which bears the same name *Nizzahon*.[31] *Nizzahon Vetus* was compiled in late 13th or early 14th century Germany but incorporates many anti-Christian traditions formerly prevalent in France.[32] *Nizzahon Vetus* § 98 contains a detailed criticism of the Christian interpretation of Isa 52:13-53:5.[33] First there is a short introduction: "The heretics refer this entire passage to Jesus because he experienced torture, death, and suffering for them." Then the nine passages of Isaiah 53 are discussed. The Jewish writer first presents them and then criticizes the Christians interpretation thereof:

1) The first phrase is ירום ונשא. This interpretation is opposed by the comment that Jesus had not yet been exalted and extolled. Assuming that Jesus was the Messiah he would have experienced this promise in his life but this has not been realized until now. Apparently this criticism was an old basic refutation of the messianic belief of the Christians because already Justin Martyr developed an idea about the Messiah's two advents: First he came as an humble Messiah and in his second coming – which according to the Christian belief is still to be realized – he will show his power. The Jewish writer, however, insists that the criterion for the messianic era is the glory of Israel.

---

[31]*Nizzahon Vetus* is edited in D. Berger, *The Jewish-Christian Debate in the High Middle Ages. A Critical edition of the Nizzahon Vetus with an introduction, translation and commentary* (Philadelphia: The Jewish Publication Society of America 1979). The text concerning Isaiah 53 is also given in Neubauer, *The Fifty-third Chapter of Isaiah* Vol 1:86-87; its translation is in vol 2: 90-91.

[32]Krauss-Horbury, *The Jewish-Christian Controversy* 246-247.

[33]The Hebrew text is in Berger, *The Jewish-Christian Debate* 66-68 and the English translation on pp. 114-116.

2) The second passage which the Jewish writer considers in his polemics is משחת מאיש מראהו ותוארו מבני אדם. If the Servant is God as Christians claim, then it should be asked "why was his face marred?" The argument is proposed that if Jesus really was God, the people could not have succeeded in hurting him. This rationalistic argument is based on the idea of philosophical monotheism which emphasizes that there cannot be any change in God – this same argument recurs also later in point 6 below. It is easy to see that the Jewish writer does not accept the Christian *kenosis* concept, apparently because he regards the philosophical argument as decisive proof.

3) כן יזה גוים רבים עליו יקפצו מלכים פיהם. The text does not say explicitly how the Christians interpret this phrase but it is contradicted by the note: "It should have said, 'So shall he bring many nations near to him' i.e., that he would gather many nations to his faith." This indicates that, according to *Nizzahon Vetus*, the Christians associated the phrase with the universal mission of the Church concerning Jesus Christ. It is worth noting that an interpretation which is attested in Alfonsi's text quoted above contains such a missionary aspect. Alfonsi's reading of Isa 52:15 is based on the Hebrew verb "sprinkle" (as in the Vulgate translation *iste asperget gentes multas*) and not the LXX reading θαυμάσονται, "will wonder". The Jewish writer, however, observes that the content of the Hebrew text is not missionary activity.

4) אשר לא־ספר להם ראו. Again the Jewish writer does not explain how the Christians understand this phrase. According to Alfonsi this verse concerns the message of the crucified Messiah which is proclaimed to the Jewish people. This provides a fitting background for the statement in *Nizzahon Vetus*. It ridicules such an understanding of the phrase by noting ironically that the Christians indeed claim that "all the prophets prophesied concerning him." This means that the Jews must have heard this message several times before because they have studied the scriptures which bear witness to Jesus.

5) וזרוע יהוה על־מי נגלתה. The Jewish writer connects this phrase too with the Christian missionary activities when he comments ironically that "the deeds of Jesus were never revealed either to sages or to prophets." This statement constitutes probably a critical assessment of the Christian mission strategy at the disputation of Barcelona in 1263 as well as the ideas presented in *Pugio Fidei*. The point is that because the Christians interpret the phrase as referring to the Christian gospel about the crucified Messiah, and this takes the form of a question, the whole idea implies that it is a novelty which has not been revealed to either the prophets (the scriptural evidence) or to the sages (the Talmudic evidence as argued by Pablo Christiani in Barcelona and as presented in *Pugio Fidei*).

6) לא־תאר לו ולא הדר ונראהו ולא־מראה ונחמדהו. *Nizzahon Vetus* contrasts this statement about Jesus with another Christian interpretation of Psalm 45:2-3 which, in turn, emphasizes that he was beautiful. Thus we have here the same polemic as was mentioned in *Milchamot ha-Shem*. It is clear that such an idea was based on actual knowledge of the Christian argumentation because many Church Fathers interpret both Isaiah 53 and Psalm 45 in conjunction with each other (see sect. 8).

The Jewish writer refers to a possible additional argument from the Christian side: "If he will reply that in his life he was handsome but in his death he had no form, the answer is: If he [the Servant] is God, what sort of death did he suffer and what change should have taken place in his appearance?" The belief that God is immutable derives from the philosophic monotheism and was regarded as valid during the medieval period.

7) וכמסתר פנים ממנו נבזה ולא חשבנהו. *Nizzahon Vetus* regards this phrase "and when he hid his face from us, he was despised and we esteemed him not" in Isa 53:3 as "very confusing words (דברי תהפוכות), because everyone knows that it was before he died and became hidden from people (ונסתר מם הבריות) that he was not esteemed, while after his death people erred by following him and thinking that he ascended to

372

heaven." This comment should be understood so that the Jewish writer emphasizes that the hiding of the face according to the MT occurred when Jesus was taken to the Heaven. This idea is not on a par with Alfonsi's interpretation. He understood this phrase to mean that "the look of Christ was hidden because the splendor of divinity hid itself under his flesh." As we have seen in sect. 8, such a view was typical in early Christian understanding of Isaiah 53. Therefore, the constructed contradiction by the Jewish writer does not consider the Christian understanding of the passage.

8) אכן חלינו הוא נשא. As far as this phrase is concerned, *Nizzahon Vetus* asks critically: "If you will say that it refers to his forgiving of their sins, was there no forgiving of sin before Jesus was born?" Then there is a longer argumentation that already in the Hebrew Bible many references are made to forgiveness of sins. Then follows another possible Christian counter-argument: "You may argue that this forgiveness did not save them from hell but only from punishment and suffering." Then reference is made to Ex 32:27-28 where punishment was meted out to those who worshiped the golden calf. The theological problem which the Jewish writer articulates here was treated already in the New Testament (Rom 3:21-26; the Letter to the Hebrews).[34] Therefore, it is no wonder that the Jewish writer was aware of this aspect of Christian theology.

---

[34]The Christian idea was rooted in the Second Temple Jewish expectation that the decisive atonement will be performed in the eschatological future and this has now been fulfilled in the death of Jesus. See A. Laato, "The Eschatological Act of *kipper* in the Damascus Document," in: Z.J. Kapera (ed), *Intertestamental Essays in honour of Jósef Tadeusz Milik Volume 1* (Qumranica Mogilanensia 6; Cracow: Enigma 1992) 91-107; idem, "The idea of kipper in Judaisms of late antiquity," *Khristianskij Vostok* (= Christian Orient) 1 (1999) 155-193; see also my Finnish study *Anteeksiantamus ja Uhri. Sovitus Vanhassa testamentissa, juutalaisuudessa ja Uudessa testamentissa* [Forgiveness and Sacrifice. Atonement in the Old Testament, Judaism and in the New Testament] (Iustitia 16, Helsinki 2002).

9) הוא מחלל מפשענו מדכא מעונתינו. This is the last expression of Isaiah 53 which is explained in *Nizzahon Vetus*. It is noted that the Christians say "that he [Jesus] suffered all his tortures for their sins, i.e., to redeem them from hell. However, according to them this fate was not a result of transgressions and iniquities, for they say that even those without sins (בלא פשע ועון) went down to hell. Thus, it was not because of our transgression that he had to suffer death but in order to nullify his decree that all men, good or evil, must descend to hell." It seems that the Jewish writer tries to articulate here the Christian idea of original sin. He struggles to formulate it in Christian terms because he does not accept the idea that all men are sinners from the outset. After all, no Christian theologian would ever say that there are "those without sins" but the writer emphasizes here to his fellow Jews that even those who, according to the Jewish view, have committed no sin are regarded as an object of Jesus' saving death. *Nizzahon Vetus* ends the discussion of Isaiah 53 by nullifying Jesus' saving acts and the Christian way of life: "If you will then say that it was for the sake of his believers and because of their sins that he suffered all this – for his death expiates all the sins of those who believe in him – then all his believers are free of any commandments and need not hesitate to rob, steal, murder, or commit adultery since all is expiated by his death. Thus, the good he did is really an evil which brings a curse to the world." Similar criticism of the Christian way of life is voiced by Joseph Kimhi in his *Sefer Ha-Berît*.[35]

What is interesting is that there is neither a description nor any criticism of the Christian interpretation of Isa 53:6-12 in this context. A little later in § 109 there is a reference to a correct interpretation of Isa 52:12-13 and 53:8-9.[36] The passage refers to Israel. There is no discussion here of how Christians understand the verses.

---

[35]See F.E. Talmage, *The Book of the Covenant of Joseph Kimhi* (Toronto: The Pontifical Institute of Mediaeval Studies 1972) 24-25, 32-35.

[36]The Hebrew text is in Berger. *The Jewish-Christian Debate* 72 and the English translation on p. 122.

374

Summing up we may conclude that the *Nizzahon Vetus* presents a more balanced picture of the Christian theology than does Jacob ben Reuben's *Milchamot HaShem*. Nevertheless, it too contains biased tendencies because its main aim was to defend the Jewish position against Christian missionary activities.

Rabbi Shem Tob ben Isaac Shaprut

Our final example of a Jewish anti-Christian text is R. Shem Tob b. Isaac Shaprut's work *Eben Bochan* (Touchstone).[37] In 1379 he and cardinal Pedro de Luna of Aragon disputed in Pamplona. The disputation took place in the cardinal's palace and was a massive public event attended by theologians and a great number of people. Pedro de Luna later became the anti-pope Benedict XIII. The main subjects of the disputation were the advent of the Messiah – whether or not he has already come – and the doctrine of original sin. This disputation prompted Shem Tob to write his work. The fourteen chapters of this book were completed in 1380 or in 1385 in Tarazona. After reading Abner of Burgos's (or Maestro Alfonso's) answer to Jacob ben Reuben's *Milchamot Ha-Shem* (Wars of the Lord), Shem Tob added the fifteenth chapter which is a refutation of Alfonso.[38]

Like Jacob ben Reuben's work so also *Eben Bochan* is a dialogue between *meyached* ("the confessor of Unity") and *meshallesh* ("the confessor of Trinity"). It is significant that Shem Tob does not call his Christian opponent pejoratively *mekached* ("denier") as Jacob ben Reuben did. Isaiah 53 and its interpretation is discussed in chapter 8

---

[37]The first chapter of *Eben Bochan* has been edited in J.-V. Niclós, *Šem Tob ibn Šaprut, "La Piedra de Toque" (Eben Bohan). Una obra de controversia Judeo-Cristiana* (Madrid: Consejo Superior de Investigaciones Cientificas 1997).

[38]See these historical details in Krauss & Horbury, *The Jewish-Christian Controversy I History* 167-168; Niclós, *Eben Bohan* 50-55.

(section 19) and chapter 15.[39] In chapter 8 the Trinitarian, according to Shem Tob, interprets Isaiah 53 as follows:

> In this Parashah it is asserted that just as the exaltation of God's servant had been great, so the humiliation which succeeded it was great likewise (52:13-14); that he was to rule over many nations (52:15); that he was despised in the eyes of the Jews (53:1-3); that he was God, smitten and afflicted (53:4); that by his stripes the sin of Adam was healed for us (53:5); that he met death for our sakes (53:6); that he met it voluntarily (53:7); that there was no one who knew his generation, i.e. his seed, and that death came upon him in consequence of the transgressions of the people (53:8); and that he was hung between two thieves (53:9). In a word, the whole passage, rightly expounded, bears witness in every line to the history of Jesus our Messiah and to the things that befell him.

When this description of the Christian interpretation outlined by Shem Tob is compared with Alfonsi's interpretation (quoted above) there are no apparent contradictions. Like Jacob ben Reuben's so also Shem Tob's description emphasizes the fact that Isaiah 53, according to the Christian view, bears "witness in every line to the history of Jesus". Nevertheless, there are some minor differences between Alfonsi's interpretation and Shem Tob's characterization of the Christian interpretation. For example, according to Shem Tob, Christian exegesis emphasizes that 53:4 is evidence of the Servant's divinity. In Alfonsi's interpretation this emphasis is made in 53:3. According to Shem Tob, 53:5 was used as proof that "the sin of Adam was healed for us" but Alfonsi related this emphasis to his interpretation of 53:6: "The Lord forgives and washes away through him (that is, through the baptism that he gave) the original sin in which all are entangled." In 53:8 Shem Tob allows the Christian antagonist to emphasize the miraculous birth – a belief which was articulated among Christians since the interpretation of Justin Martyr and

---

[39]See Niclós, *Eben Bohan* 20, 50-51. The text concerning Isaiah 53 is published in Neubauer, *The Fifty-third Chapter of Isaiah* Vol 1:88-94; its translation is in vol 2: 92-98.

also appears in Alfonsi's text: "... he pronounced this with respect to his divine generation."[40] Thus it seems obvious that Shem Tob knew Petrus Alfonsi's work and gives a critical evaluation of his interpretation of Isaiah 53.

After presenting the Christian interpretation Shem Tob proceeds to criticize it. His five first arguments parallel to those put forward by Jacob ben Reuben, but are clearly more sophisticated:

1. Christians use both Isaiah 53 (his marred outlook) and Psalm 45 (his beautiful form) when they describe Jesus – a circumstance which leads to contradiction.

2. The Servant who, according to the Christian interpretation is God, will become "high and exalted" but, according to Isa 57:15 God is "high and exalted" from all eternity.

3. Jesus is not said to be constantly ailing which contradicts Isaiah 53 according to which the Servant is "man of pains".

4. Isaiah 53 states that the Servant was smitten by God but in the case of Jesus it would be more accurate to say that he was smitten by men. And if Jesus was "smitten by God" how can he be God?

5. The Hebrew text in 53:10 which reads in the plural "there was a stroke upon them" is read by the Christians as "there was a stroke in him".

Shem Tob adds several arguments against the Christian interpretation of 53:10 and thereby develops Jacob ben Reuben's argumentation in *Milchamot ha-Shem*. It may well be that even these additional critical remarks are copied from some other Jewish anti-Christian polemical works because Shem Tob writes: "Since the Nazarenes make a great point of this prophecy for their religion, so much so indeed that, in my

---

[40]Concerning this, see sect. 8 and A. Laato, "Isaiah 53 and the Biblical Exegesis of Justin Martyr," in: A.Laato & J. Van Ruiten (eds), *Rewritten Bible Reconsidered: Proceedings of the Conference in Karkku, Finland August 24-26 2006* (SRB 1, Winona Lake: Eisenbrauns; Turku: Åbo Akademi University 2008) 215-229.

estimation, it seems to be founded upon it, it is my intention to be a little diffuse, and to add four objections of my own" (p. 94). Shem Tob's additional remarks against the Christian interpretation of Isa 53:10 are as follows:

1. If the Christians interpret 53:10 "when his soul makes a trespass-offering" it indicates that he must have sinned. If, however, the Christians interpret "trespass-offering" as referring to the death of Jesus "then the soul of Jesus died." This contradicts the Christian interpretation which asserts that "the flesh alone died" (שהבשר לבדו מת). This argument does not corroborate the classical Christian doctrine which emphasizes that Jesus – as true God and true man – died on the cross. An attempt to distinguish between dying flesh and living soul is a Jewish fabrication or an irrelevant Christian rumor which Shem Tob has heard. Nevertheless, it is worth noting that Alfonsi interprets the expression "his soul makes a trespass-offering" as referring to the vicarious death of Jesus.

2. The Servant "will prolong his days" (53:10) can only refer to the length of the physical life. Jesus was crucified when only 32 years old. It is worth noting that in the Jewish martyr theology Isa 53:10 is understood as referring to the resurrection and the life after death (see sects. 3-4).

3. The expression "he will see seed" (53:10) cannot be taken to refer to the disciples of the Servant. Then the word "sons" would be required. "The word seed denotes such as are born by carnal generation." Shem Tob seems to give an accurate Christian understanding of this passage because Alfonsi interprets "he will see seed" as referring to the spiritual heirs of Jesus, i.e. his followers.

4. "It is also derogatory to the Godhead (גנאי הוא לאלוהות) to be called servant throughout the passage: the language in 53:10 refers to Israel." This argument does not reflect the Christian idea of *kenosis* but repeats the basic Jewish belief that the Servant in Isaiah 53 is a loyal adherent of the Torah of Yhwh.

At the end of his criticism of the Christian interpretation of Isaiah 53 Shem Tob presents his own findings. These four observations clearly indicate that Shem Tob is not familiar with Christology.

1. It is said that the Servant "will understand". "From this it is evident that previously he must have been devoid of any such attribute: but how can such language be used of God?" (p. 94). Alfonsi understands Isa 52:13 simply so that it tells of the Servant who will comprehend, who will appear and have great understanding.

2. "If the words מוכה אלהים mean, as you say, that he, God, was smitten, then this contradicts the teaching of your own religion: for you assert that only his flesh (הבשר) suffered." This argument shows that Shem Tob is ignorant of the Christological doctrine of *communicatio idiomatum*.[41] The Christian theologian who is aware of the Christological statements of the First Council of Ephesus (431) and the Council of Chalcedon (451) would never state that only the flesh of Jesus suffered.

3. "How can God in any sense be said to be smitten?" This argument is not ingenuous. It reiterates the Jewish position against the concept of incarnation and is based on philosophical monotheism according to which God is impassible and cannot suffer.[42]

4. The expressions in Isa 53:11-12 imply that the soul of the Servant endured labour and death (מעמל נפשו יראה). According to Shem Tob, this contradicts the Christian dogma that "only his flesh underwent death (שלא סבל המיתה רק הבשר)." Again we have here an example of how Shem Tob formulates the Christian position without considering *communicatio idiomatum*.

---

[41] According to the Catholic Encyclopaedia "it means that the properties of the Divine Word can be ascribed to the man Christ, and that the properties of the man Christ can be predicated of the Word."

[42] See further sect. 8 where we discussed about the axiom of divine impassibility and Isaiah 53 in early Christian teaching.

Summing up we may conclude that Shem Tob is dependent on earlier Jewish arguments when he criticizes the Christian understanding of Isaiah 53. The basic concept behind these Jewish counter arguments originate in philosophical monotheism. Shem Tob shows that he is unaware that the Christian theologians considered and rejected such approaches long ago when they formulated their creeds and clarified the Christological dogma in conjunction with the Greek philosophy.

In chapter 15 of Eben Bochan Shem Tob replied to Mastro Alfonso's (Abner of Burgos, 1270?-1346/50) work *Mostador de la Justicia*.[43] Abner was a Jewish apostate who wrote many works in order to convert Jews to Christianity.[44] *Mostador de la Justicia* contains a refutation of Jacob ben Reuben's *Milchamot Ha-Shem*. In this context Shem Tob allows his Christian antagonist to formulate the following arguments:[45]

> Why do you raise an objection on the ground of the words 'his countenance marred beyond man'? No argument can be derived from what Jeremiah says (11:16), because, as a man's circumstances change, so is he himself changed likewise. The words have reference to Christ's manhood: and in this respect God is really superior to him[46]. Then the expressions, a 'man of pains' and 'known to sickness' allude to the time when they set him at nought before his death, and were known to be true to all Israel who went up to the feast. He is called 'smitten of God', because the foolish and wicked men who condemned him thought they were punishing his transgressions in accordance with the law. 'The Lord was pleased to bruise him' viz. in respect of his manhood: 'because of the transgressions of my people', etc.; this resembles verse 11 'their

---

[43]See this text W. Mettmann (ed), *Alfonso de Valladolid (Abner aus Burgos)*, *Mostrador de Justicia* Band I-II (Abhandlungen der Nordrhein-Westfälischen Akademie der Wissenschaften 92, Opbladen: Westdeutscher Verlag 1994).

[44]Concerning Abner of Burgos see Y. Samir, *Rabbi Moses Ha-Kohen of Tordesillas and His Book 'Ezer ha-Emunah* (Leiden: Brill 1975) 40-54.

[45]The text is given in Neubauer, *The Fifty-third Chapter of Isaiah* Vol 1:93-94; its translation is in vol 2: 97-98.

[46]In the Hebrew: וטעם ... מצד האנושות ומזה הצד יש אלוהים ממעל לו.

iniquities he will bear', because the murderous death which they wreaked upon him is 'a blow for them', inasmuch as in consequence of it, they will be in perpetual exile, as Scripture says, Ps 81:16. Lastly, by seed are signified his disciples, who will prolong their days for ever; and by the expression 'poured out his soul to die' the prophet means to indicate his yielding up of the ghost.

This evaluation of the Christian interpretation of Isaiah 53 is more accurate than Shem Tob's unbalanced views presented earlier in which he allows the Christian argument to be formulated without any attempt to consider the *communicatio idiomatum*. The Christian antagonist emphasizes the manhood of Christ when he speaks of the sufferings and comments that God in this respect is superior to him.

Conclusions

We saw in chapters 11-12 that the interpretation of Isaiah 53 illustrates the conflict between the Jewish and Christian biblical exegesis. In this section we focused on the way in which Jewish polemicists described the Christian interpretation of Isaiah 53. We saw that while Jacob ben Reuben had a limited knowledge of the Christian interpretations, or alternatively he intentionally conveyed a skewed picture of the Christian understanding of Isaiah 53, the later Jewish polemicists could give a more accurate view. Nevertheless, bias against Christology manifest in every attempt to describe the Christian understanding of Isaiah 53. This is dependent on the overall philosophical concepts which the Jewish (and Muslim) experts adopted in the Middle Ages in order to define their monotheism. This explains why Christology is presented in medieval Jewish polemical sources in such a way as to refer to classical Christological heresies which were refuted in the early Church when there were various attempts to formulate Christian doctrines in the context of the philosophical traditions. The philosophical discourse practiced in Judaism was directed mainly against the Trinity and the incarnation as Lasker demonstrates in his work *Jewish Philosophical Polemics against Christianity in the Middle Ages.*

On the other hand, Jewish polemical texts were written for Jews, not for Christians so that the arguments which did not convey accurate picture of the Christian doctrines were sufficient. But we can assume that Christian theologians would have vehemently opposed these arguments because they were familiar with early Christological heresies which were apparently unknown to Jewish polemicists.

We have also argued that the Jewish polemicists must have known (or even read) Petrus Alfonsi's work *Dialogue Against the Jews* because the picture given in their anti-Christian writings is often parallel with Petrus' interpretation. They also mention that Isaiah 53 was treated in the mandatory disputations when the Christian party attempted to find support in rabbinical writings for their understanding of Isaiah 53. As we saw in sect. 11 such a perverse reading of the rabbinical writings receive no support from any Jewish document.

13 Conclusions

In this study we have followed the course whereby Isaiah 53 – which was described as "an erratic block" by Klaus Koch – found its way to the Hebrew Bible, and what kind of interpretations it provoked in Jewish and Christian writings.

We accepted a long-standing scholarly opinion that behind the servant figure of Isaiah 40-55 looms a royal ideology, and argued that this may also be related to Isaiah 53. Josiah was regarded as a loyal adherent of Deuteronomistic covenant theology and therefore greatly glorified in 2 Kings 22-23. His death at Megiddo was difficult to reconcile with the favourable evaluation of his loyalty which is given in 2 Kgs 23:25: "Neither before nor after Josiah was there a king like him who turned to Yhwh as he did – with all his heart and with all his soul and with all his strength, in accordance with all the Law of Moses." Instead of seeking evidence that Josiah sinned and therefore brought his death upon himself the Deuteronomistic Historian blames Manasseh (2 Kgs 23:26-27): "Nevertheless, Yhwh did not turn away from the heat of his fierce anger, which burned against Judah because of all that Manasseh had done to arouse his anger. So Yhwh said, 'I will remove Judah also from my presence as I removed Israel, and I will reject Jerusalem, the city I chose, and this temple, about which I said: My Name shall be there'." How should we understand this statement?

The Hebrew Bible indicates that many lamentations were composed about Josiah and his death. They are cited in 2 Chr 35:25: "Jeremiah composed a lament for Josiah, and to this day all the male and female singers commemorate Josiah in their laments. These became a tradition in Israel and are written in the Laments." It is of importance to find traces of these lamentations in the Old Testament. If so, what would be their content? We have suggested in this study that Psalm 89, Zech

12:10-13:1 and Isaiah 53 reflect these laments for Josiah. All three texts refer to an individual who was killed but who did not deserve his fate. This being the case they are parallel to the judgement which was passed on Josiah in the Deuteronomistic History. The sufferer was righteous but for some reason Yhwh decided to beat him. In these three texts Josiah himself is not the focus but traditions of lamentations for his death have been reinterpreted. Josiah's death opened new hermeneutic questions concerning the validity of the covenant theology and, consequently, theological reflections in the laments for his death were disregarded.

In covenant theology it was taken as self-evident that the people (alternatively the righteous king representing the people) who fulfils the stipulations of the covenant will receive blessings in this life – a pledge which Deuteronomy 28-29 presupposes. The fate of Josiah gave a reason to challenge this view and created a dissonance which required an hermeneutic solution to the covenant theology. The proposal which we submit in this study is that the lamentations for Josiah dealt with his righteous life and his unjust death which led to hermeneutic processes to explain this theodicy.

Psalm 89 probably received its final form during the exile. The Psalm refers to the destruction of the Judahite kingdom which is presented in a way which in terms of both language and theology is reminiscent of the Deuteronomistic theology. According to this theology the Judahite kingdom was practically destroyed in consequence of the death of Josiah as becomes clear from 2 Kgs 23:26-27 quoted above. In the light of Josiah's righteousness we can understand the questions posed by the Deuteronomistic writer (Ps 89:38-39): "But you have rejected, you have spurned, you have been very angry with your anointed one. You have renounced the covenant with your servant and have defiled his crown in the dust."

Zech 12:10-13:1 is related to the postexilic messianic programme which failed. The people are accused of this failure in Zechariah 9-14. The prophet was asked to play the role of the Messiah (the good shepherd in Zech 11:4-14). The rejection of the prophet's message meant the postponement of the messianic era which Yhwh wanted to bestow on his people. Zech 12:10-13:1 compares this failure with the catastrophe which ensued at Megiddo when Josiah died but prophesies that eventually the people will confess their responsibility for the postponement of the messianic programme. The prophet sees a connection with the death of Josiah and predicts that in the future the people will repent and be pardoned and saved when they confess their guilt for the death of the Messiah (i.e. the messianic programme presented by the prophet). This is on a par with the content of Isaiah 53 which we explained as containing reflections on the lamentations for Josiah.

In the interpretation of Isaiah 53 we set the passage in the context of Deutero-Isaiah where Israel is called the servant of Yhwh. We argued that Isaiah 53 describes the sufferings of the righteous Israelites which benefit the whole people. Thus the righteous members of Israel lead the whole people to Yhwh (Isa 49:3, 5-6): "He said to me, 'You are my servant, Israel, in whom I will display my splendor' ... And now Yhwh says – he who formed me in the womb to be his servant to bring Jacob back to him and gather Israel to himself ... he says: 'It is too small a thing for you to be my servant to restore the tribes of Jacob and bring back those of Israel I have kept. I will also make you a light for the Gentiles, that my salvation may reach to the ends of the earth."

We have argued that the vivid picture of the suffering and dying servant whose death will benefit others can best be explained if it is traditio-historically associated with the fate of Josiah. Our proposal is that the idea of vicarious suffering and death in this "erratic block" can be explained as originating from the lamentations for Josiah. Josiah there was described as one who must suffer and die for the sins of others – in parallel with the idea in 2 Kings 23 according to which the sins committed during the time of Manasseh prevented God from blessing Josiah who acted according to the Deuteronomic programme. This concept was then developed in the lamentations so that the death of Josiah was regarded as vicarious inasmuch as it will benefit the people on their return to Yhwh and his covenant. Such a belief was difficult to reconcile with the idea of retribution – one of the cornerstones of the Deuteronomic covenant theology. Therefore, the Chronicler, who was familiar with many lamentations for Josiah and who represented a very strict retribution theology, introduced an interesting theory concerning the fate of Josiah at Megiddo. He argued that Josiah had to die because he was not loyal to the prophet, i.e. the Pharaoh Necho, who exhorted him in the name of Yhwh not to war against him (2 Chr 35:20-24). This being the case the Chronicler showed how such a theology contradicted the covenant theology and its principle of retribution. Nevertheless, the situation of the exile showed that the theology (expressing the idea of vicarious sufferings) could enter the focus of religious thought because it gave hope of a new beginning. Such a theology could explain, spiritually, the problem of theodicy: why must the righteous suffer in the time of the exile. According to the answer formulated in Isaiah 53, such a suffering pleased Yhwh who will pardon his people and lead it back to Jerusalem. The crisis of the exile required such a vicarious atoning theology which explains why it found its way to the Hebrew Bible (sect. 2).

The concept of the vicarious suffering remained at the periphery of Jewish theology in the postexilic period. Isaiah 53 became an erratic block, inasmuch as no other passage expressed this idea (so clearly) in the whole Hebrew Bible. Nevertheless, during the time of crises when the adherents of the covenant theology must suffer, this theology came into focus once more. In the Maccabean period Isaiah 53 influenced Jewish martyr theology. The Servant who had to suffer and die vicariously illustrated the martyr theology according to which the martyrdom of the innocent righteous will benefit the whole people. Furthermore, Isaiah 53 readily merged with the idea of resurrection which was attested also in Isa 26:19; 66:24 when these verses were read in a new apocalyptic milieu (Dan 12:2). There is evidence that Dan 11:33-12:4 were formulated with the aid of Isaiah 53 and the martyr theology of 2 and 4 Maccabees was influenced by this same Isaianic passage (sect. 3).

From the Maccabean period onwards we have evidence that Isaiah 53 was interpreted as referring to suffering righteous (LXX and Wisdom 2-5). However, there was an interpretive tendency to deprecate the idea of the vicarious atoning suffering. In the LXX translation the passages referring to vicarious and atoning sufferings were belittled to some extent although not totally disregarded. Such a translation tendency explains why in Wisdom 2-5 – which uses the LXX of Isaiah 53 to describe the oppressed righteous – there is no mention of vicarious suffering. In Wisdom 2-5 the righteous servant (of Isaiah 53) will receive his reward at the last judgment while his ungodly oppressors will be punished. There is an interesting revision of the concept of the suffering Servant in Isaiah 53: the wicked ones will not be pardoned because of the sufferings of the righteous Servant (sect. 4).

In light of the literary evidence of Wisdom 2-5 it is obvious why the theology of Isaiah 53 was an erratic block in the Hebrew Bible. It remained at the periphery of Jewish religious thought in the Second Temple period. Wisdom 2-5 also give a perspective on why there is no literary evidence from the pre-Christian period to support the view of Joachim Jeremias according to which some circles in Palestine Judaism would have expected the Messiah who would suffer and die vicariously on behalf of the sinful people. Nor did Martin Hengel succeed in rendering this hypothesis more attractive (sect. 5).

The Targum Jonathan translation of Isaiah 53 is another example of the interpretive tendency which belittled the vicarious suffering of the Servant. The remarkable feature of the Targum translation is that the Servant has been interpreted in terms of the Messiah. This has caused much discussion, as has, in particular, the Targum's relation to the Christian understanding of Isaiah 53. We rejected the view that behind the Targum Jonathan was an earlier version where a suffering and dying Messiah was depicted. On the other hand, we regard it as plausible that the Targum translation was somehow related to the Christian interpretation. Its content embodies typical Jewish messianic ideas but does not lend itself to their connection with Isaiah 53. Therefore, we asked whether such a tendentious translation (but not a tendentious messianic expectation!) could have been established in the synagogal liturgy in order to refute possible Christian attitudes (sect 6). However, we cannot overestimate the intention of the Targum's forced translation technique to belittle vicarious suffering because such a tendency was visible already in the pre-Christian period in the Wisdom of Solomon (sect. 4).

The Christian era opened a new interpretive horizon on the significance of Isaiah 53. It seems that Isaiah 53 was used as a "fifth" Gospel because its content seems so well suited to the suffering and death of Jesus on his Via Dolorosa. There was no need to rewrite Isaiah 53 but give a sensitive interpretation to the passage and single out certain sophisticated nuances from its wording. We argued that the historical Jesus did not identify himself with the Servant of Isaiah 53 at first hand but with the messianic figure of Zechariah 9-14. The Messiah is humble (Zech 9:9-10), will be rejected by the people (Zech 11:4-14) and suffer martyrdom (Zech 12:10; 13:7). The historical Jesus combined the Zecharian Messiah with the Son of Man. Through this identification Zech 11:13 and 12:10 together with the Danielic vision of the Son of Man (Dan 7 and Dan 3:25 where the Son of Man epithet appears) explain why the first disciples of Jesus developed high Christology so rapidly. Quite soon after the decisive Easter Isaiah 53 began to play a major role in the Christian message of the Messiah. 1 Cor 15:1-11 presents strong evidence of how the Christian kerygma was formulated with the aid of Isaiah 53 (sect. 7).

In the patristic writings Isaiah 53 was used in diverse ways, and certain lines of development emerge. We disagree with Markschies that there was a development from the martyrological use of Isaiah 53 (when Jesus is helpless before his executioners, i.e. the total God-forsakenness) to a more sophisticated Christological use (when it is emphasized that Jesus is God who cannot suffer but himself controls his bodily suffering, i.e. the impassibility axiom). We demonstrated that Markschies's understanding of Origen on this point is one-sided and that these two tendencies 1) the "total God-forsakenness" and 2) Jesus' willingness to sacrifice himself are already attested in the New Testament – as Origen noted. Then we showed how Isaiah 53 was used in many and diverse literary contexts in the early Church, in particular, in catechumenic instruction. The use of Isaiah 53 in the preparation for baptism implies that the passage must have been one of the key-texts in the early Church. The text was also important for the Christian self-understanding contra Judaism and paganism and was quoted when different heresies were refuted (sect. 8).

The formative period of rabbinical Judaism produced a large amount of material which was mainly related to the interpretation of *halakhah*. References to Isaiah 53 can be found only sporadically and do not give us any coherent interpretation tradition. Isaiah 53 was used in rabbinical writings with reference to suffering righteous. Those to whom Isaiah 53 was applied included rabbi Akiba, Moses and the Messiah. The messianic expectations are not prominent in the rabbinical writings. There is no indication that the messianic interpretation of Isaiah 53 contains the belief that the Messiah will suffer and die vicariously. We also rejected the opinion of Mitchell that such a view could be applied to Messiah ben Ephraim/Joseph (sect. 9).

The vicarious sufferings of the Messiah were developed in Pesiqta Rabbati, the collection of rabbinical homilies for Jewish Festivals. The Messiah is depicted in some of these homilies as a pre-existent individual who is eagerly waiting to help his people. However, he must bide his time, and the yoke of sufferings is laid upon him in his pre-existent life. The Messiah is willing to bear the sins of the people and the promise is given to him that he will bring a great salvation to the world when he once appears. A similar messianic expectation concerning the sufferings of the Messiah was developed in the Zohar (sect. 10). This development in the Jewish midrashic Bible exegesis was apparently intended to answer the rabbinical tradition concerning how Isaiah 53 can be interpreted in terms of the Messiah. The influence from the Christian side is not excluded but this messianic understanding of Isaiah 53 then involved a challenge of the Christian interpretation. The concept of the suffering Messiah in Pesiqta Rabbati and Zohar enabled a literal interpretation of the sufferings of the Servant, as indicated in the Hebrew text of Isaiah 53 without major midrashic alterations and reinterpretations as in Targum Jonathan.

The contrast between the Jewish and Christian interpretations of Isaiah 53 is manifest in the medieval literary sources. Medieval Judaism had to face Karaite attack on rabbinical traditions including their midrashes as well as the Christian misuse of midrashes in mandatory disputations. The development of the *peshat* interpretive method in the Middle Ages under the influence of Muslim *kalam* resulted in new opportunities to challenge these attacks. In the medieval Jewish exegesis Isaiah 53 was interpreted in its literary context, or by emphasizing linguistic parallels to other biblical texts. Saadiah Gaon's Jeremiah-interpretation was an early attempt to relate some expressions in Isaiah 53 to similar wordings in the Book of Jeremiah. Rashi established another *peshat* interpretation of Isaiah 53 by taking into consideration the literary context of Isaiah 40-55. He argued that the passage refers to the sufferings of the righteous ones in Israel. This interpretation was probably suggested by the massacre of Jews by German crusaders in 1096. However, the Israel-interpretation had its pre-history already in antiquity – as attested indirectly by Origen – but the new *peshat* method made it popular in medieval Judaism. It was followed by many medieval Jewish interpreters. Abraham ibn Ezra presents it as an accurate interpretation even though he also gives an alternative understanding of the passage as referring to the prophet as in Isa 42:1; 49:3. David Kimhi and Nahmanides adopted Rashi's interpretation. Besides the Israel interpretation Nahmanides also wrote an explanation of how the messianic interpretation of Isaiah 53 should be understood if some Jews are willing to follow a rabbinical tradition that the passage refers to the Messiah. Nahmanides's interpretation was written after the famous Barcelona disputation in 1263 when Christians attempted to show that the messianic interpretation of Isaiah 53 in rabbinical midrashes implies that the Christian doctrine of the suffering and dying Messiah was accepted by scholars. Nahmanides's work shows how the new aggressive mission strategy of the Christian Church was taken seriously. The situation became even more acute when Raymundus Martini wrote *Pugio Fidei* in 1278. All available Jewish material from rabbinical writings (which could be used to support the Christian doctrines in various sophisticated but uncritical ways) was therein collected and carefully analyzed. The work was intended as a handbook for friars who discussed with Jews in mandatory disputations. Since it was not published officially the Jewish party could not examine it (sect. 11).

Discussions with Christians (in forced disputations) also produced many Jewish anti-Christian writings where Jews denigrated Christian interpretations of Isaiah 53. In these writings Christology was presented in simplistic philosophical terms without regard for how the Christian Church already in antiquity had refuted many versions of such a philosophical approach. In any case, these simplistic refutations were worded to convince a large Jewish audience to hold fast to the Jewish tradition and it seems that they were effectual (sect. 12).

The reception history of Isaiah 53 conveys a wonderful picture of the exegetical history of this passage of the Hebrew Bible. This difficult passage remained there as an "erratic block". However, in the course of its interpretation history it has shown its vitality and importance first in early Jewish martyr theology, then in a marvelous way in the Christian gospel about the suffering and dying Messiah, and finally in medieval Judaism when Jews must withstand the pressure of the Christian Church. The history of interpretation shows that Isaiah 53 was able to answer the questions beyond the stage where the possibilities of the covenant theology and its retribution principle ended. Isaiah 53 opened a new path to understanding that those who sought to be in a covenantal relationship to Yhwh may have been forced to suffer because "it was Yhwh's will to crush the Servant and cause him to suffer."

14 Bibliography

Abegg, M.G.   "Messianic Hope and 4Q285: A Reassessment," *JBL* 113 (1994) 81-91.

Ådna, J.   "The Servant of Isaiah 53 as Triumphant and Interceding Messiah: The Reception of Isaiah 52:13-53:12 in the Targum of Isaiah with Special Attention to the Concept of the Messiah," in: B. Janowski & P. Stuhlmacher (eds), *The Suffering Servant: Isaiah 53 in Jewish and Christian Sources* (Grand Rapids: Eerdmans 2004) 189-224.

Ådna, J.   *Jesu Stellung zum Tempel: Die Tempelaktion und das Tempelwort als Ausdruck seiner messianischen Sendung* (WMANT 119, Tübingen: Mohr Siebeck 2000).

Albeck, C.   *Midrash Bereshit Rabbati* (Jerusalem: Mekize Nirdamim 1940).

Alès A.D.   "La doctrine de la récapitulation en S. Irénée," *RSR* 6 (1916) 185–211.

Alexander, P.   "Targum, Targumim," *ABD* 6:320-331.

Allegro J.M.   *Qumran Cave 4, I (4Q 158 - 4Q 186)* (DJD 5; Oxford: Clarendon 1968).

Alobaidi, J.   *The Messiah in Isaiah 53: The Commentaries of Saadia Gaon, Salmon ben Yeruham and Yefet ben Eli on Is 52:13-53:12. Edition and translation* (Bern: Lang 1998).

Astren, F.   *Karaite Judaism and Historical Understanding* (Columbia: University of South Carolina Press 2004).

Baer, Y.   "The Disputations of R. Yechiel of Paris and of Nachmanides" (Hebrew), *Tarbiz* 2 (1931) 172-187.

Bailey, D.P.   "Concepts of Stellvertretung in the Interpretation of Isaiah 53," in: W.H. Bellinger & W.R. Farmer, *Jesus and the Suffering Servant: Isaiah 53 and Christian Origins* (Harrisburg: Trinity Press International 1998) 223-250.

Bailey, D.P.   "'Our Suffering and Crucified Messiah' (Dial. 111.2): Justin Martyr's Allusions to Isaiah 53 in His Dialogue with Trypho with Special Reference to the New Edition of M. Marcovich," in: B. Janowski & P. Stuhlmacher (eds), *The Suffering Servant: Isaiah 53 in Jewish and Christian Sources* (Grand Rapids: Eerdmans 2004) 324-417.

Banitt, M.   *Rashi: Interpreter of the Biblical Letter* (Tel Aviv: Chaim Rosenberg School of Jewish Studies 1985) [Hebrew].

Bardy, G.   *Eusèbe de Césarée: Histoire Ecclésiastique Livres V-VII* (SC 41, Paris: Les Éditions du Cerf 1955).

Basser, H.W.   "Exegesis of Scripture, Medieval Rabbinic," in: J. Neusner, A.J. Avery-Beck, W.S. Green (eds), *The Encyclopaedia of Judaism Volume I* (Leiden: Brill) 266-280.

Becker, J. *Untersuchungen zur Entstehungsgeschichte der Testamente der zwölf Patriarchen* (AGJU 8, Leiden: Brill 1970).

Beentjes, P.C. "Wisdom of Solomon 3,1-4,19 and the Book of Isaiah," in: J. van Ruiten & M. Vervenne (eds), *Studies in the Book of Isaiah: Festschrift Willem A.M. Beuken* (BETL 132, Leuven: University Press 1997) 413-420.

Behr, J.W. *The Writings of Deutero-Isaiah and the Neo-Babylonian Royal Inscriptions: A Comparison of the Language and Style* (Publications of the University of Pretoria III:3; Pretoria 1937).

Bekkum van W.J "Anti-Christian polemics in Hebrew liturgical poetry (piyyut) of the sixth and seventh centuries," in: J. Den Boeft & A. Hilhorst (eds), *Early Christian Poetry: A Collection of Essays* (Leiden: Brill 1993) 297-308.

Berg, M. (ed), *The Zohar 1-23 with The Sulam Commentary by Rav Yehuda Ashlag* (New York: Kabbalah Centre International 2003).

Berger, D. "Christian Heresy and Jewish Polemics in the 12. and 13. Century," *HTR* 68 (1975) 287-303.

Berger, D. *The Jewish-Christian Debate in the High Middle Ages: A Critical Edition of the Nizzahon Vetus* (Judaica, Texts and translations; no. 4; Philadelphia: Jewish Publication Society of America 1979).

Berger, D. "Mission to the Jews and Jewish-Christian Contacts in the Polemical Literature of the High Middle Ages," *American Historical Review* 91 (1986) 576-591.

Berger, D. "The Barcelona disputation," *AJS Review* 20 (1995) 379-388.

Berger, D. *The Rebbe, the Messiah, and the Scandal of Orthodox Indifference* (The Littman Library of Jewish Civilization 2001).

Berges, U. "The Literary Construction of the Servant in Isaiah 40-55: A Discussion about Individual and Collective Identities," *SJOT* 24 (2010) 28-38.

Betz, O. "Die Übersetzung von Jes 53 (LXX, Targum) und die Theologia Crucis des Paulus," in: O. Betz, *Jesus, der Herr der Kirche: Aufsätze zur biblischen Theologie II* (WUNT 52, Tübingen: Mohr 1990) 197-216.

Betz, O. "Jesus and Isaiah 53," in: W.H. Bellinger & W.R. Farmer, *Jesus and the Suffering Servant: Isaiah 53 and Christian Origins* (Harrisburg: Trinity Press International 1998) 70-87.

Beuken, W.A.M. "Servant and Herald of Good Tidings: Isaiah 61 as an Interpretation of Isaiah 40-55," in: J. Vermeylen (ed), *The Book of Isaiah* (BETL 81, Leuven 1989) 411-442.

Biblia Patristica *Index des citations et allusions bibliques dans la litterature patristique. Centre d'analyse et de documentation patristiques* (Paris: Editions du Centre national de la recherche scientifique, 1975-1995).

Bietenhard, H. *Der tannaitische Midrash Sifre Deuteronomium Übersetzt und erklärt von Hans Bietenhard mit einem Beitrag von Henrik Ljungman* (Judaica et Christiana 8, Bern: Peter Lang 1984).

Billerbeck, P.   "Hat die alte Synagoge einen präexistenten Messias gekannt?" *Nathanael* 19 (1903) 97-125; *Nathanael* 21 (1905) 89-150.

Billerbeck, P.   *Kommentar zum Neuen Testament aus Talmud und Midrasch von Hermann L. Strack und Paul Billerbeck Vol I-V* (Munich: Oskar Beck 1922-1928).

Bingham, D. J.   "Justin and Isaiah 53," *Vigiliae Christianae* 54,3 (2000) 248-261.

Black, M.   *The Book of Enoch or 1 Enoch: A New English Edition with Commentary and Textual Notes* (SVTP 7, Leiden: Brill 1985).

Blanc, C.   *Origene: Commentaire sur Saint Jean Tome II* (SC 157; Paris: Les Éditions du Cerf 1970).

Blenkinsopp, J.   *Opening the Sealed Book: Interpretations of the Book of Isaiah in Late Antiquity* (Grand Rapids: Eerdmans 2006).

Börner-Klein, D.   "Das Buch des Bundes: Josef Qimchis Diskussion zwischen einem Gläubigen und einem Ungläubigen," in: C. Thoma, G. Stemberger, J. Maier (eds), Judentum - Ausblicke und Einsichten: Festgabe für Kurt Schubert (Frankfurt a.M.: Lang 1993) 209-251.

Borret, M.   *Origène: Contra Celse Tome I* (SC 132; Paris: Les Éditions du Cerf 1967).

Borret, M.   *Origène: Contra Celse Tome II* (SC 136; Paris: Les Éditions du Cerf 1968).

Borret, M.   *Origène: Contra Celse Tome III* (SC 147; Paris: Les Éditions du Cerf 1969).

Braude, W.G.   *The Midrash on Psalms* (New Haven: Yale University Press 1959).

Braude, W.G. & Kapstein, I.J.
        Pesikta de-Rab Kahana: R. Kahana's Compilation of Discourses for Sabbaths and Festal Days (Philadelphia: Jewish Publication Society of America 1975).

Braun, R.   *Tertullien: Contre Marcion Tome III* (SC 399, Paris: Les Éditions du Cerf 1994).

Breytenbach, C.   "The Septuagint version of Isaiah 53 and the early Christian formula 'he was delivered for our trespasses'," *NT* 51 (2009) 339-351.

Brock, S.   "The Christology of the Church in the East in the Synods of the Fifth to Early Seventh Centuries: Preliminary Considerations and Materials," in: G.D. Dragas (ed), *Aksum - Thyateira: A Festschrift for Archbishop Methodios of Thyateira and Great Britian* (London: Thyateira House 1985) 125-142.

Brownlee, W.H.   "The Servant of the Lord in the Qumran Scrolls," *BASOR* 132 (1953) 8-15

Bultmann, R.   *Theologie des Neuen Testament* (Tübingen: Mohr 1965).

Burns, R.I.   "The Barcelona 'disputation' of 1263; conversionism and Talmud in Jewish-Christian relations," *Catholic Historical Review* 79 (1993) 488-495.

396

Byrskog, S.   *Story as History – History as Story: the Gospel Tradition in the Context of Ancient Oral History* (WUNT 123; Tübingen: Mohr Siebeck 2000).

Camelot, P.T.   *Ignace d'Antioche, Polycarpe de Smyrne: Lettres, Martyr de Polycarpe* (SC 10, Paris: Les Éditions du Cerf 1998).

Carroll, R.P.   *When Prophecy Failed: Reactions and Responses to Failure in the Old Testament Prophetic Traditions* (London: SCM Press 1979).

Carmignac J.   "Les Citations de l'Ancien Testament et spécialement des Poèmes du Serviteur dans les Hymnes de Qumran," *RevQ* 2 (1960) 357-394.

Cathcart, K.J. & Gordon, R.P.
                The Targum of the Minor Prophets (The Aramaic Bible 14, Edinburgh: Clark 1989).

Chadwick, H.   *Origen: Contra Celsum Translated With an Introduction & Notes* (Cambridge: Cambridge University Press 1953).

Chamberlain J.V "The Functions of God as Messianic Titles in the Complete Qumran Isaiah Scroll," *VT* 5 (1955) 366–72.

Chavel, C.   *Kitvei Rabbenu Moshe ben Nahman. 2 Volumes* (Jerusalem: Mossad Harav Kook 1971).

Chazan, R.   "Joseph Kimhi's 'Sefer ha-Berit'; Pathbreaking Medieval Jewish Apologetics," *HTR* 85 (1992) 417-432.

Chazan, R.   "The Barcelona 'Disputation' of 1263; Christian Missionizing and Jewish Response," *Speculum* 52 (1977) 824-842.

Chazan, R.   "An Ashkenazic anti-Christian treatise," JJSt 34, 1 (1983) 63-72.

Chazan, R.   "The Christian Position in Jacob Ben Reuben's Milchamot Ha-Shem," in: J. Neusner, E.S. Frerichs, N.M. Sarna (eds), *From Ancient Israel to Modern Judaism. Intellect in Quest of Understanding. Essays in Honor of Marvin Fox . Vol. 2: Judaism in the Formative Age: Theology and Literature. Judaism in the Middle Ages: the Encounter with Christianity, the Encounter with Scripture, Philosophy and Theology* (Atlanta: Scholars Press 1989) 157-170.

Chazan, R.   *Barcelona and Beyond: The Disputation of 1263 and Its Aftermath* (Berkeley: University of California 1992).

Chazan, R.   *European Jewry and the First Crusade* (Berkeley: University of Californian Press 1996).

Chazan, R.   "Daniel 9:24-27: Exegesis and Polemics," in: O. Limor & G.G. Stroumsa (eds), *Contra Iudaeos: Ancient and Medieval Polemics between Christians and Jews* (Texts and Studies in Medieval and Early Modern Judaism 10; Tübingen: Mohr Siebeck 1996) 143-159.

Chazan, R.   *God, Humanity, and History: The Hebrew First Crusade Narratives* (Berkeley: University of California Press 2000).

Chazan, R.   "The Anti-Jewish Violence of 1096: Perpetrators and Dynamics," in: A. Sapir Abulafia (ed), *Religious Violence between Christians and Jews: Medieval Roots, Modern Perspectives* (New York: Palgrave 2002) 21-43.

Chazan, R.   *Fashioning Jewish Identity in Medieval Western Christendom* (Cambridge: Cambridge University Press 2004).

Chazan, R.   *The Jews of Medieval Western Christendom 1000-1500* (Cambridge: Cambridge University Press 2006).

Chilton, B.D.   *The Glory of Israel. The Theology and Provenience of the Isaiah Targum* (JSOTSS 23, Sheffield: JSOT Press 1983).

Chilton, B.D.   *The Isaiah Targum* (The Aramaic Bible 11, Wilmington: Michael Glazier 1987).

Chilton, B.D.   "Two in One: Renderings of the Book of Isaiah in Targum Jonathan," in: C.C. Broyles & C.A. Evans (eds), *Writing & Reading the Scroll of Isaiah: Studies of an Interpretive Tradition Volume Two* (VTSup 70:2, Leiden: Brill 1997) 547-562.

Chilton, B.D.   "(The) Son of (the) Man, and Jesus," in: B. Chilton & C.A. Evans (eds), *Authenticating the Words of Jesus* (Leiden: Brill 1999) 259-287.

Chilton, B.D.   "Targum Jonathan of the Prophets I," in: J. Neusner & A.J. Avery-Peck (eds), *Encyclopaedia of Midrash: Biblical Interpretation in Formative Judaism Volume II* (Brill: Leiden 2005) 889-908.

Chilton, B.D.   "Targum Jonathan of the Prophets II," in: J. Neusner & A.J. Avery-Peck (eds), *Encyclopaedia of Midrash: Biblical Interpretation in Formative Judaism Volume II* (Brill: Leiden 2005) 908-927.

Clines, D.J.A.   *I, He, We, & They: A Literary Approach to Isaiah 53* (JSOTSS 1, Sheffield: Sheffield Academic Press 1983).

Cohen, J.   *The Friars and the Jews: The Evolution of Medieval Anti-Judaism* (Ithaca: Cornell University Press 1982).

Cohen, J.   "Scholarship and Intolerance in the Medieval Academy: The Study of Evaluation of Judaism in European Christendom," in: J. Cohen (ed), *Essential Papers on Judaism and Christianity in Conflict: From Late Antiquity to Reformation* (New York: New York University Press 1991) 310-341.

Cohen, J.   "Christian Theology and Anti-Jewish Violence in the Middle Ages: Connections and Disjunctions," in: A. Sapir Abulafia (ed), *Religious Violence between Christians and Jews: Medieval Roots, Modern Perspectives* (New York: Palgrave 2002) 44-60.

Cohen, M.   "The Qimhi Family," M. Saebø, *Hebrew Bible / Old Testament: The History of Its Interpretation. Volume 1: From the Beginning to the Middle Ages (Until 1300). Part 2: The Middle Ages* (Göttingen: Vandenhoeck & Ruprecht 2000) 388-415.

Cohen, M.A.   "Reflections on the Text and Context of the Disputation of Barcelona," *HUCA* 35 (1964) 157-192.

Collins, J.J.   *Between Athens and Jerusalem: Jewish Identity in the Hellenistic Diaspora* (New York: Crossroad 1983).

Collins, J.J.   *Daniel* (Hermeneia, Minneapolis: Fortress 1993).

Collins, J.J.   *The Scepter and the Star: The Messiahs of the Dead Sea Scrolls and Other Ancient Literature* (New York: Doubleday 1995).

398

Collins, J.J. "The Son of Man in Ancient Judaism," in: T. Holmén & S.E. Porter (eds), *Handbook for the Study of the Historical Jesus Vol 2: The Study of Jesus* (Leiden: Brill 2011) 1545-1568.

Colpe, C. ὁ υἱος τοῦ ἀνθτρώπου, *ThWNT* 8 1969 cols. 403-481.

Cross F.M. & Freedman, D.N.
Studies in Ancient Yahwistic Poetry (Grand Rapids: Eerdmans 1997).

Dahl, N.A. "Messianic Ideas and Crucifixion of Jesus," in: J.H. Charlesworth (ed), *The First Princeton Symposium on Judaic and Christian Origins. The Messiah: Developments in Early Judaism and Christianity* (Minneapolis: Fortress 1992) 382-403.

Dalman, G.H. *Der leidende un sterbende Messias der Synagoge im ersten nachchristlichen Jahtausend* (Berlin: Reuther 1888).

Dalman, G.H. *Jesaja 53: das Prophetenwort vom Sühnleiden des Gottesknechtes mit besonderer Berücksichtigung des jüdischen Literatur (Leipzig: Hinrischs'sche Buchhandlung 1914).*

deSilva, G.A. *4 Maccabees* (Guides to Apocrypha and Pseudepigrapha; Sheffield: Sheffield Academic Press 1998).

Duhm, B. *Das Buch Jesaja* (Göttingen: Vandenhoeck & Ruprecht 1922).

Dunn, J.D.G. "Jesus, Table-Fellowship, and Qumran," in: J. Charlesworth (ed), *Jesus and the Dead Sea Scrolls* (The Anchor Bible Reference Library, New York: Doubleday 1992) 254-272.

Dunn, J.D.G. *Jesus Remembered* (Christianity in the Making, Vol. 1; Grand Rapids: Eerdmans 2003).

Eaton, J.H. *Festal Drama in Deutero-Isaiah* (London: SPCK 1979).

Eisenman, R. & Wise, M.
The Dead Sea Scrolls Uncovered (Shaftesbury: Element 1992).

Ekblad, E.R. *Isaiah's Servant Poems According to the Septuagint: An Exegetical and Theological Study* (Contribution to Biblical Exegesis and Theology 23; Leuven: Peeters 1999).

Elliger, K. *Studien zum Habakuk-Kommentar vom Toten Meer* (BHT 15, Tübingen: Mohr 1953).

Elliott, M.W. *Isaiah 40-66* (Ancient Christian Commentary on Scripture Old Testament XI, Downers Grove: InterVarsity Press 2007).

Engnell, I. "Till frågan om Ebed Jahve-sångerna och den lidande Messias hos 'Deuterojesaja'," *SEÅ* 10 (1945) 31-65.

Engnell, I. "Profetia och tradition: Några synpunkter på ett gammaltestamentligt centralproblem," *SEÅ* 12 (1947) 110-139.

Engnell, I. *The 'Ebed Yahweh Songs and the Suffering Messiah in "Deutero-Isaiah"* (Reprinted from BJRL 31 [1948] 54-93; Manchester: The Manchester University 1948).

Euler, K.F. *Die Verkündigung vom leidenden Gottesknecht aus Jes 53 in der griechischen Bibel* (BWAT IV:14; Stuttgart: Kohlhammer 1934).

Eynikel, E. *The Reform of King Josiah and the Composition of the Deuteronomistic History* (OTS 33; Leiden: Brill 1996).

Evans, C.A. "Prophet, Sage, Healer, Messiah, and Martyr: Types and Identities of Jesus," in: T. Holmén & S.E. Porter (eds), *Handbook for the Study of the Historical Jesus Vol 2: The Study of Jesus* (Leiden: Brill 2011) 1217-1243.

Falls, T.B. *St. Justin Martyr: Dialogue with Trypho* (Transl. by Thomas B. Falls; rev. and with a new introduction by Thomas P. Halton; ed. by Michael Slusser. Washington: Catholic University of America Press 2003).

Fascher, E. *Jesaja 53 in christlicher und jüdischer Sicht* (Aufsätze und Verträge zur Theologie und Religionswissenschaft 4; Berlin: Evangelische Verlagsanstalt 1958).

Field, F. *Origenis Hexaplorum Quae Supersunt; Sive Veterum Interpretum Graecorum in Totum Vetus Testamentum Fragmenta* (Oxford: Clarendon 1867).

Fine, L. "Kabbalistic Texts," in: B.W. Holtz (ed), *Back to the Sources. Reading the Classic Jewish Texts* (New York: Thouchstone 1984) 304-359.

Finkelstein, L. *The Commentary of David Kimhi on Isaiah* (Columbia University Oriental Studies 19; New York: Columbia University Press 1926).

Finkelstein, L. *Siphre ad Deuteronomium* (Berlin: Jüdischer Kulturbund in Deutschland 1939).

Finkelstein, L. *Sifra on Leviticus: According to Vatican Manuscript Assemani 61 with Variants from the Other Manuscripts, Genizah Fragments, Early Editions and Quotations by Medieval Authorities and with References to Parallel Passages and Commentaries* (New York: The Jewish Theological Seminary of America 1983-1991).

Fischer, G. *Das Trostbüchlein. Text, Komposition und Theologie von Jer 30-31* (SBB 26, Stuttgart: Katholisches. Bibelwerk 1993).

Fischer, J.A. *Die apostolischen Väter* (Schriften des Urchristentums. Erster Teil, Darmstadt: Wissenschaftliche Buchgesellschaft 1986).

Fitzmyer, J.A. "4Q246: The 'Son of God' Document from Qumran," *Bib* 74 (1993) 153-174.

Fox, M. "Nahmanides on the status of Aggadot; perspectives on the disputation at Barcelona, 1263," *JJS* 40 (1989) 95-109.

Friedländer, M. *The Commentary of Ibn Ezra on Isaiah* (New York: Philipp Feldheim 1873).

Friedländer, M. *Pirush Rabbenu Abraham Eben Ezra al Jesa`ya* (New York: Feldheim 1873).

Friedländer, M. *Essays on the Writings of Abraham ibn Ezra* (London: Truebner 1877).

Funk, F.X. *Didascalia et Constitutiones Apostolorum Volumen I* (Paderborn: Schoeningh 1905).

Funk, R.W., Hoover, R.W. and Jesus Seminar
  The Five Gospels: The Search for the Authentic Words of Jesus (New York: Scribner 1996).

400

Gambero, L.   *Mary and the Fathers of the Church: The Blessed Virgin Mary in Patristic Thought* (San Fransisco: Ignatius Press 1999).

García Martínez, F. & Tigchelaar, E.J.C.
    The Dead Sea Scrolls: Study Edition 1-2 (Leiden: Brill, Grand Rapids: Eerdmans 2000).

Gaster, T.H.   *The Dead Sea Scriptures in English Translation with Introduction and Notes* (Garden City: Doubleday 1957).

Gelles, B.J.   *Peshat and Derash in the Exegesis of Rashi* (EJM 9, Leiden: Brill 1981).

Gereboff, J.   *Rabbi Tarfon: The Tradition, the Man, and Early Rabbinic Judaism* (Brown Judaic Studies 7, Missoula: Scholars Press 1979).

Gerhardsson, B.   *Memory and Manuscript: Oral Tradition and Written Transmission in Rabbinic Judaism and Early Christianity* (Acta Seminarii Neotestamentici Upsaliensis 22; Lund: Gleerups 1961).

Gerhardsson, B.   *The Reliability of the Gospel Tradition* (Peabody, Mass.: Hendrickson Publishers 2001).

Gnilka, J.   *Das Evangelium nach Markus (Mk 8,27-16,20)* (EKK zum Neuen Testament II/2; Zürich: Benziger, Neukirchen-Vluyn: Neukirchener 1979).

Goldstein, J.A.   *I Maccabees* (AB 41, Garden City: Doubleday 1977).

Goldstein, J.A.   *II Maccabees* (AB 41 A; Garden City: Doubleday 1983).

Gómez Aranda M.
    "Jacob's Blessings in Medieval Jewish Exegesis," in: E. Koskenniemi & P. Lindqvist (eds), *Rewritten Biblical Figures* (Studies in Rewritten Bible 3, Winona Lake: Eisenbrauns & Åbo Akademi University 2010) 235-258.

Goodspeed, E.J.   *Die ältesten Apologeten. Texte mit kurzen Einleitungen* (Göttingen: Vandenhoeck & Ruprecht 1984).

Goppelt, L.   *Theologie des Neuen Testaments* (Göttingen: Vandenhoeck & Ruprecht 1978).

Goshen-Gottstein, M.
    R. Judah ibn Bal'am's Commentary on Isaiah: The Arabic Original According to MS Firkowitch (Ebr-Arab I 1377) with a Hebrew Translation, Notes and Introduction (Ramat Gan: Bar-Ilan University Press 1992).

Gould, E.P.   *A Critical and Exegetical Commentary on the Gospel According to St. Mark* (Edinburgh: Clark 1921).

Goulder, M.   "Jesus without Q," in: T. Holmén & S.E. Porter (eds), *Handbook for the Study of the Historical Jesus Vol 2: The Study of Jesus* (Leiden: Brill 2011) 1287-1311.

Grabbe, L.L.   *Wisdom of Solomon* (Guides to Apocrypha and Pseudepigrapha; Sheffield: Sheffield Academic Press 1997).

Green, A.   "Introduction," in D.C. Matt, *The Zohar: Pritzker Edition* (Stanford CA.: Stanford University Press 2001) XXXI-LXXXI.

Green, A.   *A Guide to the Zohar* (Stanford CA.: Stanford University Press 2003).

Greenstein, E.L. "Medieval Bible Commentaries," in: B.W. Holtz, *Back to the Sources: Reading the Classic Jewish Texts* (New York: Simon & Schuster 1992) 213-260.

Grillmeier, A. *Christ in Christian Tradition Volume One: From the Apostolic Age to Chalcedon (451)* (Atlanta: John Knox 1975).

Grimm, W. *Weil ich dich liebe: Die Verkündigung Jesu und Deuterojesaja* (ANTJ 1, Frankfurt: Lang 1976).

Grimm, W. & Dittert, K.
 Deuterojesaja: Deutung - Wirkung - Gegenwart (Calwer Bibelkommentare, Stuttgart: Calwer 1990).

Grossinger, H. "Die Disputation des Nachmanides mit Fra Pablo Christiani, Barcelona 1263," *Kairos* 19 (1977) 257-285; 20 (1978) 1-15, 161-181.

Grossman, A. "The School of Literal Jewish Exegesis in Northern France," in: M. Saebø, *Hebrew Bible / Old Testament: The History of Its Interpretation. Volume 1: From the Beginning to the Middle Ages (Until 1300). Part 2: The Middle Ages* (Göttingen: Vandenhoeck & Ruprecht 2000) 321-371.

Gruber, M.I. *Rashi's Commentary on Psalms 1-89* (South Florida studies in the history of Judaism 161, Atlanta: Scholars Press 1998).

Gruber, M.I. *Rashi's Commentary on the Book of Psalms* (Leiden: Brill 2004).

Guinot, J.-N. *Theodoret de Cyr: Commentaire sur Isaïe Tome III* (SC 315, Paris: Les Éditions du Cerf 1984).

Gunneweg, A.H.J. *Esra* (KAT 19/1, Gütersloh: Mohn 1985).

Gunneweg, A.H.J. *Nehemia* (KAT 19/2, Gütersloh: Mohn 1987).

Haag, E. "Die Botschaft vom Gottesknecht: Ein Weg zur Überwindung der Gewalt," in: N. Lohfink (ed), *Gewalt und Gewaltlosigkeit im Alten Testament* (Quaestiones disputatae 96 Freiburg: Herder 1983) 159-213.

Haag, H. *Der Gottesknecht bei Deuterojesaja* (EdF 233, Darmstadt: Wissenschaftliche Buchgesellschaft 1985).

Hägglund, F. *Isaiah 53 in the Light of Homecoming After the Exile* (FAT II/31, Tübingen: Mohr Siebeck 2008).

Hampel, V. *Menschensohn und historischer Jesus: Ein Rätselwort als Schlüssel zum messianischen Selbstverständnis Jesu* (Neukirchen-Vluyn: Neukirchener Verlag 1990).

Hanson, P.D. "The World of the Servant of the Lord in Isaiah 40-55," in: W.H. Bellinger & W.R. Farmer, *Jesus and the Suffering Servant: Isaiah 53 and Christian Origins* (Harrisburg: Trinity Press International 1998) 9-23.

Harrington, D.J. & Saldarini, A.J.
 Targum Jonathan of the Former Prophets (The Aramaic Bible 10; Wilmington: Michael Glazier 1987).

Harvey, R. *Raymundus Martini and the Pugio Fidei: The Life and Work of a Medieval Controversialist* (Diss. London 1991).

Hayward, C.T.R. *The Targum of Jeremiah* (The Aramaic Bible 12, Wilmington: Michael Glazier 1987).

Hegermann, H. *Jesaja 53 in Hexapla, Targum und Peschitta* (Gütersloh: Mohn 1954).

Heinemann, J. "The Messiah of Ephraim and the Premature Exodus of the Tribe of Ephraim," *HTR* 68 (1975) 1-15.

Hengel, M. *Studies in the Gospel of Mark* (Philadelphia: Fortress Press 1985).

Hengel, M. *The Cross of the Son of God Containing The Son of God, Crucifixion, The Atonement* (London: SCM Press 1986).

Hengel, M. *Judentum und Hellenismus: Studien zu ihrer Begegnung unter besonderer Berücksichtigung Palästinas bis zur Mitte des 2. Jh.s v. Chr.* (WUNT 10, Tübingen: Mohr 1988).

Hengel, M. *The Zealots* (Edinburgh: T.T. Clark 1989).

Hengel, M. "Die Septuaginta als 'christliche Schriftensammlung', ihre Vorgeschichte und das Problem ihres Kanons," in: M. Hengel & A.M. Schwemer (eds), *Die Septuaginta zwischen Judentum und Christentum* (WUNT 72, Tübingen: Mohr 1994) 182-284.

Hengel, M. "Jesus, the Messiah of Israel: The Debate about the 'Messianic Mission' of Jesus." In: B. Chilton & C.A. Evans, *Authenticating the Activities of Jesus* (Leiden: Brill 1999), 323-349.

Hengel, M. "The Effective History of Isaiah 53 in the Pre-Christian Period," in: B. Janowski & P. Stuhlmacher (eds), *The Suffering Servant: Isaiah 53 in Jewish and Christian Sources* (Grand Rapids: Eerdmans 2004) 75-146.

Hengel, M. & Schwemer, A.M.
  Der messianische Anspruch Jesu und die Anfänge der Christologie (WMANT 138, Tübingen: Mohr Siebeck 2003).

Henten van, J.W. "Datierung und Herkunft des Vierten Makkabäerbuches," in: J.W. Henten & H.J. de Jonge et al. (eds), *Tradition and Re-interpretation in Jewish and Christian Literature* (Leiden: Brill 1986) 136-149.

Henten van, J.W. *Die Entstehung der jüdischen Martyrologie* (Studia Post-Biblica 38, Leiden: Brill 1989).

Henten van, J.W. *The Maccabean Martyrs as Saviours of the Jewish People: A Study of 2 and 4 Maccabees* (SupSJS 57, Leiden: Brill 1997).

Hermisson, H.-J. "Der Lohn des Knechts," in: J. Jeremias & L. Perlitt (eds), *Die Botschaft und die Boten. Festschrift für H.W. Wolff zum 70. Geburtstag* (Neukirchen-Vluyn: Neukirchener Verlag 1981) 269-287.

Hermisson, H.-J. "Israel und der Gottesknecht bei Deuterojesaja," *ZThK* 79 (1982) 1-24.

Hermisson, H.-J. "Voreiliger Abschied von den Gottesknechtsliedern," *TR NF* 49 (1984) 209-222.

Hermisson, H.-J. "Deuterojesaja-Probleme: Ein kritischer Literaturbericht," *VF* 31 (1986) 53-84.

Higgins, A.J.B.   "Jewish Messianic Belief in Justin Martyr's Dialogue with Trypho,"
                   NT 9 (1967) 298-305 [reprinted in L. Landman, *Messianism in the
                   Talmudic Era* (New York: KTAV Publishing House 1979) 182-189].

Hoffman, H.-D.   *Reform und Reformen: Untersuchungen zu einem Grundthema der
                   deuteronomistischen Geschichtsschreibung* (ATANT 66, Zürich:
                   Theologischer Verlag 1980).

Hofius, O.   "The Fourth Servant Song in the New Testament Letters," in: B.
                   Janowski & P. Stuhlmacher (eds), *The Suffering Servant: Isaiah 53
                   in Jewish and Christian Sources* (Grand Rapids: Eerdmans 2004)
                   163-188.

Holladay, W. L.   *Jeremiah 2* (Hermeneia, Philadelphia: Fortress Press 1989).

Hooker, M.D.   *Jesus and the Servant* (London: SPCK 1959).

Hooker, M.D.   "Did the Use of Isaiah 53 to Interpret His Mission Begin with Jesus?"
                   in: W.H. Bellinger & W.R. Farmer, *Jesus and the Suffering Servant:
                   Isaiah 53 and Christian Origins* (Harrisburg: Trinity Press
                   International 1998) 88-103.

Horgan, M.P.   *Pesharim: Qumran Interpretations of Biblical Books* (CBQMS 8,
                   Washington: The Catholic Biblical Association of America 1979).

Hultgård, A.   *L'eschatologie des Testaments des Douze Patriarches II:
                   Composition de l'ouvrage textes et traductions* (Acta Universitatis
                   Upsaliensis, Historia Religionum 7; Stockholm: Almqvist & Wiksell
                   International 1982).

Hurwitz, B.P.   *Fidei Causa et Tui Amore: The Role of Petrus Aphonsi's Dialogues
                   in the History of Jewish-Christian Debate* (Diss. Yale University
                   1983).

Hvalvik, R.   *The Struggle for Scripture and Covenant: The Purpose of the Epistle
                   of Barnabas and Jewish-Christian Competition in the Second
                   Century* (Oslo: Det teologiske Menighetsfakultet 1994).

Hyldahl, N.   "Tryphon und Tarphon," *StTh* 10 (1956), 77-88.

Ibn Ezra   *Ibn Ezra's Commentary on the Pentateuch: Genesis* (Bereshit).
                   Translated and Annotated by H.N. Strickman & A.M. Silver (New
                   York: Menorah Publishing Company 1988).

Idel, M.   *Kabbalah. New Perspectives* (New Haven: Yale University Press
                   1989).

Jahnow, H.   *Das hebräische Leichenlied im Rahmen der Völkerdichtung* (Giessen:
                   Töpelmann, 1923).

Janowski, B.   *Stellvertretung: Alttestamentliche Studien zu einem theologischen
                   Grundbegriff* (Stuttgarter Bibelstudien 165, Stuttgart: Katholisches
                   Bibelwerk 1997).

Janowski, B.   "He Bore Our Sins: Isaiah 53 and the Drama of Taking Another's
                   Place," in: B. Janowski & P. Stuhlmacher (eds), *The Suffering
                   Servant: Isaiah 53 in Jewish and Christian Sources* (Grand Rapids:
                   Eerdmans 2004) 48-74.

Janowski, B.   *Ecce Homo: Stellvertretung und Lebenshingabe als Themen Biblischer Theologie* (Biblisch-Theologische Studien 84, Neukirchen-Vluyn: Neukirchener Verlag 2007).

Japhet, S.   "Theodicy in Ezra-Nehemiah and Chronicles," in: A. Laato & J.C. De Moor (eds), *Theodicy in the World of the Bible* (Leiden: Brill 2003) 429-469.

Jeremias, Chr.   *Die Nachtgesichte des Sacharja: Untersuchungen zu ihrer Stellung im Zusammenhang der Visionsberichte im Alten Testament und zu ihrem Bildmaterial* (FRLANT 117; Göttingen: Vandenhoeck & Ruprecht 1977).

Jeremias, G.   *Der Lehrer der Gerechtigkeit* (WUNT 2, Göttingen: Vandenhoeck & Ruprecht 1963).

Jeremias, J.   παῖς θεοῦ in *TWNT* 5 (1954) 676-713.

Jeremias, J.   W. Zimmerli & J. Jeremias, *The Servant of God* (SBT 20, London: SCM Press 1965).

Joachimsen, K.   *Identities in Transition: The Pursuit of Isa. 52:13-53:12* (SupVT 142, Leiden: Brill 2011).

Johnson, S.R.   *Historical Fictions and Hellenistic Jewish Identity: Third Maccabees in Its Cultural Context* (Hellenistic culture and society 43; Berkeley: University of California Press 2004).

Kaiser, O.   *Der königliche Knecht: Eine traditionsgeschichtlich-exegetische Studie über die Ebed-Jahwe-Lieder bei Deuterojesaja* (FRLANT 52; Göttingen: Vandenhoeck & Ruprecht 1959).

Kannengiesser, C   *Sur L'Incarnation du Verbe* (SC 199, Paris: Les Éditions du Cerf 2000).

Kelly, J.N.D.   *Early Christian Creeds* (Essex: Longman 1991).

Kelly, J.N.D.   *Early Christian Doctrines* (London: Black 1993).

Klauck, H.-J.   *4. Makkabäerbuch* (JSHRZ III/6, Gütersloh: Gütersloher Verlagshus 1989).

Klausner, J.   *The Messianic Idea in Israel from Its Beginning to the Completion of the Mishnah* (New York: Macmillan 1956).

Knapp, H.M.   "Melito's Use of Scripture in *Peri Pascha*: Second-Century Typology," *Vigilae Christianae* 54 (2000) 343-374.

Kobak, J.   "Jacob ben Elia: 'Letter to the Apostate Saul'," *Jeschurun* 6 (1868) 1–34. [Hebrew]

Koch, K.   "Sühne und Sündenvergebung um die Wende von der exilischen zur nachexilischen Zeit," *EvTh* 26 (1966) 217-239.

Koch, K.   "Messias und Sündenvergebung in Jesaja 53 – Targum: Ein Beitrag zu der Praxis der aramäischen Bibelübersetzung," *JSJ* 3 (1972) 117-148.

Kooij van der, A.   *Die alten Textzeugen des Jesajabuches: Ein Beitrag zur Textgeschichte des Alten Testaments* (OBO 35, Freiburg: Universitätsverlag, Göttingen: Vandenhoeck & Ruprecht 1980).

Koskenniemi, E. & Lindqvist, P.
"Rewritten Bible, Rewritten Stories", in A. Laato & J. van Ruiten (eds), *Rewritten Bible Reconsidered: Proceedings of the Conference in Karkku, Finland, August 24-26 2006* (Studies in Rewritten Bible 1, Åbo: Åbo Akademi University & Winona Lake: Eisenbrauns 2008) 11-39.

Kraabel, A.T.   "Melito the Bishop and the Synagogue at Sardis: Text and Context," in: D.G. Mitten, J.G. Pedley, J.A. Scott (eds.), *Studies Presented to George M.A. Hanfmann* (Mainz: Philipp von Zabern 1971) 77-85.

Kraft, R.   "Barnabas' Isaiah Text and the 'Testimony Book' Hypothesis," *JBL* 79 (1960) 336-350.

Kraft, R.   "Barnabas' Isaiah Text and Melito's Paschal Homily," *JBL* 80 (1961) 371-373.

Krauss, S. & Horbury, W.
The Jewish-Christian Controversy from the Earliest Times to 1789 Volume 1: History (Tübingen: Mohr Siebeck 1995).

Kreplin, M.   "The Self-Understanding of Jesus," in: T. Holmén & S.E. Porter (eds), *Handbook for the Study of the Historical Jesus Vol 3: The Historical Jesus* (Leiden: Brill 2011) 2473-2516.

Kugel, J.   *Early Biblical Interpretation* (Library of Early Christianity 3; Philadelphia: Westminster Press 1986).

Kugel, J.   *Traditions of the Bible: A Guide to the Bible As It Was at the Start of the Common Era* (Cambridge MA.: Harvard University Press 1998).

Kutscher, E.Y.   *A History of the Hebrew Language* (Jerusalem: The Magnes Press, The Hebrew University 1984).

Laato, A.M.   *Jews and Christians in De duobus montibus Sina et Sion: An Approach to Early Latin Adversus Iudaeos Literature* (Åbo: Åbo Akademi University Press 1998).

Laato, A.   "The Seventy Yearweeks in the Book of Daniel," *ZAW* 102 (1990) 212-225.

Laato, A.   "The Composition of Isaiah 40-55," *JBL* 109 (1990) 203-224.

Laato, A.   "The Eschatological Act of *kipper* in the Damascus Document," in: Z.J. Kapera (ed), *Intertestamental Essays in honour of Jósef Tadeusz Milik Volume 1* (Qumranica Mogilanensia 6; Cracow: Enigma 1992) 91-107.

Laato, A.   *Josiah and David Redivivus: The Historical Josiah and the Messianic Expectations of Exilic and Postexilic Times* (ConBOT 33; Stockholm: Almqvist & Wiksell International 1992).

Laato, A.   *The Servant of YHWH and Cyrus: A Reinterpretation of the Exilic Messianic Programme in Isaiah 40-55* (ConBOT 35; Stockholm: Almqvist & Wiksell International 1992).

Laato, A.   '2 Samuel 7 and Ancient Near Eastern Royal Ideology,' *CBQ* 59 (1997) 244-269.

406

Laato, A. *A Star Is Rising: The Historical Development of the Old Testament Royal Ideology and the Rise of the Jewish Messianic Expectations* (International Studies in Formative Christianity and Judaism, Atlanta: Scholars Press 1997).

Laato, A. *About Zion I Will Not be Silent: The Book of Isaiah as an Ideological Unity* (ConBOT 44; Stockholm: Almqvist & Wiksell International 1998).

Laato, A. *Monotheism, the Trinity and Mysticism. A Semiotic Approach to Jewish-Christian Encounter* (Frankfurt am Main: Peter Lang 1999).

Laato, A. "The idea of kipper in Judaisms of late antiquity," *Khristianskij Vostok* (= Christian Orient) 1 (1999) 155-193.

Laato, A. *Anteeksiantamus ja Uhri: Sovitus Vanhassa testamentissa, juutalaisuudessa ja Uudessa testamentissa* [Forgiveness and Sacrifice: Atonement in the Old Testament, Judaism and in the New Testament] (Iustitia-serien 16, Helsinki 2002).

Laato, A. "Theodicy in the Deuteronomistic History," in: A. Laato & J.C. De Moor (eds), *Theodicy in the World of the Bible* (Leiden: Brill 2003) 183-235.

Laato, A. *Emmauksen tiellä: Miten ensimmäiset kristityt selittivät Vanhaa testamenttia?* [On the Way to Emmaus: How the First Christians Interpreted the Old Testament?] (Åbo: Åbo Akademi 2006).

Laato, A. "Isaiah 53 in Jewish Perspective: Four Misunderstandings in Christian Exegesis," in: J. Svanberg, A. Holmberg & N.G. Holm (eds), *Kritisk läsning och ärliga ord: Vänskrift till Siv Illman* (Religionsvetenskapliga skrifter 71, Åbo: Åbo Akademi 2007) 127-141.

Laato, A. "Beloved and lovely! Despised and rejected. Some reflections on the death of Josiah," in: J. Pakkala & M. Nissinen (eds), *Houses Full of All Good Things. Essays in Memory of Timo Veijola* (Helsinki, Göttingen 2008) 115-128.

Laato, A. "Isaiah 53 and the Biblical Exegesis of Justin Martyr," in: A.Laato & J. Van Ruiten (eds), *Rewritten Bible Reconsidered: Proceedings of the Conference in Karkku, Finland August 24-26 2006* (SRB 1, Winona Lake: Eisenbrauns; Turku: Åbo Akademi University 2008) 215-229.

Laato, A. "Justin Martyr Encounters Judaism," in A. Laato & P. Lindqvist (eds), *Encounters of the Children of Abraham from Ancient to Modern Times* (STCA 1, Leiden: Brill 2010) 97-123.

Laato, A. "Gen 49:8-12 and Its Interpretation In Antiquity – A Methodological Approach to Understanding of the Rewritten Bible," in: E. Koskenniemi & P. Lindqvist (eds), *Rewritten Biblical Figures* (SRB 3, Turku: ÅAU, Winona Lake: Eisenbrauns 2010) 1-26.

Laato, A.	"Interpreting the Hebrew Bible with Different Hermeneutical Models," in: S.-O. Back & M. Kankaanniemi (eds), *Voces Clamantium in Deserto: Essays in Honor of Kari Syreeni* (Studier i exegetik och judaistik utgivna av Teologiska fakulteten vid Åbo Akademi 11; Åbo: Åbo Akademi University 2012) 163-183.
Landman, L.	*Messianism in the Talmudic Era* (New York: KTAV Publishing House 1979).
Lange de, N.	*Origen and the Jews: Studies in Jewish-Christian Relations in Third-Century Palestine* (University of Cambridge Oriental Publications 25; Cambridge: Cambridge University Press 1978).
Lapide P. & Moltmann, J.	*Jüdischer Monotheismus – Christliche Trinitätslehre: Ein Gespräch* (Munich: Chr. Kaiser 1979).
Lasker, D.J.	*Jewish Philosophical Polemics against Christianity in the Middle Ages* (New York: Ktav Publishing House 1977).
Lasker, D.J.	"The Jewish critique of Christianity under Islam in the Middle Ages," *PAAJR* 57 (1991) 121-153.
Lasker, D.J.	"Jewish-Christian Polemics at the Turning Point: Jewish Evidence from the Twelfth Century," *HTR* 89 (1996) 172-201.
Lasker, D.J.	"Jewish-Christian Polemics in Transition: From the Lands of Ishmael to the Lands of Edom," in: B. Hary, J. Hayes & F. Astren (eds) *Judaism and Islam: Boundaries, Interaction, and Communication* (Leiden: Brill 2000) 53-65.
Lasker D.J. & Stroumsa, S.	*The Polemic of Nestor the Priest. **Qissat Mujādalat al-Usquf** and **Sefer Nestor Ha-Komer** Volumes 1-2* (Jerusalem: Ben-Zvi Institute for the Study of Jewish Communities in the East 1996).
Lehmann, M.	"'Yom Kippur' in Qumran," *RdQ* 3 (1961/62) 119-124.
Levey, S.H.	*The Targum of Ezekiel* (The Aramaic Bible 13; Wilmington: Michael Glazier 1987).
Levey, S.H.	*The Text and I: Writings of Samson H. Levey* (edited by S.F. Chyet; South Florida Studies in the History of Judaism 166, Atlanta: Scholars Press 1998).
Levine, E.	"The Biography of the Aramaic Bible," *ZAW* 94 (1982) 353-379.
Levine, E.	"Targum, Conceptual Categories of," in: J. Neusner & A.J. Avery-Peck (eds), *Encyclopaedia of Midrash: Biblical Interpretation in Formative Judaism Volume II* (Brill: Leiden 2005) 908-927.
Liber, M.	*Rashi* (London: Mazin 1911).
Licht, J.	"Taxo, or the Apocalyptic Doctrine of Vengeance," *JJS* 12 (1961) 95-103.
Lieberman, S.	"Raymund Martini and His Alleged Forgeries," *Historia Judaica* 5 (1943) 87-102.
Liebes, Y.	*Studies in Zohar* (SUNY Series in Judaica: Hermeneutics, Mysticism, and Religion, New York 1993).
Limor, O.	"Beyond Barcelona," *Jewish History* 9 (1995) 107-119.

408

Lindblom, J.   *The Servant Songs in Deutero-Isaiah: A New Attempt to Solve an Old Problem* (Lund 1951).

Litwak, K.D.   "The Use of Quotations from Isaiah 52:13-53:12 in the New Testament," *JETS* 26 (1983) 385-394.

Lohfink, N.   "Israel in Jes 49,3," in: J. Schreiner (ed), *Wort, Lied und Gottesspruch: Beiträge zu Psalmen und Propheten: FS Joseph Ziegler* (Bd. II; FzB 2; Würzburg: Echter, 1972) 217-229.

Lohfink, N.   "Der junge Jeremia als Propagandist und Poet. Zum Grundstock von Jer 30-31," in: P. M. Bogaert (ed.) *Le livre de Jérémie. Le prophète et son milieu, les oracles et leur transmission* (BETL 54, Leuven: Peeters 1981) 351-68.

Lohfink, N.   "Die Gotteswortverschachtelung in Jer 30-31," in: L. Ruppert, P. Weimar, E. Zenger (eds), *Künder des Wortes: Beiträge zur Theologie der Propheten Josef Schreiner zum 60. Geburtstag* (Würzburg: Echter Verlag 1982) 105-119

Lohmeyer, E.   *Kyrios Jesus: Eine Untersuchung zu Phil. 2, 5-11* (Sitzungsberichte der Heidelberger Akademie der Wissenschaften, Philosophisch-historische Klasse; 1927/28, Abh. 4; Heidelberg : C. Winter 1928).

Lüdemann, G.   *Jesus after Two Thousand Years: What He Really Said and Did* (London: SCM 2000).

MacKenzie, I.M.   *Irenaeus's Demonstration of the Apostolic Preaching: A Theological Commentary and Translation* (Aldershot: Ashgate 2002).

Macoby, H.   *Judaism on Trial: Jewish-Christian Disputations in the Middle Ages* (London: The Littman Library of Jewish Civilization 1993).

Maier, W.A.   "Hadadrimmon," *ABD* 3:13.

Malter, H.   *Saadia Gaon: His Life and Works* (Hildesheim: Olms 1978).

Mann, C.S.   *Mark* (AB 27, New York: Doubleday 1986).

Mann, J.   *The Jews in Egypt and in Palestine under the Fatimid Caliphs: A Contribution to Their Political and Communal History Based Chiefly on Geniza Material Hitherto Unpublished. Volumes I-II* (New York: KTAV Publishing House 1970).

Marcovich, M.   *Iustini Martyris Apologiae pro Christianis* (Berlin: de Gruyter 1994).

Marcovich, M.   *Iustini Martyris Dialogus cum Tryphone* (Berlin: de Gruyter 1997).

Marcus, J.   *Mark 8-16* (AB 27A, New haven: Yale University Press 2009).

Margulies R.   *Sefer Wikuach Rabbenu Jehiel mi-Paris* (Lwow 1928).

Markschies, C.   "Jesus Christ as a Man before God: Two Interpretive Models for Isaiah 53 in the Patristic Literature and Their Development," in: B. Janowski & P. Stuhlmacher (eds), *The Suffering Servant: Isaiah 53 in Jewish and Christian Sources* (Grand Rapids: Eerdmans 2004) 225-320.

Martini, Raymundi
                  Pugio fidei Adversus Mauros et Judeos cum Observationibus Josephi de Voisin, et Introductione Jo. Benedicti Carpzovi (Paris 1667).

Matt, D.C.   *Zohar: The Book of Enlightment. Translation and Introduction* (New York: Paulist Press 1983).

Matt, D.C.	*The Zohar: Pritzker Edition. Volumes 1-5* (Stanford CA.: Stanford University Press 2004-2009).
McCarthy, D. J	'II Samuel and the Structure of the Deuteronomistic History,' *JBL* 84 (1965) 131-138.
McNamara, M.	*The New Testament and the Palestinian Targum to the Pentateuch* (AnBib 27A, Rome: Biblical Institute Press 1978).
Melugin, R.F.	"On Reading Isaiah 53 as Christian Scripture," in: W.H. Bellinger & W.R. Farmer (eds), *Jesus and the Suffering Servant: Isaiah 53 and Christian Origins* (Harrisburg: Trinity Press International 1998) 55-69.
Mettinger, T.N.D	"Die Ebed-Jahwe-Lieder: Ein fragwürdiges Axiom," *ASTI* 11 (1977/78) 68-76.
Mettinger, T.N.D	*The Dethronement of Sabaoth: Studies in the Shem and Kabod Theologies* (ConBOT 18, Lund: Gleerups 1982).
Mettinger, T.N.D	*A Farewell to the Servant Songs: A Critical Examination of an Exegetical Axiom* (Scripta Minora 1982-1983:3, Lund: Gleerups 1983).
Metzger, M.	*Les Constitutions Apostoliques Tome I* (SC 320, Paris: Les Éditions du Cerf 1985).
Mitchell, D.C.	"Rabbi Dosa and the Rabbis Differ: Messiah ben Joseph in the Babylonian Talmud," *RBJ* 8 (2005) 77-90.
Mitchell, D.C.	"Messiah ben Joseph: A Sacrifice of Atonement for Israel," *RRJ* 10 (2007) 77-94.
Mittmann-Richert, U.	*Der Sühnetod des Gottesknecht: Jesaja 53 im Lukasevangelium* (WUNT 220, Tübingen: Mohr Siebeck 2008).
Mowinckel, S.	*He That Cometh* (Oxford: Blackwell 1956).
Mutius von, H.-G	*Die Christlich-Jüdische Zwangsdisputation zu Barcelona* (Judentum und Umwelt 5, Frankfurt am Main: Lang 1982).
Na'aman, N.	"The Kingdom of Judah under Josiah," *Tel Aviv* 18 (1991) 3-71.
Nelson, R.N.	"Realpolitik in Judah (687-609 B.C.E.)," in: W. W. Hallo, J. C. Moyer & L. G. Perdue (eds), *Scripture in Context II. More Essays on the Comparative Method* (Winona Lake: Eisenbrauns 1983) 177-189.
Neubauer, A.	"Jewish Controversy and the 'Pugio Fidei'," *The Expositor* 38 (1888) 81-105; 39 (1889) 179-197.
Neubauer, A.	*The Fifty-Third Chapter of Isaiah According to the Jewish Interpreters. I: Texts* (Varda Books 2005)
Neubauer, A. & Driver, S.	*The "Suffering Servant" of Isaiah According to the Jewish Interpreters Translated by S.R. Driver and A. Neubauer* (Eugene: Wipf and Stock 1999).
Neusner, J.	*Messiah in Context: Israel's History and Destiny in Formative Judaism* (The Foundations of Judaism: Method, Teleology, Doctrine 2; Philadelphia: Fortress Press, 1984).

410

Neusner, J.   *Sifre to Deuteronomy: An Analytical Translation Volume Two: Pisqaot One Hundred Forty-Four through Three Hundred Fifty Seven* (Brown Judaic Studies 101, Atlanta: Scholars Press 1987).

Neusner, J.   *Sifra: An Analytical Translation Volume One* (Brown Judaic Studies 138, Atlanta: Scholars Press 1988).

Neusner, J.   *The Components of the Rabbinic Documents From the Whole to the Parts I: Sifra* (South Florida Academic Commentary Series 75; Atlanta, Ga.: Scholars Press 1997).

Neusner, J.   *A Theological Commentary to the Midrash, Volume 6: Ruth Rabbah and Esther Rabbah I* (Studies in Ancient Judaism, Lanham: University Press of America 2001).

Nickelsburg, G.W.E.
    Resurrection, Immortality, and Eternal Life in Intertestamental Judaism and Early Christianity (Harvard Theological Studies 56, Cambridge: Harvard University Press 2006).

Nickelsburg, G.W.E. & Baltzer, K.
    1 Enoch: A Commentary on the Book of 1 Enoch 1-36; 81-108 (Hermeneia; Minneapolis: Fortress 2011).

Niclós, J.-V.   *Šem Tob ibn Šaprut, "La Piedra de Toque" (Eben Bohan).* Una obra de controversia Judeo-Cristiana (Madrid: Consejo Superior de Investigaciones Cientificas 1997).

North, C.R.   *The Suffering Servant in Deutero-Isaiah: An Historical and Critical Study* (Oxford: Oxford University Press1963).

Novak, D.   *The Theology of Nahmanides Systematically Presented* (Brown Judaic Studies 271, Atlanta: Scholars Press 1992).

Nyberg, H.S.   "Smärtornas man: En studie till Jes. 52,13-53,12," *SEÅ* 7 (1942) 5-82.

O'Connor-Visser, E.A.M.E.
    Aspects of Human Sacrifice in the Tragedies of Euripides (Diss. Amsterdam 1987).

The Old Testament Pseudepigrapha.
    The Old Testament Pseudepigrapha. Vol. 1-2. Ed. by James H. Charlesworth (Garden City: Doubleday 1983).

Osborn, E.F.   *Justin Martyr* (Tübingen: Mohr Siebeck, 1973).

Osborn, E.F.   *Irenaeus of Lyons* (Cambridge: Cambridge University Press 2001).

Paul, S.M.   "Deutero-Isaiah and Cuneiform Royal Inscriptions," *JAOS* 88 (1968) 180-186.

Pelikan, J.   *Jesus Through the Centuries* (New Haven and London: Yale University Press, 1985).

Perler, O.   *Méliton de Sardes: Sur la Pâque et Fragments* (SC 123, Paris 1966).

Pesch, R.   *Das Markusevangelium II. Teil Kommentar zu Kap. 8,27-16,20* (HTKNT 2; Freiburg: Herder 1977).

Pickup, M.   "The Emergence of the Suffering Messiah in Rabbinic Literature," in:
                 J. Neusner (ed), *Approaches to Ancient Judaism. New Series Vol 11*
                 (South Florida Studies in the History of Judaism 154, Atlanta:
                 Scholars Press 1997) 143-162.

Popper, W.   *The Censorship of Hebrew Books* (New York: KTAV Publishing
                 House 1969).

Puech, E.   "Fragment d'une Apocalypse en Araméen (4Q246 = pseudo-Dan^d) et
                 le 'Royaume de Dieu," *RB* 99 (1992) 98-131.

Puech, E.   "Fragments d'un apocryphe de Levi et le personnage eschatologique:
                 4QTestLevi^{c-d} et 4QAJa," in: J.T. Barrera & L.V. Montaner (eds),
                 The Madrid Qumran Congress Volume 2 (STDJ 11/2 Leiden: Brill
                 1992) 449-501.

Puech, E.   "Notes sur le fragment d'apocalypse 4Q246 – 'Le fils de Dieu'," *RB*
                 101 (1994) 533-558.

Rahlfs, A.   *Septuaginta* (Stuttgart: Deutsche Bibelgesellschaft 1982).

Rembaum, J.E.   "The Influence of Sefer Nestor Hakomer on Medieval Jewish
                 Polemics," *PAAJR* 45 (1978), 155-185.

Rembaum, J.E.   "The Development of a Jewish Exegetical Tradition Regarding Isaiah
                 53," *HTR* 75 (1982) 289-311.

Rembaum, J.E.   "Medieval Christianity confronts Talmudic Judaism," *Judaism* 34
                 (1985) 373-384.

Remus, H.   "Justin Martyr's Argument with Judaism," in: S.G. Wilson (ed.),
                 *Anti-Judaism in Early Christianity. Volume 2: Separation and
                 Polemic* (Waterloo: Wilfrid Laurier University Press 1986) 59-80.

Resnick, I.M.   *Petrus Alfonsi. Dialogue against the Jews.* (The Fathers of the
                 Church. Mediaeval Continuation. Washington: The Catholic
                 University of America Press 2006).

Robles Sierra, A. *Raimundi Martini: Capistrum Iudaeorum I* (CISC Series Latina 3/1,
                 Würzburg: Echter Verlag 1990).

Robles Sierra, A. *Raimundi Martini: Capistrum Iudaeorum II* (CISC Series Latina 5,
                 Würzburg: Echter Verlag 1993).

Rosengård, N.   *We Want Moshiach NOW! Understanding the Messianic Message in
                 the Jewish Chabad-Lubavitch Movement* (Turku: Åbo Akademis
                 förlag 2009).

Rosenthal, J.M. *Milhamot ha-Shem* (Jerusalem: Mossad ha-Rav Kook 1963).

Rosenthal, J.M. *Joseph ben Nathan Official, Sepher Joseph Hamekane* (Jerusalem:
                 Mossad ha-Rav Kook 1970).

Rousseau, A.   *Irénée de Lyon: Contre les Hérésies Livre I* (SC 264, Paris: Les
                 Éditions du Cerf 1979).

Rousseau, A.   *Irénée de Lyon: Contre les Hérésies Livre II* (SC 294, Paris: Les
                 Éditions du Cerf 1982).

Rousseau, A.   *Irénée de Lyon: Contre les Hérésies Livre III* (SC 211, Paris: Les
                 Éditions du Cerf 1974).

Rousseau, A.   *Irénée de Lyon: Contre les Hérésies Livre IV* (SC 100, Paris: Les
                 Éditions du Cerf 1965).

412

Rousseau, A.   *Irénée de Lyon: Contre les Hérésies Livre V* (SC 153, Paris: Les Éditions du Cerf 1969).

Rousseau, A.   *Irénée de Lyon: Démonstration de la Prédication Apostolique* (SC 406, Paris: Les Éditions du Cerf 1995).

Runciman, S.   *The First Crusade* (Cambridge: Cambridge University Press 2007).

Ruppert, L.   *Der leidende Gerechte: Eine motivgeschichtliche Untersuchung zum Alten Testament und zwischentestamentlichen Judentum* (FzB 5, Würzburg: Echter Verlag 1972).

Ruppert, L.   *Jesus als der leidende Gerechte? Der Weg Jesu im Lichte eines alt- und zwischentestamentlichen Motivs* (SBS 59, Stuttgart: KBW Verlag 1972)

Ruppert, L.   *Der leidenden Gerechte und seine Feinde: Eine Wortfelduntersuchung* (Würzburg: Echter Verlag 1973).

Saadiah Gaon   *The Book of Beliefs and Opinions* (translated by S. Rosenblatt; New Haven: Yale University Press 1976).

Saadiah Gaon   *The Book of Theodicy: Translation and Commentary on the Book of Job* (translated from the Arabic with a philosphic comment by L. E. Goodman; Yale Judaica Series 25; New Haven: Yale University Press 1988).

Saadiah Gaon   *Sefer Emunut ve'Deot: First Edition, Constantinople 1562* (Reprint; Jerusalem: Makor Publishing 1972).

Saebø, M.   *On the Way to Canon: Creative Tradition History in the Old Testament* (JSOTSS 191, Sheffield: Sheffield Academic Press 1998).

Samir, Y.   *Rabbi Moses Ha-Kohen of Tordesillas and His Book 'Ezer ha-Emunah* (Leiden: Brill 1975).

Sanders, E.P.   *The Historical Figure of Jesus* (Allen Lane: The Penguin 1993).

Sapp, D.A.   "The LXX, 1QIsa, and MT Versions of Isaiah 53 and the Christian Doctrine of Atonement," in: W.H. Bellinger & W.R. Farmer (eds), *Jesus and the Suffering Servant: Isaiah 53 and Christian Origins* (Harrisburg: Trinity Press 1998) 170-192.

Sarachek, J.   *The Doctrine of the Messiah in Medieval Jewish Literature* (New York: Hermon Press 1932).

Sawyer, J.F.A.   *The Fifth Gospel: Isaiah in the History of Christianity* (Cambridge: Cambridge University Press 1996).

Shatz, D.   "The Biblical and Rabbinic Background to Medieval Jewish Philosophy," in: D.H. Frank & O. Leaman (eds), *The Cambridge Companion to Medieval Jewish Philosophy* (Cambridge: Cambridge University Library 2003) 16-37.

Schäfer, P.   "Bibelübersetzung II. Targumim," *TRE* 6:216-228.

Schenker, A.   *Knecht und Lamm Gottes (Jesaja 53): Übernahme von Schuld im Horizont der Gottesknechtslieder* (Stuttgarter Bibelstudien 190, Stuttgart: Katholisches Bibelwerk 2001).

Schiffman, L.H.   *The Eschatological Community of the Dead Sea Scrolls* (SBL MS 38, Atlanta: Scholars Press 1989).

Schiffman, L.H. *Reclaiming the Dead Sea Scrolls: The History of Judaism, the Background of Christianity, the Lost Library of Qumran* (Philadelphia: The Jewish Publication Society 1994).

Schiller-Szinessy, S.M.
    "The Pugio Fidei," *Cambridge Journal of Philosophy* 16 (1888) 131-152.

Schmid H. *Šalôm. 'Frieden' im Alten orient und im Alten Testament* (SBS 51, Stuttgart: Katholisches Bibelwerk 1971).

Scholem, G. *Major Trends in Jewish Mysticism* (New York: Schocken 1941).

Scholem, G. *The Messianic Idea in Judaism and Other Essays on Jewish Spirituality* (New York: Schocken 1971).

Schreiner, S. "Isaiah 53 in the Sefer Hizzuk Emunah ('Faith Strengthened') of Rabbi Isaac ben Abraham of Troki," in: B. Janowski & P. Stuhlmacher (eds), *The Suffering Servant: Isaiah 53 in Jewish and Christian Sources* (Grand Rapids: Eerdmans 2004) 418-461.

Schwartz, D.R. *2 Maccabees* (CEJL, Berlin: de Gruyter 2008).

Schwartz, J. "Gallus, Julian and anti-Christian polemic in Pesikta Rabbati," *Theologische Zeitschrift* 46 (1990) 1-19.

Schwemer, A.M. *Studien zu den frühjüdischen Prophetenlegenden Vitae Prophetarum* (Two Volumes, TSAJ 49-50, Tübingen: Mohr Siebeck 1995-1996).

Seeligman, I.L, *The Septuagint Version of Isaiah and Cognate Studies* (FAT 40, Göttingen: Mohr Siebeck 2004).

Segal, A. *Two Powers in Heaven. Early Rabbinic Reports about Christianity and Gnosticism* (Leiden: Brill 1977).

Septimus, B. "'Open Rebuke and Concealed Love': Nahmanides and the Andalusia Tradition," in: I. Twersky (ed), *Rabbi Moses Nachmanides (Ramban): Explorations in His Religious and Literary Virtuosity* (Cambridge MA: Harvard University Press 1983) 11-34.

Sicherman H. & Gevaryahu, G.J.
    "Rashi and the First Crusade: Commentary, Liturgy, Legend," *Judaism* 48 (1999) 181-197.

Simon, U. "Ibn Ezra between Medievalism and Modernism: The Case of Isaiah XL-LXVI," in: J.A. Emerton (ed), *Congress Volume: Salamanca 1983* (VTSup 36, Leiden: Brill 1985) 257-271.

Simon, U. "Abraham Ibn Ezra," in: M. Saebø, *Hebrew Bible / Old Testament: The History of Its Interpretation. Volume 1: From the Beginning to the Middle Ages (Until 1300). Part 2: The Middle Ages* (Göttingen: Vandenhoeck & Ruprecht 2000) 377-387.

Simons, J. *The Geographical and Topographical Texts of the Old Testament: A Concise Commentary in XXXII Chapters* (Leiden: Brill 1959).

Sirat, C. *A History of Jewish Philosophy in the Middle Ages* (Cambridge: Cambridge University Press 1995).

Sjöberg, E. *Der Menschensohn im äthiopischen Henochbuch* (SMHVL 41, Lund: Gleerups 1946).

414

Skarsaune, O. *The Proof from Prophecy. A Study in Justin Martyr's Proof-Text Tradition: Text-Type, Provenance, Theological Profile* (SupNT 56, Leiden: Brill 1987).

Skarsaune, O. "The Development of Scriptural Interpretation in the Second and Third Centuries – except Clement and Origen," in: M. Saebø (ed), *Hebrew Bible Old Testament. The History of Its Interpretation I/1: Antiquity* (Göttingen: Vandenhoeck & Ruprecht 1996) 373-442.

Skehan, P.W. "Isaias and the Teaching of the Book of Wisdom," *CBQ* 2 (1940) 289-299.

Smallwood, E.M. *The Jews under Roman Rule: From Pompey to Diocletian* (Leiden: Brill 1976).

Smith, C. "Chiliasm and Recapitulation in the Theology of Ireneus," *VC* 48 (1994) 313-331.

Smolar L. & Aberbach, M.
    Studies in Targum Jonathan to the Prophets (New York: KTAV; Baltimore: Baltimore Hebrew College 1983).

Spieckermann, H. *Martyrium und die Vernunft des Glaubens: Theologie als Philosophie im vierten Makkabäerbuch* (Nachrichten der Akademie der Wissenschaften zu Göttingen. I. Philologisch-Historische Klasse 2004:3, Göttingen: Vandenhoeck & Ruprecht 2004).

Steck, O.H. *Israel und das gewaltsame Geschick der Propheten* (WMANT 23, Neukirchen-Vluyn: Neukirchener Verlag 1967).

Stemberger, G. *Introduction to the Talmud and Midrash* (Minneapolis: Fortress 1996).

Stenning, J.F. *The Targum of Isaiah* (Oxford: Clarendon Press 1949).

Stewart-Sykes, A. "Melito's anti-Judaism," *Journal of Early Christian Studies* 5 (1997) 271-283.

Stroumsa, S. "Saadya and Jewish *kalam*," in: D.H. Frank & O. Leaman (eds), *The Cambridge Companion to Medieval Jewish Philosophy* (Cambridge: Cambridge University Library 2003) 71-90.

Stuhlmacher, P. "Der messianische Gottesknecht," *JBT* 8 (1993) 131-154.

Stuhlmacher, P. "Isaiah 53 in the Gospels and Acts," in: B. Janowski & P. Stuhlmacher (eds), *The Suffering Servant: Isaiah 53 in Jewish and Christian Sources* (Grand Rapids: Eerdmans 2004) 147-162.

Suggs, M.J. "Wisdom of Solomon 2:10-5: A Homily based on the fourth Servant Song," *JBL* 76 (1957) 26-33.

Sweeney, M. *King Josiah of Judah: The Lost Messiah of Israel* (Oxford: Oxford University Press 2001).

Syrén, R. *The Blessings in the Targums: A Study on the Targumic Interpretations of Genesis 49 and Deuteronomy 33* (Åbo: Åbo Akademi Press1986).

Syrén, R. "Targum Isaiah 52:13-53:12 and Christian Interpretation," *JJS* 40 (1989) 201-212.

Talmage, F.E. "R. David Kimhi as Polemicist," *HUCA* 38 (1967) 213-235.

Talmage, F.E.   *The Book of the Covenant of Joseph Kimhi* (Toronto: The Pontificial Institute of Mediaeval Studies 1972).

Talmage, F.E.   *Sefer ha-berît ûvikûhe RaDaQ 'im hannazerôt* (Jerusalem: Bialik Institute 1974).

Talmage, F.E.   *David Kimhi: The Man and the Commentaries* (Cambridge MA: Harvard University Press 1975).

Theisohn, J.   *Der auserwählte Richter: Untersuchungen zum traditions-geschichtlichen Ort der Menschensohngestalt der Bilderreden des äthiopischen Henoch* (SUNT 12, Göttingen: Vandenhock & Ruprecht 1975).

Thurén, J.   *Sardeen piispa Meliton: Pääsiäisen salaisuus* (Helsinki: Suomen Luterilainen Evankeliumiyhdistys 1968).

Thurén, J.   "'Der Herr ist einer' in Neutestamentlicher Sicht," in: K.-J. Illman & J. Thurén (eds), *Der Herr ist einer, unserer gemeinsames Erbe* (Åbo: Åbo Akademi 1979) 98-121.

Thurén, J.   *Sovituspaikka ja sovinto: Uuden testamentin käännössehdotuksen tarkastelua* (Kirkon tutkimuskeskus Sarja B 65, Tampere: Raamattu-talo 1991).

Thurén, J.   *Markuksen evankeliumi* (Helsinki: SLEY-Kirjat 1996).

Tishby, I.   *The Wisdom of the Zohar. An Anthology of Texts. Volumes 1-3* (Oxford: Oxford University Press 1989).

Tomes, R.   "Heroism in 1 and 2 Maccabees," *Biblical Interpretation* 15 (2007) 171-199.

Trebilco, P.   *Jewish Communities in Asia Minor* (SNTS MS 69, Cambridge: Cambridge University Press 1991).

Tromp, J.   "Taxo, the Messenger of the Lord," *JSJ* 21 (1990) 200-209.

Twersky, I.   *A Maimonides Reader* (Springfield: Behrman House 1972).

Twersky, I. (ed)   *Rabbi Moses Nachmanides (Ramban): Explorations in His Religious and Literary Virtuosity* (Cambridge MA: Harvard University Press 1983).

Valle de, C.   "Jacob ben Rubén de Huesca. Polemista. Su patria y su época," in: J. Maier (ed), *Polémica Judeo-Christiana estudios* (Madrid: Aben Ezra Ediciones 1992) 59-65.

Varner, W.   *Ancient Jewish-Christian Dialogues: Athanasius and Zacchaeus, Simon and Theophilus, Timothy and Aquila* (Lewiston: The Edwin Mellen Press 2004).

Varner, W.   "In the Wake of Trypho: Jewish-Christian Dialogues in the Third to the Sixth Centuries," *EQ* 80 (2008) 219-236.

Veijola, T.   *Verheissung in der Krise: Studien zur Literatur und Theologie der Exilszeit anhand des 89. Psalms* (AASF B 120, Helsinki 1982).

Vermes, G.   "The Oxford Forum for Qumran Research: Seminar on the Rule of the War from Cave 4 (4Q285)," *JJS* 43 (1992) 85-90.

Vermes, G.   *The Dead Sea Scrolls in English* (Revised and Extended Fourth Edition; London: Penguin Books 1995).

Vetus Latina   *Vetus Latina 12 (Pars II): Esaias.* Ed. R. Gryson (Freiburg: Herder 1987-

Vielhauer, P.   "Gottesreich und Menschensohn in der Verkündigung Jesu," in: idem, *Aufsätze zum Neuen Testament* (TBü 31, Munich: Kaiser 1965) 55-91.

Visotzky, B.L.   "Anti-Christian Polemic in Leviticus Rabbah," PAAJR 56 (1990) 83-100.

Wald, S.G.   "Baraita, Baraitot," *Encyclopaedia Judaica* 3:124-128.

Watts, R.E.   "Jesus' Death, Isaiah 53, and Mark 10:45: A Crux Revisited," in: W.H. Bellinger & W.R. Farmer (eds), *Jesus and the Suffering Servant: Isaiah 53 and Christian Origins* (Harrisburg: Trinity Press International 1998) 125-151.

Weinfeld, M.   *Deuteronomy and the Deuteronomic School* (Winona Lake: Eisenbrauns 1992).

Weiss Halivni, D.*Peshat and Derash: Plain and Applied Meaning in Rabbinical Exegesis* (New York: Oxford University Press 1991).

Wengst, K.   *Didache (Apostellehre) Barnabasbrief Zweiter Klemensbrief Schrift an Diognet* (Schriften des Urchristentums Zweiter Teil; Darmstadt: Wissenschaftliche Buchgesellschaft 1984).

Whybray, N.R.   *Thanksgiving for a Liberated Prophet. An Interpretation of Isaiah Chapter 53* (JSOTSS 4, Sheffield: Sheffield Academic Press).

Wilken, R.L.   *Isaiah Interpreted by Early Christian and Medieval Commentators* (Grand Rapids: Eerdmans 2007).

Williamson, H.G.M.
     1 and 2 Chronicles (The New Century Bible Commentary, Grand Rapids: Eerdmans 1982).

Winston, D.   *The Wisdom of Solomon* (AB 43, Garden City: Doubleday 1981).

Winston, D.   "Theodicy in the Wisdom of Solomon," in: A. Laato & J.C. De Moor (eds), *Theodicy in the World of the Bible* (Leiden: Brill 2003) 525-545.

Wolff, H.W.   *Jesaja 53 im Urchristentum. Mit einer Einführung von Peter Stuhlmacher* (Giessen: Brunnen 1984).

Woude van der, A.S.
     Die messianischen Vorstellungen der Gemeinde von Qumran (SSN 3; Assen: van Gorcum 1957).

Wright, A.G.   "Numerical Patterns in the Book of Wisdom," *CBQ* 29 (1967) 524-538.

Wünsche, A.   *Midrasch Tehillim oder haggadische Erklärung der Psalmen* (Hildesheim: Georg Olms 1967).

Ziegler, J.   *Untersuchungen zur Septuaginta des Buches Isaias* (Alttestamentliche Abhandlungen 12:3; Münster: Aschendorffschen Verlagsbuchhandlung 1934).

Ziegler, J.   *Sapientia Salomonis* (Septuaginta: Vetus Testamentum Graecum, Auctoritate Societatis Litterarum Gottingensis editum XII,1; Göttingen: Vandenhoeck & Ruprecht 1962).

Ziegler, J.	*Isaias* (Septuaginta, Vetus Testamentum Graecum, Göttingen: Vandehoeck & Ruprecht 1967).
Ziegler, J.	*Eusebius Werke Neunter Band: Der Jesajakommentar* (Berlin: Akademie Verlag 1975).
Zillesen, A.	"Jesaja 52, 13 – 53, 12 hebräisch nach LXX," *ZAW* 25 (1905) 261-284.
Zobel, M.	*Gottes Gesalbter: Der Messias und die messianische Zeit in Talmud und Midrash* (Berlin: Schocken & Jüdischer Buchverlag 1938).
Zunz, L.	*Die Gottesdienstlichen Vorträge der Juden: Ein Beitrag zur Altertumskunde und biblischen Kritik zur Literatur- und Religionsgeschichte* (Hilsesheim: Georg Olms Verlagsbuchhandlung 1966).

15 Indexes

15.1. Author index

15.2. Index of passages

E. Apostolic Fathers and Patristic texts

432

G. Medieval Jewish and Christian documents

CPSIA information can be obtained
at www.ICGtesting.com
Printed in the USA
BVHW040541140521
607207BV00011B/63